LAND, PEOPLE AND POWER

LAND, PEOPLE AND POWER

An Anthropological Study of Emerging Mega City of New Town, Rajarhat

Kakali Chakrabarty
Krishna Mandal
Janak Kumari Srivastava
Sudhansu Gangopadhyay
Asok Kumar Mukhopadhyay
Sumitabha Chakrabarty
Rapti Pan
K.M. Sinha Roy

Anthropological Survey of India
Government of India, Kolkata - 700016

GYAN

ISBN: 978-81-212-1258-8

Price: ₹ 960

First Published, 2015

Published by
Gyan Publishing House
5, Ansari Road
Daryaganj, New Delhi-110002
Phones: 9811692060
E-mail: books@gyanbooks.com

Printed at: G. Printers, Delhi

Cataloging in Publication Data--DK

Courtesy: D.K. Agencies (P) Ltd. <docinfo@dkagencies.com>

Land, people and power : an anthropological study of emerging mega city of new town, Raharhat / Kakali Chakrabarty ... [et al.].
p. cm.
Includes bibliographical references.
ISBN 9788121212588

1. Eminent domain--India--Rajarhat. 2. Urban anthropology--India--Rajarhat. 3. Economic development projects--India--Rajarhat. 4. New town (Rajarhat, India). I. Chakrabarty, Kakali.

DDC 307.76095414 23

Contents

Foreword

The present volume is the outcome of a short-term research project on 'Anthropological Study of the Emerging Issues Related to Development', undertaken by the Anthropological Survey of India during 2011-2012. The main objective of this project was to empirically understand the immediate as well as long-term effects of the development on the different social strata. The strength of Anthropological Survey of India is its field work and first hand information from the people *in situ.* Development programmes have various facets. They affect differently to different layers of the society depending on the basic needs of the people, which of course is not the same in every society. In the last few years, controversies have emerged out of the development scenario involving the issue of land acquisition, very prominently in the State of West Bengal. Civil societies, professionals and media became vocal on this issue, on behalf of the affected people, who otherwise were marginalised with poverty, social deprivation, discrimination, and powerlessness. Against this backdrop, the present project was taken up to unearth the ground realities through scientific methods of anthropological studies. One methodological strong point of this work is that a multi-disciplinary team comprising the anthropologists, psychologists, linguists and human ecologists has conducted this research and it has largely succeeded in bringing out people's perspective in their report prepared with rich empirical data, organised in quantitative and qualitative terms.

The case studies and experiences reveal the fact that the rural people, who primarily subsisted on agriculture and pisciculture, taking advantage of their unique eco-system of wet-land, became the worst victims of development projects of the Mega city while their urban and affluent counterparts are on the gaining side. This social contradiction further aggravated inequity between the social strata, making affluents more prosperous and forcing marginal to poverty, deprivation from elementary rights and privileges, in addition to their voicelessness. The study also reveals that the major victims of this land acquisition issue were the weaker sections of the society, particularly the Scheduled Castes and Scheduled Tribes, who were vulnerable otherwise. One point is important that these people mainly practised subsistence agriculture which assured food security for the society. These people now face the problems of poverty, hunger, unemployment, which lead to loss of mental health giving rise to intra-community and inter-community tensions. The team of researchers deserves our appreciation for contributing to such a valuable treatise on this issue.

The book is an important contribution to the study of emerging issues related to the planned development. I am confident that it would be beneficial to the social scientists in general and specialists on the subject in particular, besides anthropologists and experts of development agencies, including the development planners.

Prof K.K. Misra

June, 2013

Director, Anhropological Survey of India,
Kolkata

Preface

In last couple of years, India witnessed strong peasant unrest over the land acquisition policy of the government. West Bengal also came in limelight due to the same reason. Acquisition of land particularly of arable land for various development projects of the government made the poor peasants upset and resulted spontaneous organised movement against the land acquisition policy of the government. The civil society, the professionals, the elites, the media came out with varied observations and people were polarised greatly on the issue. The socio-political scenario in the West Bengal was changed in view of the appearance of new political force through electoral poll 2011. Anthropological Survey of India, the premier institute of its kind with a consistent history of anthropological and multi-disciplinary researches in various aspects of human societies always extended its research interest to various issues cropped up time to time in the society against the varied scenario of development. In continuation of such research activities a short-term project on 'Anthropological Study of the Emerging Issues Related to Development' has been initiated by the Anthropological Survey of India in the later phase of 2011, and the present volume is an outcome of that project.

Keeping in view the current issue of land acquisition, particularly of agricultural land in large scale and people's spontaneous contention against it, the present project on Rajarhat issue was proposed to understand the impact of 'development' on the rural project affected people in the perspective of their present socio-economic situation. The case of Rajarhat attracted attention of media and the civil society much later than the actual happenings of land acquisition in the area, only after the people's protest against the government notification of land acquisition in Nandigram, in the district of Purba Medinipur (West Bengal). Thereafter, Rajarhat issue occupied the major headlines in almost all leading newspapers, both in English as well as local Bengali language. Anthropological Survey of India probed into the situation from purely academic view and came out with untold truth, the unforgettable saga of land losers. For the researchers, it was altogether a different experience, witnessing directly the worst ever instance of deprivation of the poor, socially and economically marginal, voiceless people by a democratic government of the state in the interest of powerful and affluent society. The volume could not bring out account of the total affected area due to lack of time and manpower. To be honest to the ethics of the discipline of anthropology it requires detail probe into the situation covering the total area of the affected villages, taking a stock of land losers, who are yet to find out an alternative livelihood; who are yet to receive their dues from the government; who are yet to hear a word 'sorry' from their urban counterpart.

The villagers, under the banner of Jami Bachao committee (*jami*= the land, here the agricultural land, *bachao*=to save), filed a case in the Calcutta High Court for justice. We were shocked to learn from the villagers that during the hearing of the case the Justice of the Division Bench, Pinaki Chandra Ghosh with great anger shouted on the villagers 'go back to the age of cave-dwelling and make fire with the help of stone (*guhay fire jan ar chakmaki diye agun jalan*)'. It has become a history now. One great leader of the Left party expressed pity to the peasants, who work in agricultural field in mud and water round the year. Their toil hurt him so much that he decided to make them free from such misery (*ora jale kaday kaj kare, ki kasto, eta chalte dewa jay na,* i.e., they work in water and mud, how miserable it is, this cannot be allowed to continue). Thus, they were ousted from their land and from their age-old occupation of agriculture and fishing. Perhaps the leader never came across the concepts like subsistence agriculture and food security. We came across many such untold stories during our study.

Rajarhat is also one of the hazardous examples of the violation of environmental policy. The vast wet- land, which was the oxygen producer for the city of Kolkata, has been filled up ruthlessly for the Mega-city. More than 15 lakhs trees were cut down in Rajarhat. The figure is increasing day by day. This volume, based on first hand field data, may help to frame developmental programmes for the benefit of the people.

While this mnuscript is press-ready, we received two publicaions: one in Bengali, titled Operation Rajarhat by Raghab Bandyopadhyay, published by Bhabani Books, Kolkata (2013); and the other titled Beyond Kolkata, Rajarhat and the Dystopia of Urban Imagination by Ishita Dey, Ranabir Samaddar and Suhit K. Sen, (series Editor: Sujata Patel), published by Routledge, New Delhi (2013). The first one deals with the facts in the form of a novel and the later one is a research publication. Both the publications uncovered the crude reality of the situation of Rajarhat before and after land acquisition and very much in tune to our study. Though, we could not discuss or refer their findings and views in the discourse of our understanding in the text but we take the opportunity to acknowledge them for their valuable contribution on the question of land acquisition and development.

Every study has a time frame, and so was with the present study. We had to wind up from field work for the desk work. But we feel that no research work can actually be winded up and in reality we could never come to a halt in regard to Rajarhat project. People of Rajarhat approached us continually and took us in their confidence for sharing their various constrains due to loss of livelihood, their feelings, their day-to-day problems, their frustrations, their hope and aspiration which they could not share with their neighbourhood. They wanted us to write on each and every point they shared with us. We could not do justice to their continued spontaneous interaction till date as somewhere we had to come to a halt for the sake of publication of the data and unfolding the findings to a greater community of readers. We could accommodate some of them under 'Addendum', of course in brief in the press-ready format. We are thankful to all of them for their trust on us. As researcher, this is the greatest ever reward for all of us.

The book, we hope, will add some important dimensions in the area of studies related to development. The authors will be highly obliged, if the volume becomes useful to the social scientists in general and specialists of the development studies in particular.

Let us remember the words of Blaise Pascal, the French philosopher and mathematician, Human kind is only a small link in the immense web of nature, but it is the only one that through thought understands nature, it is the only species on earth to be responsible for the earth, and to be able to transform it for better or for worse.' Do we really behave in a responsible way towards Earth?

Authors

Acknowledgements

The success story of any research work stands on encouragement, co-operation and academic as well as administrative support from different personalities at different stages and different capacities. None of these supports is comparable to each other as each in its own perspective is great to the researchers. Starting from the very inception of the project, till the publication of this volume, sincere efforts and co-operation from different people were involved.

We express our deep sense of gratitude to Prof K.K. Misra, Director, Anthropological Survey of India, for his constant encouragement and academic support on research work. This short-term project was conceived by him and completed under his able guidance. We are thankful to D. N. Pandey, Senior Human Ecologist and Head of Office, Head office, Kolkata for his help and co-operation in making the project successful. Dr Abhijit Guha, Reader, Vidyasagar University, West Bengal, has gone through this report and offered his valuable suggestions. His study on land acquisition in Medinipur remained as an academic resource for this volume and as much we are extremely thankful to him. We express our sincere gratitude to Debashis Sen, Chairman, West Bengal Housing Infrastucture Development Corporation Limited (WBHIDCO) for his help and co-operation during our fieldwork. He allowed us to get access to various reports of HIDCO which helped us to understand the project as well as the area. We are also thankful to Prasanta Bhattacharya, General Manager (T and P), HIDCO, for his co-operation. He spared us his valuable time in discussion which helped us to understand the scenario. We received full co-operation from District Authorities for our study. Our sincere gratitude goes to each one of them. We are indebted to the officials of the DM Office, North 24 Parganas, Barasat, for their co-operation during our field work.

We express our heartfelt thanks and sincere gratitude to all the people of Ghuni, Jatragachhi, Sulanggari, Thakdari, Patharghata, Chhapna and Akanda Kesari *moujas* for their kind co-operation and help during the field work. It was confessed honestly to them that we are not in a position to help them in removing their sufferings; what best we can do is to share their experience. They trusted us, attended us and shared their experiences and problems with us, hold detailed discussion on various issues which helped us in developing insight of the problem. We owe to them so much. Our special thanks go to Prahlad Mandal, Ranjit Naskar, Gobinda Biswas, Sahidul Islam, Gobinda Mandal and Amala Mandal of Rajarhat villages for their support and help during the field work. Without their active co-operation this study would not be possible. We also express our sincere gratitude to Sujali Mandal, Panchayat Pradhan of Jangra-Hatiara Gram Panchayat-2, Ghuni, Sri Ashok Naskar, Panchayat Pradhan, Patharghata Gram Panchayat, Sulata Mandal, ex-Panchayat Pradhan, Jangra-Hatiara Gram Panchayat-2, Ghuni, Abdul Mannan Mandal, BLRO, Rajarhat, Sri Biplab Sarkar, SRO (II), Land Revenue Department, Barasat, Yasmin Bari, Joint BDO, Rajarhat Block and Sandhya Pramanik, Panchayat Pradhan, Mahisbathan Gram Panchayat for their kind co-operation. We are thankful to Nilotpal Dutta, for his co-operation and prolonged discussion with us. He was associated with the '*jami bachao*' movement at Rajarhat since its inception and took an active leadership role with much success. We got access to many important documents through his collection, some of which are incorporated in the appendices. He provided us a lot of old photographs from his personal collection which are valuable visual document on erstwhile Rajarhat. We express our thankfulness to Prof Asit Kumar Roy, a geologist turned environmentalist, for his kind co-operation in providing relevant document to us. Still we might have missed some of those who extended their helping hand in different stages of our study; we express our gratitude to all of them.

Ashok Sarkar and Sridam Kundu of Anthropological Survey of India deserve special thanks for photographic coverage. Dipa Saha computerised the data with utmost sincerity and helped us in many ways. We are thankful to all of them.

Last but not the least we offer our thanks to Subhodeep Dey and other members of the Publication Division of the Anthropological Survey of India for their co-operation in bringing out the publication within a short span of time.

1

Introduction

In the eastern part of Kolkata and adjacent to its satellite city of Salt Lake Town, there emerged a planned Mega city named New Town over an area of more than three thousand hectares of arable land stretching over the Rajarhat Block of North 24 Parganas district and a portion of Bhangar-II Block of South 24 Parganas district. The new city was a planned project of the government of West Bengal (the then Left Front government) to decongest the over congestion of Kolkata, the capital city of West Bengal, as has been proposed by CMDA (the Calcutta Metropolitan Development Authority), a West Bengal Government Undertaking, in their concept plan submitted to the government of West Bengal in the year 1994. In the said plan, it was indicated that the project area at Rajarhat, though outside the CMA (Calcutta Metropolitan Area) boundary, but being bordering to it likely to share the increased population of CMA.

The State Planning Board estimated the rise of population in CMA from 11.86 million in 1991 to about 14 million in 2001, to 17 million in 2011 and to 20 million in 2021. The Project area of Rajarhat was identified as new planning area to be annexed to CMA, and it was anticipated that the New Town would accommodate a population of five lakhs other than the population in the existing settlements within the project area. Initially (in the year 1994), there was a proposal for a Project Area covering 2750 hectares of cultivable land which was increased to 3075 hectares in the year 2000. In 2005, the project area was proposed to cover 5,000 hectares and finally it reaches up to 5400 hectares (De, 2011, p. 23). Besides, there was a planning area shown in the Drawing No. 4 of the CMDA Concept Plan (Appendix-1) although the total planning area was not disclosed. In the next phase, there was a proposal of BRADA (Bhangar Rajarhat Area Development Authority) engulfing another 4000 hectares of arable land.

However, the proposal of BRADA has been dropped after the recent political changeover of power in the state following West Bengal's Assembly Election result in 2011. The then Left Front government of West Bengal proposed the plan of New Town in Rajarhat area in the year 1993 where both IT-hub and real estate development had been proposed. The plan was implemented through West Bengal Housing Infrastructure Development Corporation Limited (WBHIDCO, popularly referred to as HIDCO). HIDCO emerged as a government owned nodal agency in the year 2000 under Town and Country planning Act of 1979 with a mission to acquire land for New Town mega city. Under the project, huge amount of cultivable land had been acquired from the villagers of this area leaving only the settlement area, i.e., the homestead under their disposal. According to the concept plan of CMDA, the site of New Town comprised seventeen (17) *moujas* (full or part) and the area within the project boundary was 3382 hectares out of which 2574 hectares were claimed vacant and 808 hectares were occupied by the existed settlement (c.f. Dutta and Banerjee, 1996: 2). The project area as identified by CMDA is located within Rajarhat police station and extends from Rajarhat road in the north to the Krishnapur Kata Khal in the south. The eastern boundary of CMA is on its west. Bidhannagar (Salt Lake Township) is located to the south-west of the site. Netaji Subhas Chandra Bose International Airport area is about 1km to the north-west of the northern boundary of the project area while the 'Calcutta Wet Lands and Waste Recycling Region' is located in the south of the area. The Kazi Najrul Islam Sarani runs north-south about 1.5 km on the west of the site.

Agricultural area along with its settlements lies in the eastern side of the project area. A vast area of '*bheris*' located within the 'Calcutta Wet Lands and Waste Recycling Region' (12500 hectares). Since no urban development is permitted in this area the southern boundary of the project area will always remain open allowing fresh cool breeze in the summer months (*ibid*: 4). However, more *moujas* had been added to the project area and altogether twenty-four (24) *moujas* from the two blocks (Rajarhat and Bhangar-II) were included finally. About the existing villages in the project area the same report stated that existing settlements within the project area cover about 24 per cent (808 hectares) of the total land (3382 hectares) within the project area. Settlements of considerable size exist in Noapara, Rekjuni, Ghuni, Sulanggari, Chandiberia, Tarulia, Mahishgot, Mahisbathan, Jatragachhi, Chak Panchuria, Baligari, Chhapna and Kadampukur *mouzas* (*ibid*: 5).

At the outset, it may be made clear that the present study was a post-project review and thus, the impact of 'development' on the Project Affected Persons (PAP) in the perspective of their present socio-economic situation remained the main focus. The objective was to understand the impact of development project of a mega city on an agrarian society that was to deal with with a new kind of economic and socio-cultural situation which was not experienced earlier.

It may be mentioned here that the agricultural land in Rajarhat were most fertile land of West Bengal and produce three crops a year, besides vegetables. The Bagjola, Krishnapur (commonly pronounced as Kestopur) and Nawai canals remained the major sources of water supply to these lands. In 1970s, the River Lift Irrigation (RLI) Scheme was introduced in these canals as a part of 20-point Programme of the Central Government for the benefit of the agriculturists. In about six years, the installation of RLI scheme was complete in the area and with this facility agriculture had flourished in a big way and almost all the cultivable lands turned into '*tin fasali jami*', i.e., started yielding three major crops a year. On nominal rent of rupees 80.00 per bigha for paddy cultivation and even lower for vegetable cultivation, peasants used to get the benefit out of it. Initially, the rent was far lower and gradually increased to rupees 80.00 in recent years. The waste water of the canals also worked as natural fertiliser to their land and those could produce good crops with relative ease. Besides, the low-lying wet-land and water bodies remained major resource for fisheries and pisciculture. Fisheries had been developed in this area in a big way due to low-lying lands. Rajarhat villages used to supply tons of rice, fishes and vegetables to the markets of Kolkata and adjoining urban areas. This area also

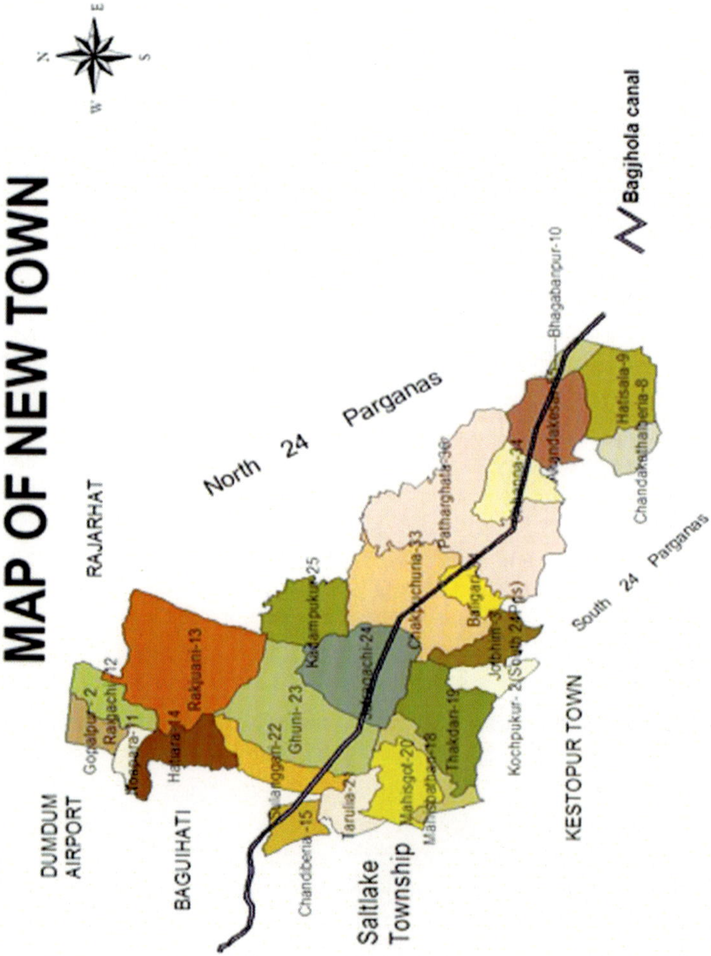
MAP OF NEW TOWN
N
E
S
W
RAJARHAT
North 24 Parganas
South 24 Parganas
DUMDUM AIRPORT
BAGUIHATI
Saltlake Township
KESTOPUR TOWN
Bagjhola canal
Bhagabanpur-10
Rakjuani-13
Ghuni-23
Kadampukur-25
Chakpachuria-33
Patharghata-36
Thakdan-19
Mahisgot-20
Chandiberia-15
Tarulia-21
Hatisala-9
Chandakathaberia-8
Kochpukur- 2(South 24 Pgs)

supplied flowers to the city markets. According to a report by Sanhati (August 29, 2008) that after satisfying the demands of the local markets the Rajarhat peasants could satisfy 20 per cent to 25 per cent of the demands of Kolkata and its suburbs. In 2002, the RLI scheme had been forcibly withdrawn by the Left Front government following people's protest against the land acquisition.

The villages of Rajarhat used to supply milk to the city in addition to agricultural produce. There was no dearth of pastures for the cattle. According to the local people, Rajarhat was inhabited by four categories of people: (1) marginal peasants, (2) cultivators and labourers, (3) small petty traders and salaried (service) people, and (4) share-croppers and agricultural labourers.

While talking of land acquisition and development of Rajarhat, one should keep in mind that this area falls under the East Calcutta Wetland (ECW) zone, and plays a significant role not only in maintaining the ecological balance and bio-diversity but also provides livelihood for a large number of socially and economically marginalised people who depend on subsistence agriculture and fish cultivation. On February 3, 2000, an area of 12,500 hectares of this East Calcutta Wet-Land had been designated as Ramsar site. This ECW (now called EKW, i.e., East Kolkata Wet-land) is 'world-renowned as a model of a multiple use wet-land. The site's resource recovery systems, developed by local people through the ages, have saved the city of Calcutta from the costs of constructing and maintaining waste water treatment plants. The wet-land forms an urban facility for treating the city's waste water and utilising the treated water for pisciculture and agriculture, through the recovery of nutrients in an efficient manner, i.e., the water flows through fish ponds covering about 4,000 ha, and the ponds act as solar reactors and complete most of their bio-chemical reactions with the help of solar energy. Thus, the system is described as "one of the rare examples of environmental protection and development management where a complex ecological process has been adopted by the local farmers for mastering the resource recovery activities" (RIS).' (Courtesy: http://www. ramsar. org). In the same site, it is also stated that the wet-land provides about 150 tonnes of fresh vegetables daily, as well as some 10,500 tonnes of table fish per year, the latter providing livelihoods for about 50,000 people directly and as many again indirectly.'

The phenomenon of this magnificent waste water recycling system of ECW was discovered by Dhrubajyoti Ghosh (proxied.changemakers.net/journal/98october/ghosh.cfm) in 1980's. He noticed that, "Retention of waste water in the ponds, before the initial stocking of fish, allowed bacteria to act upon the organic matter in the sewage and decompose the organic waste. The growth of these beneficial bacteria was supported by the algae that thrived in these shallow ponds under the ample sunshine. The algae also provide food for the fish. This eco-system provides a natural kidney for the city's organic waste-water. So, a double boon was taking place: The organic sewage was being treated by the natural eco-system, and was producing rich quantities of fish food on which the local varieties thrive."

Historically, Rajarhat was an integral part of ECW (supported by the historicity of the land and recent research findings, discussed in due course). Surprisingly, in none of the reports by HIDCO, CMDA, IIT, Kharagpur and Ghosh, Bose and Associates, giving clearance to the New Town Project, admitted this aspect of universal importance for Rajarhat. Rather it was argued that the present Mega city project area lies beyond ECW.

The Comprehensive environmental impact assessment and environmental management plan report prepared by Ghosh, Bose and Associates Pvt. Ltd. for HIDCO says 'the environmental importance and sensitivity of the East Calcutta Wet-lands is well-recognised and the project site lies entirely outside this zone' (5.1.7; p. ES-5). The concept plan submitted by CMDA (p.13) also claimed the project area was lying outside of the Calcutta wet-land and recycling region. It also claimed that the area did not contain large ponds or water bodies or *bheris,* and therefore, did not qualify for being regarded as an area under preservation for ecological and environmental purposes. Contrary to this the 'State of environment Report' published by the Department of Environment (*Paribesh Daptar*) of the Government of West Bengal in the year 1998 says, 'Recent development proposal for setting up of a satellite township at Rajarhat (by Housing board), Central leather complex at Karaidanga and the Sonarpur Satellite Township, all within the designated wet-land of east Calcutta call for critical appraisal and year round impact assessment study. These are some of the examples of contingent responses made to a very complex problem of land conversion for urbanisation and consequent degradation of environment...It may be mentioned that east Calcutta has long been acknowledged as an ecologically fragile area providing immense service to the city. The government has recognised that East Calcutta Wet-Lands and the canal side agricultural fields should be considered as "No Development Zone." It has also decided to set up a Leather Complex at the heart-land of east Calcutta and a new township at Rajarhat in north east Calcutta. These are examples of contradictions. The point to note is that habitat improvement programme has to be made eco-friendly. This is critically required in tracts with fragile eco-systems like the coastal zone, the Sundarbans, Darjiling hills as also the wet-land of East Calcutta" (c.f. De, 2011: 4-5).

Chattopadhyay (2001:11) also identified the area under study as wet-lands. According to him (*ibid:* p. 3) 'the main biotic feature of wet-land ecosystem is the low depth of water cover over the soil'. In his report, it is observed that for wet-lands, One determining feature that could be considered as the basis of getting waste water recycling status was using waste water for agriculture as well as pisciculture. But, in spite of having this character, some neighbouring *moujas* were left out of the official map...Six such *moujas* of adjoining Rajarhat police station...had been identified as wet lands by our research team and were brought under the present study. *Moujas* under Rajarhat police station of 24 Parganas (N) district are: Ghuni, Jatragachi, Mahisbathan, Mahisghot, Rekjuani and Thakdari' (*ibid*). The present study also covered these *moujas* except Rekjuani. The other *moujas* under study like Patharghata, Chhapna and Akanda Kesari also come under the wet-lands considering the very nature of the land and the determining factors as discussed by Chattopadhyay (quoted in the previous lines). The Asian Bureau (1991) defined wet-lands of south and west Asia as "Estuaries and deltas, salt marshes, mangroves and mud flats, coastal lagoons, fresh water lakes and marshes oasis, seasonal flood plain wet-lands, swamp forests, rivers and streams, man-managed systems such as rice fields, fish ponds and reservoirs" (*ibid*:3). (More have been discussed under section Diminution of Wet-Land and loss of aquatic bio-diversity in New Town). Rajarhat is very prominently satisfying all the characters of wet-lands contradicting the claims of the HIDCO and other reports. Till date some low-lying lands and *gheri* (small fish embankment) are surviving in and around Chhapna and Akanda Kesari *mouja* and about 100 acres of Ghuni *bil* (*bil* =local word for huge area of natural low-lying land having low depth of water throughout the year or swamps) is still surviving as an integral part of the proposed eco-tourism park within the New Town mega city. All these certainly speak of the very nature of the land in pre-urbanised Rajarhat, apart from people's submission during the course of present study.

The total scenario of Rajarhat during and after acquisition of land tells the sad stories of deprivation of the common people mostly the marginal population by the powerful people, here the Government bodies under the leadership of a democratic government (the Left Front government). The present study tried to probe into the problem of land acquisition from the perspective of both government and the affected people critically. Simultaneously, as unearthed from empirical data, the environmental aspect particularly the wet-lands issue was also attended critically.

The study had been undertaken in a short period and accordingly strategies had been developed. The study was initiated on 20th of September 2011 but it took more than a month to make contact with the administrators at different levels, i.e., the District, Block, Panchayat and the Project Authority (HIDCO) depending on the availability of the concerned officials. Taken clues from the officials from different bodies a list of most affected villages was prepared and out of the list six *moujas* were selected for the present study. The six *moujas* were: Ghuni, Jatragachhi, Sulanggari, Patharghata, Chhapna, Akanda Kesari and Thakdari. All the studied villages were primarily agriculture-based. Fisheries were reportedly profound in Thakdari, Ghuni and Jatragachhi *mouja* and observed in Akanda Kesari and Chhapna also though not as much as the above said *moujas*. Field work in villages was conducted for about three months by the team from November 2011 to middle of March 2012. The selected six *moujas* were distributed into three Gram Panchayats (GP) as follows:

Thakdari *mouja* under Mohisbathan GP;

Ghuni, Solangguri and Jatragachhi *moujas* under Jangra-Hatiara GP 2; and

Chhapna, Patharghata, Akandakeshari *moujas* under Patharghata GP.

As the villages were large and field work was of limited duration it was difficult to cover each and every house in household census schedule. Hence, it was not possible to follow any established sampling method. Another important factor had to be considered during fieldwork was that the villages had actually been passing through a transitional phase of transformation from a completely rural-based society to a marginal city dwelling society and this had a tremendous effect in their settlement pattern, which often disrupted with the outward migration of the old residents and intrusion of people from the urban suburbs of Kolkata, resulting to a kind of unstability in social relations which the villagers were yet to be acquainted with both mentally and physically. Being ousted from settled livelihood, i.e., agriculture they were in search of suitable job and were on move frequently. Therefore, we were to go for random interview with the villagers depending on their availability physically. Besides, key informants were interviewed in each of the visited villages. Key informants included Panchayat Pradhan (present and past), Panchayat members, school teachers, villagers who were in government organisations, government officials related to land revenue, librarian of the Panchayat office library, leading members of syndicates, and available members of the Rajarhat Jami Bachao committee (committee to save land; *jami*=land, *bachao*=save) and so on. Some detailed interviews were also recorded by the investigators on specific issues of land acquisition. The present study covered 80 households in Ghuni, 29 households in Thakdari, 15 in Patharghata, six in Akanda Kesari, 18 in Chhapna, and 11 in Sulanggari *mouja* besides key informants and group interviews organised at different locations.

It may be mentioned here that the three *moujas* namely Solangguri, Ghuni and Jatragachhi were located in between Baguihati, a suburb and extension of Kolkata city and emerging New Town, and therefore more prone to rapid urbanisation while the other three *moujas* (Patharghata, Chhapna and Akanda Kesari) are relatively in interior location from the newly built six-track road connecting Salt Lake City and Kolkata Airport. The present study also included psychological analysis of the Project Affected People where established psychological methods were applied to collect the information. The findings were presented in a separate section under mental state (Appendix-2).

(For all the photographs under this section the authors are thankful to Nilotpal Dutta).

Pre-acquisition Wet Land Character of Rajarhat.

Pre-acquisition Wet Land Character of Rajarhat.

Pre-acquisition Wet Land Character of Rajarhat.

Pre-acquisition Wet Land Character of Rajarhat.

Pre-acquisition Wet Land Character of Rajarhat.

Pre-acquisition Wet Land Character of Rajarhat.

Pre-acquisition Wet Land Character of Rajarhat.

Pre-acquisition Wet Land Character of Rajarhat.

Rajarhat Wetland Under the Grasp of Destruction.

2

Land and People

Erstwhile Rajarhat

According to the District Census Handbook, 2001 the North 24 Parganas district is the youngest of all the deltaic districts of West Bengal located on the huge thickness of alluvium deposited during recent and sub-recent geological era. It traced the early history of this district from the references found in the writings of several early Greek navigators, historians and geographers between the first century B.C. and third century A.D. All of them referred to the country of a people variously called the Gangaridae, Gangaridai, Gangaritai, Gangaraeoi and Gangarides. In 17th century A.D. Chinese pilgrim Heuen Tsiang (Yuan Chwang) described the district as low-lying country bordering the sea that might have formed a part of 'Samatata'.

Rajarhat is one of the administrative blocks under Barasat sub-division of North 24 Parganas district. It comprises 55 *moujas* (*mouja* is an administrative boundary consisting of one or more villages) of which 39 *moujas* come under the rural area and distributed under six panchayats. Of the 39 *moujas* one *mouja* namely, Mahisbathan was described as uninhabited in District Census Handbook, 2001 although the census records of 1961 showed Mahisbathan populated with 186 households. In the same Census all 55 *moujas* were described as rural areas (District Census handbook 1961). The census record about Mahisbathan was important for the present study as several references described Mahisbathan area as wetland full of water bodies which were filled up and converted to agricultural lands time to time under various political reasons.

Rajarhat was an agriculture-based Block; even in Municipal areas also agriculture was the mainstay of the people. Dhupir *bil* and Bagjola-Ghuni-Jatragachhi basin were the main two water bodies that acted as sink for the rainwater and huge waste water of Rajarhat Barrackpur Mohakuma. The excess water was passed to the Bagjola canal through four bypass channels (*Rajarhate Jami Dakatir Itihas:* p. 5, in Bengali). According to the local people the present Nawai canal was once Labanyaprabha River. It was so said that Raja Sabarna Choudhuri, while on his way through this river, was passing across this area and halted for some time here (the present Rajarhat police station). On the gracious arrival of the king the local traders immediately placed their produces for sale and it took a shape of a *haat* (temporary market) and the area became known as Rajarhat, i.e., 'a *haat* for Raja', the king. 'After introduction of Martin Rail, Rajarhat became an important centre for communication between the city and this wet-land area and from here the produced vegetables, fish and milk had been transported to Belgachhia and Patipukur area (city and surroundings). Though Martin Rail was abolished in the year 1956, but with the development of the roadways and transport system the peasants of this locality managed to sale their produces to the City' (*ibid:* 6) since the installation of the RLI Scheme and deep and shallow tube-wells for irrigation in seventies, agriculture flourished greatly.

From the available published materials on Rajarhat at different times it is certain that this area was a part of wetland. The vast horizon of swamp and marshy land, worth mentioning of which were Ghunir *bil*, Dhupir *bil* and Bagjola basin together constitute 2095 hectare were located at Rajarhat. Dhupir *bil* alone constituted 95 hectares of land (Sambad Nagarik Mancha, November 2009: 9). Besides, there were numbers of *bheri* (large fish embankment), *gher* (relatively smaller fish embankment), *khol* (local categorisation of water body) and *pukur* (pond) in and around the area (Sambad Nagarik Mancha: November, 2009, *Rajarhate Jami Dakatir Itihas*).

For the development of the mega city New Town, 19 *moujas* from Rajarhat Block and five *moujas* from Bhangar-II Block had been acquisitioned leaving their settlements only (808 hectares according to R.N. Dutta, p. 2). All these affected *moujas* were inhabited by the marginal people including Scheduled Castes and Scheduled Tribes, who were primarily peasants and fish cultivators.

The total area under the mega city project (according to HIDCO records) is 3075 hectare. It was observed that total area of 24 *moujas* of the said two Blocks was 5627.1417 hectares (calculated on 1961 District Census Hand Book data) and the entire area was shown as rural in character. According to the said data (Census 1961) in respect of land area of the affected *moujas*, the total excess land is left out to the extent of 2552.1417 hectares. It is assumed on the basis of the information provided by the villagers that about 25 per cent of the total geographical land of the said 24 *moujas* comes under settlements and adjoining area which were exempted from the acquision. The rest amount of land was taken for the development of adjoining municipality or census town such as Noapara, Hatiara, Gopalpur or Raigachi etc.

Geographical Position and Terrain

Geographically, Rajarhat is bounded by Barasat Police Station and Madhyamgram on its north, South and North Dumdum municipalities on its west, Salt Lake City (Bidhannagar) on its south and Kashipur, Bhangar in the east. The geographical location of this area is under 22°37'N to 22°61'N north latitude and 88°31'E to 88°52'E east longitude. It is principally north-eastern fringe of Kolkata. The terrain pattern is flat in general with low-lying areas with water bodies in the south of Mahishbathan and Thakdari area, as well as in adjacent area of Ghuni and near Chhapna *mouja*. The area is covered by alluvial deposition brought by the Hooghly river and tributaries. Soil texture is silt and clayey. It is the most fertile area having upland and low marshy land on which the local peasants used to produce two to three varieties of principal crops during *kharif* and *rabi* season. Villagers grew varieties of vegetables (peas, cabbage, cauliflower, brinjal, tomatoes, carrot, capsicum etc.,) in their upland fields (*unchu shali jami*). In the low lying areas, different types of small fishes, like, *Koi*, *puti*, *kholsey*, *nadosh*, *mourala, shole, singhi* etc., were available in the water bodies. In this wet land, there were about 170 varieties of small green phyto-planktons, which have more capacity to generate oxygen than the trees (De, 2011: 3-4).

Apart from two canals Bagjola and Kestopur, the Nawai *khal* passess through the northern side of the study area. These canals used to supply water for irrigation during pre-urbanisation set up. According to Madhumita Mukherjee, Deputy Director of West Bengal Fisheries Department, the specialty of Rajarhat is in its relief and variation of water bodies. There are large number of water bodies–*doba*, *pukur* (pond), *noynajuli*, *jhil*, *bil*, *khol*, *koni*, abundant river channel, waste water land, swamps etcetera in Rajarhat (*Bipanna Paribesh*, Madhumita Mukhopadhyay, 2000, Kolkata, Pragya Prakashani, in Bengali). Such low-lying areas were seen adjacent to Ghuni and south of Kestopur *khal*. There were also huge water bodies in and around Chhapna *mouja* locally known as Chhapna *bil*. The water of the low-lying areas was used for irrigation. The comprehensive report on Environmental Assessment by Ghosh, Bose and Associates (2000: 5.5.3.3) states that the area is having good quality of ground water and water supply is drawn by about 9,000 individual and 2,000 community hand tube wells, besides deep tube-wells in two Gram Panchayats.

People

The Panchayat records show that different *moujas* are inhabited by various concentrations of people from Hindu and Islamic religious sects. Both the Hindus and Muslims are numerically large groups. Among the Hindus the Scheduled Castes form the majority. Three major such castes are the Paundra Kshatriya, Namasudra and Rajbanshi. According to Census of India, 2001, the Scheduled Caste (SC) population contributes 35.93 per cent and Scheduled Tribe population contributes 0.6 per cent to the total population (145,381 persons) of Rajarhat. The total rural population of Rajarhat has been enumerated as 138,652 heads against the total urban population of 6729 heads. The sex ratio was 932. According to SC population the Block ranks third in the district with a proportion of 72.7 values and the proportion of ST is top in ranking with 74.3 values. Literacy-wise it ranks fifth in the district with a proportion of 74.8 values. All the studied *moujas* are having educational institutions (primary, middle and secondary), medical institutions (PHC, PHS, dispensary), supply of drinking water through pipeline in addition to tube-wells, Post and Telegraph offices, commercial and co-operative banks, agricultural, non-agricultural and other credit societies and recreational centres.

The *moujas* are well-connected by bus, auto-rickshaw, pulling rickshaw etc., and are approached by primary village road or metalled road. Bidhannagar (Salt Lake city) and Kolkata are the nearest cities. According to census records, 2001, all the *moujas* of Rajarhat had electric power supply. Sometimes there are caste or community specific hamlets (*para*) within the *moujas,* like, in Ghuni *mouja* there are Naskarpara (dominated by the Naskar, by caste Namasudra, a scheduled caste), Mollahpara (dominated by the Mollah, a group of Muslim), Ghoshpara (dominated by Ghosh, i.e., the *goala* (milkman) caste), Mondalpara (dominated by the Muslim, having surname as Mondal) and so on.

The land acquisition in Rajarhat is not a new phenomenon. In census of India 1961, entire Rajarhat was recorded as rural area while census data of 1971, onwards shows urban area in Rajarhat. An analysis of census data reveals a process of land acquisition over decades. The following table gives a glance on this fact:

Table 1: Area Transferred to Towns

	Transferred to urban areas in Census Years (hectare)				
	1951	1961	1971	1981	1991
Rajarhat	Nil	Nil	1108.56	2301.78	2581.79

(c.f. Chattopadhyaya, 2001:38)

The wet-land of Rajarhat started getting threat since nineteen seventies.

Empirical data and Panchayat records show the population composition of the studied *moujas* as follows:

Thakdari *mouja* (GP Mahisbathan): Major castes include Namasudra, Paundra Kshatriya and Rajbansi. Rajbansis are numerically dominant. Christian population is also present in small numbers.

Jatragachhi, Ghuni, Sulanggari *moujas* (GP Jangra-Hatiara-2): Namasudra is in majority in Jatragachi *mouja*, while Mollahs (Muslim) are in the highest concentration in the Ghuni *mouja.* Karmakar, an OBC caste is also present in considerable number.

Patharghata, Akanda Kesari, Chhapna *moujas* (GP Patharghata): The Chhapna *mouja* is inhabited exclusively by the Muslims (particularly of Mollah community). Patharghata *mouja* is predominantly inhabited by the Hindus. Among the Hindus majority belong to Scheduled Caste category, namely, Paundra Kshatriya, Rajbanshi and Namasudra. In

Patharghata, Paundra Kshatriya is numerically dominant. Rajbanshis are less in number in these *moujas.* The villages of west Patharghata are dominated by the Muslim followed by Paundra Kshatriya and Namasudra. Very few households belong to Brahmin caste. Akanda Kesari is dominated by the Paudra Kshatriyas.

The decadal growth of population in Rajarhat (CD blocks) shows that the rural population remained almost unchanged since 1991 (138,708) to 2001 (138,652) while urban population has been decreased radically from 147,348 in 1991 to 6,729 in 2001 with decadal variation of -95.4 per cent (Census of India, 2001).

In the district hand book 2001, it is explained that the urban area (municipality) of Rajarhat became smaller because of land acquisition due to the expansion of Kolkata Air port and formation of mega city New Town project.

The table-2 shows a decline in household number and population size in Thakdari *mouja* from 1991 to 2001. During the field work, it was reported that many people whose cultivable land had been taken away in mega city project, sold out their homestead land to the private broker and settled in farthest area to Bhangar or Haroa. Just an opposite picture was found in all the other five *mouzas* (Ghuni, Sulanggari, Jatragachi, Chhapna, Patharghata), where both household number and population size were increased. The maximum increase was noticed in Ghuni followed by Sulanggari *mouja*. While discussing with the people it was revealed that three *mouzas*, namely, Jatragachi, Ghuni and Sulanggari were very near to the proposed mega city and had a good connectivity with Rajarhat in one hand and Baguihati, an urban extension of Kolkata in its northern extremities, on the other. The nearness of Baguihati over a long period already had an urban impact on these *moujas* and hence we found the process of urbanisation due to mega city was comparatively faster in these areas.

The proposed New Town at Rajarhat attracted people from urban areas to these *moujas* and they started purchasing land in the settlement areas. As the price of land hiked a lot and people were afraid of dispossession of their land at any point of time they availed the suitable opportunity of selling out their lands to the individual buyers in a profitable price.

Table 2: Population of studied villages in two census years (1991 and 2001)

Name of moujas	1991 Census Figures			2001 Census Figures				
	Area (ha)	No. of house hold	Total population	Area (ha)	No. of household	Differences	Total population	Differences
Thakdari	250.37	729	3940	250.4	669	– 60	3114	–826
Ghuni	398.18	1700	9332	389.2	3116	+1416	15382	+6050
Sulanggari	96.52	793	3935	96.5	1918	+1125	8393	+4458
Jatragachi	290.93	809	4254	290.9	1010	+201	5118	+864
Chhapna	119.92	297	1671	119.9	378	+81	2088	+417
Patharghata	572.72	958	5428	572.7	1349	+391	6905	+1477

Economy: The traditional occupations of the inhabitants of the studied villages were primarily of two types: cultivation and fishery. Both the occupations were accompanied with livestock rearing. Cultivation was greatly pronounced in all the *moujas* especially in Thakdari, Patharghata, Chhapna, Akanda Kesari, Ghuni (among studied villages), besides Mohisgot, Chakpachuria, Tarulia; Raigachi and Kadampukur *moujas*, the other affected villages in Rajarhat. Three major canals namely Bagjola, Kestopur and Nawai were also a great factor for sound agricultural economy. The RLI (River Lift Irrigation) system further accelerated the production. In the back-drop of agricultural development livestock rearing was popular and selling of milk was also an important subsidiary source of income to the people.

Besides, rearing of poultry birds and ducks was also popular. There was no dearth of ready supply of feeds for the pets because of sound agricultural economy. Fishing is also a subsidiary source of income due to availability of traditional fishes in the low-lying areas. After land acquisition people, who were the small peasants are presently engaged in labour work in construction sites, masonry work, *bidi* rolling, etc. Young people are involved in supplying and selling of building materials through syndicates.

Cultivation: Before land acquisition in Rajarhat, three crops of paddy (*dhân*) were cultivated, such as *âman*, *boro* and *âus*. Aman paddy is generally cultivated (broadcasting and transplanting) in the month of *Pous* (December-January), *boro* is cultivated in the months of *Chaitra-Baisakh* (March-May) and *aus* is cultivated in the month of *Sraban* (July-August). Besides, the villagers used to grow varieties of vegetables in their upland fields (*unchu shali jami* in local usage). It was informed by the villagers that the quality of agricultural land of Patharghata and Chhapna *moujas* were relatively more fertile than that of Ghuni and Jatragachhi *moujas* and there the peasants used to produce *til* (sesame), pulses and mustard as cash crops. Fruit garden and flower cultivation was subsidiary economic resource for many. All these could have been possible with the well-developed irrigation system through canals and water bodies.

There were numerous *bil*, *koni*, *doba*, *pukur* (local identification of water bodies according to their nature and size) in the area besides *khal*/canals and *bheri* (fish embankment). During monsoon season, when the low-lying lands were filled up with rain water numerous local varieties of fishes (*puti, nadosh, kholsey, mourala* etc.) became abundant in the water bodies and were available for the villagers for their consumption as well as for sell. A few other varieties of fishes namely *koi, singi, magur* were also naturally grown in low-marshy land during monsoon. All these added extra nutrition to the dietary pattern. The crop pattern of the area was as follows.

Major cereal: Rice.

Oil seeds: Rape, sesame and mustard.

Pulses: Chickpea, lentil.

Winter vegetables: Cabbage, cauliflower, brinjal, tomato, carrot, turnip, radish, spinach, lettuce, bottle gourd, country bean, and garden pea.

Summer vegetables: Pumpkin, snake gourd, ladies finger, etcetera

Leafy vegetables: Spinach, red spinach, etc.

Fruit plants: Banana, pineapple, papaya, melon and jackfruit.

Besides, jute, sugarcane, green chillies, etc., were also produced in the area.

According to the estimate of the village people, the fertile lands produced 8.40 quintal of paddy per bigha on an average. The annual produce was claimed as follows:

Paddy: 4400 tonnes, wheat: 40 tonnes, oil seeds: 2000 tonnes besides the huge quantity vegetables and fruits (which cannot be exactly measured). About irrigational facilities there were about 203 shallow machines run by the private owners apart from the shallow and deep tubewells installed by the government, about 58 numbers of RLI spout that lifted water from Kestopur-Bhangar *Kata Khal* and from Bagjola canal. Besides, water was lifted from innumerable water bodies, ponds, *doba* (small waterbodies, local categorisation) etcetera for irrigation. In one estimate about one lakh fifty thousand people were surviving on agriculture in the project area.

The villagers informed that prior to the installation of RLI system (in early nineteen seventies) most of the land in Rajarhat used to produce single crop in a year (*ek fasali jami*). But with RLI system the situation changed totally; all the land turned into *tin fasali jami,* i.e., started producing three crops in a year.

Fishery: Fish cultivation is one of the major economic resources in the ECW in general. Rajarhat is also a part of it. The district as a whole also contributes effectively to the pisciculture. The census of India (2001) reported, 'there was 20,589 hectares of area under effective pisciculture from where 194,962 quintal of fishes was harvested as per District Fisheries Office's statistics. The district contributes considerably to the growing prawn export market of the state...' In the studied area, there were large number of water bodies, swamps and wet-lands before the onset of urbanisation process. Fish cultivation was effectively practised in Thakdari, Jatragachi, Ghuni, Akandkesari, Chhapna *moujas* among the studied villages. During the present study a lot of *gheri* (*gheri* is smaller fish embankment while *bheri* denotes larger fish embankment) had been noticed in the Chhapna *mouja* adjacent to the settlement. The Mahisbathan *mouja* (under Mahisbathan G.P.) was also identified as predominantly fishing lands by the people of the other villages/*moujas* namely, Thakdari and Mohisgoth (under the same Gram Panchayat) as well as by the people from other *moujas* of the study area. The record of 186 households in Mahisbathan by the census of India in 1961 also supports our views that Mahisbathan was mainly comprised water bodies.

The old history of the area spoke of a large number of *bheris* in Mahisbathan. Sanhati reports (August, 2008) 'apart from a couple of embankments now belonging to the present day Bhangor of South 24 Parganas, the rest were all in the Mahishbathan region of the undivided Rajarhat. Prominent among these fish embankments were *Boro Paresh, Choto Paresh, Bather bherry, Diller bherry, Sardar bherry, Patrabaad 1,2,3, Nalban, Munshir bherry, Chinta Singh, Narkeltolar bherry, Mollahr bherry, Bonghery, Daktar bherry* etc. Many people from Thakdari, Mahishgoth, Mahishbathan, Krishnapur, Nayapatti, Polenait, Khash Mahal used to work here.'

Some officials of Land Revenue Department shared their experiences that in their youth they used to visit this area for site seeing by small boats. Then there were vast water bodies in the area. During those days only one crop could be cultivated. Attention was also drawn on the impact of development of Salt Lake Township on the wetland as of Rajarhat. The Bidhannagar Township (or Salt Lake City in popular terms) was developed during 1958-1965 to accommodate urban affluent population of Kolkata. The township was built on a reclaimed salt-water lake which gave rise to its popular name of 'Salt Lake City'. Dr Bidhan Chandra Roy, the then Chief Minister of West Bengal was instrumental in formulating the plan to build this satellite township.

The filling up of this vast wetland which was neighboring to Rajarhat gradually made great impact in elevating the land in Rajarhat and making it further suitable for agriculture. The field data also revealed the fact that before nineteen seventies Rajarhat was mainly single crop producing area. Agriculture flourished remarkably with the development of irrigation facilities in the area since later part of that decade.

Live stock: Livestock is a part and parcel of any agrarian society and Rajarhat also shows the same feature. In the words of a peasant woman '*gol goru gola*' are the characteristics of a peasant society (gol=cattle-shed, *goru*=cow, *gola*=granary). People used to domesticate varieties of live stocks, such as cow, bullock, buffalo, goat, duck etc.

Bullock helps them in agricultural operation. Husk of paddy were used as fodder for their pets. But after land acquisition there is no paddy cultivation, so there is no husk. Now they find it difficult to rear up their livestock as fodder is also to be purchased from market. The open pasture for cattle as well as water bodies for the ducks is also diminishing quickly with the process of urbanisation. For this reason, the number of live stock is decreasing fast. Table 3 shows the village-wise decreasing trend of livestock pattern.

Interestingly, women in the family were considered as custodians of the pets and the animal products were solely at their disposal. The animal products like milk, egg etc., helped the village women to earn some money to meet up their personal requirements like cosmetics, *saris,* or other objects of their desire. Sometimes they sold out goats, hen and ducks also for extra requirement of cash money. The loss of such earnings placed the women at a disadvantageous state, totally dependent on their menfolk for petty requirement in their day to day life. Often their needs were not attended with care and this sometimes leads to quarrel between the spouses. The village women took this very seriously.

Table 3: Livestock Pattern

Moujas	Hh. No.	Past (before land acquisition)						Present (during field work)					
		Cattle				Bird		Cattle				Bird	
		Cow	Ox	Buffalo	Goat	Duck	Hen	Cow	Ox	Buffalo	Goat	Duck	Hen
Chhapna	17	39	36	—	33	63	110	18	10	—	07	48	92
Ghuni	80	250	180	14	130	207	237	35	04	—	33	29	90
Patharghata	16	29	12	—	25	45	33	05	04	—	11	28	24
Thakdari	30	82	24	26	52	87	82	03	—	02	12	38	61
Akandkeshari	02	04	02	—	—	04	02	—	—	—	—	—	—
Sulanggari	06	23	02	—	03	—	—	03	—	—	02	05	—

Table 4: Land use Pattern

Name of the mouja	*Pre-landacquisition before 2000*	*Post-land acquisition after 2000*	*Pre-land acquisition before 2000*	*Post-land acquisition after 2000*
	Cultivated land	*Cultivated land*	*Fishing land*	*Fishing land*
Thakdari (29 households)	165.5 bighas	11.5 bighas	8.5 bighas	Nil
Ghuni (80 households)	414.5 bighas	51.5 bighas	28.5 bighas	Nil
Chhapna (25 households)	235.5 bighas	72.5 bighas	4.0 bighas	2.5 bighas
Patharghata (15 households)	183.5 bighas	27.5 bighas	2 bighas	0.5 bighas
Sulanggari (6 households)	23 bighas	Nil	2 bighas	2 bighas
AkandaKesari (6 households)	37.5 bighas	9 bighas	Nil	Nil

Table-4 and figures (1 and 2) depict the situation concerning individual land holdings in the studied villages before and after land acquisition. The table and figures reflect empirical data. Table-4 clearly reflects that in three villages the fishing land, i.e., water bodies have been reduced to nil in respect of studied households. Similarly, the cultivated land is also reduced radically and in one village (Sulanggari), no cultivable land is left with the households under study. The village Sulanggari is adjacent to Baguihati, an urban extension of Kolkata. Again majority of the villages indicate the presence of water bodies, i.e., wet-lands before the land acquisition in 2000.

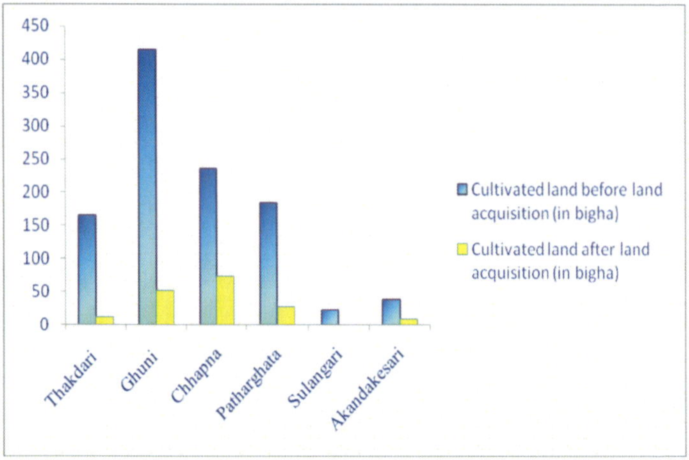

Fig. 1: Land use Pattern (Cultivated Land)

The census 2001 recorded the operational land holding (in the district as a whole) of more than 80 per cent under marginal (below 1.0 acre) size of holding in the district. So, it can be said that people of that area are small or marginal farmers. Moreover, according to the records of Directorate of Agriculture, Government of West Bengal, '8,812 hectares of vested agricultural land have been distributed among 98,672 beneficiaries of which 31.30 per cent belong to Scheduled Castes and 19.13 per cent to Scheduled Tribes during the year ending on 30.09.2000.' This means, total 50.43 per cent of the land was distributed among the Scheduled Caste and Scheduled Tribe population. In our country, several welfare schemes are planned and implemented for the protection and uplift of the socially marginal and backward people but at Rajarhat they were ousted from their livelihood in which they were specialised.

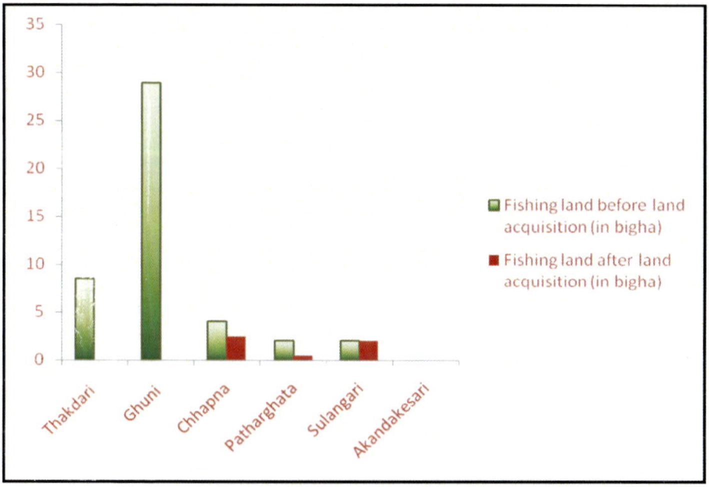

Fig. 2: Land use Pattern (Fishing Land)

The question arises is that how the Government can take such a stance against these marginal people? Now, they were simply pushed towards insecurity of livelihood and became occupational refugees.

Changing Occupations

'Others' include various types of works, like working at a shop, teaching, various kinds of petty jobs, collecting and selling of waste plastics, papers (rag-picking materials), *bidi* rolling etc.

Petty business includes *pan* (betel) shop, small tea stall, plastic toys vendor, grocery shop and so on.

Table 5: Primary Occupations of the Studied Households: Before Land Acquisition

Name of the mouza	*Cultivator*	*Fisher man*	*Business man*	*Others*	*Total*
Chhapna	15	0	1	1	17
Ghuni	71	1	3	5	80
Patharghata	12	0	1	3	16
Thakdari	26	0	2	1	29
Akandkeshari	2	0	0	0	02
Sulanggari	4	0	1	1	06
Total	**130**	**1**	**8**	**11**	**150**

Table 6: Primary Occupations of the Sample Households: After Land Acquisition

Name of the mouza	*Cultivation*	*Fishing/Fish cultivation*	*Petty Business*	*Non-Agri Labour*	*Others*	*Total*
Chhapna	2	0	6	5	4	17
Ghuni	4	0	32	35	9	80
Patharghata	0	0	9	5	2	16
Thakdari	0	0	12	9	8	29
Akandkeshari	0	0	1	0	1	02
Sulanggari	0	0	4	0	2	06
Total	**6**	**0**	**64**	**54**	**26**	**150**

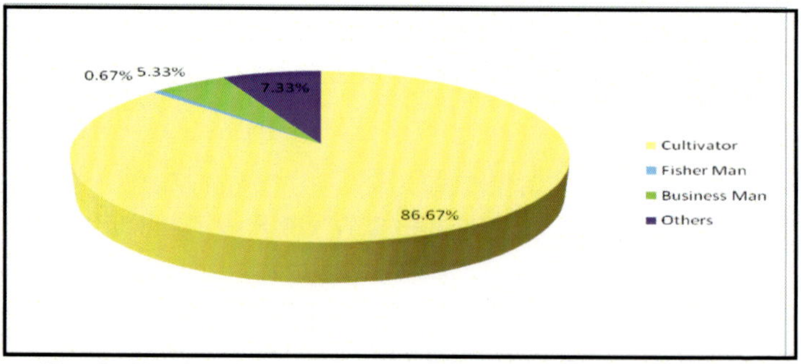

Fig. 3: Showing the primary occupation of studied households: Before land acquisition.

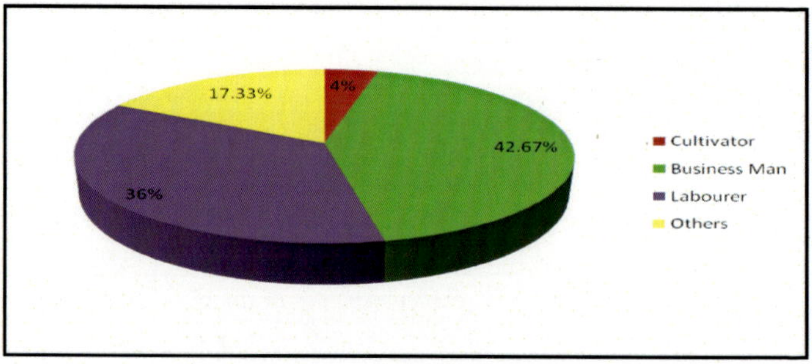

Fig. 4: Showing the primary occupation of studied households: After land acquisition.

The table 5 and 6 and Fig. 3 and 4 show the sharp fall in the occupation of cultivation indicating the extent of loss in their livelihood pattern. A solitary case is found among the studied families (0.67 per cent) engaged in fishery as a secondary source of livelihood. It is clearly portrayed that after the land acquisition, the scenario has been changed radically. They were uprooted from their age-old livelihood and forced to be diverted to varied occupations.

Fig.5 shows the occupational diversities among various groups of people in project affected villages. In Ghuni, a large number of people were found involved in *bidi* rolling.

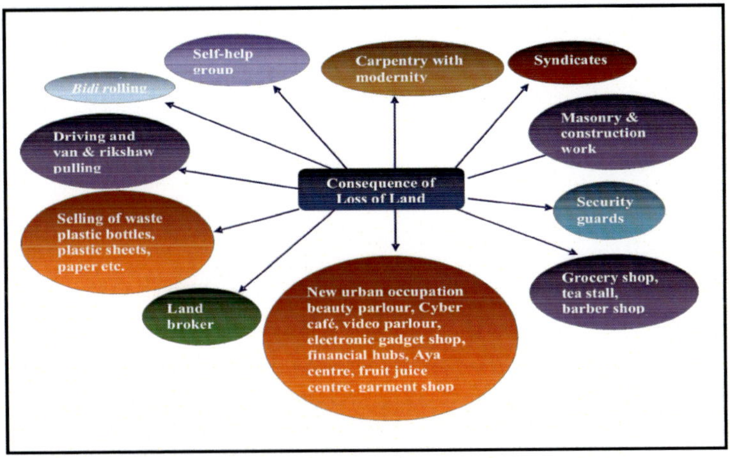

Fig. 5: Occupational Diversity: Emergence of New Occupation.

Aya centres, beauty parlour, cyber café, video game parlour etcetera were the new avenues. In previous days, *bidi* rolling was practised as secondary occupation; in post-project situation more people than earlier times were engaged in this occupation wherein womenfolk also started participating.

The doctors in Primary Health Centre identified the job of *bidi* rolling as one of the responsible factor for Tuberculosis which was prominent in the area. The beauty parlour, cyber café, video game parlours were certainly the result of urbanisation. Furniture shops were also growing fast in these villages. When people received a large amount of money against their land, their first preference was to build a *pucca* (brick-built) house, followed by acquiring furnitures of modern style. Hence, business of furniture emerged in a big way. A large number of people were reportedly engaged in the job of security guard and as wage labourers in construction sites in the coming up city. The security guards were mainly appointed at different offices or at different residential complexes of the New Town. The wage labourers were engaged in masonry as well as other kinds of work in building construction. They mainly work as day labourers. Sometimes for more money they perform duties in evening shift also and earn double wages. Wage labour in construction sites was the urgent need for the growing mega city. Hence, people have ample opportunity to get such kind of jobs. The rag and waste material pickers in Ghuni were actually outsiders, who started living in the outscurt of the village in recent past. Now, a few people from the village also joined them for earning their bread. Some people were engaged in different syndicates. But these types of jobs were not very secured (as observed by the people).

Those who were engaged in construction work suffered from tremendous job insecurity. Their question was: how long they would earn their bread from this type of job? The day would come when all the buildings would be ready; then what will be their fate? According to the villagers, before the land acquisition they had a secured life because they had their land. In the field, father and sons could jointly work to earn the livelihood. Parents want a secured future for their children. But now they have been suffering from insecurity. What would be the fate of their children in future? In fact, being social observant we had no answer. It was also an important observation of the research team that land brokery was a new entry in the occupational categories. The people who could have saved some amount of land from acquisition due to the locational advantage were at a favourable position in post-project time as land price had gone too high, in lacs of rupees per cottah which was earlier priced in a few thousands only. This opportunity was fully utilised by the land brokers and they started mobilising the people for selling their lands. More and more people were joining this profitable business.

Self-help groups were also reported increasing (from the Gram Panchayat records). Some were successful and flourishing, some not. For the unsuccessful cases internal conflict among the members was responsible. There were instances where money was taken for poultry firms but were invested in some other purpose mainly in money-lending business. In such cases vested interest worked and consequently the group became defunct.

Co-operative and Syndicates

After land acquisition HIDCO faced a real crisis and that was of supply of labour. It was of great concern to them that from where a huge cheap labour force would be available for various toilsome works, like, digging and filling-up of land, digging up of canals, construction works etc. The potential labour force before them was the project affected people, who were earnestly in search of a livelihood. HIDCO quickly formed co-operatives of various natures, viz., labour co-operatives, engineering co-operatives and service co-operatives etcetera under the rehabilitation programme for the affected people.

According to the statement of a senior officer of HIDCO, the co-operatives were formed with the idea to provide alternative economic avenues for the affected people and initially 55 numbers of co-operatives (one engineering co-operative, six service co-operatives and 48 labour co-operatives) were formed.

Altogether 2965 members were initially enrolled in co-operatives. It has also been reported that in labour co-operative maximum people came from land-loser families, while a few joined in service co-operatives (as line-man in cable connection, courier service, gardening etcetera). In an initial stage of sufferings people thought that the job of wage labour would possibly satisfy their needs of livelihood. As days passed, gradually improved technology with modern machineries had entered into the project sites and the scope of manual labour work got minimised and at one point of time they became jobless. Later the labour co-operative system had totally been defunct and people presently involved in construction labour work at their individual capacity.

It was also informed that the supply of building materials excepting the iron rods and cement was also an important activity of the co-operatives. The supply orders to the co-operatives were normally channelised through HIDCO only. In due course of time, co-operatives lost its importance and syndicates had cropped up. Now co-operatives function through syndicates only. Each co-operative has a number of syndicates having political background. HIDCO place the requirement of building materials like stone-chips, varieties of sand, bricks etcetera to the co-operatives through which the syndicates get the orders of supply.

At a time, a syndicate can supply one item only. Iron, rods and cement are purchased directly from the concerned companies. While discussing with the officials of HIDCO, it was revealed that co-operative was a registered body having affiliated through Banks. On the other hand, syndicates are unregistered bodies and get the affiliation through Panchayat. co-operatives and syndicates in the area have political affiliation at the local as well as state level and thereby produce tension time to time.

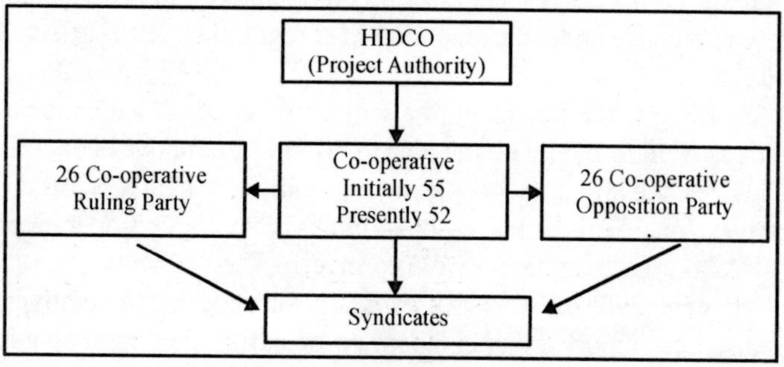

Fig. 6.

Syndicate emerged in the scenario during 2005, and the ruling Left Front Party played an important role to involve their party cadre in the syndicates. Altogether 56 syndicates were formed, which were initially governed by the politicians of the then powerful Left Party. While discussing with the people, it was revealed that most of the syndicates were controlled by economically well-off people and had support of the Left Party. To form a syndicate at least 20 members are required and all are to bear a part of the financial burden for initial investment. It is reported by the people that syndicates were formed by handful of moneyed and politically powerful persons with their vested interest and other members were collected from poor people without monetary investment; so they always remained under the control of moneyed group. These non-affluent people work for the syndicate, arrange raw materials and were paid minimum wages for their labour.

The dominating group distributes the duty of procurement of materials to them according to their need. It was informed by one such member that for enrollment they are to offer bribe to the dominant group. If any such member is reluctant to pay the bribe then his membership is ceased on some or other ground. The very way of working reveals the exploitation and internal corruption of the syndicates (Appendix 17).

Cultural Bonanza: Rituals and Festivities

In the empirical situation it was found that the life of the Rajarhat peasants revolved around land and agriculture.

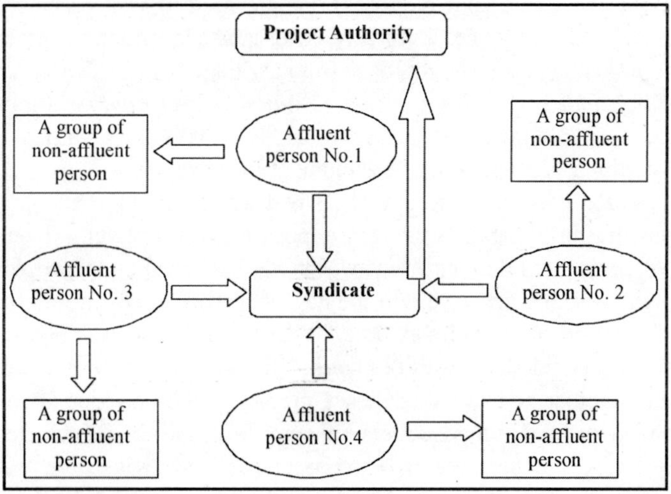

Fig. 7: Structure and Functioning of Syndicate.

The three major attributes that formed the very basis of their cultural practices were '*gol* (cattle shed), *goru* (cattle) and *gola* (granary)' in their own expression. This very phrase signified the importance of agricultural land and livestock in their life. Some of their traditional practices are described below.

Rannapujo: This particular ritual, related with agriculture, observed in the *sankranti* (last day) of the month of *Shravan* (July-August) according to Bengali calendar. It was informed by the people that before the land acquisition when they had enough land for cultivation every agriculturist household used to observe this ritual. On that day, the household deities were worshipped and the female member of the household used to make necessary arrangement for worship, after taking bath. The worship (*puja*) was necessarily been done by a *purohit* (priest from *Brahmin* caste). The married women arranged five numbers of *pan* (betel leaf), five *supari* (betel nut), some amount of newly produced *dhan* (paddy), mustard oil (a bowl full) and *kori* (cowrie) and placed them in front of the sacred place with a lit earthen lamp. All the female folk of the house observed fast until *puja* is over.

A feast was arranged with rice, varieties of vegetarian dishes and *kheer* (a sweet delicacy prepared by new rice boiled with milk and *khejur gur* (date palm molasses). People used to visit each other's house on the very occasion freely. After land acquisition this ritual is no more practised. The response from a villager: '*gola bhara dhan-o ar nei; gai, goru sab hariechhe ei notun saharer daulate*' (granary does not contain paddy any more; we have lost cattle, etc., everything because of the development of this city).

Nabanna: This agricultural festival was common to all agrarian societies in Bengal. This was a post harvest festival. The term (*Nabanna*) was derived from two words like *nabo* and *anno* which literally means new rice. On the day of festival *payas*, a traditional delicacy prepared with new rice, milk and molasses, was offered to the household deity. Besides, *pithe* (indigenous small rice cakes) were another home made delicacy prepared with new rice and used to be dedicated to the Goddess Lakshmi first, and then distributed to all family members as *Prasad* (consecrated food). Kins were invited to participate in this ritual. After this *nabanno* festival only, the new rice was taken for consumption by the family. This festival was generally performed in the month of *Poush* (December-January). The big land holders and well of families used to perform this festival with great enthusiasm. But after land acquisition this ritual had been faded away.

Sadh-dhaka: It was also an important ritual for this peasant society. The ritual was observed in the month of *Kartik* (October-November) following the first flowering of paddy. On an auspicious day, all the members including males and females of the household used to assemble in the field in early morning after having bath for worshiping the rice field offering incense sticks, fruits and sweets. Offerings were left behind in the field itself. But with the loss of agricultural land such kind of rituals and festivities are no more observed.

Boani: *Boani* was the celebration of harvesting of paddy. The ritual was performed in the field itself on the preceeding day the

Poush Sankranti, the last day of the month of *Poush* (in January every year). On that occasion, people used to make a small bundle with *tulsi* (Basil), flower, *gur* (molasses) and paddy and offer it to the God and pray; 'God, thank you for such a good harvest this year and please give us more crops in the next year'.

Sadh Khawano: On certain day of *Kartik,* the agriculturists observed *sadh khawano* where a palm sheaf (*taler-anti*) was implanted in the agricultural field symbolically. To them the land is their mother. Crops come out of her womb. When they sowed the seeds the mother became pregnant. It was their duty to offer *sadh* (a ritual to satisfy all desires of a pregnant lady, a Bengali custom) to their mother nature. They used to offer *puja* in the agricultural field and sing a song jointly:

> '*Aswin gelo Kartik elo,*
> *Choto baro dhan gorve porlo,*
> *Ma lakkhi sadh khao*'.
> (The month of Aswin is over, Kartik is started
> Small and large paddy is set in the womb
> Mother goddess Lakshmi have your *sadh*).

Poush Sankranti: This festival was performed on the last day of the month of *Poush* (14th January every year) of Bengali calendar. Indigenous cake (*pithe*) of ground new rice was the main attraction of the festival. Every household used to prepare *pithe* lavishly and consumed with great enjoyment. The tradition was to offer *pithe* first to a bullock. The tradition shows how a bullock was culturally attached to the psyche of an agrarian society.

Alakkhi Biday: This ritual was associated with the *Lakshmi puja* (the worship of goddess Lakshmi, the deity of wealth and well-being of the family) where in a symbol of *Alakkhi* (inauspicious) was prepared out of cow dung cake and taken out of the house to the village path by beating of winnowing fan. It symbolises to drive away the malevolent power from the house.

Gomâtâr Pujâ/Bhagabatir Pujâ/Goâl Pujâ: It was the worship of cow. In Hindu belief cow is equated with mother goddess *Bhagabati* (*go*=cow, *mâtâ*= mother). In Rajarhat this ritual was learnt to be observed in every house of cultivators on the first day of *Baisakh* (15th April every year) according to Bengali calender. First of all, they used to clean the cowsheds applying cow dung paste and water, and then with cow dung they used to prepare a structure signifying Mother Goddess *Bhagabati*. Washing the feet of cows and bullocks and applying vermillion on the forehead of cows and on the horns and feet of bullocks was compulsory part of the ritual. This they used to observe with reverence and they bowed down their heads to the feet of bullocks and cows.

Gochh Banne: On the first day of *Asâd* (in June) in every Bengali calender year, the owner cultivator used to plant bunch (*Gochh*) of paddy seedlings in the field and on returning home, he was served with boiled green *deshi amra* (local variety of Hog-plum) along with rice by his mother or wife. The belief was that as a small green *amra* grows and ripe so would be the bunch of seedlings into flowering plant.

Hal Panne: This was observed by the cultivators in the month of *Jaistha* (May-June) but there was no fixed date. On a convenient day and time, the cultivator used to take his plough and bullock to the field and round them two and half times in the field. Before going to the field, the cultivator was to draw the image of lord Shiva on the *Jowal* (the long piece of wooden plank placed on the shoulder of the two bullocks) with the help of oil and vermillion paste.

Kather Alo: This ritual was performed with the hope of getting good crops. On the day of *bhatri-ditiya* (second day of the bright fortenight in the month of *Kartik;* the day signifies the affectional ties between bothers and sisters) a bunch of dried *Patkathi* (which comes out after extracting raw jute) was lit with fire and after the flame extinguish, the sticks were planted into the fields. It was perfomed in the agricultural field only. On the occasion, a song was sung addressing mother Lakshmi:

"*Kather Alo dey*
Ma Lakshir bey
Ma Lakshmi ante jabe
Phul batasa de".
(With *Kather alo*
Mother Lakshmi's marriage
Mother Lakshmi will be brought
With flower and *batasa*/sugar cake).

This ritual is usually held in the evening. After returning home they compulsorily eat *at kalai bhaja* (a mixture fried grains and pulses).

Jamai-shashti: This was a social function observed commonly in Bengal for the welfare of the married girl and the son-in-law of a family. The ritual was performed in the month of *Jaistha* (May-June) according to Bengali calendar. On this occasion, goddess *Shasthi* was worshipped by the female-folk. *Shasthi* is a folk deity, who brings prosperity and well-being for a family. On that day, the female-folk performed various rituals. Delicious food items were prepared and served ceremonially to son-in-law.

But this social tradition was affected adversely in the process of land acquisition. When land acquisition process started there were protests from the peasants and many refused to attend the hearing to show their unwillingness. To win over this standstill situation, the powerful Left politicians played a shrewd game through brokers and men in their confidence. They approached the married girls of the families to attend the hearings and to receive cheque issued by HIDCO. Many got entrapped and for the sake of cash or under pressure from the in-laws they attended the hearings without knowledge of their natal families. This very act on the part of the married girls adversely worked on the movement of the people. Such incidences invoked conflict between the father and daughters, brothers and sisters and broke up family ties. In many families the observance of *Jamai-shasthi had* been stopped. Sometimes economic reason (due to loss of lands) was cited for not practising *Jamai-shasthi*.

Bhatri Ditiya (Bhai-phonta): This ceremony signifies the bond of love between brothers and sisters. Sisters observe this ceremony for the welfare of their brothers. Sisters used to apply a *tika* with sandal paste on the forehead of their brothers reciting a *mantra* (here it is a folk verse): *Bhaiyer kapale dilam phonta/jamer duare porlo kanta* (with the tika she closed the door of Jam, the god of death signifies a prayer for the long life of her brother). Brothers were offered a good feast; brothers reciprocate with gift to the sisters. But similar to *Jamai-shashti* the celebration of *Bhai-phonta* had also been affected badly on the issue of land (already discussed under *Jamai-shashti*).

There were innumerable such practices around the cultivable land, each of which was a festive occasion for these marginal communities. These were also the occasions for the mutual interaction between the people and communities. All such traditions were lost for ever with the loss of land. It affects greatly to their mental and social horizon.

While taking account of their rituals and festivities, the villagers requested us to note down one of their earlier practice, *Panta Bhat Kere Khaowa*, which though not a ritual but used to be a event of enjoyment for them and it earned immense importance in their life.

Panta Bhat Kere Khaowa: In the villages when men were at work in field their food was usually brought to the field by the family members. The morning food was normally *panta-bhat*, the wet/ soaked boiled rice. Such rice used to be added with salt, fried chillies/ green chillies/boiled potato and vegetable curry if available. It was a common joke between the neibouring cultivators to snatch each others *panta bhat* and eat them joyously. The person whose food was eaten by others had to ask for more *panta bhat* from home and mutually shared that with the co-cultivators. At the end of the day, the person who was on the losing end was to invite the co-cultivators to his house and to present each of them a *gamchha* (local word for handloom towel) as a token of love, goodwill and joy. This simple joke and the presentation of *gamchha* speak of the cordial relation between the people. The villagers remember the old days with a great sigh from their heart.

Proposed Mega City: New Cultural Landscape

The proposed mega city of New Town had been inaugurated officially by the then state government (Left Front) on 2nd June, 1995. Altogether 24 *moujas* with 19 *moujas* from Rajarhat Block and five *moujas* from Bhangar-II Block were taken into the project area (see appendix for the list).

The imposition of restriction on registration over selling and purchasing of land with proclaiming order of the Governor of the state in August 1999, invoked a great repercussion in the mental horizon of the people inhabiting the area and having hold of lands. The post-project scenario leads slowly in changing the landscape of agricultural and fishing lands to urban landscape through the allotment of residential space, business and commercial complex, cultural, education, recreational, health facilities and establishment of major arterial and linkroads. It also proposed open space and water bodies to be used for the eco-cultural purposes which not only diminishing the area in wetland, but also damaging the wet-land by way of filling up of surrounding area.

The proposed mega city takes up land of all 24 villages of Rajarhat and Bhangar-II Block leaving only settlement and little bit adjoining area with village settlement. Thus, the emergence of new cultural landscape has not only replaced the existing landscape for the proposed New Town, but also affects the character of the existing landscape of the left out areas by way of changing the surrounding landscape including wet-land and gradual depletion of *gol* (cattle-shed), *goru* (cattle), *gola* (storehouse of grains) and loss of functional relation of these three elements with the existing landscape. The existing villages started to show inclination towards new urban economy with the setting up of co-operatives and syndicates in a haste way leading tension and unrest among the people of new set-up in some cases.

Basic Objective of the Proposed Town (Left Front Government's Perspective)

The basic aim (according to HIDCO reports) of setting up New Town Rajarhat as mega city was to check further intensification of congested Kolkata city, to prevent urban sprawl in the fringes and to boost up emerging industrial and economic activities through provision of a new centre of business instead of existing the central business district of Calcutta Metropolitan Area (CMA). The New town has also aim to provide social infrastructure, better education and health facilities, markets, cultural and recreational centres etc. There is also anticipation that New town would be able to create efficient drainage system leading to benefit of the entire sub-region. Significantly, the proposed meg city project is dovetailed with Government of India declaration towards establishing 100 such new towns of population 0.5 million by 2020.

The environmental quality in the context of proposed New Town would be maintained by way of preservation of East Calcutta Wet-lands, treatment of waste water comprehensive in waste water treatment plants, scientific disposal of solid waste as sanitary land free in suitable identified area within project site, arrest of pollution by aforestation and plantation programmes, landuse and development control plan (LUDCP) to ensure the development in harmonies and sustainable way, development of adjacent villages with water supply, rural electrification, drainage and road development.

Proposed Land Use

The proposed land use in the context of setting up of New Town mega city would provide space primarily for residential town (HIDCO Project Report, 1999, p. 13; Ghosh *et al* 2000, p. 4.11). Therefore, the principal use of the development of land would be for residential purpose along with ancillary service and community facilities. Another important use will be for clean industries. The central business complex and other commercial area will also receive due importance. According to Master Land use plan published by HIDCO the New Town would be environment-friendly city with large areas of open green land, waterbodies, plantations etc. The landuse breakup as per report is attached in appendix-3.

Residential Areas

Considering the total project area of 3075 hectares, the New Town is planned for a total residential population of 7.5 lakhs. It will give rise in density of population of about 244 persons per hectare in the changing situation. It may also be added in this context that the population of Rajarhat Block was seven persons per hectare considering the 1991 census population of 1,19,650.

In addition, the expected floating population per day would be about 2.5 lakhs for business and commercial function. The land for residential use would be 1555 hectare, i.e., about 50 per cent of total project area. Considering residential areas, residential density would be 482 persons per hectare. High quality infrastructure and community facilities particularly efficient public transport system had been proposed. There would be provision of service village at different points of the city. The service village will provide facilities for work and living for the service population. The location of service village will be near to existing settlement within the project area.

Industrial and Commercial Area

The New Town will provide 200 hectare of land for development of non-polluting, in-offensive and non-hazardous industries. These areas would provide accessibility to goods movement.

New Business District and Other Commercial Areas

New Town would provide a business district to act as a supplementary Commercial Business District of the metropolis. The total land area to be used for the new business district and two commercial sub-centres would be 140 hectares. The major facilities would include office complex, offices of different institution including financial centres and banks, LIC, etc., offices of airlines, hotel complex, shopping complex,cultural-complex with commercial and recreational facilities.

Open Space, Recreational Area and Landscape

A unique feature of the New Town as proposed is that about 20 per cent of total land use for bulk open space with green areas, water bodies and large lakes etc. In this connection, it is to be mentioned that an eco-tourism park has been proposed centering round a portion of *Ghunir Bil.* The park will be developed on 480 acres of land including 100 acres of waterbodies (*Ghunir Bil*). The existing ponds within the project area cover an area of 45 hectares, which would not only be maintained but enlarged also to a total area of 165 hectares.

The preservation of the East Calcutta Wet-lands would be made an integral part of the project.

Proposed Water Supply and Drainage System

The proposed mega-city requires a huge and dependable supply of water of proper quality in the context of establishment of incoming inhabitants of 7.5 lakhs population and setting up business, commercial and industrial complex.

The future water demand shall be as under:

(a) Residential population of six lakhs at the rate of 140 lpcd
=85 mld

(b) Day-time population of 2.5 lakh 45 lpcd

Total 95.25 mld

Say 100 mld. (c.f. Concept plan: p. 26).

The PHE Department has already prepared a preliminary report of comprehensive Water Supply Scheme. A feasibility report for interim water supply plan has also been completed by the PHE Department. In order to cope with the first phase development of the

New Town, an interim water supply scheme has been prepared with ground water as the source of supply. There will be arrangement for continuing monitoring of water quality till the scheme for water supply from the Hooghly River is completed. Similarly, comprehensive drainage scheme is prepared for improvement of the lower *Bagjola Khal* from VIP road to the outfall of Kultigong.

Two important drainage arteries available are *Bagjola Khal* and Kestopur (Krishnapur) *Kata Khal*. The two *khals* have outfalls in the river Kultigong. These two *khals* would be used as the drainage of waste water flowing from neighbouring urban centres as well as proposed New Town. Rapid urbanissation has caused heavy siltation with depth of silt at places being as high as 1.5 meters. The irrigation and water ways department of West Bengal has undertaken a detail survey of the *Bagjola Khal.*

Rajarhat Land Before Acquisition (Courtesy: Nilotpal Dutta).

Before Acquisition Scenario. (Courtesy: Nilotpal Dutta).

Before Acquisition Scenario. (Courtesy: Nilotpal Dutta).

Before Acquisition Scenario. (Courtesy: Nilotpal Dutta)

Before Acquisition Scenario. (Courtesy: Nilotpal Dutta)

Before Acquisition Scenario. (Courtesy: Nilotpal Dutta)

Before Acquisition Scenario. (Courtesy: Nilotpal Dutta)

Before Acquisition Scenario. (Courtesy: Nilotpal Dutta)

Before Acquisition Scenario. (Courtesy: Nilotpal Dutta)

Before Acquisition Scenario. (Courtesy: Nilotpal Dutta)

Fertile Land Under Acquisition for Township.

Fertile Land Under Acquisition for Township.

Fertile Land Under Acquisition for Township.

Fertile Land Under Acquisition for Township.

Fertile Land Under Acquisition for Township

Fertile Land Under Acquisition for Township.

Fertile Land Under Acquisition for Township.

Local Market.

3

Process of Land Acquisition in Rajarhat

Empirical Findings

The plan of a mega city in Rajarhat was conceived by the Left Front government in the year 1993. The department of housing, government of West Bengal constituted a Technical committee in May 1993 for preparation of a preliminary report of the New Town. The Housing Directorate prepared a preliminary base map in August 1993. The Technical Committee in its second meeting held on 03.09.93 decided that the CMDA (Calcutta Metropolitan Development Authority) should prepare a draft Concept Plan taking into consideration of the relevant factors. Accordingly, the Directorate of Planning and Development, CMDA prepared a concept plan for the housing department of West Bengal government in May 1994 and this was accepted by the Technical Committee. In May 1994, the Housing Department constituted a Task Force comprising senior technical officers of Force, 1995; p. 1). The Task Force report described the project area (2750 ha) as vacant low yield Housing Department, Housing Board, Public Health Engineering Department, Environment Department, Irrigation and Waterways Department and other experts. The Task Force felt the need for modifying the Concept Plan and provided guidelines for necessary revision (Report of the Task agricultural land and stated that 'there is no existing fishery or '*Bhery*' or permanent wetland in the project area' (*ibid.*, 5: 2.3.1). While assessing the preliminary cost the same report estimated a cost of Rs 241.40 crore to fill up an area of 2095 hectares, taking into consideration the average depth of 1.5 metres constituting a volume of fill as 314.25 lakh cuM. (Low-lying agricultural lands with average depth of 1.5 metres are certainly the wet-land as per the very nature of the land in the area).

However, the Housing Department (vide their D.O. letter no. SH-1402, dated 15th November, 1994) requested the Department of Architechture and Regional planning. I.I.T., Kharagpur to review the Concept Plan of the proposed New Town at Rajarhat between Bidhannagar and Netaji Subhas Chandra Bose International Airport in the district of 24 Parganas, prepared by CMDA. The I.I.T., Kharagpur submitted their review report in 1996 accepting all the proposals of the Concept Plan. The project was formally inaugurated on 2nd June, 1995 by the then Chief Minister Jyoti Basu. On 6th December, 1996, restriction was imposed on registration over selling and purchasing of land at Rajarhat with proclaiming order of the then Governor of the state. (However, according to its officials, HIDCO purchased about 100 acres of land from the villagers at the rate of rupees 6000-7000 per cottah as 'sample purchasing of land'). Afterwards, with the instruction of the High Court environmental impact assessment was done through the firm Ghose Bose and Associates. The said Environmental Impact Assessment Report was submitted in 2000. The report totally denied the existence of wetland in Rajarhat and described the agricultural land as single crop producing with low production rate. It also did not report about the effective irrigation system in the area through RLI scheme, deep and shallow tube-wells besides the canal water.

The land acquisition process officially started in Rajarhat in the months of April-May 1999. Initially, vide notification number 1423/HG/NTP/IM-1/98 dated, 27/08/1999 and subsequent partial modification in 2001, 2006, 2008 (737-HI/HG/NTP/IM-1/98 dated 26/07/01, 650-111/IM-198 dated 22/11/06, 392 HI/HG/NTP 3C-2/2005 dated 21/07/2008) all total 23 villages of Rajarhat of North 24 Parganas and 16 villages of Bhangar-II Block of South 24 Parganas were taken in planning area of the proposed New Town.

However, at last 19 villages of Rajarhat Block and five villages of Bhangar-II Block were acquisitioned as project area for implementation of proposed New Town. Initially, acquisition notice was issued for

2750 hectares of land; later some other *Moujas* were added to the plan and notice was issued for 3075 hectares of cultivable land (All the lands were under cultivation at that time). The landowners and the *Bargadars* were sent notices to that effect. 'According to the documents of the land revenue department the number of recorded landowners was over 30,000 while 5,000 were recorded *Bargadars*. The number of unrecorded *Bargadars* was double of that. Long before the government notification, and land acquisition process had started the land mafia started buying the land from the poor farmers.' (Sanhati, August 29, 2008)

In the beginning of this process, all the farmers of Mahishgoth and Thaakdnari declined to accept the notice primarily because the compensation package decided upon for each cottah was rupees 5,000 to 6,000 which was far lower as compared to the officially government registered price from rupees 40,000 to 50,000. More importantly for the major section of people here, farming was their assured resource and they knew no other way of earning their livelihood.

Also various promises were made to the land loser regarding possible employment in various jobs. However, all these could not divert the farmers from their path of agitation. Even the eminent political figures and administrators failed to sway the farmers in spite of holding more than one public meeting in Rajarhat. Sanhati (August, 2008) reported 'The sad fact is that nobody stood by these helpless people. Bourgeous political parties had already turned their back towards them. If the news media and the intelligentsia, who are so vocal against the land grabs in Singur-Nandigram of the Left Front government enamoured with SEZ, and its inhuman repression and mass murder of common people had shown even a fraction of that solidarity for the people of Rajarhat perhaps so many people would not have lost their lives.'

To stop people's voice the Left Front government used all its functionaries including Police Force, RAF, and political cadres. Random arrest and suppression of the leading people caused a set back to the spontaneous movement of the affected people. In 2001 from 5th to 8th June, there was strong protest movement in Ghuni *Mouja* against the forceful land acquisition by the government. Women from the peasant families lay down *en masse* on the cultivable land as a gesture of protest. Let us hear from the people in their own words:

'The untold story of Rajarhat is that here lands had been occupied forcibly by the government. The green bench of High Court allowed 622 hectares of land for development. But government acquired 3075 hectares of land. The Left Front (LF) government claimed that the villagers surrendered their lands willingly which is not only a distortion of the fact but also a total lie. The Rajarhat Jami Bachao Committee and Howrah Ganatantrik Nagarik Committee filed an appeal to the High Court against the land acquisition which was not decided upon (see Appendix 5). Besides there were 28 land cases pending with the Calcutta High Court. The vital role played by the cadre (LF) force, political goons, police force and the *dalals* (middlemen) in Rajarhat was the worst ever instances in the working procedure of the Left Front government. Only a handful big landlords were the beneficiaries and poor and the marginal peasants became pauper' viewed by Sri Prahlad Mandal of Patharghata.

The housing department said that the lands of Rajarhat were not much productive and also denied the existence of vast water bodies (already cited reference in p. 4 and p. 25). In a discussion with the HIDCO personnel, it was told to us that the mass of land choosen for the project area was mostly vacant land, low-marshy in character (it is contradictory to another interview in later date where an official said that there was no major water bodies in the project occupied area), where single crop was grown in a limited quantity and the agriculturists used to get a minimum yield from the field. In contrast, according to the District Statistical Hand book, North 24 Parganas, Bureau of Applied Economics and Statistics, Government of West Bengal (c.f. Dey, 2011: pp. 19-20), 'in 2000-01, the total agricultural land was 3958 hectares of which 60 per cent was multi-crop land. In 1993-94 about 819 hectares of land was under fish cultivation and the annual fish production was 10388 quintals'. In the government report of 1993-94, there was mention of RLI scheme, shallow and deep tube wells and ponds along with two canals for the purpose of irrigation. The total irrigated land was 2667 hectares. In 2000-01 report, though there was no mention of canals and there was decrease in the number of ponds still the irrigated lands were recorded as 2104 hectares, i.e., about 53 per cent of lands were under irrigation. The people also contradicted the observation by the housing department. There was Municipality as well as six Panchayats in Rajarhat. 'There were about 15 RLI Schemes, three deep tube-wells and innumerable shallow machines for irrigation with the help of which we produced paddy, jute, Rabi-crop, flower as cash crop and also there were *bheris* where people used to cultivate fish. The Left Front government made the RLI schemes electric-operated which further improved agriculture in this area. But Kharagpur IIT's report totally distorted the fact. At the first instance, HIDCO got hold of the *parcha* (LR) for 25 *moujas* from BLR Office. So, the peasants could not do mutation of their lands. Secondly, registration over selling and buying of land was restricted for five years. Thirdly, the Left Front supported middlemen approached the married sisters for attending the hearings over land and tempted them for money. Next step was to make propaganda among the poor peasants that whoever would refuse to surrender land his/her money would be deposited to CD (court). It would be then a great difficulty for them to get the money. But people protested. To stop their voice people were arrested at random.

Sri Ranjit Naskar, Prahlad Mandal, Pulak Chatterji, Adhir Mandal of Patharghata and Sabir Ali Siddiki, Sabil Ali Naskar and Mohinddin Molla of Baliguri *mouja* were arrested and the case against them had not been withdrawn till date. While they were in jail, the Left Front government with the help of police force forcibly occupied the 3-4 crops producing lands from the peasants on the gun point. The brick-kiln of Nishikanta Mandal was forcibly occupied, destroyed and he was abducted; till date he could not be traced. HIDCO wanted to plant high tension power cables through the lands of the peasants. But, with the kind intervention of Kakoli Ghosh Dastidar, the TMC (Trinamool Congrss) MP, in time that was stopped. The CPI-M (Communist Party of India-Marxist) Party promoted 58 syndicates for the supply of building materials to the growing city which were controlled by their own people only. Afterwards in the changing post election scenario the TMC occupied about 50 per cent of them. The Left Front allotted land to the influential and established people of Kolkata from the Chairman's quota (see appendix 10). So, we poor people were at the receiving end' said Ranjit Naskar of Patharghata village.

'HIDCO sent notice for acquisition; asked me to receive the cheque from Salt Lake office. I had low-lying land where they created a *jhil* (water body) but I did not get any compensation against it; because, I was not willing to give the land. I did not appear for hearing. Government (LF) said that people surrendered land willingly; no, that is not correct. People surrendered their land under fearful situation. The Left government cordoned the area with Police Force, not less than four/five thousand. There was no other option but to surrender, remembered Akhtaf Uddin.' His experience: 'For an eight cottah of land I received a cheque of rupees 40 thousand only while the price in their terms amounts to rupees 64 thousand only. While they sent the cheque, there was no mention of the amount of acquired land. Total amount of land acquired was nine bighas only. But no more compensation was given. All these lands were *dhan jami,* i.e., paddy producing lands. After acquisition in fact there is dearth of room for a big family.'

'People did not come forward for surrendering their lands. Government acquired the land forcefully. In Rekjoani *mouja,* government promised to pay rupees 10,000/- per cottah but actually paid rupees 6,000/- per cottah. Government promised to provide job at least for one person from every affected household. So many pomises were made by the then Chief Minister, Ministers, political leaders before land acquisition, but after acquisition they forgot all the promises. People were told that if they fail to receive cheque within specified date they will be required to collect it from court. Many people did not collect their cheque at that time, their payment are still pending' said Sardar from Sulanggari village.

A responded aged 39 years from Ghuni *mouja,* remembered those days. In his words, 'about 3.5 bighas of my land was acquired. For about four years registration of land was stopped by the government. People were in economic trouble. Because in villages land is the only asset and in crisis peoples either sell out or mortgage a portion of it to meet up the immediate need. So, when in 1998, government announced that whoever would sell their lands government would pay them, and the big landholders and locally prominent people volunteered to surrender their lands for the proposed project, some poor people also followed them. But later people understood that there was foul play underneath, and these were for the eyewash of the poor people. The big landholders mostly surrendered their disputed lands and managed to get their good lands away from acquisition. They started advising people to surrender their lands to the government for the sake of their self-interest only. They posed themselves as if they were speaking for the interest of the people. Out of fear many people surrendered their lands. Some people purchased land but did not register in their name they suffered a lot as the cheques were issued in the name of landholder. There were so many problems.'

Our interaction with the villagers recorded countless such experiences. The above are to mention a few. The field data unveiled the fact that the land acquisition process of the then LF government was not transparent and was a planned conspiracy of the Ruling power against the marginal people with vested interest from the part of the then political leaders. This clearly speaks of violation of people's right by the government. On 19th June, 1997 the Additional District Magistrate and District Land and Land Reform Officer in a letter wrote to the Joint Secretary of the Housing Department of the State government that 'I would like to bring to your notice that the West Bengal Housing Board has sponsord the names, of eleven companies for mutation of the RORs in their favour by the BLLRO, Rajarhat. The total quantum of land is about 94.0 acres in the *mouzas* of Thakdari, Mahisgot, Mahisbathan. Initially, the companies could not be served notice at their recorded address; as such offices do not appear to exist. Thereafter, it was seen that all the companies have appointed one Anil Maheswari to deal with all the matters relating to mutation/conversion. ...These companies ostensibly formed for trade/manufacture of different products like film, PVC pipe etc., do not exist on the ground. Nor are they found in possession. The concerned plots are to be in cultivating possession of RS recorded *raiyats* as seen by the Revenue Officer. In such a situation, mutation cannot be allowed in favour of these companies which appear *prima-facie* fictitious....' (c.f. Dey, 2011: 9). The letter unearths the vested interest of a section of people under the patronage of political power.

Rajarhat is perhaps the worst example of violation of environmental protection rules also. Water bodies, marshland and agricultural fields were being rapidly filled up and multi-storied buildings were being erected at a breakneck pace (see photographs though unfortunately there is no trace of the water body at present. Also see the photograph of a little portion of *Ghunir bil* that exists till today. It is proposed to be a part of the Eco-Tourism Park covering 480 acres of land).

It may be pointed out here that the natural drainage system of Kolkata and its adjoining areas irrevocably damaged and the ecological balance being destroyed by the steady acquisition of all the arable land and water bodies of Rajarhat. The environmentalists of the state filed a case with the Green Bench of Kolkata High Court. As per the verdict of the Calcutta High Court Green Bench, the government can acquire 622 hectares of land for the development of township.

We quote Prahlad Mandal, a project affected person and an active member of the Rajarhat Jami Bachao Committee 'there are multi-lane roads, rows of multi-storied buildings, market complexes, Malls, schools, hospitals, IT sectors and so on. All these are being constructed over our lands soaked with our blood and tears.' This has been echoed by every land loser.

In their own words 'while the farmers were paid only Rs. 5,000 to 6,000, the same land was being sold by the government to the businessmen at Rs.7,00,000 to 3,00,000 or more per cottah, while the promoter and developers in turn are making more profit out of it. A small 450 square feet flat costs Rs. 15 lakhs initially. It is costing more nowadays. See, how much they are earning, but whatever they are earning is at the cost of our livelihood.'

Land Acquisition Act, 1894 and Rajarhat Issue

(For this section, we are greatly indebted to Guha, 2007, 47-55: different stages of the LA Act are quoted from him).

As a backdrop of the Land Acquisition Act, Guha (2007:47-48) observed that 'In India, the system of keeping records of cultivable land by the state for the purpose of revenue collection originated in pre-colonial period, while a systematic legal and administrative machinery for acquiring land from private owners developed during the colonial regime. The all-embracing nature of the colonial state power found one of its successful expressions through the enactment of the Land Acquisition Act of 1894. The succession of some landmark events, which led to the enactment of this enabling piece of legislation, showed a consolidation of British colonial power in the Indian sub-continent. This consolidation of the colonial power was not only a political phenomenon, but it also ushered in a chain of technological as well as economic events which needed a well-organised legal and bureaucratic structure...The succession of events, which led to the enactment of this Act, clearly showed that it was the need of the time. Mining, plantation, establishment of railway lines, manufacturing industries, beginning of major irrigation works, and road building all needed land which again was already under various forms of state controlled and customary tenure systems that existed from the pre-colonial period. This enabling Act empowered the state to acquire any privately owned as well as common property land for public purposes. The Act provided the legitimacy behind the acquisition which otherwise would have to be done with the application of brute force. After Independence, the Government of India did not abolish this piece of colonial legislation and acquisition of private land continued with the help of the Land Acquisition Act 1894. The first major change in the Act was introduced in 1984 through an amendment by the Central Government. The said amendment resulted in some beneficial changes for the Project Affected People (PAP) which is enumerated below:

1. Payment of 12 per cent per annum interest on land value to the person whose land has been acquired commencing from the date of notification to the date of declaration of the compensation award.'
2. Payment of solatium (i.e., compensation for losses suffered or injured feelings) at the rate of 30 per cent. Earlier it was 15 per cent.
3. A provision was made to those not satisfied with the collector's award to apply for a redetermination of the compensation.
4. The amendment also tried to minimise the undue delay that characterises land acquisition proceedings.

But along with above beneficial changes the amendment had also conferred greater discretionary power on the government and introduced the acquisition of land for private companies. Before the amendment, private companies procured land from the market by paying the market price. The amendment enabled the private companies to get land from government, which meant that the latter had to acquire land beforehand on behalf of the company.'

For acquiring land by the government under the Land Acquisition

Act (LA Act) there are certain administrative stages which are interconnected. We must mention here that in India Land Acquisition Act 1894 is still followed.

1. According to Land acquisition Act, the state can exercise its right of *eminent domain* (India-West Bengal) wherein it is the ultimate owner of all land, which it can acquire for public purposes after paying full compensations calculated on the market value.
2. At the first stage a notification under Section 4 of LA Act is issued by the government stating the purpose for which the land is to be acquired. This notification is to be published in the Government Gazette as well as in two daily newspapers of which one should be in regional language. The District Collector also should issue a public notice at convenient places in the area.
3. In the following stage any person, who has interest in land (e.g., landowner or share-cropper) may file an objection under Section 5-A against acquisition within 30 days from the date of publication of the notice and the Collector may give an opportunity to the objector of being heard and after making any further enquiry will submit the case to the government, although the decisions of the Collector on the objections is final.

   [Section 5-A- Hearing of objections— (1) Any person interested in any land which has been notified under Section 4, sub-Section (1), as being needed or likely to be needed for a public purpose or for a company may, within thirty days from the date of the publication of the notification, object to the acquisition of the land or of any land in the locality, as the case may be. (2) Every objection under sub-Section (1) shall be made to the Collector in writing, and the Collector shall give the objector an opportunity of being heard in person or by any person authorised by him in this behalf or by pleader and shall, after hearing all such objections and after making such further inquiry, if any, as he thinks necessary, either make a report in respect of the land, which has been notified under Section 4, sub-Section (1), or make different reports in respect of different parcels of such land, to the appropriate Government, containing his recommendations on the objections, together with the record of the proceedings held by him, for the decision of that Government. The decision of the Appropriate Government on the objections shall be final. (3) For the purpose of this section, a person shall be deemed to be interested in land that would be entitled to claim an interest in compensation if the land were acquired under this Act. (C.f. De, 2011:16-17)].

4. Next stage is that under Section 6, a declaration notification is issued by the government which is conclusive evidence that the land is needed for a public purpose or for a company. This declaration is made within one year from the date of publication of notice.
5. In the fourth stage, a notice is issued by the Collector under Section 9 of LA Act to all those persons, who have an interest in the land. Through this notice, the Collector invites 'interested persons' to claim compensation.
6. In the fifth stage, the Collector conducts an enquiry under Section 11 against the claim of the interested person and also makes an 'award'. The LA Act stipulated that the 'award' would have to be made within two years from the date of publications of the declaration under Section 6. This 'award' becomes final under Section 12 of the Act. If any dispute arises, the Collector may refer the matter to the Court for its decision under Section 30.
7. Stage 6. At this stage, that is, after the declaration of the 'award' the Collector can take possession of land under Section 16 of the Act. But in case of urgency, the Collector may immediately after the notification under Section 9, can take possession of land under Section 17 without making an 'award', although in this case the Collector will have to make 80 per cent of the estimated compensation to the land losers.

   [Section 17 – Special powers in cases of urgency – (1) In cases of urgency, whenever the appropriate Government so directs, the Collector, though no such award has been made may, on the expiration of fifteen days from the publication of the notice mentioned in Section 9, sub-Section (1), take possession of any land needed for a public purpose, such land shall thereupon vest absolutely in the Government, free from all encumbrances.

   (2) Whenever owing to any sudden change in the channel of any navigable river or other unforeseen emergency, it becomes necessary for any Railway administration to acquire the immediate possession of any land for the maintenance of their traffic or for the purpose of making thereon a river-side or *ghat* station, or of providing convenient connection with or access to any such station, or the appropriate Government considers it necessary to

acquire the immediate possession of any land for the purpose of maintaining any structure or system pertaining to irrigation, water supply, drainage, road communication or electricity, the Collector may, immediately after the publication of the notice mentioned in sub-Section (1) and with the previous sanction of the appropriate Government, enter upon and take possession of such land, which shall thereupon vest absolutely in the government free from all encumbrances;

Provided that the Collector shall not take possession of any building or part of a building under this sub-Section without giving to the occupier thereof at least forty-eight hours' notice of his intention so to do, or such longer notice as may be reasonably sufficient to enable such occupier to remove his moveable property from such building without unnecessary inconvenience.

(3) In every case under either of the preceding sub-Sections, the Collector shall at the time of taking possession offer to the persons interested, compensation for the standing crops and trees (if any) on such land and for any other damage sustained by them caused by such sudden dispossession and not except in Section 24 and in any case such offer is not accepted, the value of such crops and trees and the amount of such other damage shall be allowed for in awarding compensation for the land under the provisions herein contained.

(3-A) before taking possession of any land under sub-Section (1) or sub-Section (2), the Collector shall, without prejudice to the provisions of sub-Section (3),

(a) tender payment of eighty per centum of the compensation for such land as estimated by him to the persons interested entitled thereto, and (b) pay it to them, unless prevented by some one or more of the contingencies mentioned in Section 31, sub-Section (2), and where the Collector is so prevented, the provisions of Section 31, sub-Section (2), (except the second proviso thereto), shall apply as they apply to the payment of compensation under that Section.

(3-B) The amount paid or deposited under sub-Section (3-A), shall be taken into account for determining the amount of compensation required to be tendered under Section 31, and where the amount so paid or deposited exceeds the compensation awarded by the Collector under Section 11, the excess may, unless refunded within three months from the date of the Collector's award, be recovered as an arrear of land revenue.

(4) In the case of any land to which, in the opinion of the appropriate Government, the provisions of sub-Section (1), or sub-Section (2) are applicable, the appropriate Government may direct that the provisions of Section 5A shall not apply, and if it does so direct, a declaration may be made under Section 6 in respect of the land at any time after the date of the publication of the notification under Section 4, sub-Section (1). (c. f. De; 17-18)]

8. Guha has discussed about Sections 23 and 24 under stage 8. These Sections of LA Act deal with the parameters to be used by Court as well as the Collector for the assessment of the compensation. The parameters include, (i) the market value of the land on the date of publication of notification under Section 4, (ii) damage caused to crops etc., while taking possession of land or during measurement, (iii) damage to earnings or property while taking over a part of property, (iv) cost of change of residence or place of business as a result of acquisition, and (v) loss of profit between date of publication of declaration and the actual time of taking possession of land.
9. Next stage deals with the payments of compensation. In case of delay in the payment of compensation, an interest in the valuation of the land ranging from nine per cent to 15 per cent per annum would have to be paid.

From the above discussion we see that there are a number of stages in the process of acquisition of land but almost all are skipped in case of Rajarhat as the land for New Town was acquired on urgency under Section 17 of LA Act. Under this Act, land can be acquired by the government under urgency (of course for public purpose) and the Collector can take possession of land immediately after notification under Section 9 of the Act.

The Supreme Court of India has observed in a case *Union of India and Ors* vs. *Krishan Lal Arneja and Ors* on 28th April, 2004:

> "Section 17 confers extraordinary powers on the authorities under which it can dispense with the normal procedure laid down under Section 5-A of the Act in exceptional case of urgency. Such powers cannot be lightly resorted to except in case of real urgency enabling the Government to take immediate possession of the land proposed to be acquired for public purpose. A public purpose, however, laudable it may be, by itself is not sufficient to take aid of Section 17

to use this extraordinary power as use of such power deprives a land owner of his right in relation to immoveable property to file objections for the proposed acquisition and it also dispenses with the inquiry under Section 5-A of the Act ... Normally, urgency to acquire a land for public purpose does not arise suddenly or overnight but sometimes such urgency may arise unexpectedly, exceptionally or extraordinarily depending on situations such as due to earthquake, flood or some specific time-bound project where the delay is likely to render the purpose nugatory or in fructuous. A citizen's property can be acquired in accordance with law but in the absence of real and genuine urgency, it may not be appropriate to deprive an aggrieved party of a fair and just opportunity of putting forth its objections for due consideration of the acquiring authority. While applying the urgency clause, the State should indeed act with due care and responsibility. Invoking urgency clause cannot be a substitute or support for the laxity, lethargy or lack of care on the part of the State Administration." (C.f. De, 2011: 17-19).

In the light of the aforesaid discussion together with the empirical findings following observations are made:

(a) The expression 'public purpose' is nowhere defined in the Act as has also been discussed by Guha. Neither was it defined by the government in Rajarhat case. The reason for urgency was also not made public. In case of Rajarhat, the land was acquired mainly for Real Estate development (as proposed by the HIDCO more than 50 per cent of the land would go for housing; here it is Real Estate development.

    Now, the question arises is that whether Real Estate Development can be called as 'Public Purpose' and that too on 'urgency'? As per the version of LA Act Section 17 (discussed above) Real estate cannot be defined under 'urgency'.

(b) The word market value is also not clarified clearly; whether it implies the government's rate or the local rate prevailing between the peasants. The local rate always remains low. In a village society where majority are marginal farmers, land is being sold only on utter necessity like marriage, health ground, other absolute social obligation and the transaction is mostly restricted among the villagers. Therefore, the selling price always remains low.

They also do not go for registration as there always been an understanding between the parties that whenever the situation changes the land would be taken back by the original owner on payment of money. It is also true in case of Rajarhat.

In case of Rajarhat when lands were acquired the price was fixed on the rate as fixed by the HIDCO (Rs 6000.00 to Rs 7000.00 per cottah). Neither, it was the prevailing rate in the villages (which was certainly lower) nor was the rate fixed by the government (which was Rs 40,000/- to Rs 50,000/- per cottah).

The rate fixed as market rate was actually of HIDCO.

On 6th December, 1996 Government of West Bengal imposed restriction (by order of the then Governor of West Bengal) on selling and registration of land in 21 *moujas* of Rajarhat to private parties through public notification. During 1996-97 Housing Board through HIDCO purchased 241 acres of land directly from the peasants at the rate of Rs 6,000/—Rs 7,000/- per cottah while the local rate was far lower than that. This was taken as the market value by the government.

In a discussion between us and the HIDCO official the very fact was unearthed and the official admitted that the market rate had to be the one as fixed by HIDCO. The HIDCO officials knew very well that the price fixed by them would be considered as the market rate as the legal transaction in local market was restricted by the government since last couple of years. It was also foreseen by the government about the lucrative future prospect of these lands.

If analysed sincerely the whole scenario would unveil the very motive of the then Left Front government to deprive these poor marginal people from their right to livelihood (or to live!) for the interest of the priviledged group of people. (From the list of the elite beneficiaries as provided in the appendix, we can very well get a generalised idea about the interest of the government functionaries).

De (2011:14) observed from various sources that in the year 1997, the Housing Board purchased land, mainly the cultivable land (*shali jamin* in local usage) at Rs 6050 per cottah. On this basis, the market value was fixed at Rs 6352.50 per cottah in 1998.

In 1998-99, the Housing Board sold the land at Rs 60728.00 per cottah. In the year 2004, it sold the land at Rs 2, 00,000/- and more per cottah. In depreciation of that value at the rate of five per cent the rate comes around Rs. 1.49 lakh per cottah. This fact was noticed by the Comptroller and Auditor General (CAG) also. In CAG report, 2007, it was stated (*ibid.*, 15-16) 'While determining the market price of 635.13 ha. of land in four *moujas* (Ghuni, Thakdari, Raigachi and Recjoani), the LAC (Land Acquisition Collector), at the instance of the Company and the Department, fixed the rates at two to 41 per cent below the prevailing market rates worked out on the prevailing rates of 1995. Consequently, 26,565 land owners were deprived of Rs. 33.45 crore from 1998 to 2002, calculated at 1995 price loaded with five per cent premium per annum… at Gopalpur *mouja,* the LAC acquired 73.52 ha. of land at the rate of Rs. 16.72 to Rs. 50.29 lakh per hectare after depreciating (by $33^1/_3$ per cent) the rates as per sale records of 1996. The LAC ignored the current market value of Rs. 25.54 to Rs. 76.62 lakh per hectare determined on the sale rates for 1995. Consequently, 3012 land owners were deprived of Rs. 16.89 crore … Thus, fixation of awards for 708.65 ha. of land below the prevailing rates in deviation of legal provisions resulted in depriving the land owners of getting additional award of Rs. 50.34 crore (Para-2.1.14)'.

It appeared in a daily newspaper in recent time that HIDCO receive Rs. 58.5 crore bids for seven plots, all within Action Area I and II. The agency (HIDCO) received the highest bid of Rs. 34 crore for the four institutional plots on two acres of land. For the 20-cottah mercantile retail plot, HIDCO received Rs. seven crore bid. This amounts to Rs. 21 crore per acre. For the 20-cottah restaurant project plot, a bid of Rs. 50 crore has been placed. For two health sector plots of 30 cottah each, HIDCO received bids of Rs. Seven crore and six crore respectively, which sum up to Rs. 14 crore and Rs. 12 crore per acre respectively. The authorities have already given offer letters to the highest bidders. So far seven highest bids accumulate to Rs. 58.5 crore for about 3.6 acre. On an average, commercial plots in Rajarhat New Town now cost about Rs. 10 crore per acre. It was decided earlier that all plots in Rajarhat from now onward will be sold through commercial bidding only. Earlier, the government had sold two 50-acre plots to Infosys and Wipro for Rs. 75 crore each, amounting to Rs. 1.5 crore per acre (*Times of India,* Kolkata, June 25, 2012).

On August 19, 2012 the same daily reported record bid for Rajarhat plot where 2.5-acre land at Action Area II fetched Rs. 51.13 crore and retail-cum-office complex to come up. It reported that the land, priced at more than Rs. 20 crore per acre or Rs. 34 lakh per cottah, has broken all land sell records in Rajarhat, New Town. It also observed that selling these plots in Rajarhat, New Town has proved to be quite lucrative for HIDCO. On November 13, same year another news coverage appeared in the said daily that a 22 cottah plot of land was auctioned in Action Area I of Rajarhat has fetched Rs. 6.85 crore, which is as goods to land sold at the rate of Rs. 18.45 crore per acre.

From all these we can infer very well that HIDCO is now acting as land selling agent on exorbitant profit at the cost of these poor and marginal people, leaving them at the mercy of FATE !

(Roughly 20 cottah=1 bigha; 3 bighas=1 acre though the villagers measure land in terms of decimal, in local usage it is *satak*; 33.33 decimal=1 bigha (=20 cottah), 100 decimal=1 acre (=roughly 60 cottah).

Based on T.O.I. News (25.06.2012, 19.08.2012, 13.11.2012) Land Price is Given Below (d=decimal)

Price (in lakh)	*Purpose (in lakh)*	*Price/cottah*	*Price/decimal*
Rs. 34 crore	120 cottah (200d) for institutional plots	28.33	17.00
Rs. 7 crore	20 cottah (33d) Mercantile retail plot	35.00	21.00
Rs. 4.5 crore	20 cottah (33d) plot for restaurant	22.50	13.50
Rs. 7 crore	30 cottah (50d) healthcare facility	23.33	14.00
Rs. 6 crore	30 cottah (50d) Health-care facility	20.00	12.00
Rs. 51.13 crore	150 cottah (250d) for retail-cum-office complex	34.09	20.45
Rs. 10.00 crore	120 cottah (200d) for setting up a high school	8.42	5.05
Rs. 6.85 crore	22 cottah (37d) for setting up a polyclinic-cum-day care centre	31.12	18.52

(c) Compensation on market value does not consider the various socio-economic dimensions of land ownership in an agrarian society. A glance at these issues:

(i) The acquisitioned land may not be high priced in the market at the time of acquisition but it is priceless for the peasants as it not only supports the families for the present generation but also supports a number of generations, both ascending and descending. Moreover, it promises a secured livelihood as well as security of food for future generations. The same observation is applicable to the peasants of Rajarhat also.

(ii) While the government record shows a single person/family to lose land, in all practical purposes a number of persons or families are actually losing their lands as well as livelihood because land has always been perceived as a family property (sharing among grand father, father, uncles, brothers of an ego) in village India despite the fact that it may officially belong to a single person. For instance, a piece of land may be officially registered in the name of X but it is the economic resource for Y and Z, the sons of X, A and B, the grandsons of X, C and D, the brothers of X and so on. Rarely, the legal procedure is maintained while land is shared among the heirs as from the core of their heart they perceive the land as their *sthabar sampatti*, the immoveable property. The division of property among the heirs is very informal. Therefore, a piece of land legally belongs to a particular peasant is actually cultivated and shared by his sons, grandsons as well as secure the livelihood of those who have not yet born. (We have shown the fact using genealogical tool in appendix). Arbitrarily, if we say that X is losing the land, therefore one person is evicted from land. Let us see what actually happens. X is a married person therefore, he has a wife. X has one son Y who is also married. Y has one son Z. All live on the same piece of land. So, when theoretically (here in government record) one person is displaced actually 1 (X) + 1 (wife of X) + 1 (Y) + 1 (wife of Y) + 1 (son of Y) = five persons are displaced. Considering the average family size in rural India we can very well visualise the adversity of the situation (see genealogy in appendix-4).

(iii) Ownership of land can empower a family and increase the social status and prestige in the local social milieu. This is the expression of all the people whom the present team of researchers interacted to. Some of the expressions are quoted below:

Mubarak Molla of Patharghata feels that with the loss of land, he lost his superiority in social status and became at per with the landless labourers; this is humiliating for him.

A woman of Patharghata *mouja* expressed, 'we lost our land. We knew no other job. So, we have taken land on lease and are cultivating. We have not changed our occupation but the difference is that we were land owners and now tenant'.

Sher Ali of Chhapna *mouja* said 'we are not happy now. Apparently, the village is looking promising as brick built houses are coming up. But people are spending their compensation money after the *pucca* houses. Now, they have no secured livelihood. We lost our lands but yet to get compensation on certain amount of land. We were landholders; people used to work in our land on wage. Now, we have become wage earner, our children are working on wage. We have lost our social dignity. It is so depressing for me. I don't know how our children and grand children will survive and earn their livelihood. I cannot provide any social and economic security for them. I feel so sorry for them.'

Md. Noor Hussain was a farmer. In his own words, 'we have lost our land and with that we have lost our social identity as well as dignity.'

There are many such expressions that arose from the core of their heart. But any attention to such social values was totally denied by the then government machinery. The present study recorded them sincerely and would reflect them as many as possible under concerned sections.

(iv) It not only supports the livelihood of the owners but also creates employment opportunity for a large section of landless families throughout the year. As the lands of Rajarhat yield throughout the year hence the employment opportunity was also high.

(v) It provides a sense of security to the people, not only for the present generation, but also for the future generations as well.

(vi) The socialisation process made them knowledgeable about the methods and the process of utilisation of the land, i.e., the traditional knowledge of the peasant society.

(vii) Likewise it serves various social, political and psychological functions to its owner.

(viii) All these important dimensions of land in an agricultural society are always overlooked while calculating the compensation.

(d) The people who will be affected with government's decision have no role/say at all in such decision although they will be the victims/worst sufferers of the situation.

In *The Land Acquisition Act And You* (1990) published by Multiple action Research Group (MARG) the authors observed on the same issue (pp. 110-113) that the LA Act does not provide any power to the affected people by which the acquisition can be prevented. Project affected people by going to courts and raising legitimate objections can only delay the process of acquisition and enhance the rate of compensation (Vaswani, Dhagamwar and Thukral, 1990; c.f. Guha, 2007: 55). In case of Rajarhat because of strong protest and movement by the peasants the compensation money had been enhanced later to Rs. 13,000/- per cottah by the government for certain villages only (while it was Rs. 6,000/- to 7,000/- per cottah initially). In Patharghata *mouza* the enhanced rate was given while in Ghuni, Jatragachhi and Sulanggari *mouza* simply the initial rate was paid. As the land was acquired under LA Act 17 (already discussed) hence they were not allowed the stipulated time to file any objection against the rate of compensation.

(e) The acquisition of land under Section 17 of LA Act raises certain issues.

(a) Report from HIDCO says that more than 50 per cent of the land would be used for housing. From empiricism it is found that a major share of land were sold out to Realty business agencies and high rise complexes now form the skyline of the mega city.

(b) The question raised here is that, can the real estate business be considered as urgency?

(f) In an agriculturist family often with the expansion of family especially due to the marriage of youngsters new houses are constructed on the *shali Jami,* i.e., the agricultural land without converting the nature of land officially. These villagers never foresaw this situation of land acquisition and never felt the need of undergoing such official procedure as in their inner sense the land belongs to them. But while measuring the cultivable land the government officials never considered this social fact. For them, government record is the ultimate one ignoring the social fact and physical existence of the house. Our team encountered a number of such cases where lands were measured and acquisition notices were served for the land with one or two storied buildings on it. The inhabitants of those houses reported that when they protested the surveyers threatened them that if they did not allow them to measure they would write that the land in question were under cultivation. The helpless villagers withdrew represention and went on waiting for their fate. The houses were brick-built and occupied by the families since long.

(g) The Land Acquisition Act does not deal with rehabilitation of Project Affected Persons (PAP). With the payment of compensation the government's responsibility is over. Moreover, the share-croppers are never considered for compensation. This is the view shared by the villagers with the researchers. Guha (*ibid.*, 50) observed the same.

Restriction Imposed on Selling of Land by the Government (Courtesy: N. Dutta).

A Message—Poor People should not be Deprived of their Land (Courtesy: N. Dutta).

A-message—Acquisition of 30 thousand Bigha of Wet Land will Lead to Submerging of Huge Area Kolkata including Dum Dum.

Movement Against Land Acquisiton (Courtesy: N. Dutta).

Movement by Jami Bachao Committee (Courtesy: N. Dutta).

Movement by Jami Bachao Committee (Courtesy: N. Dutta).

Celebrities on the Stage of Jami Bachao Committee (Courtesy: N. Dutta).

Movement Against Land Acquisiton (Courtesy: N. Dutta).

Movement Against Land Acquisiton (Courtesy: N. Dutta).

Movement Against Land Acquisiton (Courtesy: N. Dutta).

After Acquisition (Courtesy: N. Dutta).

After Acquisition (Courtesy: N. Dutta).

After Acquisition (Courtesy: N. Dutta).

Dumping Soil on Riped Crop (Courtesy: N. Dutta).

4

The Story of Land Losers: People's Voice

Introduction

Land acquisition was a traumatic experience for the majority of the villagers of all the affected *moujas* in Rajarhat. During our interaction with the villagers in all studied *moujas* (Ghuni, Sulangari, Thakdari, Chhapna, Patharghata, Akandakesari), we came across varied experiences and views of the affected people. During nineteen nineties, when the planning of Mega city Township was just adopted, land sharks became proactive and land grabbing became a common feature in Rajarhat. Numerous private land purchasers from Kolkata and surroundings started acquiring land with the help of goons and brokers. Many miscreants happened. The villagers were often exploited and deprived of their dues. A few years (four-five years) prior to land acquisition, Government stopped land registration. No one could buy or sell their land. Detailed discussion with the villagers revealed how land acquisition was done on whims and wish of the authority, regulated by the political leaders of the then ruling party.

This chapter deals with the experiences of the affected villagers of Rajarhat. Experiences were described in their own version without distorting their language and expressions. All kinds of views were taken into consideration , both pro and anti-acquisition. But overall impression goes against the government's decision of acquisition of agricultural land, the very resource of their livelihood and their social existence. Observations from our part on their expression have been discussed in the section summary and observation.

Case Study: 1

In the first instance, Prahlad Mandal, aged 52 years, resident of Patharghata was an agriculturist, a marginal peasant having cultivable land of 3.5 bighas in joint ownership with brothers and sisters (sisters never claimed share of cultivated produce). He is a graduate from Calcutta University. His family was economically sound enough to run the daily life. In his own version, 'the notice (for land acquisition) was first published in *Ganashakti,* the political organ (newspaper) of Communist Party of India (Marxist) followed by some other Bengali daily, perhaps *Bartaman* (a Bengali newspaper). Some other villagers said that notice was published in various leading newspapers also. After that BLRO office send notice to the respective person according to the *dag* number. The notice contained that respective person had to appear for hearing in respect of his/her respective land. People became afraid because, ruling party had spread the news that if anybody did not appear for hearing, then the cheque would be deposited to the treasury and getting the cheque would be very difficult.

Mr Goutam Deb, Ex-minister, held several public meetings at Rajarhat before land acquisition started and had promised publicly that Government would provide job to one person from every land loser family. He also promised that Government would allot a shop space (stall) for each land loser family and when New Town would come into being, then opportunity for business would rise tremendously. But in reality, the scenario is largely different from their announcement. No promise was maintained from the part of the government/ministers.

There are so many syndicates existing in New Town, Rajarhat. Those syndicates are for the land loser's families. But in reality, those people, who are associated either with the Left Party or with the TMC party (Trinamool Congress) acquire more supply orders forcefully. During the ruling of Left Front government the syndicates having members of Ruling party supporters used to grab 90 per cent of the total orders while the rest would go to TMC. But when the TMC party came into power, the local TMC leadership formulated a *Samanvaye* committee involving the cadres from CPI-M also to solve the local issues. The committee is functional in the area. Now, the syndicates with TMC supporters came in an understanding with the other syndicate groups in terms of order supply and managed a considerable number of orders in their favour. So, it is very clear that here political colour is more important than the benefit of the land loser. In the locality, the incidence of theft has been increased, as young people now steal iron rods, cement, sands etc., from the construction cites. Often women are also involved in such kind of activities. They are earning a good amount of money by doing such kind of mischieve. With the cash in hand youths are getting addicted to alchoholism and drugs. In the day-time, publicly they are consuming alcohol which was beyond imagination in the past. The syndicate people are also involved in various miscreant acts which go beyonds ethics.

In the year of 1995, local people formed Jami Bachao Committee because they did not want to give their land for the mega city project. The mode of action of the committee was to convince the cultivators so as not to give land and to file case against the acquisition.

First of all they filed a case against the Land Acquisition Act of 1894. The land of this area was very much fertile and there were lots of trees. A case was filed to the Calcutta High Court on that ground. After that seven members of Jami Bachao Committee were arrested and put into the jail custody for fourteen days. They were I (Prahlad Mandal), Ranjit Naskar, Pulak Chatterjee and Adhir Mandal from Patharghata *mouja* and Sabir Ali Laskar, Mohiuddin Molla and Sidhikali Molla from Baligori. In the custody, we faced tremendous mental and physical torture by the police as well as by the regular prisoners. The case has not been withdrawn till date…

The Barasat Agricultural Department (Barasat Krishi Daptar) recognised Rajarhat New Town area as one of the most fertile places of West Bengal. In that place, people can cultivate crops with minimum expenditure. RLI scheme was launched in nineteen seventees and productivity of the land profoundly increased. For this scheme the cultivators used to pay Rs. 80 per bigha for paddy cultivation for three months and Rs. 25 per bigha for vegetable cultivation for three months. So, question must be raised that how government said Rajarhat lands were barren? And how HIDCO occupied such type of land?

Low lands where water stagged in the rainy season were filled up. The vast *Dhupir bil* was left with a small water body, rest were filled up. Local people used to catch varieties of fishes from the *bil*. There were atleast 40 kinds of fishes. Trees were also cut down. About 15 lakhs of trees were cut down.

A case was filed at the Calcutta High Court against the land acquisition under the auspices of Rajarhat Jami Bachao Committee. But the Justice of the Division Bench, Pinaki Chandra Ghosh with great anger shorted 'they should go back to the age of cave dwelling and to make fire with the help of stone (*guhây fire jân âr chakmaki diye âgun jâlun*)'. We believe that Justice Pinaki Chandra Ghosh gave judgment in favour of the Left Party and in exchange he got a plot of 4.485 *katha* (cottahs) in HIG category area in Rajarhat New Town through the minister's special quota. We are not sure that what happened exactly, but from internet we got his plot no. as AC 90 of AAI area. Now people are free to judge…' (see appendix).

He came out with his experience that 'at the first instance the rich people with large land holdings came forward to sell their lands to the government. Actually, they handed over their disputed land but the Government showed that the people are giving lands voluntarily. They were backed by the then ruling party also. The poor people got influenced and gave their land…'

He further informed that 'Government took the help of '*harmad bahini'* (a local vocabulary for goons and anti-social people) to occupy the lands forcefully. They were paid in cash, rupees 100 per day. When the land acquisition operation was completed, the goons were treated with grand feasts.

One thing you are to know that initially the government declared to acquire land for building up of roads and bridges which were the need of the local people also. Thus, people were ready to spare some land for the development work. But later the actual intension of the government to grab our land came into limelight and we had gone for the protest'.

In this connection, it may be mentioned that the case against them has been settled in 2012. The court found them not guilty for any kind of offence and they were freed from any such complains as lodged under the Left party rulers. This also clearly speaks of the political torture and humiliation of the Left government to the local people in their own interest.

In a recent interaction, he came out with his view on certain issues, "I tell you that we had expection for justice from the present government. We thought the changeover of political power in the state would bring end to our sufferings. In a meeting at Chinar Park the Chief Minister announced that (i) 10 per cent of the acquired land would be returned to the landlosers, (ii) LA-4 would be withdrawn in regard to those land which are still under the captive of the peasants, and (iii) the unwilling peasants (a coinage came up in connection with land-issue in recent years meant those, whose land have been acquired against their will; the opposite word is willing peasants, i.e., those who willingly handed over their land to the government agencies) would be paid at a higher rate. Presently, the TMC leadership of Patharghata *mouja* and HIDCO reconsidered the rate per katha (cottah) of land at rupees 58,000.00 only. Those who did not receive the cheque under protest would get the benefit. Another thing I would like to point out that the version of the hearing notice issued by HIDCO earlier, i.e., during the time of acquisition and now (presently) is not same rather significantly different. The earlier notice was of land acquisition from the part of HIDCO while the present notice (in Bengali) is drafted in such a way that it will appear that the land owner/peasant is offering the land to HIDCO. This is perhaps a treachery to the people'.

Case Study: 2

In the second case, the respondent from Mondalpara under Ghuni *mouja* is a middle aged man (aged about 44 years). He studied upto primary level of education. With distress he also stated about the economic condition in agony, 'mega-city is a curse for us. It has taken away everything from us. With the support of the ruling party the new city emerged at the cost of our livelihood.

In the name of development of new modern city, the Left Front government sucked the blood of the poor villagers; looted huge agricultural land, destroyed the livelihood pattern, broken down the personal relationship among the relatives especially between brothers and sisters, fathers and daughters, minimised socio-religious values and so on. In the consequences of land acquisition, majority of the villagers are in great trouble; whatever cash money they got at a time as compensation package was spent to satisfy their bare necessities and sometimes to get some modern facilities like cell phone, motorbike etcetera. So, their money was drained away in no time. On the other hand, many villagers like me became dependent on market for every food items including rice; what we could produce a few years back are now to be purchased from the market in cash. The villagers, who had a nexus with the Left Front party at that time made money by cheating their relatives, constructed RCC houses, started business, dealership and what not. But the poor villagers, who received the cheque-notice unwillingly they are facing real problems; many *dag* numbers of their land had gone under acquisition but not properly compensated. Because of illiteracy they suffered and got into the clutches of a few shrewd and cunning villagers, who with the support of left party political leaders had pilfered other poor villager's plots of land and got compensation. The physical condition of livelihood of the poor villagers became distressful; poor became poorer.' The respondent and his wife are engaged in *bidi* rolling these days and work hard day and night to earn their livelihood. As supportive income, he sells waste renewable materials like broken tube light, chair, rubber products, rusty iron rods etc. He viewed: 'New Town Mega city is now a pleasure city of great political leaders, film stars, great business houses. Who really bothers for us?'

Case Study: 3

In the third instance, the respondent from Polenite, Thakdari *mouja* aged 32 years, is a young energetic man. He recalls 'Thakdari was the first affected zone under mega-city project. When land acquisition started, miles after miles of lands (fields) were lush green with paddy. People protested but they were killed by the goons. Ganesh Mondal, Probodh Sardar, Tonu Meyo, Basudev Naskar and many more sacrificed their lives for the sake of land. Villagers were terrorised by the *mastaan* (muscle-men/goons) and miscreants who demanded to hand over their Rajarhat land to them; after that the *maastan* or miscreants sold it to the private business houses, real estate companies at exorbitant price; whoever denied the proposals he was either tortured brutally or simply killed. Then land acquisition started by the order of District Magistrate, and local people faced another problem; miles after miles of green paddy field had to be handed over to the government against cheque-notice. Whenever villagers showed any collective agitation against that they were killed by the goons, who were backed by the then ruling party and were involved in malign activities against the people and in favour of the Project authority. You can note down the name of Ganesh Mondal, Probodh Sardar, Tonu Meyo, Basudev Naskar of Thankdari, who were killed by the goons as they protested against land acquisition. I must say that the authority forcefully and brutally snatched land from the local people by employing the *maastan* in one hand and a huge troop of RAF on the other; sometimes bulldozers were applied to destroy the crops. In this way, mega city has been coming up and people are facing crisis for mere subsistence. To get rid of harsh economic condition, the villagers involved in diversified ways of earning like wage labour, auto-rickshaw driving, some opened up small shops and so on. Nowadays, as mega city is becoming cosmopolitan in nature, local people especially the younger generation got involved in various activities keeping aside their cultural values, relationship bondage and social obligations.'

Case Study: 4

In the fourth instance, Ramala Mandal, aged 60 years, wife of Nishikanta Mandal from Akanda Kesari village is a housewife. She narrated her experience, 'my husband Nishikanta Mandal was a retired school teacher. At the time of land acquisition, he was aged about 70 years. He was a supporter of the then ruling party, i.e., CPI-M till the land acquisition process started. Besides cultivating about 20 bighas of land he started a brick kiln at Akanda Keshari village on 18 bighas of land in the year 2000. Out of 18 bighas we owned 11 bighas (dag no. 383, 381, 363) and rest were taken on lease. Two hundred families were working there as labourer, who used to stay in the quarters constructed for them in the brick field. Nishikanta also used to stay at the brick field often. In the year 2006, we received acquisition notice from HIDCO. Then it was a running business. So, we did not want to dispossess the kiln. But HIDCO made hearing for seven bighas of land from the brick field. Nobody from my family attended the hearing but the land was acquired. One day, HIDCO officials came with the full force of Police, Fire Brigade and the goons and massacred the area with bulldozer; the labour quatters were mercilessly smashed without giving opportunity to the poor labourers to take their belongings out of it, and their little children could escape narrowly. The brick kiln which was in operation at that moment was extinguished by water by Fire Brigade. Then the kiln was demolished with dynamite. My husband and sons requested earnestly to allow them to take out the finished and the *kacha int* (unfinished brick) which were left under the process to sundry only. But they did not care to listen to them and destroyed everything there ruthlessly. Not a single piece of brick could have been saved. At that moment there were about 20 lakhs finished bricks, 10 to 12 lakhs unfished *kachha* bricks lying in the brick field apart from those were in the kiln. Just imagine the loss. My husband was tremendously shocked and helpless as for running the brick field he took loan of 36 lakhs from the UCO and State Bank and another 44 lakhs from the market. That loan remained unpaid. He then joined Trinamool Congress and I also contested in the Panchyat election. Nishikanta approached the leaders for justice. My son then filed a case against the damage and also for compensation. The case remained unsettled. Besides, we also had about 10 bighas of agricultural land in the project area which was filled up with soil by HIDCO forcefully over the produces. The field full of '*sonar dhan*' (a Bengali phrase literally means golden paddy, actually meant the ripen crop) had gone under the soil. Just imagine how much toil and money was invested to grow them and the HIDCO people just destroyed it by dumping soil over it. After that my sons went to Mayukh Bhavan to collect compensation cheque against the 10 bighas land. There they were informed that the cheque had already been received by one Nishikanta Mandal. It was some other person bearing the same name with same father's name. Such incidences are rare but it happened in our case. HIDCO did not verify whether the actual person was getting the cheque or not. For this matter we have talked to Dr. Kakoli Ghosh Dastidar of the present ruling government, who assured us to look into the matter sincerely.

On 27th February, 2007, my husband (Nishikanta Mandal) went to Mayukh Bhavan. My son (Ashok Mandal) accompanied him. He sat in a tea stall for rest. He was 72 years old at that time. He sent Ashok to the office building for enquiry. After about an hour when Ashok came back to the tea stall he found his father missing. Nobody could tell him about his father. We lodged a missing report at the Barasat Police Station. Since then he is untraceable. We tried our level best to trace him out but all in vain. I do not know whether I am a *sadhaba* or *bidhaba* (*sadhaba*=whose husband is alive, *bidhaba*=whose husband is dead). I do not get his family pension as he is missing. His pension is being deposited in his account, but we cannot withdraw the money. Bank people said that after 14 years from the date of missing I can withdraw the money as a nominee. Government has not given any compensation for the brick field. I had in my name three bighas of land. That cheque I have received. We had 10 numbers of cows but now all are sold. Where is the pasture? *Gol, Goru, Gola kichhui nei* (cowshed, cow, granary-nothing is there now). *Age hans, murgi sab chhilo, akhon ke pusbe*? *Ki khaoabe* (earlier we had ducks, hens everything, now who will take the responsibility? how we will feed them?). Earlier byproducts of paddy were used as fodder for the animals and birds. Now, with the dispossession of land all have been lost.'

Ramala's sons could not repay this huge amount of loan. Now, loan amount plus interest is about one crore. 'The Bank people are pressurising us for repaying of loan. If we get the compensation money for the brick field then only we can repay loan. Recent development is that HIDCO has agreed to compensate rupees 35 lacs for the brick field but on the condition that we won't demand any more in future. This will be one time payment and we are to sign on the agreement.' Ramala and her sons ar helpless before the cruelty of administration and only thing they pray to the administration that to repay the loans on their behalf. Ramala's sons are now earning their livelihood from wage labour excepting the eldest one who is in government job (Appendix 12).

Case Study: 5

In the fifth instance, the respondent, aged 65 years a resident of Thakdari, had three bighas of land which were acquired by the HIDCO. 'At the time of acquisition land was full of crops. I was not given any chance to harvest the crops. HIDCO filled up land, dumped earth over the ripe crops and the crops were just buried under the mud. I had a pond on 10-12 cottah of land, which was also acquired by the HIDCO forcefully.'

He further narrated that 'when HIDCO decided to acquire the land, the Pradhan of the Gram Panchayat held a meeting with three people, namely Guru Das, Robin Mondal and Tapan Talukdar. Those people have a large amount of land in this area. Pradhan asked them to hand over their land to HIDCO for New Town. They were well-known faces in the locality and so, if they agreed to give their land in primary phase, then other people would be motivated easily. Ultimately, those people gave their land and following them, other people also gave their lands.

When we had the land, we got good amount of paddy every season. After storing the needed amount for whole year's consumption, we used to sell a large surplus amount. But now we have to search for new jobs. I opened up a grocery shop in the village and my two sons sells vegetables on the road-side, but the family income has been decreased. Before land acquisition, I used to get 3000 kg of paddy after harvesting. I used to cultivate paddy twice in a year. But the golden days are gone now and now I have to struggle a lot for very survival'. The two sons of respondent who sell vegetables couldn't manage any permanent stall-space in the market. They are to sit on the roadside with their items. On almost every day, police drive them out from the road-side on the reason of traffic control and thus, they go on changing the place to avoid bitter interaction. Often they are to pay bribe to the policemen for a space on the roadside even. All these bitter experiences of life led them to feel for their past livelihood pattern, 'See, when we had the land we cultivated vegetables also, we had bullock for cultivation. We also had cows and used to get enough milk for consumption of our children. There was no dearth of food in the family. Now, the question is how long we will be able to adjust with the policemen for a livelihood? Is this the real objective of urbanisation that is being witnessed by the poor villagers? The reality is that a group of rich people got settled in their new flats and another group of poor people are displaced and are made more impoverished earning rupees 2000-3000/- per month only.'

Case Study: 6

In the sixth instance, the respondent, aged 32 years, a resident of Ghuni *mouja* is the great grandson of a big landlord. His father inherited the property from his father, and in turn the property succeeded to the respondent. In his version, 'HIDCO told that if anybody fails to receive the cheque, it would go to the treasury and then getting the cheque would be difficult. Whether willing or not willing, people had to give land for the project (New Town). Fearing for the worst most of the people surrendered their land. I had one eight cottah land on which the canal was supposed to go through. When I went to Mayukh Bhawan for collecting the cheque, I got a cheque for Rs. 40,000 only. At that time HIDCO paid Rs. 7,935 per cottah, i.e., I got price for five cottah only. But the total eight cottah of land was already acquired by HIDCO. Then I asked for money for the remaining three cottah, but from Mayukh Bhawan I didn't get any satisfactory answer. The officers of the Mayukh Bhawan told me that they got order from their higher authority for making a payment of Rs. 40,000 in my name. I also had some land on the roadside of New Town mega city and that was already acquired by HIDCO but for that land also I didn't get the proper amount of compensation. In total I didn't receive the price for 62 cottah of land. The *dag* numbers were 1791, 1732, 1766, 1785, 1873, 1874, 1869 and 1866. When I asked about those lands the officers of HIDCO replied that those numbers were not present in their records, so, I am not supposed to get any more money for those lands. Now, the question is how can a government agency like HIDCO acquire one's property without due compensation?'

Case Study: 7

In the seventh instance, the respondent from Thakdari, aged 38 years, narrated that 'At the time of development of 'mega city', acquiring of land was started in the side of the Keshtopur canal by creating a panic atmosphere in the village with firing of pistol and bomb. Despite that few villagers dared to raise their voice against them. The authority harassed them economically and socially with the help of muscle men; they choose some politically influential youth from every locality; trapped them with huge money, trained them with arms and ammunition. Those people then started doing the job of negotiating villagers' land in exchange of a fixed amount in favour of the authority following breach of conduct. They met with few notorious people (Gour of Mahishghoat, Siddhi of Polenite) and turned them into a gang of 'mastaan' or 'land mafia' of that area, who helped in land acquisition with the help of the then ruling political party. Thus, the land was transferred, and the local people like us turned into daily wage labourer from land owner, subsistence with canal fishing; we do not get any benefit from them, what they promised at the time of capturing their lands forcibly.

Case Study: 8

The respondent from Thakdari, aged 55 years, a resident of Polenite Ward No.14, described his experience, 'in 1993 Panchayat election, famous anti-social Ruidas Mondal, alias Ruhis or Lewis of Mahishbathan No. 2, Thankdari area contested as a candidate of Left Front. Earlier, he was a famous miscreant involved in stabbing, looting, robbing in the whole of Mahishbathan and its adjacent area. The basic intention of his enrollment in politics was to terrorise the local people of this area and to get his help in acquisition of land. He won the election and after getting the post of Secretary in Panchayat the malign activities (as said above) increased its pace with the help of political domination and direct support of the police force. At the same time, with his presence his party men forcefully acquired the consent of handing over the ownership rights of land from the poor villagers. They grabbed away bighas after bighas of our land by terrorising with pistol, bomb and other ammunitions and handed over those to their choice person who were either the party men or retained by themselves. Even some of us did not get any money but lost our land. Overlooking all these terrorist activities, few villagers, who were still not agreed to handover the land, they were horribly tortured; many people of us were absconded, many were killed, many of our houses were broken. In this way, about 30 local people were killed from Mahishghoat and Thankdari area. When some of us refused to accept the 'cheque notice', the authority silently informed other family members especially the married daughters and handed over the cheque to them and acquired the consent. In this way, the process of land acquisition also damaged our family relationship and created a separatist attitude amongst the family members'.

'My father had fifteen bighas of agricultural land and we are three brothers, each inherited five bighas of land. I personally purchasd two bighas, therefore, I had seven and half bighas of land under my possession. Of my land 2.5 bighas was in Mohishghoat *mouja,* four bighas in Jothbil *mouja* and one bigha was located in Thankdari *mouja*. All my land was agricultural land only. I used to cultivate paddy in six bighas for two times, during monsoon season (*barshar dhan*) and during winter months (*boro dhan*). On one and half bigha, there was a pond surrounded by fruit trees. During pre-acquisition period there was no scarcity of food; approximately 300 and 400 gunny bag full rice were grown. Keeping apart for consumption I used to sale a good quantity. It would earn me a good amount. Nowadays, I have no landed property; all my 7.5 bighas were acquired by HIDCO against a compensation of Rs. 6,000.00 per katha (cottah). With the compensation money I purchased a homestead land in Mahishbathan area and started a business of flour mill. My son sells *phuchka* (a typical local food item). Whatever compensation amount I received from HIDCO was spent within a short spell. I must say that land was our asset. It gave me foodgrains on one hand and on the other hand it gave me security; whenever any cash money was required either for daughter's marriage or for higher education of children I could manage that by mortgaging my land. But now it is not possible; HIDCO snatched away that security from us.

Case Study: 9

The respondent from Mollah Para, aged 78 years, shared his experience: 'The Left Front government ruthlessly destroyed the huge chunk of agricultural land of Rajarhat in the name of 'Mega city'. The huge paddy fields with golden ripen paddy were smashed away with tractors, huge areas of yellow mustard field was bulldozed, hundreds of hectare of agricultural land was cordoned by the people with pistol and dagger in their hands and red bands around their foreheads and wrist, accompanied with RAF and Police Force. Ranjit Naskar, Pulak Chatterjee, Prahlad Mandal and others, altogether seven farmers were arrested from Ghuni area. The male members absconded in fear, the femalefolk showed their protest out of lying on the field to save the lands from filling up and labelling work for the proposed project site. In this way, in the year 2001, a strong agitation was going on in Ghuni *mouja* against the land acquisition. But it did not last long; the political leaders of Opposition party joined hand with the ruling party. The condition of the local people remained same and was not freed from the trouble; one after another plot of land was grabbed away. Some of them who collected the cheque notice under protest they faced much trouble and did not get the part of compensation money even today. A few people like me did not get the compensation of some portion of their lands; even they did not know how their land had been acquisitioned. My father also did not receive compensation for a number of plots (*dag* numbers include 1147,

1282, 1283, 1298, 1299, 939, 940, 945, 946, 947, 954, 955, 957, 958, 959,1132,1133,1318, 1292, 1293, 1439 and some more).'

Case Study: 10

The respondent from Majherpara, Ghuni *mouja*, aged 58 years, talked about, 'in the process of land acquisition the big land owners generally got the benefit, because they were the headmen of the area and people used to pay respect to them, the other small land owners followed them. In this way, when the land acquisition had started in Ghuni village many small and marginal landowners gave their consent eagerly to the authority (HIDCO) against compensation money. At that time, the market price of land in Ghuni was very low; so, whatever rate of compensation price received by the villagers was quite enough for them, but we people could not utilise the money properly and intelligently. Liquid asset money was drained out quickly by making *pucca* houses, buying motorcycle, colour television set, furnitures and other household items. We never thought of the future. Nowadays, the people are in crisis; in one hand local peoples' agricultural land had been acquired and the compensation money is exhausted, on the other hand, there are no permanent avenues of income. At the same time, it was very shameful in what way the HIDCO forcefully commenced the land acquisition with full support of the then ruling party. Primarily, the land acquisition authority promised to provide services to at least one person of the land-loser family but that was in vain; the condition of business promotion was as poor as before. The overall bad effect of land acquisition has to be borne by the local people. Nowadays with the rising price of land in Rajarhat, they think in despair that if land had not been acquired earlier, we would become millionaire'.

Case Study: 11

In the version of the respondent, aged 56 years, of Ghuni *mouja*, 'in Ghuni there were so many leaders, such as Abdul Hamid, a leader of Congress party, Tanmoy Mondal, a leader of TMC party and Wajid Ahmed, one of the leader of Left Front party, who gave their land for the project area overwhelmingly. At that time, a red coloured car used to come regularly from Mayukh Bhawan. It was used to be parked in front of the Panchayat office. Officers of the Mayukh Bhawan came by this car and the people, who were willing to give their land came and collected cheque from that car. In Ghuni, those leaders collected their cheque at the first instance. A packet of sweets and a packet of biriyani were also presented to them. Their photographs were published in the leading newspapers. By this process, some people became tempted and collected their cheques. After this, the leaders of all the party started convincing the poor people by saying that, Government is going to establish some industries in their lands, so the local people will get job, and the Government planned this project only for the poor villagers. With their promise and propaganda the poor villagers) started dreaming.' In his words '*tâkâ pâbâr pore jakhan meyer jonnye bor khujte jâi, takhon pâtro pokkho beshi kore pan chây. Târâ bole je tomrâ to tâkâ peychho to pan debe nâ keno? Amâder sochoniyo abasthâr kathâ keu bojhe nâ*' ('after receviong money when we go for negotiating daughter's marriage the groom's family ask for heavy amount in cash as dowry. They say that you have received enough money (against land); so why don't you pay dowry? No one understands our wretched condition').

Case Study: 12

The respondent, aged 42, a resident of Ghuni *mouja*, recalled his past experience: 'one day there was news that Government was giving job; one was to dig soil and Government would pay double the market rate. Most of the youth went to the field for digging soil and then a huge number of policemen cordoned them. The news spread like a fire that HIDCO came for marking their boundary line. All villagers rushed to that spot and protested. At that time people's leader was Tanmay Mondal. But in front of a huge police force, the people had to retreat. Tanmay Mondal tried to convince people that 'in the field, your brothers are working. If you protest, then police will open firing, then either you people will die or the men working in the field will die. Then what will be the future of your family members?' The people became afraid and they withdrew themselves. There was another reason that most of the youth of the village were working in the field and only some old men and women were present in the house. Then who will protest? Can a movement stand on old people and children? The answer is a big no. It was the conspiracy of both the Government and the opponent party and we had been victimised. How can we trust our leader? The ruling party was main accused and the leaders of the opponent party were sold out, then who will speak for us? Answer is nobody. Then we were bound to give our land, as there was no other alternative for us. As a result, we became landless and the rich people got their new habitat in the place of our paddy field. I often go to that place, but I cannot recognise my own land; my land where I used to go regularly and cultivated so many crops. I cultivated with my own hands but where is my place? There is multi-storied flat that are coming up at that place. I can't control my tears. I beg in front of all of you to please return my land. Leaders said that this project is only for us. We shall get job but where is the room for us. We lost our land and occupation. Land was not only our source of income, it was our property also. It was helpful during our crisis; we lost it forever.'

Case Study: 13

The respondent, aged 59 years, a resident of Ghuni *mouja* had 14 bighas of land which had been acquired by HIDCO. Presently, he is an owner of a small daily-need shop. He had a very small fruit garden which was also occupied by the HIDCO. He shared his feelings like this, 'I planted varieties of fruit plants which were nurtured with my own hands. To me, those were my children. I brought them up very carefully. I did watering of them everyday. Those plants grew up and started yielding fruits. I felt so happy. Those were close to my heart. But in one fine morning I was served the notice from HIDCO for acquisition of that garden. I hugged those, I cried, please don't snatch my children…I can't live without those trees but who would listen to my scream. The garden was acquired by the government. The trees were cut down.'

Case Study: 14

Ranjit Naskar, aged 57, residing in his parental house at Patharghata with his daughter and wife, was a peasant. Before land acquisition, he used to cultivate varieties of crops throughout the year. In response to land acquisition and RLI scheme, he expressed that 'earlier days were fine, from dawn to dusk we worked in the field, produced a good yield of crops, atleast the tension of livelihood was not there. Now after land acquisition, we face tremendous insecurity of livelihood, in spite of compensation money that we received.

RLI scheme was an important aspect for us. It was introduced in the year 1972 under 20-point development programme on agriculture.

Originally, it was initiated by Late Prime Minister Indira Gandhi. On the basis of this scheme, about 12 pump sets were installed at different locations (Naskarhat, Akanda Kesari, Patharghata and so on) of Rajarhat Block to irrigate peasant's land. It benefitted all the cultivators. The waste water of Bagjola canal was supplied through these pump sets and irrigated a vast area of cultivable land. By this RLI scheme, the lands got two benefits simultaneously; one, lands received water during winter months also for winter paddy and second, lands received fertiliser with those waste ingredients. But after land acquisition when HIDCO, the project authority, started to develop the new township they took out the RLI pump sets from Patharghata during night beyond the knowledge of the villagers. As a result, the local peasants could not use the irrigation system and they failed to produce the winter crops.'

Case Study: 15

The respondent, aged 38 years, a resident of Patharghata, inherited ancestral cloth business and he was involved in the same for about last fifty years. He narrated, 'for Rajarhat New Town our ten bighas of land was acquired by the Government in the year 2005-2006. But those lands were not cultivable. We received rupees three lakh as compensation for our land. We have twenty-five bighas of land under our possession. My father, aged about seventy-eight, is involved in local politics.' He lives in a joint family with his parents and two brothers with their wives and chilren. He looks after the cloth business and his brother is an employee of Rajarhat-Gopalpur Municipality. To him Rajarhat New Town is a boom to the locality with the increasing scope of employment and it also increased the scope of real estate business. From the compensation money he has built house and purchased four magic cars (hoodless four wheeled vehicle) which ply between the villages as public transport. He finds the development of mega city is good for all of them.

Case Study: 16

The respondent, aged seventy years, a resident of Gayenpara, Patharghata, retired from government job, had two bighas of land in his father's name which was acquired by the Government. 'We received compensation of rupees five lakh sixty thousand only. Our land yielded three crops in a year. That yielded paddy, jute, wheat, mustard, pulses and other seasonal vegetables etc. As the land was very fertile, we were not willing to dispossess the lands but were compelled to do so. In return, the compensation which we got from the authority was totally unjustified'.

To him New Town, Rajarhat is not good for them as they used to yield paddy from the land. 'We never required to purchase rice from the market, rather we could enjoy *pitha* and *payas* (delicacy of traditional sweet dishes prepared with rice powder, molasses and milk) lavishly. For emergency need such as marriage of daughters we could mortgage or sell the land. For the poor daily labourers, it is difficult time as they have lost the scope of earning as daily labourers in the land. It has been boom to the people, who still have considerable amount of land under their possession as they are now selling those lands on exorbitant prices. But the communication system has been improved a lot with urbanisation. Earlier there were roads but connectivity with the city was poor. However, according to my view, urbanisation has brought little benefit to me as well as to the poor people of working class as they have to spend their days with more misery and grief as they had in the past.'

Case Study: 17

The respondent, aged forty years, a resident of Patharghata *mouja*, engaged as a labour in a private sector at Salt Lake. His family lost two bighas of land for the mega city and received compensation of rupees five lakh sixty thousand only in return. The money was distributed among seven members woith equal proportion including , his parents, three brothers, two married sisters and he himself. Therefore, he got little cash in his hand. He finds great difficulty to maintain his small family comprising his wife and two children. He said that 'the local price of land at the time of acquisition was rupees eight thousand per cottah, but Government paid compensation at the rate of rupees four thousand per cottah. Initially, HIDCO acquired low agricultural lands but later on acquired high lands, fruit gardens also and gave compensation at the rate of rupees thirteen thousand per cottah.' According to him, New Town has not been beneficial to them, because at present due to the loss of land they are on the verge of starvation as their main sources of livelihood is lost. 'For our survival, we have to purchase rice from the market which is beyond out capacity and nowadays somehow managing our both ends meet;

had we not lost our land, we could produce paddy and other seasonal crops and could get money by selling the surplus. We even could arrange fund for emergency need like marriage of daughters and education of children by selling or mortgaging the lands.'

Case Study: 18

The respondent from Ghuni *mouja* reported, 'I had inherited seven bighas of land from my father; it was on the northern side of the village. I got into the clutch of a land broker. He acted as a middleman between me and HIDCO. But I did not receive any compensation for that land (*dag* numbers include 45, 46, 65, 66, 67, 80, 81, 96, 97, 98, 99, 202, 203, 204, 215, 216, 338, 335, 489, 497, 498, 502, 692, 693, 694, 751, 903, 904, 914, 915, 932, 933, 1124, 1125, 1146). Earlier my father was also exploited by the land mafia, backed by the then prominent political leaders who misappropriated most of his lands. Those plots of land, altogether 72 bighas, were recorded under *Khatiyan* number 616.

Case Study: 19

The respondent, aged 65, a resident of Mandalpara under Ghuni *mouja,* jointly owned 100 bighas of land with two brothers. Of the land, 20 bighas were vested. 'About 40 bighas of lands were not notified under Land Acquisition Act-4 (LA-4). But HIDCO acquired that land without giving any compensation. . Of rest which was acquired under LA-4, we did not receive compensation for *dag* numbers 691, 692, 699, 749 and 2396.'

Case Study; 20

The respondent, aged 73, a resident of Mollapara, Ghuni, a commerce graduate from Motijhil College, Dum Dum. He was from an economically solvent family. He stated that the then state Government took right approach of urbanisation and planned to develop a satellite township similar to that of Salt Lake. According to him, land acquisition was an important step done in the right way following the Land Acquisition Act 1894, and under Sections 4 and 6 of LA Act the land was acquired by the consent of District Magistrate. In his own words, 'Ghuni *mouja* was a low-lying area with numerous water bodies, locally known as *bil*, *doba*; during monsoon days that low-lying areas were filled up with water and turned to a *koni* (local categorisation of water body), where small local varieties of fishes were available in plenty. Due to low-lying nature, the market value of these lands was very low at that time, about rupees one thousand per cottah. The villagers used to cultivate single crop when the water was completely drained out from the field. In some years, they got good yields, sometimes not. The compensation money, about Rs. 7,800 per cottah as given against land acquisition for the mega city project, brought a golden opportunity; all the people earned more or less a good amount; those who had the futuristic outlook they started business of varied nature, like grocery shop, fast food stall, laundry, readymade garment shop etc.; moreover due to mega city project the standard of life of the local people have developed; English medium schools have been opened up in the area and the villagers send their children for good education; autorickshaw have started plying inside the area by which one can reach Baguiati or New Town in less time; regular market has come up where people can procure various items. I feel development of mega city is definitely a good step, taken by the Government.'

Case Study: 21

The respondent, aged 62 years from Ghuni village was happy with New Town. 'In earlier days, people used to cultivate paddy only. They used to earn too little amount of money. They often used to eat once a day. Livelihood standard was also very low. There was no television in those days, very few families had radio. There were mostly mud-built thatched houses. *Pucca Bari*, the brick-built house was rare. Conditions of the roads were poor. Communication was a serious problem. Majority of the population were engaged in cultivation. Usually, they didn't buy fish from the local market. For consumption they used to catch fish from the low lying areas. The rate of literacy was also very low in the community. People had very less amount of money in their hands. In previous days, nobody had motor-cycle or four-wheeler. But the scenario has been changed totally after the advent of HIDCO. Almost all young men have a two-wheeler vehicle now. As a result of urbanisation, the land prices raise very sharply. Before urbanisation, the price of one cottah of land was just three to four thousand rupees but now the price of that land is six to seven lakh rupees per cottah. The people, whose land was not included in the project area, are now benefitted mostly. They can sell their lands in high price. Many people now are engaged in realty business. Now in local market there are varieties of fishes. The price of fishes ranges from 100 rupees to 350 rupees per kg. In previous days, people couldn't afford to buy fishes with such amount of money. In every village, most of the houses are now *pucca*.'

He added, 'people gave their land on their own. Nobody forced them and no revolt had ever occurred. One day Nilotpal Dutta, one of the leaders of the *Rajarhaat Krishi Roksha Committee*, invited people to gather at a place. Dutta wanted to protest but nobody was present there. The people who are saying that the Government created pressure for giving the land or other negative attitude to the urbanisation are all supporters of TMC party' (This statement was not acceptable to the present reasearchers as the empirical fact was just opposite).

He further added that 'we kept our political affiliations and inclinations aside when we were in the field. When we went to the field we saw the real grudges of the people. We don't know whether they all are the supporters of the TMC or not but we must look the fact neutrally.'

Case Study: 22

The respondent, aged 35 years, a resident of Akandakeshari village and a member of Patharghata Gram Panchayat said that about 90 per cent of the people of Patharghata *mouja* were cultivators and about 10 per cent were engaged in salaried job in various government and private organisations. He informed that initially about 100 bighas of land in Akandakeshari village was out of LA- 4 but afterwards it was brought under acquisition and HIDCO wanted to fill it up. But people resisted and HIDCO could not fill up the land. He viewed that those who were having big landholdings and managed to retain some land under their possession even after land acquisition are now in a comfortable situation because now they can sell their land at higher prices. He said, 'people having land of below 10 bighas used to cultivate their land of their own; produced seasonal crops and vegetables and earned enough to maintain their families. Now, they have become landless and are forced to live with great misery and hardships. Of course some who were educated managed to secure jobs and they have been able to improve their standard of living. In general, land acquisition at Rajarhat for mega city did not bring any good to us.'

Case Study: 23

The respondent, aged 50 years, resident of Chhapna village of Patharghata Gram Panchayat, was an agriculturist by occupation. He lost five bighas of land under land acquisition for the mega city. His compensation is still pending with the Government. In Chhapna *mouja,* Government faced a strong opposition from the villagers and could not acquire all the lands. The matter has not yet been settled. 'The lands in this village were very fertile because of the good irrigation facilities of waste water from Bagjola canal through River Lifted Irrigation Scheme, launched by the Late Prime Minister Smt Indira Gandhi in the year 1972. Four hundred bighas of land in this village were irrigated by this Bagjola water scheme. By paying a nominal tax to the Government for this scheme, the cultivators were able to produce three crops in a year such as paddy, jute, mustard, pulses, onion, potato and other seasonal vegetables. With this they could improve their financial position and standard of living as well. After land acquisition the HIDCO dismantled the RLI scheme overnight beyond the knowledge of the villagers. Thus, they lost the RLI irrigation facility. Then we had to spend more money after fertiliser and water. Now, for irrigation through the help of shallow pumps we are to bear huge electricity charges. Such situations affected the production and in turn our income. Now, we are to live in misery. Many people have been compelled to perform various jobs in construction sites on wage. Some are associated with syndicates as labourers. Urbanisation has not been proved good for us.'

Case Study: 24

The respondent, aged 50 years, a resident of Patharghata *mouja*, had 20 bighas of land of which 18 bighas had been acquired by HIDCO leaving two bighas as homestead land. 'As we were not willing to surrender the land we filed case to the Barasat court. But even under subjudice condition the land had been acquired by HIDCO. The compensation against *dag* numbers 1238, 1262, 1269, 1386, 1381, 1428, 1429, 1432, 1430, 1431, 1683, 1684, 1759, 1764, 1746, 1766, 1773, 1738, 1692, 1412, 1747, 1689, 1690, 3911 and 2568 are still pending. In *dag* number 2568 simplex building is now under construction. It would be a 42-storied building. Presently, I am involved in real estate business.'

Case Study: 25

The respondent, a resident of Chhapna *mouja*, is a veterinary practitioner. He narrated that 'before land acquisition, the situation was something different from nowadays. Every landowning household had enough number of cattle, birds (hen and duck) and his veterinary practice was going on smoothly. As the mega-city project grasped the agricultural land of the villages the local people became landless and as an obvious result livestock became decreasing in numbers, nowadays it is almost vanished.' So Rabiul shifted his profession from veterinary practice to quack healer, use to give allopathic medicine to the villagers. He feels, 'people become very conscious and go to the Primary Health Centre (PHCs) for any kind of ailment. So, my business is not running well. Now, I get involved in various medical camps organised time to time in different areas, like medical camp at Gangasagar, in bird flu affected areas, sometimes in hazardous areas like incidence of mass death due to illicit liquor consumption, and so on.' Through such detailed description about his insecured earning, he just wanted to make us understand the sufferings of the village people due to sudden ousting from their livelihood for the cause of New Town mega-city.

Case Study: 26

The respondent from Chhapna village recalled, 'before acquisition of land for the mega city project very few amount of land was sold to the private parties, who came from outside Rajarhat. Lands used to be sold to the outsiders only on acute crisis of money either at the time of daughter or sister's marriage or to meet up the huge debt. But this happened for limited cases only. The general practice was to mortgage a portion of land to fellow cultivators against money and solve the immediate crisis. To us the land worked as source of subsistence as well as an emergency fund.' He further viewed that 'land should not be given for real estate development; rather it may be given to the industries or any famous institution, which would generate employment opportunity for the local people. Real Estate industry does not generate employment opportunity. I tell you, there were two pump sets at the left side of Bagjola canal under the jurisdiction of Chhapna *mouja* and that two pump sets used for irrigation during dry season. When HIDCO started land acquisition in

Chhapna and the villagers did not volunteer to hand over 300 bighas of fertile, canal side land to HIDCO, those two pump sets were taken away immediately by the then ruling party and the whole operation was done during night without knowledge of the villagers. That patch of 300 bighas of land is still remained with the villagers but they face a tremendous problem in irrigating the land during winter crop cultivation. Any one can tell you that at the time of acquisition how HIDCO authority made us fool. It was announced in several public meetings that the youths of land-loosing families will get employment in different sectors according to their educational level; others will be employed as labour. But in reality the HIDCO authority employed labour-force from outside the area, also from the districts of Birbhum, Murshidabad and even from Bihar.'

Case Study: 27

The female respondent from Ghuni *mouja* informed that 'all the lands were fertile and multi-crop ones. Share cropping was common in paddy cultivation. Before the mega-city project, we used to cultivate paddy twice in a year, one crop during monsoon months (*barsha kaler dhan*), and another during summer months (*tetor dhan*). In share cropping yield is shared equally between the land owner and the share cropper. All the cost of cultivation was to borne by the share cropper excepting during the monsoon cultivation when the land-owner was to bear the cost of manure only.' They are no more cultivators.

Case Study: 28

The respondent, aged 32 years, resides in the Dhalipara of Thakdari area. He studied upto higher secondary level. His father had 10 bighas of land, from which he inherited five bighas, which was totally acquired by HIDCO. With great annoyance he said, 'presently, there is neither any *bheri* nor any marshy land in the planning area of New Town. Earlier, it was all agricultural fields, where paddy was grown in huge quantity; only a few *doba* or *koni* (small water bodies) were present. At that time, about 60 kg in one bag was grown from one katha of land; there were uplands (*uporer jami*) and low lands (*nichur jami*) in the project area; during monsoon days, the low lands were filled up with rain water where varieties of fishes were available. After monsoon, the same patch of land was used as agricultural field. There were pump sets in Thakdari area, through which canal water was lifted for irrigation during the winter months. So, the villagers could produce sufficient amount of *boro* variety of paddy. I feel that development is necessary everywhere but it should be done at the cost of the poor local people.' He described how his lands helped him at the time of his daughter's marriage.

Case Study: 29

The respondent, a resident of Ghuni *mouza* is a teacher in Hatiara High School. His subject of teaching is history. He owned five bighas of low land. During 1970, the then ruling party (CPI-M) distributed land to the villagers and he was one of them. He feels that for the development of New Town, the villagers of Ghuni, Sulangari, and Jatragachi got benefitted. People are enjoying well connectivity for their movement to Baguiati or to New Town. Due to development of New Town, kindergarten schools are coming up. In Ghuni *mouza* also such schools have come up; small flats are coming up gradually. He also feels that when land was acquired the rate was low in these areas and whatever compensation the villager got was right. His five bighas of land was also acquired and he is satisfied with the rate of compensation money, rupees 6,000 per katha (cottah). He opines that due to development of roads and transport system, the children of Ghuni, Sulangari and Jatragachhi enjoy the opportunity to study in the famous Bodhicharia Higher Secondary School.

Case Study: 30

The respondent from Pathorghata *mouja,* aged 41 years, practising quack medicine remarked, '*Râjârhât habâr phale kichu unnoti hayechhe, jemon âmâder ekhâne current (electricity) chilo nâ, current eseche, kintu âmâder jibone to ondhokâr neme esechhe. Jomi chilo to âmrâ kheye pore bâchte pârtâm, akhon jibon onek beshi kothin*' ('Consequent upon Rajarhat, he meant New Town'). Some development is visible like earlier electrcity was not available; now we have electricity, but our life has become difficult and covered with darkness, (i.e., became miserable). There was land, so we could maintain our livelihood (food and clothes); now, we are facing more hardship.

Case Study: 31

The female respondent from Ghuni *mouja,* aged 55 years, is a home-maker. She stated that, '*takhon âmrâ swâmir sâthe kândhe se kândh milie thaktam. Swâmi râ mâthe kâj korto âr âmrâ bârite dhân theke châl bânâtâm, muri bhâjtâm, hâns-murgi, gâi-garur jatno nitâm. Khât te hoto kintu jibone anek anondo chilo. Bârite jakhon golâ bhorti dhân uthto takhon khub bhâlo lâgto. Ekhon sab kichhu âmâder kato tâkâ die bâjâr theke kine ânte hay.*' (At that time, i.e., during pre-acquisition we used to work together with our respective husbands. Men used to work in the field and we used to make rice out of paddy, fry *muri* (fried rice), rear ducks and hens, take care of cows. We had to work hard but there were happiness in our life. We used to feel very happy when our granaries were full. But now we have to purchase everything from the market which is beyond our reach as we don't have any source of income).

The case studies described above expressed the varied views of the project by the affected people. There are hundreds, thousands of such people, who have gone through the agony of similar experiences. We have potrayed only a few out of them. They mostly spoke of their deprivation, especially those who could not rehabilitate themselves in a proper way. They were largely suffering from food insecurity and were dissatisfied with the process of land acquisition. It is a matter of their discontent that the then ruling Government never informed them properly about the massive project. Some of them were victims of misappropriation of their property by the land-mafias. They often were deprived of compensation money. Therefore, they were at the victims of dual deprivation, one the loss of land and consequently exposed to economic and food insecurity and on the other hand deprivation of compensation which could have been used for rehabilitating themselves.

Moreover, many areas of land of the local people were acquired forcefully without following the legal ways. It is their viewpoint that some people who had political linkages with the ruling party got benefitted and others became loser. There were people who find the mega city project as opportunity for better living. They were mostly big land-holders with lesser incumbent. Hence, they earned enough money and a better livelihood. They invested their money in business, mostly in syndicates, joined political parties and utilising various avenues. But in Rajarhat, majority was small and medium peasants with a number of incumbent. One of the Panchayat Pradhan informed that he received rupees fifty thousand only as an incumbent of a property of eight bighas of land as his married sisters also were claimant of the compensation. But they never placed any claim over the crops and thus, there were enough surpluses of grains after consumption by the family. Because of large landholdings, he also enjoyed high position in village society. He was actively involved in the movement against land acquisition. In contrast, another Panchayat Pradhan welcomed the urbanisation process. She is a member of the CPI-M party and elected in the Panchayat under the banner of the same party. So, there were varied interest groups in the study area. But in an average, the feeling of deprivation overwhelmed the scenario.

From the narrations of the affected people, it is understood clearly that land acquisition for the development of proposed mega city had been done without prior and proper intimation to the villagers, who were to lose their land. They did not get any chance to appeal legally against the massive land acquisition. In all the cases, the government authority determined the price of land and the farmer/ land-owner had no choice. Many of them felt deprived as in post urbanisation days land price increased at a high pace, much higher than five per cent appreciation/depreciation to the average price that was fixed by the then political authority. It was a great economic loss for them as neither did they receive the amount just to them nor they could retain their agricultural land. It was observed during the field work that the affected people were mostly cultivators and used to produce multi-crops.

During field work we often encountered a common vocabulary, 'cheque-notice'. They meant the notice issued by the government inviting them to receive compensation-cheque against their respective lands. It was observed that in general, people received the cheque-notice under protest. In the Ghuni *mouja,* people informed that many of the *dag* numbers of acquisitioned land were not mentioned in the cheque-notice.

There were instances, when a land-ower did not accept the cheque-notice under protest, the agents of the then ruling party approached his married sisters and brothers-in-law and convinced them to accept the compensation. On many occasions, the married sister, being an incumbent accepted the 'cheque-notice' and the unwilling land-owner found himself in a loosing battle. Such instances destroyed the kinship relations between brothers and sisters and between close relations.

Fertile Land After Acquisition.

Fertile Land After Acquisition.

Fertile Land After Acquisition.

Fertile Land After Acquisition.

Land Adjacent to Acquisitioned One

Acquisitioned but Not Utilised.

Fertile Land Sold in Pieces—After-effect.

Under Acquisition.

Measured as Cultivable Land.

Researchers and Villagers.

5

Diminution of Wet-land and Loss of Aquatic Bio-diversity

Introduction

While talking of the early history of East Calcutta Wet-lands, Chattopadhyay (2001: 5) describes 'Being a part of the mature delta of the river Ganga, the wet lands of eastern Calcutta were marshes. Before the establishment of Calcutta, the salt-water lake was a backwater swamp and spill area of the Bidyadhari river. The tidal flow from the Bay used to increase salinity in water. The vast expanse of the water bodies located to the east of the city had long been known as salt-water basin. ...The natural elevation of city Calcutta is six to seven meters along the levee of the river Hooghly and 26 meter at the existing wet-land sites.' The same report *(ibid.,* pp. 5-6) says, 'Calcutta has been described by many as ecologically subsidised city for its two special geographical features. One is the existence of river Hooghly on the west as the source of drinking water. The other is the vast low-lying area on the east that plays the role of a sink... Moreover, Calcutta has no sewage treatment plant. The only one that was installed at Bantala had long been left out of order. It is the wet-lands that act as bio-treatment plant and treat the sewerage without involving any cost.'

The emergence of New Town as mega city and large scale land acquisition process since 2,000 has not only replaced agriculture, the major landuse of the area, but also affected wet land of the area developed adjacent to Ghuni, Jatragachi and south of Kestopur canal or southern side of Mahisbathan, Thakdari or Mahisgot *mouja* and Chhapna *bil* adjacent to Chhapna settlement. The situation leads to disturb the water containing capacity of the area and also cause the loss of aquatic diversity. It affects irrigation situation also. Like ECW, Rajarhat wet land includes *bil*, *khol*, ponds, *bheri* and canals.

In some respect, East Calcutta wet-land may be compared with Loktak wet land of Manipur. As Loktak is considered as Sub-basin of Manipur River, so ECW is the sub-basin of the Hooghly River (Chattopadhyay, 2001:57). It is also characterised by paddy cultivation by the majority and fishing and human habitation as seen in case of Loktak wet land. Unlike problems of vegetal cover with construction of Ithahi barrage in Loktak wet land, conversion of water bodies to urban use with increasing siltation of the canals are the major problems of ECW and Rajarhat wet land particularly when it is affected by large scale land acquisition since 2000.

In an observation on environmental conservation and valuation of East Calcutta, wet-lands, Chattopadhyay (*ibid:* 2) stated that 'the total area of water body has been reduced by 2/3 during last 40 years in East Calcutta and still it is under threat.' (The damage of the wet-lands to build up the present Salt lake Town may be cited here. The vast salt-water lake and a number of large *bheris* (fish embankment) have been filled up to develop the town. Daser *bheri,* Baro *bheri*, Nortala *bheri,* Bidyadhari Spill Co-operative Society *bheri*, are to name a few. In an interview, the principal secretary of Urban Development Department of West Bengal (*The Economic Times*, 3rd July, 2012) stated 'Salt Lake (township), when it was conceived 50 years, was a swampy area that was later filled up using various sophisticated technologies). This threat is now rampant in the land acquisition issue of Rajarhat. Chattopadhyay (*ibid*) described the wet- lands of Calcutta as critical zone resources. A critical zone resource can be replenished until threshold of irreversible depletion has been reached. In this context, the ecological and economic function of wet-land should be viewed for sustainable existence of the greater metropolis, Calcutta in general and New Town with adjoining villages in particular.

In recent days, it appeared in a national daily (*Times of India,* June 24, 2012) the committee tasked with preparing a draft policy on wet-lands suggested the filling up of wet-lands and any construction on them should be banned across the state. The report said, 'A major problem is that tracts of wet-lands are declared as agricultural land and then converted to industrial or residential land, adding that this should be stopped'. We can add our observation with this that according to the definition of wet-land agricultural land also comes under wet-land. However, the situation in Rajarhat was same as the report said. The report said that Bengal is blessed with wide varieties of wet-lands but ECW is the only Ramsar site. The draft policy advocates banning the use of any kind of wet-land, irrespective of size, even for public interest projects. It is suggested by the committee that the government should reject all construction plans on wet-lands or any other forms of water bodies like *jala, khal, bil, doba*, and even on paddy fields. The committee also observed that apart from being vital to the ecological balance, wet-lands is important for income generation, livelihood and well-being of the communities and suggested a call for ten years awareness programme and restoration of all degraded and filled up wet lands and water bodies.

Definition of Wet-land

The wet-lands are the lands transitional between terrestrial and aquatic systems where the water level is unusually at or near the surface. Wet-lands must have one or more of the three attributes: (i) at least periodically, the land supports predominantly hydrophytes; (ii) the substrate is predominantly undrained hydride soil and (iii) the substrate is unsoiled and is saturated with water (Vass, K.K. 1998; c.f. Chattopadhyay: 2). This definition is widely accepted by wet-land scientists all over the world. According to Ramsar Convention (1971), wet-lands are, 'areas of marsh, fen, peat land or water, whether natural or artificial, permanent or temporary, with water that is static or flowing, fresh brackish, or salt, including areas of marine water the depth of which at low tide does not exceed six meters' (*ibid.*, 3). According to Science and Environmental Education Society, New Delhi, wet-lands are those areas that remain water-logged or submerged under water, seasonally or throughout the year. All these attributes are very well relevant to Rajarhat project area.

Wet-land as a Supplier of Energy and Source of Products

The shallow coverage of water allows sunlight to penetrate up to bottom. With the help of solar energy and existing nutrients, wetlands allow there luxuriant growth of plants, the primary producer in food chain. These plants in turn support the lives of secondary and tertiary producers (*ibid.,* 3). The products that are produced in wetlands are forest resources, wild life, fisheries, agricultural resources, water supply, energy resources etc.

New Town Wet-land

The low-lying areas of Rajarhat Block are considered as wetlands of New Town and a part of the East Calcutta Wet-land (ECW). Recorded as *Dhupir bil* it stretches from Dum Dum Airport to Salt Lake and locally identified by various names like *Ghunir bil, Jatragachhir bil*; it has also different names in diverse location ((Memo No.774, dated 26/08/1999 Fisheries Department, Meen Bhawan, North 24 Parganas, Barasat).

The location of *Dhupir bil* was an existence centering round Ghuni, Jatragachi *mouja.* The wet land of new town practically extends from South of Rajarhat Road in the north to almost Bagjola Khal in the south though it is farther extended upto Kestopur canal. The contour map of the area reads that *Dhupir bil* descends from four feet in the northern side, i.e., Rajarhat road to almost zero feet m.s.l towards south, i.e., Bagjola khal. This kind of wet-land is greatly affected due to road development and urban landscape. The *Dhupir bil* was also divided by Bagjola canal. It also used to play an important role and drainage system of northern part of Calcutta Metropolitan Areas carrying highly concentrated waste water.

The said memorandum of Fishery Department of West Bengal stated that thousands of fishermen used to practise aquaculture following traditional, extensive and improved extensive methods. Thus, emergence of New Town has a great bearing on ECW economically and ecologically. The wet-lands act as bio-treatment plant and treat the sewerage without involving any cost.

It has already been discussed that six *moujas* under Rajarhat Police Station namely Ghuni, Jatragachi, Mahisbathan, Mahisgoat, Rekjoani and Thakdari have been identified as wet-lands by the research team of environmental conservation and valuation of East Calcutta wet-lands in 2001. During the present investigation, it was observed that the above six *moujas* and the other *mouja* under study had a strong attachment on agriculture and fishing which is reflected in the peoples view and household survey.

Change in Land-use in Wet-land of New Town and East Calcutta

The conservation of ECW in respect of landuse was made mandatory by the 1992 ruling of the Calcutta High Court with the designated area of East Calcutta Wet-lands. But during investigation the traditional land-use pattern (agriculture and fishing) is found greatly disturbed due to land acquisition process since 2000 in connection with the initiation of urban process in New Town, Rajarhat.

In an investigation on environmental conservation and valuation of East Calcutta Wet-land (*ibid.*, 38), it shows that there is increasing trend in transfer of land to urban areas in Rajarhat and Bhangar during census years 1971 to 1991.

Table 7: Area Transferred to Towns

Police Station	*Transferred to urban areas in Census years (hectare)*				
	1951	1961	1971	1981	1991
Rajarhat	Nil	Nil	1108.56	2301.78	2581.79

(*Courtesy:* Chattopadhyaya, 2001:38).

The table clearly depicts the fact that land acquisition in Rajarhat is not a new phenomenon. Till census 1961, the whole of Rajarhat was recorded as rural area while since 1971 census urban areas had been reported. So, the wet-land of Rajarhat started getting threat since nineteen seventies. The situation of transfer of land for urbanisation was further aggravated since 2000, when land acquisition took place in a large scale in the 19 *moujas* of North 24 parganas and five *moujas* of South 24 Parganas (Bhangar Block).

The same study shows reflection on the strength of general land-use on agricultural and fishery in respect of average operational land per household under agriculture, fishery and average productivity of paddy and fish. Accordingly, average operational land per household under agriculture in Rajarhat Police Station was .48 ha., average operational land holding per household under fishery in Rajarhat Police Station was .09 ha.

In almost identical investigation on land holding during the present investigation in 2012, it is observed in all the villages under study that the fishing land, i.e., water bodies and the cultivated land has been reduced radically in respect of studied households (see Table 4).

Chattopadhyay (*ibid.,* 41; Tables: 5.11, 5.12) showed the average productivity of paddy in Rajarhat Police Station was 55.00 quintal per hectare of land, while in ECW it was 48.71 quintal per hectare; the average productivity of fish in Rajarhat was 19.82 quintal per hectare while in ECW it was 31.00 quintal per hectare. The loss in amount of paddy production in Rajarhat is estimated by him as 600 hectares of land with 33,000 quintal paddy production.

Wet Lands of New Town Rajarhat as Perceived by Local People

The shallow low-lying area in this zone, i.e., south of Ghuni and south of Kestopur canal lying under Mahisgot, Thakdari and Mahisbathan *mouja* is perceived by the local people in the name of *Beler khol, Putimarar khol, Dhupir bil, Tangrakhaler bil* which also signify the low-lying area of local terrain. Another low-lying area, namely, Chhapna bil situated in the south eastern part of present New Town area. According to local people, the recent built up HIDCO building, Tata hospital, DLF buildings—all were built up on Dhupir bil, the vast natural water body. The Shrachi residential complex with adjacent mall was built up on the ponds and *gheris* owned by the local people. The Balaka Apartment was also on the water-bodies partly. The vast natural swamp, namely, Ghunir bil was also filled up largely leaving only a portion (about 100 acres approximately) which is to be included in the proposed eco-tourism park. Besides, there were large number of *gheri* and *kkol* in the surroundings of the settlement areas which were filled up and high rises are coming up on them. The people also talked of Bagjola basin which has left no trace in post acquisition scenario. The villagers expressed that they find it difficult to identify the location of their lands and water-bodies on which they lived over years.

Water Birds of Wet-land of New Town Rajarhat

With the loss of water bodies due to filling up of lands in view of large scale urbanisation, the local water-birds, namely *bak, samukkhol, senkhol, itting, bilchari, salik* gradually disappeared from the scenario. This kind of birds used to eat insects and warms which indirectly helped growth of crops without using chemical fertiliser.

***Zeol* Fish of Wet-land of New Town Rajarhat**

In these low-lying area different kinds of fishes such as *Koi, Mâgur, Singhi, Letha, Shol* known as zeol type of fishes used to be available in the shallow water in rainy season. These kinds of fishes are also in great demand for sale in the nearby market in Baguihati and Dum Dum area. The common fishes available in wet land of Rajarhat are given against the scientific name.

Names of Common Fishes at East Calcutta Wet-lands

Sl. No.	*Common name*	*Scientific name*
1.	Letha	*Channa punctatus*
2.	Sol	*Channa striatus*
3.	Rohu	*Labeorojita*
4.	Katlâ	*Catla catla*
5.	Mrigel	*Cirrihinus mrigala*
6.	Silver crap	*Hypophthaimichthys molitrix*
7.	Common crap	*Cyprinuscaripo*
8.	Tilâpiâ	*Tilapiamysambica*
9.	Lalantica	*Oreochromis nilotica*
10.	Mâgur	*Clarias batrachus*
11.	Koi	*Anabastudineus*

Sanghati (August, 2008) talked of many low-lying areas and *bheris* in erstwhile Mahisbathan area such as Boro Paresh, Choto Paresh, Batherbheri, Dilerbheri (150 bighas), Sarderbheri, Munshirbheri (200 bighas), Narkeltolarbheri (600 bighas), Mollahrbheri (200 bighas), Daktarbheri which are no more traceable.

In this way with the diminution of wet land due to urbanisation at New Town, there is a loss of bio-diversity. In addition to this, large scale filling up of land has posed a threat for inundation of water during rainy season in this area as well as surrounding places of Salt Lake, Dum Dum and Baguihati as these wet-lands used to act as store house of surplus water. The loss of bio-diversity will certainly pose a threat to the delicate ecological balance in a fragile environment and eco-system, the micro-climatic condition of the region, habitat for a variety of flora and fauna and living organisms endemic to wet-lands and purify the air that citizens breathe.

(For this section we are greatly indebted to Chattopadhyay, Kunal: 2001)

Once Famous Ghunir Bil, The Wet-land.

Filled Up Ghunir Bil.

Wet-land Tranformed into Township.

Akanda Kesari Village—Wet-land Character Still Visible.

Ghunir Bil Changing to Eco-tourism Park.

Eco-tourism Park Coming up on Ghunir Bil.

Rajarhat, Transitional Phase from Wet-land to Township.

Rajarhat, Transitional Phase from Wet-land to Township.

6

Mental State: A Psychological Analysis

(This section aimed to (i) evaluate the attitude of the affected people, (ii) know the people's attitude about urbanisation, and (iii) to know the actual mental state of the affected people. Standard psychological methods have been used).

Introduction

In studying the mental state altogether, 103 affected people including males and females from the Ghuni, Sulanggari, Patharghata and Chhapna *mouja* were interviewed. Out of them 39 people were from Ghuni, 28 from Patharghata, 25 from Chhapna and 11 from Sulanggari. During field work initially the respondents showed reluctance to come out with their genuine problem. After establishing proper rapport they came up willingly with their views and feelings. They submitted for that they were in the impression that they may face problem in near future if they express the real problem publicly. More so, it was observed that there was a tendency among the respondents to give socially desirable response. These 103 persons belonged to same number of families as only one person was interviewed from one selected household. The reason was that in a family almost same way of thinking was noticed regarding the issue under discussion. The age of the subjects ranged within of 19 to 79 years. From analysis of the empirical data following demographic characteristics have come up:

Table 8: Demographic Characteristics (N=103)

Characteristics	*Category*	*Number*	*Percentage*
Gender	Male	90	87.37
	Female	13	12.62
Age	below 45 years	63	61.16
	45+ and above	40	38.83
Education	Illiterate	19	18.44
	Primary (I-V)	18	17.47
	Secondary (VI-X)	44	42.71
	Higher Secondary (XI-XII)	9	8.73
	Graduate	13	12.62
Occupation	Farmer	2	1.94
	Business	51	49.51
	Service	13	12.62
	Housewife	8	7.76
	Student	1	.97
	Labour (including agricultural and daily wage)	21	20.38
	Unemployed	7	6.79
Marital status	Married	98	95.14
	Unmarried	2	1.94
	Widow/widower/separated etc.,	3	2.91
Type of family	Joint	44	42.71
	Nuclear	59	57.28
Religion	Hinduism	31	30.09
	Islam	72	69.90

The studied group is classified into two: below 45 years and above 45. The logic behind this is that it has been observed during the field work that generally individuals below the age of 45 years, although they got their share from their fathers, do not hold legal ownership right over the land. So, they may perceive this issue in a different way. It is also visible from the table that literacy level is high in general in the villages (out of 103 individuals, 84 are literate). It is to submit that proportion of female informants is far less than the males. The reason is that women were not so outspoken on this particular issue when male members of the family remain present. The occupation pattern of the respondents is mixed. It is pertinent to mention here that before land acquisition about 98 per cent of these respondents were cultivators. They were either owner-cultivators, or were cultivating land taken on lease.

Table 9: Knowledge about Land Acquisition

Statements (A)	*Yes*	*No*
Are you aware about land acquisition?	97 (94.17)	6 (5.82)
Are you willing for acquiring your land?	8 (7.76)	95 (92.23)
Are you getting satisfactory compensation package?	8 (7.76)	95 (92.23)
Are you losing your own house in relation to the Rajarhat township?	4 (3.88)	99 (96.11)
Are you losing your own agricultural land? (total amount of land specify)	97 (94.17)	6 (5.82)
Whether the compensation is received?	97 (94.17)	6 (5.82)
If 'yes' mode –		
Cash	97 (94.17)	
in kind	Nil	
both	Nil	
Whether any NGO/ any organisation fight for you?	4 (3.88)	99 (96.11)

Statements (B)	*Yes*	*No*	*Can't say*
Is it right decision of Government to acquire land for Rajarhat township?	10 (9.70)	89 (86.40)	4 (3.88)
Whether Rajarhat issue is politically motivated?	88 (85.43)	9 (8.73)	6 (5.82)
What are the major agricultural products you have lost?			
(a) All type of crops, three seasons		38 (36.89)	
(b) Paddy/fish		46 (44.66)	
(c) Paddy/vegetable		17 (16.50)	
(d) march land		2 (1.94)	

The analysed data show that a very small number of peasants offered their land willingly to the government and are satisfied with the compensation money. A majority feel that Rajarhat issue was politically motivated. A small number of people lost their houses under acquisition. This is perhaps due to the fact that their houses were located in the land, which were recorded as *Sali jami* (agricultural land). Similar to any other villages in India, it is also a fact in Rajarhat that when, due to increase in the family size there is any dearth of space in the homestead, people build their house in the arable land adjacent or near their homestead land without transferring its nature in the government record. It is a common practice as they know that the land belongs to them. While measuring for acquisition government people did not consider the very social reality and acquired the land with the built in houses. So, though the percentage of such occurrence is low (3.88 per cent), but is significant from the point of deprivation of the people. The figure (Fig. 8) below shows the scenario at a glance.

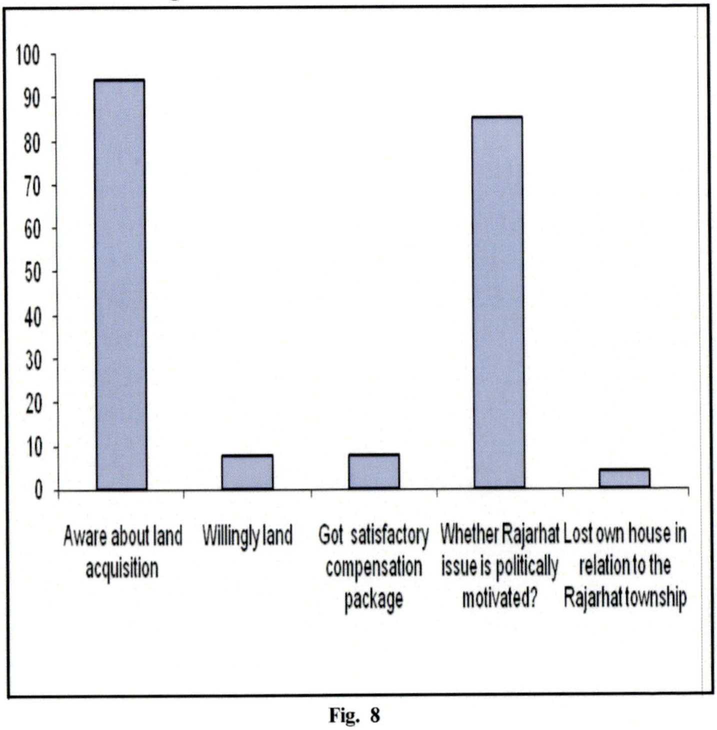

Fig. 8

Table 10: Attitude and Mental State of the Local People (N=103)

Statements (C)	*Answer*		
	Often	*Sometimes*	*Never*
Do you feel socially unhappy because of land disposition?	93 (90.29)	3 (2.91)	7 (6.79)
Do you feel you were happier when you have your land?	96 (93.20)	1 (.97)	6 (5.82)
Do you feel afraid of being unsuccessful while starting up new venture?	58 (56.31)	27 (26.21)	18 (17.47)
Do you feel that anybody can convince and mould you very easily? *	40 (38.83)	32 (31.06)	31 (30.09)
Are you very much bothered about your identity in society? **	52 (50.48)	22 (21.35)	29 (28.15)
Do you feel that others (who did not lost their land) are happier than you?	77 (74.75)	15 (14.56)	11 (10.67)
Does your fear of embarrassment or humiliation keeps you from doing things you really want to do?	33 (32.03)	43 (41.74)	27 (26.21)
Do you try to avoid social situations that cause you anxiety, if at all possible?	33 (32.03)	42 (40.77)	28 (27.18)
Has your anxiety about certain social situations interfered with your normal routine?	30 (29.12)	40 (38.83)	33 (32.03)
Has your anxiety about certain social situations kept you from having friendships or other relationships or any kind of social life?	26 (25.24)	42 (40.77)	35 (33.98)

(Cont...)

Name of the mouja	*Pre-landacquisition before 2000*	*Post-land acquisition after 2000*	*Pre-land acquisition before 2000*	*Post-land acquisition after 2000*
	Cultivated land	*Cultivated land*	*Fishing land*	*Fishing land*
Thakdari (29 households)	165.5 bighas	11.5 bighas	8.5 bighas	Nil
Ghuni (80 households)	414.5 bighas	51.5 bighas	28.5 bighas	Nil
Chhapna (25 households)	235.5 bighas	72.5 bighas	4.0 bighas	2.5 bighas
Patharghata (15 households)	183.5 bighas	27.5 bighas	2 bighas	0.5 bighas
Sulanggari (6 households)	23 bighas	Nil	2 bighas	2 bighas
AkandaKesari (6 households)	37.5 bighas	9 bighas	Nil	Nil

*If a person can be convinced and moulded very easily, then it might have happened that regarding the land acquisition issue, he could be influenced to give the land but afterwards he realised that he had done a mistake.

** Earlier those who possessed vast area of land in village enjoyed higher social status and respect as they were the resourceful persons for the landless in terms of job opportunities. They also used to help the labourers in their crisis. Now, the earlier land-owners are also landless. So, they feel the loss of prestige in the society and equate themselves with other landless people (respondent's view).

The table clearly depicts the mental state of the people. Majority of the people (90 per cent) expressed their unhappiness towards the event of land acquisition. It is important to note that majority are suffering from insecurity feeling (82.52 per cent of respondents were feeling afraid of being unsuccessful while starting up a new venture) and identity crisis (about 70 per cent expressed they are bothered about their social identity). The uncertainty of socio-economic life affected the people differently depending on one's mental make-up. While about one-third (33.98 per cent) of the respondents were found coping up with the situation about another one-third were found depressed with the situation (25.24 per cent) and keeping themselves secluded from social interactions. Almost half of the respondents were found worried about their future and lost their hope (to them their future would be dark and gloomy) and sometimes their worries reflected through somatic symptoms like headache, restlessness, amnesia, dizziness, etc. (Somatic symptoms are some physical symptoms that involve more than one part of the body, but no physical cause can be found).

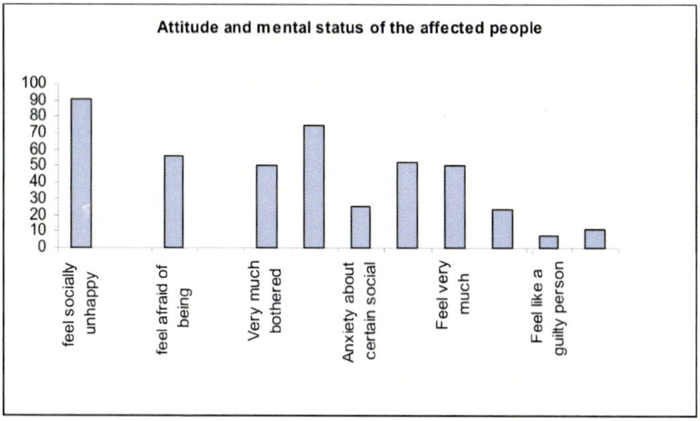

Fig. 9

The question 'do you feel that you are a guilty person who deserves to be punished?' needs clarification. It is a common value system in India that whenever anything unpleasant happens in one's life immediately that is related to one's fate or to one's any kind of mis doings in present life or past birth life (Indians, especially the Hindus believe in re-birth of soul). Interestingly about 7.76 per cent were found thinking in that way. But majority of the land losers never considered it as their destiny but a deprivation by the government. Fig. 9 depicted the situation at a glance.

Findings from Psychological Point of View

Rajarhat experienced rapid growth of urbanisation in a short period. This development has two faces: one face depicts better social amenities and facilities like better transportation, so many work places, etc., for the urban and privileged class of people while the other face brought hazards to the old inhabitants who are the marginal and underprivileged section of the society.

Social Change

Consequent upon the rapid growth of urbanisation new economic opportunities have opened up which brought a insightful transformation in the class structure, value system and in human relationship. The majority of the people living in Rajarhat were peasant. The tragedy of land acquisition fostered abrupt social changes. The changing situation as perceived by the people is discussed below in their own words.

The respondent, a local medical practitioner from Ghuni *Mouja* lives in a joint family, where his father is head of the family. There are total fifteen members in his family. His father is a retired primary school teacher, who owned five bighas of cultivable land. They used to cultivate paddy and vegetables. At present, only 12 cottah of land is left under their possession (rest have been acquired by the government). He viewed, 'due to urbanisation most affected domain is morality, social value and culture. Now-a-days feeling of brotherhood does not persist. Affection among the brothers and sisters is lost. After getting cash money most of the youth have their own vehicle, at least a motor bike. They move here and there and also involved in so many anti-social activities. Yes, quality of life developed but at the cost of morality. This urbanisation provides us only misfortune.'

The respondent from Patharghata *mouja* talked of some other social dimensions, 'society is polluted not in terms of the morality but also in terms of family relationship. The relationship between brothers and sisters is badly affected on this land issue. According to law, there should be equal share for all the children may it be a girl or a boy. But I have taken a big amount of loan for my sister's marriage. Apart from this, I also sold out some of my land to meet the expenditure. But when government sent them notice they gladly appeared for hearing and accepted the cheque. This is happened not only with me but also with so many people. You can very well see that a social custom like '*bhaiphota*' (a ceremony which signifies the eternal ties between brothers and sisters) is almost vanished.'

Conflict in Family

The respondent from Patharghata village told 'the main crisis has emerged for middle socio-economic status people. Government has no agenda for them. Whatever amount I have got, that is already spent to build house and other household things. Yes, some amount I have deposited in the bank but how long it will support me? Who belongs to low socio-economic status, they have so many jobs. The new companies have arrived. They can work as daily labourer or security guard. They are getting money, making *pucca* house. They are now getting equal status. But we cannot do such kind of job. In society we enjoyed a different type of respect which we cannot destroy at any cost. The worst situation is for the people of above 35 years old. Neither any company is giving them job because of their over-age, nor could they get the money against the land. Because land is legally owned by the elderly people, sometimes it is father, sometimes a grand father who is still alive. Money is kept with the legal owner.

Suppose, I am 50 years old and I am the land-owner. I can expect atleast another ten years I will be alive. Till then, I will never give money to my son. It is my security. So a conflicting situation is developing between sons and parents. Family system is getting weak and weak. Apart from this, anti-social behaviour is also flourishing in this area. Gambling, alcoholism and other types of anti-social behaviour, are grasping our society.' The respondent had 6.5 bighas of land of which five bighas had already been acquired by the government. For rest 1.5 bigha he was served notice under LA-4. He said that, 'for my land HIDCO has offered me a higher price, three times higher than the then market rate, i.e., Rs. 13,650 per cottah. Earlier my primary occupation was cultivation and secondary was tailoring. But now my earlier secondary occupation has become my primary occupation.' His family is small. He lives along with his wife, son, daughter-in-law and a grandson.

Emotional Crisis

A 55 years old lady from Patharghata *mouja* shared her experiences, 'my father-in-law had nine bighas of land. After his death, it was divided into six shares. But due to land acquisition we lost our land. My husband was attacked with brain stroke and he is not in a condition to work hard. Then we have to think about another option. Now, we have taken land on lease and cultivate. We have not changed our occupation. Only difference is that earlier we were land owner but now we are tenant.' The peasants who tilted the same land for generations feel an emotional attachment with the land even if it did not give return in a satisfactory way.

The respondent from Patharghata village possessed 2.5 bighas of land. But presently he is landless. According to him, '*jami thake pitriday, matriday, kanyadhayer janno* (land is for obligation of performing funeral rites of dead father (*pitriday*), mother (*matriday*), and for meeting up of the responsibility of daughter's marriage (*kanyaday*). Land is an immoveable property (*Jamin ekta achal sampatti*). If I have the land the future of my children would be secured. I acquired that land against my toil. That I have lost. I literally wept that time.'

A respondent from Chhapna *mouja* told, 'land is just like my son. If I lost my son could I get it back? Nothing happened well. Everything happened badly. So many wine shops have been opened. This type of social change occurred. Big farmers are benefitted. They are utilising their money in syndicate, business etc., they always exploit the poor.' He further told, 'my father had 20 bighas of land. The government already acquired 12 bighas of land and the rest about eight bighas is under LA-4 (that means notice has already been served under Section 4 of Land Acquisition Act; it is commonly referred to as LA-4). We are six brothers. Earlier we were farmers now we all six became businessmen. How shameful it is!'

There were instances where the legal owner of the land could not prove his ownership in a way satisfactory to the authorities of HIDCO had their land confiscated. However, HIDCO sold those lands to private companies in high price.

An old man of 76 years, Haranna Ali Naskar narrates his experience, 'before land acquisition I did not know that there was a land in my name. My parents died in my childhood. In 2004, I received a notice from HIDCO asking me to collect my cheque. Only then I came to know that I own 8.4 cottah of land in my name. I went to HIDCO office. The official asked me to prove my identity. They asked my name. I told my name is Haranna Ali Naskar. But HIDCO officers said that as per record my name was written as Harran Nasker. So they did not give me the cheque. I then approached the BLRO office and lastly in 2008, somehow I could manage to take the paper from BLRO. Since then I had been visiting HIDCO office and from there one office to another office to get the cheque. Now I am exhausted. I often think why they sent me the notice. Otherwise, I would still know that I have no land. It is better to be landless.'

Dark Future for Young Generation

The new modern sector opens up new economic avenues but those sectors require technically trained people. The Project Affected People are from poor agriculturist's families. Technological expertise as required by these modern economic sectors, are far from their reach. They get the jobs at the lower levels as security guards, daily wage labourers etc.

The respondent, a son of land loser told, 'I was recruited in a private company. But I could not survive there for not being able to speak fluently in English. The educated youths from other states have also come to work there. They are educated and are conversant in English. Do the employers expect to match us with their fluency in English? Where are convent schools in this area that would make us at par with them?'

Occupational Change

Earlier, cultivation was the main occupation of most of the people. But after urbanisation as there is no cultivating land and the occupational pattern has been changed. Big farmers became big businessmen, middle level farmers became shop-owners or involved in private job, and agricultural labourer now work as daily labourer. But shifting from one occupation to another is full of insecurity. The villagers were not confident about their success in the new occupation. Here, a kind of insecurity feeling comes.

A respondent, 59 years old, told, 'my father was a farmer. He had 14 bighas of land. We are two brothers and three sisters. We live in a joint family. Those, whom we thought our leader, gladly gave their land first, and then we had to give. Afterwards, we came to know that it was a conspiracy. (Which party they belong to I won't say.) We have to shift our occupation. Earlier we were farmers now we are shop-owners. You cannot imagine how we feel when we find a labourer, who worked in our field, is now a shop owner. We have lost our land; we have lost our social identity as well as dignity.'

Insecurity Feeling

Md. Ali lives along with his wife and two married sons and three grandsons. He had seven bighas and five cottah of lands. At present, he has two plots of land (one 1.5 bigha and another seven cottah plot) under his possession. With the loss of land, he became a mental patient. He always complains of headache and of a kind of irritating sound in his ear. Without any reason he started quarrelling with the family members as well as neighbours. He always shows aggression. He often tells that he will finish himself. He was taken to a Doctor and he is under treatment now. The medicines are very much expensive. His wife told, 'We got only 7-8 lakh rupees against our land. But now it costs crores of rupees.'

The respondent, aged 60, expressed his anxiety, 'my sugar level has increased after land acquisition. I don't know why my sugar level has increased? It may be due to anxiety or idle sitting. But whatever the reason I feel that land acquisition is responsible for my diabetes. Only five per cent people are benefitted rest 95 per cent is loser. Yes, the *mastan* (goons) took opportunities to show their *mastangiri* (muscle power). Before land acquisition by HIDCO, I never sold or mortgaged my land even in worst situation, so I have three bighas land. That time market price was Rs. 30,000 for one cottah but government gave me only Rs. 12,000 per cottah. In many cases, villagers mortgage their land and take money against the land in crisis. When situation goes better they rescue their land. This give and take process also work as bridge between the people. It enhances brotherhood and support in society. I received cheque with objection. Development has occurred but at the cost of the poor.' He lives with his wife. He has three daughters and all are married'.

Quality of Life *vs* Feeling of Deprivation

A lady from the Ghuni *mouja* told, '*Ghare jadi bhat thake noon diye khawa jay kintu na thakle ki awastha hay chinta kare dekhun*' (if we have only rice in our home we can consume it with salt only. But just think if there is no rice at home what will happen?). We were not interested to sell the land. To save the mother like land, villagers protested, fought against government but the supporters of ruling party somehow pursued the policemen through *khana-peena* (literally means food and drinks). And without any hurdle they easily acquired the land of poor villagers. Then TMC and Congress party consoled that if we elect their government they would definitely do something for us. But what happened? Nothing! All political parties are thieves. They squiz poor's blood only. Before urbanisation male members of the family used to work in agricultural field; females used to manage mainly the household chores and some jobs related to cultivation. We could get rice, fuel, food for us as well as fodder for cattle, hen and duck etc. One crop helps us in so many ways.' She did not disclose how much land her family possessed and how much money they got. But she told that earlier they were happy. She lives in a family with her two sons, their wives and three grand children.

Haffijur's father had two bighas of land. 'We are three brothers. At the time of land acquisition we lived in a joint family. We used to grow sufficient amount of paddy. The produce was that much that after meeting up the consumption for whole year, we sold the paddy of Rs. 30,000-40,000. Apart from that we also worked on daily wage as and when time was available. Life was so smooth and peaceful. After getting the money against our land my father gave our share and I opened this small tea stall. Now, only this shop is my support. We are totally smashed by the government.'

A respondent's father had about 10 bighas of land which had already been acquired. But he received money for only two bighas at the rate of Rs. 7,800 per cottah, rest eight bigha's cheque was not issued by HIDCO. 'That time the market price of that land was 40-50 thousand rupees per cottah. We are six brothers. After formation of New Town, I sold out some more land to get more money. I established a vehicle repairing workshop. Somehow I can manage my livelihood. Government formed a new township; it is hundred per cent okay. But for this purpose they should take only that much of land which was absolutely required. Why they have taken more and more land. Just because of for playing brokers game. Though I should not say like this. If the companies would come directly then farmers could get more money. Yes, I cannot say that nothing better happened through urbanisation. Yes, transport system, better public schools, and scope for business has increased. But who are the beneficiaries? Only those who have money they are enjoying the life,' he says.

Shahabuddin's father had 5.5 bighas of land. 'HIDCO paid us only Rs. 7,000 per cottah, but HIDCO sold out it to private companies at crores of rupees. That time cost of things and labourers both were cheaper. Nothing has changed due to this urbanisation for poor. We are living in a same locality and house, our children study in same *sarkari* school.'

A resident from Ghuni Lashkar para had two bighas of land, which had been acquired by HIDCO. Earlier his main occupation was cultivation. But after this, he opened a small shop. The shop runs in a very good way. He lives along with his wife and two children. According to him, he got Rs. 6,000 per cottah, but at that time local rate was only Rs. 2,000 per cottah. He told that 'leave about me. I can earn that much of money and I can manage my family in healthy way. But who had very small piece of land and who were dependent upon share cropping, what will they do? They have not got enough cash to invest in anything appropriately. Only 25 per cent are benefitted rest 75 per cent are badly loser. This social inequality is man-made.'

There were different views also. In a group interview it came out, 'in the newly-formed township (Newtown) roads, schools, hospitals, IT hubs, high-rise housing complexes, etc., are built and a modern system of administration is established. These changes intended to link the village economy more effectively. New sectors are arising. People get work there as per their ability. Definitely, the scope of earning cash money has increased. The villagers who have lost their lands are availing the opportunities.'

A resident of Patherghata village had 3.5 bighas of land. He lives in a family with his wife and two daughters. He told, 'now I am feeling very happy, because that time I had to send labour in agricultural field. But even after so much of toil we got very less production. There was no scene of cash money. We had to suffer. But now-a-days due to urbanisation development happened. And I got the opportunity to work hard and getting cash money. I can fulfil my children's demand. I am very happy.'

The respondent from Ghuni Lashkarpara is a serviceman. Apart from the service, he was also engaged in his cultivation. His father had six-bighas of land which had been acquired. After getting his share, he opened a shop. The shop runs very well. His elder son is auto rickshaw driver. There are total five members in his family. He told, 'Now the position is better than earlier. We all have liquid money and we are enjoying it. Most of the villagers built *pucca* houses, brought vehicles. Due to construction of high rise buildings we are getting the job according to our calibre. In my opinion this urbanisation provided us better life.'

Abdul told, 'I am very happy to be a part of this land acquisition. Though I have received the cheque with objection but I know that when land was acquired by HIDCO market price of the same land was very low. HIDCO had given us three times more than market price. Yes, I cannot disagree that land was an asset that I lost. I utilised that money in my business. I must say that quality of life increased. Now ways of employment opened for all type of people. You can choose accordingly. Everything is looking in apparently. You can see roads, transportation, electricity, health, water etc., so many people are getting the job. When we had agricultural land, we cultivated but production was never sufficient. We always suffered for cash. That time we had to think ten times to buy a dress, but now-a-days we have to think ten times to select which one is better. It is a different.' He had 1.5 bigha of land and against this land he got Rs. 2,85,000. After getting the money, he opened a hardware shop and it runs very well. There were eleven members in his family.

It is observed from empirical data that the feeling of deprivation had been emerged among the villagers more and more with the passage of time. Initially, those who were little bit happy after having cash money in hand were also developing a feeling of deprivation day by day. The reason is that they are not thinking in terms of what they earned in respect of the then market price but in terms of calculating present market value that is rising exorbitantly. And they repent.

In the version of one respondent, 'my father had 2.4 bighas of land. After land acquisition my father gave me some amount. That time I was very happy. I never saw that much of amount. I bought motorcycle, colour TV, mobile phone and some money utilised in repairing of my home. I felt happy. But after 2-3 years when Jami Bachao Andolan (movement to save the land), started only then I could realise. I feel if now I have even a small piece of land I could sell out or mortgage and could get more money. I could utilise it in my daughter's education or marriage. But nothing is to do now. My dream has already been finished. Things looking better are apparent only. Earlier, who had a bicycle now having a motorcycle, those who had motorcycle now had gone for a car. Who used to eat *dal-bhat* (literally meaning pulses and rice, actually a usage in Bengali meaning simple food), now eat *mangsa-bhat* (literally meaning meat and rice signifies good/delicious food). Youths are going in wrong direction. Pleasure is only outer nothing inner. Nothing has happened well. If we get any good return from urbanisation things would have been different. Earlier who were share croppers; they are now sitting idle and trying to earn in a wrong way. I cannot blame them because what would else they do? Now, my money is finished. I have four daughters. But land could have been given us return throughout our life.'

A resident of Patherghata village told 'in general every person directly or indirectly is gainer. Earlier ten bighas land holder had to live from hand to mouth. Before township land price was maximum Rs. 50,000 per bigha. Government gave us Rs. 3,00,000 for one bigha. That time people were crazy to give their land. Peasants were ready to give their land. But, now development has already been occurred and the price of land has increased. Now, we are thinking to sell our land to private company not to government, so that we can get more money. We have got rupees three lakh against one bigha of land. If we fix it in Bank we get Rs. 24,000 per year as interest. But you cannot produce crops worth Rs. 24,000 yearly in one bigha of land, maximum you can make a profit of Rs. 1,000 or 2,000. Leave the cost of seeds, fertilisers, water and labour. If you give land on lease even then you will get only Rs. 2,000 yearly for one bigha. Earlier, there was no four wheeler vehicle in this village. But now, there are 1about 12 four wheelers in the village. Besides, there are so many two wheelers. I must say development happened, life style has changed, and standard of living has developed. Even low levels of farmer are also benefitted. They have got some *ekmushti* (handful) liquid money and they are getting job also in private companies as day labourer, security guards etc. Apart from this how we can forget that due to this urbanisation the cost of land has increased. Does it not show the betterment?'

It was observed during the course of interaction with the key informants that the people from low income group, who used to live entirely on agricultural land and day labour, were in a favourable situation in the post urbanisation scenario. Earlier, they used to earn fewer wages in agricultural field while now the rate of wage is more in construction labour which they mostly opted for. The people with big land holdings were also benefitted, though most of them dispossessed their land on compulsion. They invested their money into business and running well. The people who had moderate land holdings but had lesser shareholders also got some benefit and invested their money into profitable business. These moneyed classes of people got involved in the syndicates and were earning enough hard cash. But the majority was marginal and small peasants, who were the worst sufferers of land acquisition (this observation is also supported by the CAG report, 2007, which says 'most of the land acquired for NTP (New Town Project) was in small plots of less than 10 decimals with few large adjacent plots of land. The Panchayat Pradhan of one of the *mouja* explains, 'take my case into consideration. We had small amount of land but produce was enough for whole year's consumption. We brothers and our families were smoothly running with the land. The sisters never claimed any share of the produce. But when we received money it was to share among all the shareholders including brothers and sisters. After sharing I got rupees fifty thousand only. You can imagine very well my situation. The food security has gone. I am to think at every step how to manage the livelihood. We fought for our land but all in vein. How can poor people compete with the government? They had power; they had police force under them, more so they had goons with them. We were shattered, tortured, arrested without any reason and forcibly ousted from our land. We had no other option than to surrender helplessly.' His observation was supported by people in general whom we interacted with.

A resident of Patharghata *mouja* at first refused to talk with us. Afterwards when our key informants pushed us, he could not deny in entertaining us. When we met him he looked depressed and he could not hide his emotion. He was a big land holder and enjoyed a respect in the society. But after the distribution of the compensation money among the shareholders, he got little. He had no other option than to earn the livelihood through any kind of job. He could not opt for labour work; neither he was in an age to find a service nor he had any technical expertise. He found a job of salesman in a garment shop of a villager. He got irritated on simple reason. While interacting with us he just burst out, 'I request you to leave me. What is there to recall my earlier situation? I am now popper and working as you see. I won't tell you about myself. Everything is clear; if you have sight you can see yourself. So many people came, so many reporters, political leaders, social workers but nobody has done anything in favour of these poor villagers. One lady came; she did her Ph.D. and never showed her face. You won't do anything but keep on asking us, what is just a story for you is the hard reality for us. Now enough is enough, I won't talk to you any more'.

One can understand very well the depression, disgust and mistrust developed among these people.

Major points identified from the aforesaid empiricism:

1. Traditional social structure is negatively affected due to emergence of New Town.
2. Hostile stances have been increased with urban growth in the area.
3. The increasing socio-economic differences making it difficult for the poor to maintain a healthy relationship with the rich. Such situation further deepening the negative attitudes of the affected people and consequently there emerged social intolerance and vulnerability.
4. Impacts negatively on environment and quality of life for a majority.
5. People find themselves fully dictated by the city markets. Earlier they used to consume what they cultivated at their own will. But now they have no option but to accept what city offers.
6. Employment opportunities have increased but villagers can avail only the lowly paid jobs like wage-labour in construction sites, security guards etc. Observing the growth of urbanisation around they feel themselves further marginalised.
7. People associated with syndicates, business, etc., are earning hard cash and are coping up with the situation. Others feel deprived.
8. People who were earlier in economic affluence find hard to find out livelihood according to their aspiration.

9. It is difficult for them to accept the situation of landlessness and resultant insecurity of livelihood.
10. Loss of confidence to face an altogether new socio-economic situation.
11. The village society is passing through a transitional phase from a close-knit agrarian one to an individualistic urban conglomerate. Earlier agrarian economy indulged them into regular interaction through reciprocal labour among the relatives and neighbours, share-cropping and thereby developed a social bond. With the loss of land such interaction stopped and the social bond loosens. A kind of individualism is growing in the attitudinal level, where people are taking interest of own self only. People mostly engaged in construction sites on daily wage or in private sectors which are purely temporary and therefore no permanent social bond can be developed.

7

Development: Conflicting Scenario

Empirical data reveals a conflicting situation between the government and the people over the issue of development. According to Nobel laureate Joseph Stiglizt, 'Development is not about helping a few people to get rich or creating a handful of pointless protected industries that only benefit the country's elites... Development is about transforming societies, improving the lives of the poor, enabling everyone to have a chance at success and access to health-care and education' (*Globalisation and its Discontent,* pp. 251-52; c.f. Das, 2007:37-38).

Let us see what development meant for Left Front government (or HIDCO) in respect to New Town Rajarhat development. The researchers have a discussion with the officials of HIDCO on a number of occasions on the issues related to land acquisition.

A simple question was placed: what is your working definition of development?

The instant reply was 'acquiring of land, filling up of land and selling out of land.'

Does this view really comply with the motto of Government of India or HIDCO's own proposition?

In the HIDCO report it is observed that the New Town project was conceived and implemented in compliance with the Government of India's declaration of establishing 100 new towns of half million population by 2021. In this respect, it refers 'Lack of adequate shelter facilities, particularly of the economically weaker sections, has affected the quality of life, particularly of the children and women. The shelterless people have been forced to squat on pavements and other places with an overall deterioration of health, hygiene and basic sanitation' (Report by Ghosh, Bose and Associates, 2000). Thus, it welcomes the Government of India's declaration. In great contrast, we can refer FICCI report which speaks, '...an interesting phenomenon of the changing perception of New Town among prospective buyers from a predominantly MIG destination to a HIG destination. The number of applicants in the HIG segment is on the rise while those from the MIG segment have comparatively reduced' (c.f. Dey, 2011: 23). The Economic Times of India reported of Rajarhat Realty Pitches for Villas where it was stated that villa projects in Rajarhat are priced in excess of a minimum rupees 65 lakh and scale upto a rupees 3.25 crore a unit. Buyers are from all over, corporares, locals from Kolkata, different parts of India and NRIs. For many NRIs buying vilas are an investment considering the booming real estate market in the city (3rd July, 2012). Is there any room for those shelterless people, who have been forced to squat on pavements and other places with an overall deterioration of health, hygiene and basic sanitation as promised in the government report? Our data says 'no'. That till date, there was no provision for the poor also supported by the recent statement of the present Chairman of HIDCO. He stated, 'as far as housing is concerned in New Town, there are different types of housing here, but now the strategy we are adopting is slightly different. In last one year, the strategy was to provide houses to the poor at affordable cost...we think that the housing policy needs to concentrate upon the economically weaker section and the lower income group by making policy interventions and earmarking space for them' (*Times of India Guide,* June, 2012). Thus, the thinking about the housing for the poor is a baby of one year old and corresponds to the change of power at the state government level following the Assembly Election in 2011.

Our next question to the official was that the acquired area is a part of the East Calcutta Wet-land which is recognised under Ramsar site.

Do you feel it will affect the environment in a long run?

Ans: The project area does not cover any *bil* or water body.

HIDCO official's claim does not corroborate with the empirical data as well as secondary data based on other scientific studies (already discussed in earlier sections). All these certainly tell us the reluctance from the part of the then Left Front government to understand not only the problems of the people but also the importance of bio-diversity and the ecological balance of the country.

HIDCO officials claimed that they had done a lot towards the rehabilitation of the land loser like the development of co-operative system (which later took shape of Syndicates). It was also claimed that the development of New Town opened up plenty of avenues before the local people to earn their livelihood.

HIDCO's claim of rehabilitating the land loser was not supported by the people. The rehabilitation was given to those whose homestead was acquired by the government under the land acquisition process. But the work was not satisfactory. The example cited by the people was that of Sri Mandal of Jatragachhi *mouja,* who was allotted less than one cottah of land (600 sq ft) on lease for the house. He was to pay Rs. 20 annually as rent. Such rehabilitated people were restricted from selling off their allotted plots of land within ten years period. Sri Mandal did not receive any money for construction of his new house.

In regard of economic opportunity, we would prefer to quote people's response: We were traditionally exposed to and were engaged in agriculture only. With that we were happy and comfortable in our life. Now, we are driven out from our own land. Of course, there are avenues like labour work in construction sites, security guards, domestic help, etc., in which we were never exposed to. Our settlement is left only to get supply of menial service to the urban residents. Our females will go for the job of a housemaid. But we were land-holders and had enough food to eat. We never let our females to go out for such low job. They were the home makers in their own house and lived with dignity. Whatever we had we lived in dignity and self-respect.

The response clearly spoke of the way the land loser are looking into the whole process of so-called development by the government. About the co-operative and syndicates we have already discussed in other section. These days a lot of news appeared in daily newspapers about the corruptions that have been cropped up in syndicates (*Anandabazar Patrika*, January 12, and February 5, 8, 10 and 11, 2012), which portray clearly the vices that have been implanted in these village societies by the Left Front government. People also expressed their dissatisfaction with the working procedures of syndicates and viewed that the syndicates lead the youths to a wrong direction.

The HIDCO report (*ibid*: 3.1) says 'The New Town will primarily be a residential town.... Another important use will be for clean industries. While the residential areas occupy about 50 per cent of the total project area, industries 6.5 per cent, new business district and other commercial areas 4.6 per cent, regional cultural, educational and health facilities 0.7 per cent, major road and other transport systems nine per cent, large open spaces, green areas and water bodies account for almost 30 per cent of the total area. The New Town is planned for a total residential population of 7.5 lakh with an overall density of 244 persons per hectare.' From the Census of India report, we find the density of population is seven per hectare.

People of Patharghata reacted towards this issue: initially government asked land for roads and people willingly surrendered land with a hope for better communication with the towns and city. But afterwards it came into surface the government's intention to acquire vast lands for township. Accordingly notice came. People protested. But all efforts of people were in vain. Government forcibly took the land by police force and on muscle power of their cadres (CPI-M). Now, concrete high rises are coming up. People from different places gathered here; they are of different type, not like us. We don't know what will happen in our settlement. If we are to live with dignity we may have to go away from this area, we are not sure.

According to an ex-Panchayat Pradhan and a supporter of Left Party, 'my father who was a big farmer from Mahisbathan area gave 2.5 bighas of cultivable land to the government willingly for the construction of bridge. We were happy because it was a necessity for us also. But I don't want to comment on the acquisition of cultivable land for the city.'

From the recent newspaper clippings we find that the densely populated areas of Kolkata are facing threat of Arsenic in water (*Times of India,* June, 28, and June 30, 2012). The threat is more where high rising buildigs are located. The huge extraction of under ground water is responsible for raising the concentration of arsenic in water. A study carried out by Jadavpur University's School of Environmental Studies under the leadership of Dipankar Chakraborti identified some of the city's high rises areas with arsenic contamination in ground water. While the CMA is already over-exhausted with the basic resources then the burden of a mega city would certainly add much to the problem. A government 'development programme' deserves a serious attention to such environmental issues (Appendix-15).

The HIDCO report *(ibid.,* 4.1.5, land-use) writes 'there is no forest land within the project area. About 68 per cent of the project area consists of agricultural land with its vast majority being unirrigated. Land not available for cultivation occupies about 32 per cent of the project area.'

Under point 4.1.8 (Terrestrial Ecology) it is said 'The project area consists of low agricultural and barren land. Only one crop of paddy with *Kharif* is cultivated with poor production. Double cropping is done over limited areas. About 45 hectares of the project site consists of ponds.

Point No. 4.1.9 (*ibid:* Aquatic Ecology) states 'There are innumerable *bherries* and ponds in the study area where fish is cultivated. The East Calcutta Wet-lands lie to the south of the project boundary. The project area does not infringe on the wet-lands to any extent.'

The report also is self-contradictory. On one hand, it says, they are not damaging the wet-lands and on other hands, it describes the project area as low-lying agricultural land with innumerable *bheris* and ponds which are the characteristics of wet-land. In this regard, people expressed just opposite views.

It was stated by the people that on the acquired area (3750 hectares) comprised agricultural land and fisheries a total of 1,31,000 persons were dependent for their sustenance. They cited from government survey report that there were around 6179 marginal farmers, 2,105 small farmers, 4,605 landless labourers and more than 4,000 people engaged in piscicultute (c.f. Petition by Nilotpal Dutta and others to the Calcutta High Court, p. 6).

On government's observation of project land as vacant land the petitioners found it deliberate and willful suppression of the fact (on the part of the government) that the project area covered as many as forty villages having the total population to the extent of 1.50 lakh approximately (*ibid.,* p. 18). However, let us see the people's view from empirical data.

One view: 'The government's claim that the area produces one crop is not correct at all. It produced three crops a year (*tin fasali Jami*). Besides, there was vast natural water bodies, namely, Dhupir bil, Ghunir bil, Bagjola-jatragachhi-Ghuni basin, innumerable *bheri, gheri, koni, khal* where villagers used to do fishing and fish cultivation. The Dhupir bil was extended from Dirojio College to Chinar Park. How could a government report say a totally wrong thing?'

Another view: 'Long long back it was single crop land. Since 1970 with the RLI system introduced by the government the lands became *bahufasali* (multi-cropped land). People started having some cash money, situation developed, people's living standard also developed. We were happy. Now government acquired our land leaving us nowhere.'

Yet another view: 'If government now says the lands were not yielding much we are to say that government is misleading. We were happy because our children were secured with food and shelter. Our children got education, I could afford that. Girls of my family were all educated, some read upto higher secondary, some upto graduation standard. Weren't these called development? But now we are thrown out of our livelihood. We are to think how to manage the family. Do you think labour work opportunity is development? The very concept of development of the government is wrong, it is anti-poor. What we will get out of this mega city? You just tell me. Students come; ask about our deprivation; they are doing research; they will get a degree, with that they will get good job; but our condition? Would it be changed? So, why I should tell all the things repeatedly? I don't know how my children will pass their life? I could not leave any asset for them. Land was my only asset. Compensation? We had 30 bighas of land. There were enough surplus produce. With that money we managed our daughters marriage, could afford the cost of education. We are yet to receive cheques for some of our land. Whatever we have received shared among the brothers and sisters. Very little came in each share. I know I should not say all these things. We may get victimised if our names are published. But whatever has happened with us was not good.'

Another experience: 'I own a sweet's shop. Besides I had 30 bighas of land, 20 bighas inherited from my grand father and 10 bighas from father. We are four brothers and two sisters. We used to produce three crops a year, paddy, mustard, jute and seasame, apart from vegetables. The compensation money was shared among all six siblings. Some compensation amount is still pending from the part of HIDCO. We are yet to receive money for about 11 decimal of land at one instance, for another 46 decimal of land hearing procedure is over. We have a fruit garden. They wanted to acquire that also. We protested. Till date that is under our possession but I am not sure about its future. We filed a case; that is also pending in High Court. When my land was acquired it was full of grown up paddy, we wanted a little mercey so that at least we could harvest the produce. But they dumped earth over the riped paddy. I cannot just explain you the shocking situation. *Sonar fasal*, (meaning the golden coloured paddy). I have this shop, a running business. So I am not so much depressed. But I know the village people who were living on land only. The village lands secure our food. People have lost that security. We are forced towards a life similar to that of slum in a city. Now, high rises are coming up in our surroundings. We will be underlooked by them. People constructed brick built houses with the compensation money, but there is no dignified way of earning for them. How they will maintain their house in future? Now we are to buy rice for our consumption. Government put a notice somewhere, forcibly took the land and publicised that people have surrendered their land willingly. Government is acquiring the land under British rule. If you call it a development what we poor people can do? But from our heart we cannot support what government has played with us. The simple question I would like to ask if the people gave their land willingly what was the necessity to deploy police force in the village, why seven people were arrested and put into jail.'

'What has happened to Rajarhat was just total devastation of the life and culture of the poor people' says a young boy from Chak Pachuria, another affected village.

Prahlad Mandal of Patharghata observed that the lands acquired from villagers were sold out to the real estate businessmen. Both government and the housing promoting agencies are making exhobitant profit from their land but the affected people are not under consideration of any kind of development programmes. They are just neglected. The local people are displaced without any rehabilitation scheme.

There were many such interviews. The very basic approach of the government (through HIDCO) was contradicted by the villagers.

Some statements and proverbs came up in relation to land acquisition during our discussion, we have noted those down:

Nichutalâr kânnâ upartalây pouchhay nâ. (the cry of the people from lower stratam does not reach to the people belong to upper stratam),

Achhe goru nâ boy hâl/ târ dukkho chirokâl (the cow is there but it won't carry the plough/its shock would survive forever; expressing their depression of landlessness),

Asar bujhe gân (one should sing a song according to the audience; indicating the changing strategies of the political leaders),

Khudhârta kukurer sâmne mângsa diyechhe (meat is thrown before a hungry dog; indicating the cropping up of corruption in syndicates),

Amâder jami to Indonesiay jây ni. Jârâ babsâ korchhe târâ lâbh korchhe, târâ kothây niye jâbe, ekhânei rayechhe (our lands have not gone to Indonesia; those who are making money out of it they are our countrymen only),

Rastrer unnati ki ? krishi nirbhar deshe? (what is the development for a country which is agriculture-based?)

Hindu kâ thâkur/ sâmne chikan châkan/Pichhane kharer gâdan (the image of Hindu god/ frontal side is well-decorated/ the back side show the bared structure with straw and bamboo; satirical to the development programme of the New Town).

All these speak the strong feeling of deprivation as well as the point of differences of the people.

In a writ petition filed by Nilotpal Dutta and others (on behalf of the Rajarhat Jami Bachao Committee) in the matter of New Township Project at Rajarhat in the High Court at Calcutta the petitioners stated that 'The right of the farmers (the petitioners) to carry on agriculture in their own land is a part of the rights of life governed by Article 21 of the Constitution of India. The public element allegedly involved in the measures initiated by the Government Authorities for development of the new township on the agricultural land belonging to the inhabitants of the said area have to be *prima facie* proved. The policy of the Government of West Bengal is in essence intended to mop-up substantial revenue for the Government of West Bengal by selling the said agricultural lands acquired from the cultivators to put promoters at exorbitant prices for construction of multi-storied building and housing scheme which cannot by any stretch of imagination be deemed to be public purpose. Your petitioner states that in view of implementation of the so-called 'public project', a large number of members of public are being sought to be not only dispossessed of their landed property but also are deprived of their right to earn their livelihood which is dependent on cultivation of the said land.

Fig. 10

Hence, the so-called 'Public Project' which is bound to result in substantial members of the public being deprived of the right to earn their living cannot be deemed to be a 'Public Purpose' in the eyes of law. In the instant case, in order to determine whether the said project initiated by the Government of West Bengal is actually for 'Public Purpose' one has to determine the ratio of the pubic benefitted against the ratio of the public to whom prejudice is likely to be caused. It is no doubt true that the said project is prejudicial to the interest of the majority of the public as the number of people who are likely to suffer on account of the said project far exceeds the number who may be benefitted therefore (Point 19). Your petitioners are also aware that the said township is not also intended for providing shelter or home to the homeless' (Point No. 20). Point No. 21 of the same petition stated, 'It appears from the project report of Housing Infrastructure Development Corp (HIDCO) published on May, 1999 that there are two paddy crops (*Boro and Aman*) grown through double cropping practice in the said area. Such report is also silent about other crops, vegetables and oil seeds grown on various seasons. In page-19 under Section X, it observed 'for that in order to facilitate the people of a particular community and limited in number, a large section of the people are going to be uprooted.'

All these reflect the points of conflict between the government machinery and the people of Rajarhat. For a free observation from the readers the petition is added with the appendix (5).

From Wet-land to Township—Long Journey.

From Wet-land to Township.

From Wet-land to Township—Long Journey.

New Town Coming Up.

New Town Coming Up-yet to be Occupied.

Planned for 5 lakh Population.

No Place for Poors.

Finance Centre.

More Essential than Wet-land?

Once Wet-land.

Ghuni-entering Into New Phase.

Ghuni—New Avenues.

Brick Kiln of Nishikanta Mandal Transferred into Power Sub-Station.

Brick Kiln of Nishikanta Mandal Transferred into Power Sub-Station.

8

Summary and Observations

I

1. Lands were usually under joint holding and mostly inherited from forefathers. Often the partition/mutation of land was not done and ownership had not been changed. The land was cultivated by the heirs on mutual understanding. Therefore, a piece of land under single ownership actually supported the number of families. Thus, when a land-owner lost his land it was not that one family became landless; actually a number of families in successive generations became landless, i.e., the loss of their occupation, their livelihood. So, when in government records there was one land loser actually there were multiplied numbers of land loser. Moreover, there were landless people who lived on agricultural labour, on share-cropping or on cultivating the land taken on lease. These unaccounted people also lost their livelihood. This social reality needs immediate attention.

2. The settlement areas though spared but are not undisturbed. Surrounded with the urban multiplexes, high rise apartment houses, business centres, intrusion of urban people the villages lost their traditional social environment. It is very often expressed by the people that these settlements are kept only as the potential resource of supplying the menial class of servitors to the urban people, who are coming as residents. Under this changing situation people find themselves further marginalised in their own land.

3. It is accepted by the villagers that situation has changed a lot. Communication system has been improved a lot and urbanisation is

coming up very quickly. Apparently, the livelihood situation has been improved a lot. The houses are transformed into brick-built one; mobiles, motor bike, cars are common, thanks to the compensation money. Some people have become rich, thanks to the syndicate system. But in the core of their heart people are suffering from uncertainty of occupation and livelihood for themselves as well as for their future generations.

4. Syndicates are now appearing in the news headlines very often unearthing the corruption and irregularities in supplying the building materials. It also produces political tensions between the groups. Villagers are also not happy with them. It is often expressed that syndicate system and its corrupt way of working spoiling the village youths morally. They are earning hard cash which they are spending after liquor and many other ways that don't match with their tradition. But it is an undeniable fact that for all these malpractices cropping up in these village societies the Left Front Government cannot just escape of their responsibility because social malformation and moral deterioration in any society has a direct bearing with the disturbances in normal situation of which a society is used to, coupled with the problem of economic deprivation and insecurity.

5. From HIDCO's point of view development is nothing but acquiring of land and sell those out after filling up for real estate development mainly. Such attitude certainly contradicts the interest of the agrarian society to whom land is their lifeline.

6. Another unfortunate part of this land acquisition is that lands have been acquired, sold it out to different companies and real estate businessmen and multiplexes, high-rises have come up but in many cases the land-loser did not receive the compensation. It is a common complain of the villagers. Besides the instances discussed under the experiences of the people here, we can cite another such case (cited by the people in general) and that is Balaka Apartment. In that apartment, house flats have been sold, but the hearing of lands is still pending, compensation cheques are not issued. There are people who even refused to attend the hearing but they found apartment houses are erected on their lands. This is not happened in one or two cases, this a common experience to innumerable people. Now they are running between the tables for their compensation.

Recently on May 5th, 2012, there was an agitation in Ghuni village. They detained the Chairman of HIDCO and demanded the compensation against their land. The news appeared in a Bengali daily newspaper. We have recorded a number of such cases.

The *Anandabazar Patrika (ABP)* a Bengali daily, reported that the state would pay additional one time compensation to those of the affected villages in Rajarhat New Town who, being unwilling to be parted with their cultivable land did not receive the compensation cheque during the time of acquisition. Over the issue there was a discontent among the people. Their point of argument was that why other people would not get the benefit. *ABP* reported from government records that in last 15 years about 6100 acres of land had been acquired from North 24 Parganas district. Force acquisition was the main complain, especially from Jangra Hatiara 2, Patharghata, Rajarhat-Bishnupur 1 and 2, Mahisbathan 2 Gram Panchayats. The compensation would be paid to the unwilling peasants in the above Gram Panchayats. What is that additional compensation? HIDCO decided to pay their earlier amount of compensation with interest and an additional package of Rs. 29,000 per cottah. A government spokesman explained to ABP that this package is for North 24 Parganas only. Why additional 29,000 rupees would be paid? The answer was the new government feels that the rate per cottah of land offered to the people was less. Why the 'unwilling' peasants of South 24 Parganas district would not be paid? (*ABP* reported that about 700 acres of land had been acquisitionaed from South 24 Parganas district in the last 15 years). The spokesman said that the land in South 24 Parganas district had been acquired in later stage and HIDCO did not find any inconsistency in the rate of compensation in South 24 Parganas district. *ABP* also reported about people's view. The Panchayat Pradhan of Rajarhat-Bisnupur 2, Sri Mannan Gazi, was one among the discontented people. He viewed that 'I had two bighas of land which was acquired forcefully. I had to accept the cheque. Law should be same for all. If additional compensation is given to those, who did not accept the cheque at that time then it shoud be given to us also. At least some amount should be given. Otherwise, people would go to the court of law.' Other opinions were also there supporting the government's decision. In New Town, a section of the 'unwilling' peasants opined that like the case of Singur in Rajarhat also government can think of returning the land to the peasants. The estimated cost for additional compensation would be about 300 crores. However, the chairman and managing Director of

HIDCO said the matter is under discussion and no decision has been taken so far (*ABP*, September 7, 2012).

The attempt, if taken up fruitfully, is a welcomed step from the part of the new government of the state. However, the details of this report generate certain observation.

First, HIDCO did not disclose the actual area of acquired land in their reports. Their reports show far less area than the actual acquisitioned area.

Second, why a section of people would be given certain benefits while all the affected people are severely suffered? This may further enhance the feeling of deprivation among the PAP.

Third, there were people who, due to lack of proper legal documents were deprived of the compensation money. They require immediate attention.

Fourth, the urgent need is an extensive list of those people, who did not receive any compensation on some or other ground. A total list of affected people with all details of their land holdings, rate of compensation, amounts of compensation distributed needs to be published by the HIDCO and at the same time a document on the transaction of land by HIDCO, to whom the land has been allotted, its income and profit etcetera to be published. An extensive survey of the area can only provide the valid information. Our study revealed that there were innumerable people who were deprived of compensation money on some or other reason. From the part of the then government no prior step had been taken up to settle the legal anomalies of the land so that the affected people could get their claims.

Fifth, the present government felt that the rate fixed per cottah of land was not sufficient. But does rupees 29,000 enough when HIDCO is making profit in crores? The land price in local market has gone high enough and it was well-visioned by the planners. Thus, if at all these people are given additional compensation, a people friendly and logical stand is expected from the government.

7. It appeared in daily news papers (*TOI,* dated June 25 and July 8, 2012) that HIDCO is selling huge amount of lands through auction and e-auction to different companies and educational institutions. The news unveils the fact that in more than ten years HIDCO could not utilise the lands acquired by the government. This depicts clearly

that HIDCO acquired lands much more than its actual requirement for mega city out of depriving the marginal people.

This is not the first ever instance. *Times of India*, July 23rd, 2012 reported about the unused plots in Salt Lake township where 'plots were handed over to private companies during the Left rule for implementing projects through PPP (Public-Private-Partnership) model, but those are still lying vacant'. It further reported that apart from land for PPP projects the Urban Development Department is scrutinising the records of all lands in Salt Lake area that are lying vacant for years together.

That the lands were aquired more than requirement may be substantiated by the fact that in still undistributed land by HIDCO government planned to set-up financial hub and the Chief Minister has already flagged off but as reported by *The Times of India* (August 1, 2012) only one company so far had shown interest to invest in the said financial hub even after four months since the CM flagged off to the project. It further reported that the project is implemented by the HIDCO. A 25 acres plot has been identified for taking up the first phase of the financial hub, which could be extended up to 100 acres in the future in phases. HIDCO chairman said the authority will decide very soon as to whether a fresh expression of interest could be floated.

Earlier April 24 (2012) was fixed as the last date of submitting applications which was later extended till July 31 by HIDCO. The union minister of state for urban development said, 'we have to do aggressive marketing'. *The Times of India* reported on August 23, 2012, 'with lone-taker government hardshells fin hub.' The report said 'the department has sought the Union Urban Development Ministry's help to showcase the financial hub at a banker's meet in New Delhi on August 23, 2012, where state officials will interact with representatives of major banking and financial institutions and convince them to invest in the hub.' It further reported that, 'the state government wants large financial and banking institutions to come forward and invest in the financial hub in Rajarhat which has, so far, received lukewarm response from such institutions.'

On November 19, 2012, the same English daily reported about the invitation of tenders for Rajarhat financial hub by the state. It reported that with applications from six financial and banking institutes, the authorities now floated tenders to begin work on the second phase of the financial hub. HIDCO received bid from UBI (United Bank of India), UCO (United Commercial Bank), NIC (National Insurance Company), WBFC (West Bengal Financial Corporation), WBIDFC (West Bengal Infrastructure Development and Financial Corporation) and SREI (*TOI*, Kolkata, November 19, 2012). From the report it came out that HIDCO is trying hard to attract investment but till date the response is not satisfactory.

The *Anandabazar Patrika,* December 6, 2012 reported that in New Town a lot of plots allotted to various business institutions are lying vacant and the institutes are showing relactance to invest. Their argument is that they are afraid of investing keeping in view the present infrastructural deficiency and the role of syndicates in supply of bulding materials. According to HIDCO, source there are 1,500 acres for commercial sector. Now HIDCO started giving caution to the land-holders asking them to utilise the land immediately. HIDCO sources said that according to the policy of the government no institution can hold the land under their possession for indefinite period without utilising it. In that case, legal action may be thought of (which also include the provision of taking the land back from them).

All these point out the very fact that there was no planning for the utilisation of the acquired land beforehand and land had been grabbed without actual requirement. Therefore, the very question comes out spontaneously 'was the acquisition of such huge area of land really necessary at the cost of lakhs of people's livelihood?'

8. Rehabilitation of the people, who were dispossessed of land was not taken care of seriously by the government.

9. This is perhaps the worst-ever incidence where government played a role of land selling agent (occupied the huge cultivable land forcefully from the marginally placed people at a very low cost with an intention to sell it out at an exorbitant profit to private parties) and earned huge profit out of it.

10. A class of land brokers has emerged in the process of urbanisation.

11. The people whose lands were located outside the project area boundary are now in a favourable situation and selling out their lands in high price. Consequantly, a deep sense of deprivation is intensifying further among the people who have lost all their lands. They view their deprivation not in terms of pre-urbanisation situation but in

terms of present land price. They firmly believe that government played a foul game (crooked) with them where they were placed in losing side while the government was the gainer.

We observe that government (Left Front) was fully aware with the future prospect of the New Town and knowingly exploited these marginal people using all administrative power and force.

12. The occupation of *bidi* rolling is getting impetus because of loss of land. It is one of the causes of health hazards like T.B.

13. Some socio-cultural rituals like *Bhai phonta*, *jamaisasthi* etcetera have been evaporating to a great extent because of deteriorating interpersonal relations centering the land issue.

14. Agriculture related rituals like *Nabanna*, *Bij Bapan* etcetera are no more practised.

15. Earlier the womenfolk used to rear hens, ducks and sell the eggs. It was exclusively their earning and they were free to spend the amount at their will. The pets were fed with *khud*, *kunro* etcetera which are not available due to loss of land. They have lost these earnings which is a great shock for them as they are to ask for money on every step from their men. Often it invites misunderstanding between the spouses.

16. Occupational pattern has been changed due to loss of land. Now, they are engaged in masonry work, daily wage labour in unorganised sectors like security guards, etc., small petty business like piecemeal hotels, grocery shop, STD booth, tailoring, driving, supply of building materials. Some have shifted to business also. But they are not sure about their future and the very fact lead to a feeling of social and economic insecurity among the affected people. This feeling of insecurity also works for their future generations, who will born as landless.

17. Big farmers are benefitted in the process of urbanisation but marginal farmers and *bargadars* are not.

18. In the process of urbanisation the opportunity of work in the unorganised sectors has been increased greatly.

19. There is a growing trend among the well off families to send their children to reputed/English medium schools. The researchers also noticed English-medium nursery schools in the locality.

20. In contrast, the marginal peasants and the share-croppers are becoming poorer. They are not able to send their children for

education. A type of complexity has been developed within the village society.

21. Landless labourers, who lived entirely on wage labour, are now better placed economically. They shifted to construction labour where wage is far better than the agricultural labour.

22. It is also observed that people have hard cash in their hand.

23. Transport system has also been developed and people are availing of this facility.

24. Due to urbanisation the price of land is increasing rapidly and is going beyond the reach of general people.

25. In the villages multi-storied housing complexes are coming up where the occupants are from different urban centres. Now, the old inhabitants are facing problems in accommodating the newcomers in their social milieu because of cultural and attitudinal differences between them.

26. The land not only supports the peasant society, it also feeds the surrounding non-agricultural societies including the city-dwellers.

27. The way of development had been conceived by the then Left Front government in case of Rajarhat, it did not suit with the interest of the local people comprised marginal peasants and fish cultivators. In the development of the mega city in Rajarhat the primary thrust was on the welfare of the privileged classes of city people ignoring the basic livelihood of the marginal communities which was vehemently opposite to the very concept of development (as defined by the Nobel Laureate Joseph Stiglizt). This very approach of the then government led a conflicting situation in Rajarhat.

28. The very process of land acquisition in Rajarhat is not at all democratic in nature. The Rajarhat land acquision issue clearly speaks of violation of people's right by the government.

29. Damage to the ECW (or EKW) violates the government's policy for environmental protection. In various reports, government has manipulated the truth that Rajarhat is a part of ECW and inadvertedly reported that in the project area there was no water bodies. In recent years, the Chairman of WBHIDCO expressed 'the only way Kolkata can grow is by expanding on the eastern fringes of the city taking into account that the wet-lands are not affected (*The Economic Times,* 3rd July, 2012). The observation is contradictory to

the mega city project of New Town. Or the government is befooling the public?

The damage to ECW by the then state government (LF) is alarming. It totally destroyed the wet-land of Rajarhat in order to promote real estate business of the private developers' companies. The report published in the English daily, *Times of India,* Kolkata in August 2012 reads, 'Bidhannagar Municipality has been dumping solid waste at Mollar *Bheri* for the past five years after getting no-objection certificate from the East Kolkata Wet-land Management Authority (EKWMA) in August 2007. This might have gone on for even longer had not the State government woken up to a Central environmental rule that prohibits dumping of garbage in the protected wet-land.' It further detailed that, 'going by the rule, the Bidhannagar Municipality can't dump solid waste at Mollar *Bheri* even though it has got a no-objection certificate from the EKW Management Authority (EKWMA). The same rule throws a spanner on the Housing Infrastructure Development Corporation's (HIDCO) plan to use the the Beonta *mouza* in Rajarhat for dumping solid waste from the New Town area. The Wet-land (Conservation and Management) Rules 2010, framed by the union ministry of environment and forested under clause (iv) of Rule-4 prohibits such dumping of social waste. The clause also specifies that if such practice existed before the rules came into force it has to be phased out within six months from the commencement of the rules.

'The matter came up in the EKWMA meeting held on August 13, 2012 where environment officials pointed out that the practice was in contravention with the Central rule. But then, the Bidhannagar Municipality didn't start the dumping on its own. It chose Mollar *Bheri* for dumping solid waste only after getting a no-objection certificate from none other than the EKWMA. Officials present at the meeting held that the management body has no authority to issue such an NOC going against the Central rule. It was precisely on this ground that the EKWMA scuttled plans for dumping solid waste at Beonta in Rajarhat. CEO, KMDA Vivek Bharadwaj, who was present in the meeting, had already communicated the decision to the Bidhannagar Municipality. "I was present in the meeting and have already asked the Bidhannagar Municipality to make a fresh application for renewal of permission from EKWMA. If the municipality doesn't get the permission, it has to come out with an alternative," said Bharadwaj. The government is in a binding. Neither can it allow the municipality to continue with the dumping, nor can it stop the process in a day. "There is a distinct difference between sewer and solid waste. We have no plans to block sewer water from the city canals to flow into the EKW. In fact, that is the uniqueness of EKW. But dumping solid waste is a different thing altogether. If done without precaution it may lead to filling up the wet lands. The problem was discussed in the last meeting. Measures have to be taken to phase out the dumping of solid waste at Mollar *Bheri* as the law says," an EKWMA official said. (*The Times of India*, Kolkata, August 28, 2012).

All these unveil the hard truth that environmental protection became a farse to the then Left Front government and it is only after the recent change over of power in the state that the steps have been taken up by the government in favour of Central environmental rule as reported above.

A little off bit but closely related to the issue is the ECW (or EKW) of Dhapa. *The Times of India,* Kolkata reported 'Dhapa extension hits green hurdle'. The report said that the second Dhapa project, which was planned by the Kolkata Municipal Corporation (KMC) as an alternative to the existing Dhapa dumping ground off EM Bypass, has hit a hurdle. The National Ganga River Basin Authority (NGRBA) officials, after going through the detailed project report, have refused to give it a nod saying that it was falling within the East Kolkata Wet-lands area. The NGRBA officials have recently held a meeting with the KMC officials and expressed their views.

Interestingly, the project spread over 140 acres, was approved by the East Kolkata Management Authority (EKWMA) and the concerned state environment department. After the new KMC board was formed in 2010, a plan was chalked out by the civic authorities to extend the planning area of Dhapa. Accordingly, a rupees 265-crore project was hatched. The project plan was also sent to the Ramsar authorities in New Delhi. The NGRBA officials also said that the international environment bodies could also object to the project. It further reported that 'the existing site at Dhapa covers 17 acres. Officials said that it would only take a year and half for the dumping site to get fully exhausted, as 3,500 metric tonnes of solid waste is being dumped now at the site daily and the quantity is rising (TOI, Kolkata, August 27, 2012).

In recent years, government has taken step to protect the area under Ramsar site. 'The East Kolkata Wet-land Construct Management Authority (EKWMA) has decided to plant concrete pillars to demarcate the boundary of the Ramsar site, some environmentalists have demanded for long to curb encroachment.' (*Times of India*, Kolkata, September 20, 2012). According to the Chief Technical Officer of EKWMA, the work would begin with marking out the EKW periphery adjoining urban areas like Sonarpur, Tiljala, EM Bypass and Salt Lake that are the most vulnerable to encroachment (*ibid*).

But it should be taken into account that ECW/EKW is not restricted within the declared area of Ramsar site only; it actually extends beyond it over vast surrounding areas. As in Rajarhat such lands were never protected by the earlier governments, whosoever political party was in power, rather encroached in a ruthless way, Salt Lake Township is one such instance.

Hence, the present government is liable to to protect these wet-lands in the state.

In this respect, we feel it relevant to cite here the news coverage by *TOI* on 'Wet- land being sold in pieces' (*The Times of India,* dated July 7, 2012, *Times City,* Kolkata). It reported that 'a water body in the East Kolkata Wet-lands–a Ramsar site that the state has committed to protect has been filled up in broad daylight and demarcated into plots that are selling for Rs. 3.25 lakh per cottah. Located in Chowbagha, less than a kilometer from Collector *bheri* that *TOI* and environment activists had helped to protect the land in January, the 52 bighas water body was filled with sludge around the same time that concrete pillars and walls around, Collector *bheri* were being torn down. In the ensuing summer, the water evaporated, leaving behind a stretch of fertile land where shrubs and bushes sprouted. There's no trace of water. Instead, it looks like an island with water all around. When *TOI* visited the encroached wet-land at Pirtala in Kolkata Municipal Corporation area, a five-minute drive from Collector *bheri*, located next to Heritage school and college, around a dozen masons and labourers were engaged in constructing a wall around the 1,040 cottah plot. Overseeing the work, labour contractor Swapan Mondal surveyed the pristine area around and remarked how picturesque the location was. "The promoters want to sell off the land in three to seven cottah plots. Those who build houses here will be in the lap of nature," he said. But what were the surety that the adjoining *bheris* would also not be encroached upon and the wet-lands replaced by concrete structures. "True, there is no guarantee to that. Dozens of water bodies have been encroached over the past few years and land sharks have become more active than ever. Anyway, it does not concern us so long as we get to earn," he said. In fact, large parts of the adjoining *bheris* are slated to be grabbed by the land sharks once they build a 24-foot-wide road to woo investors to buy those plots.

Some locals, though, are distraught over the sweeping changes that have occurred in the neighbourhood and changed the very landscape. "A nexus of realtors, politicians and local toughs are wreaking havoc. They are grabbing land with impunity and no one dares to resist. Tiljala police is aware of it but will not act because it too gets a share of the pie. While they monitor each truck entering and exiting major construction sites, they turn a blind eye to tankers dumping sludge into *bheris* and construction of walls around them," said a local man.

Stone chips, bricks and sand were dumped on the adjoining *kachha* road that meandered through *bheris*. "The road, built recently by dumping rubble, will be converted into a 25-foot-wide *pucca* road. Though around five feet of the adjoining water body needs to be reclaimed to construct the road, which will not be a problem. Book the plot within a month because the price will be revised upwards soon," said to Sanjay, one of the middlemen engaged in selling the plots East Kolkata Wet-land Management Authority (EKWMA) Chief Technical Officer Arijit Banerjee, who had initiated the drive to tear down the wall around Collector *bheri*, said, he would take up the issue at the next meeting of EKWMA on July 19. "This is shocking. There is a need for resistance from locals.

Otherwise, the wet- lands and the Ramsar tag will be lost. And that would be a shame for the city," he said. Though located in Ward 108, the KMC authorities are blissfully ignorant of the development. Sanchita Mondal, the member, mayor-in-council overseeing the KMC environment department, said she would definitely look into the matter. "I will send a team of civic officials to the spot to look after the situation," she said.

Kalyan Rudra, a member of the Wet-land Conservation Committee appointed by Calcutta High Court, expressed dismay at the development. "Silt dredged from canals is being dumped into wet-lands. We have already lost all water bodies in Kolkata. Unless we protect the East Kolkata Wet lands, the very survival of the city will be at stake," Rudra said.' (See appendix). All these certainly speak of the great threat to the EKW and the survival of the city as well. A strict measure from the government is expected to stop the encroachment over the EKW. Civic society is also to come forward to co-operate the government in this regard. Awareness programme may be launched in a big way among the people, in schools, colleges, local clubs, and other institutions about the importance of and threat to ECW/EKW.

30. So far we have come across the statements of the authorities about the development of mega-city, we did not find any programme concerning the project affected people, neither of any rehabilitation programme, nor of solving the issue of non-payment of compensation money (far apart from any effective development scheme for them). But government's responsibility just not over by displacing the poor and marginal people from their livelihood and making avenues for the privileged well-off section of the society.

31. The question of rehabilitation does not restrict its implication only with the ousting of people from their homestead but also equally related with the event of ousting from ones livelihood. The people of Rajarhat were expecting much from the present government. With the development of the changing scenario of Singur (another worst case of land acquisition by the then Left Front government) where the Chief Minister announced of returning the land to unwilling peasants, the people of Rajarhat are also waiting for a similar decision from the CM in regard to their lands which are yet to be sold out by HIDCO. A rehabilitation package for their livelihood is also expected. It is to be seen how far the present government take a pro-people stand. The problem of these poor and marginal people need to be taken care of by the government as they are the worst victim of the vested interest of the powerful people in the Left Front government.

32. The field data unveiled the fact that the land acquisition process of the then Left Front government was not transperant and was a planned conspiracy of the ruling power against the marginal

people with vested interest from the part of the then political leaders. This clearly speaks of violation of people's right by the government.

33. The way development had been conceived by the Left Front government in case of Rajarhat, did not consider the interest of the local people, especially the marginal peasants, *Bargadars*, agricultural labourers and fish cultivators. The Left Front's thrust was on the welfare of the affluent city people ignoring the marginal communities which vehemently oppose the very concept of development. This very approach (of Left Front government) consequent upon a conflicting situation.

II

Some Related Issues

1. Concept of Development

The working definition of development is very important. A common conscience is necessary considering the prospect of the society as a whole. Any developmental planning requires to be formulated without hampering the interest of the under-privileged groups. Development cannot be imposed from above; it would be effective development when it starts from the grassroots level. It needs to be clear about the purpose of development: 'progress towards what and progress for whom'. Whether the achievement would greater than loss? The cost-benefit ratio would be helpful. Keeping in view the land acquisition issue in Rajarhat and the similar other situations we may suggest orientation courses and training programmes for the planners, beureacrats and administrators towards the people-oriented development. In this context, the comment by the Principal Secretary, Urban Development, Government of West Bengal and Chairman, WBHIDCO (*The Times of India*, Kolkata, July 27, 2012) may be looked at: 'The essence of core sector development is the presence of proper infrastructure such as road-rail connectivity, water supply and other allied activities. In whatever little of HIDCO land is left, we are trying to build a financial hub too in New Town. What we are trying to move at is to support housing for people directly connected with the commercial sector. Many a time, people talk about the adverse effects of development activities, especially in relation to environment. However, the population is ever-expanding.

Majority of the people are gravitating towards the cities. The urban population contributes to 60 per cent of India's GDP. Hence, for cities to function, one needs to set-up core basic infrastructure.' But does really GDP proves the development of a country? The Economist Dr Mehbub-ul-Haq of Pakistan clearly proved that there is no relationship between the increasing GDP and the development of people as a whole (c.f. Bandopadhyay, 2007: 33). Joardar (2007:24) observed, 'in many countries that in spite of the growth in GDP a large section of people remained deprived of economic and social development.' Development cannot ignore the physical aspect of the environment also. Protection to bio-diversity and ecological balance is of the utmost importance in the context of human resource development. Without orienting the bureaucrats towards the basics of development all efforts not only would go in vain but would also invite more problems for the administration including conflicts and violence as experienced in Rajarhat and in similar situations. Joardar (2007: 30) gave an account in this regard. He observed that in 1993, the incidence of conflict between the peasants and police due to land acquisition was ten thousand in number while the figure increased to seventy four thousand in 2004. The situation is alarming from the developmental point of view. The words of Blaise Pascal, a seventeenth century French philosopher and mathematician (b.1623) can still guide us, 'Human kind is only a small link in the immense web of nature, but it is the only one that through thought understands Nature, it is the only species on earth to be responsible for earth, and to be able to transform it for better or worse' (c.f. Bagchi, 2007:14).

2. People's Participation

The process of land acquisition needs to be transparent and participatory in nature. A transparent process would help people to understand the pros and cons of the land acquisition while a participatory process would have been helpful in identifying the likely impacts of the land acquisition on different groups of people. People needs to be informed well in advance, at least a year before, so that they can get the opportunity to settle down the papers related to lands and thereby would not lose the compensation.

3. Planning of Development Projects

This is perhaps the most important part of the whole process. At the planning level, a committee consisting of administrators, economists, anthropologists, sociologists, ecologists, representatives from civic society and representative from the target area may work together. But so far no government has ever taken the people other than the administrative body in confidence. Neither the target group of people was consulted. In case of Rajarhat, even the observation submitted by the Fisheries Departmrnt (already referred in the report) was also ignored by the then government as it was not in favour of implementing the project.

4. Agricultural Lands *vs* Development

The target area for land acquisition process by the government often focussed to the agricultural lands. The popular views of development (as observed in Rajarhat and similar situations), meant the real estate development, industrialisation with improved technology, IT hubs, modernised business outlets like multiplex, Malls etc., with focussed group of urban middle income groups, higher income groups, industrialists, big business communities, high profile administrators and aristrocrats. The interest of these privileged groups of people and that of the agriculture-based marginal communities are not located at the same plane. This point needs to be understood by the planners. It is also to be noted that agriculture provides food security to the marginal peasants and for that only the poor and marginal peasants save themselves from starvation. Thus, agricultural economy cannot be replaced with wage labour. Bandyopadhyay (2007:35) discussed with the support of NSSO data that while during 1983—1993/94 several industries were shut down in West Bengal and the BPL (Below Poverty Line) population decreased to a great extent wherein he found out the answer of this 'miracle' in the progress of agricultural front.

In a country like India, agriculture provides economic opportunity for a large section of population throughout the year. Agriculture could be developed as profitable industry. In West Bengal about 92 per cent of land holders are marginal peasants, who hold 60 per cent of the total cultivable lands; hence unless and until their problems are not resolved duly the total production of the state would be affected negatively (*ibid*:39).

'West Bengal Statistical Hand Book (2002), clearly depicts the land use pattern in West Bengal, which are as follows:

Net sown area: 63.5 per cent,
Current fallow: 3.3 per cent,
Forest: 13.6 per cent,
Not available for cultivation: 18.1 per cent (1.5 m hectare), and
Old fallow: 1.5 per cent.

Thus, the total land not available for cultivation (including the old waste land) amounts to 19.6 per cent, i.e., almost 20 per cent' (*ibid:* 40). Those lands can be used for industrialisation and urbanisation instead of multi-crop producting agricultural lands. Acquiring of such lands on reasonable compensation would also help the poor people to build up alternative livelihood.

5. Data base for the Projects

What is urgently required for the PAP of Rajarhat is to develop a data base. There is no baseline data available with the government about the actual number of PAP, and their present condition. How many peasants had been paid with compensation and how many of them did not receive. How much land were disputed and how many were not heard upon. How many people had been given rehabilitation and how many were pending. What was the impact of acquisition of land on their livelihood? How many needs to be rehabilitated? With a reliable data base government is to move for an effective developmental programme for this project affected people. Such data base is required for each such project.

6. Economic Rehabilitation in Rajarhat and in Similar Situation

At this juncture, (in the post-project scenario as discussed in the report) Rajarhat requires special attention of the present government. Government's function would be to open up alternative economic avenues for the affected people which suit their self-esteem. Security of livelihood would pacify the tension in the area. Simply ignoring the interest of the poor and marginal people and providing facilities to the incoming urban people (as came out from the statement of the HIDCO authorities, time to time), would not only increase the social inequality but would also further aggravate the tension between the two groups.

The huge profit earned by the HIDCO in these years may be used for the overall development and rehabilitation of the marginal section of the affected people. A portion of the profit may also be spent as additional compensation money which may ease the feeling of the people of being exploited by the government. Compensation package was insufficient and also irregular. State also failed to provide sustainable income to the affected families. These points may be taken care of under the changing political scenario.

An official help desk may be created to extend legal and administrative support to the people to regularise their land records and to help them in getting the compensation. The help desk may sort out the cases where lands have been acquisitioned but compensation is still pending; such cases need to be identified at the earliest through direct interaction with the villagers. A committee can be set-up immediately with anthropologists, members from civil society, representative from villagers to work on this issue.

7. Measures for Developing Infrastructure of the Existing Villages in Rajarhat and in Similar Situation

The infrastructure of the existing villages in terms of road, electricity, education and health facilities which is lagging behind in relation to the promising New Town are to be developed in accordance with the common need of villagers as well as in accessible condition. The educational or health facilities available at the nearby emerging mega city are far beyond the reach of the marginal section of the village people.

8. Amelioration of Land-use of Existing Villages

The existing land use categories, i.e., agriculture, wet-land and settlement area have been disturbed greatly due to mega city project. The present government may ensure the survival of the wet-land available till now in the form of *doba, bil* or *gheri* in the surroundings of the existing villages without further damage in the form of unauthorised filling or chocking. If it is done in a proper way, the villages would get the opportunity to maintain duck rearing or fishing or using surface water for domestic purpose. It would also minimise the pressure on ground water. Animal husbandry can be encouraged as far as possible with the restoration of agricultural production of profitable crops or vegetables in the left out meager land following the method of intensive farming in possible sites. This kind of farming would be helpful to get nearby urban market.

A Syndicate Office.

Ghuni in a Transitional Phase.

Ghuni in a Transitional Phase.

Ghuni—Trying Hard to Cope Up.

New Business Centre Coming Up in Ghuni.

New Generation, New Exposure.

The Curse of Growing City.

9

Concluding Remarks

The inhabitants of the Rajarhat and surrounding areas have been facing innumerable problems due to land acquisition by HIDCO and other land grabbers in a most unehtical manner. Consequently, they not only lost their permanent livelihood but also uprooted for the realty development. It is also a great shock for their self-esteem. Such kind of social situations never lead a society towards a healthy state. Should we call it 'development'?

1. Rajarhat is perhaps the first-ever incidence in West Bengal where vast areas of agricultural lands had been acquisitioned and people were ousted from their livelihood for the realty development. The villagers of Rajarhat are facing three problems at a time: one is the loss of livelihood, second is the absence of any rehabilitation scheme for alternative livelihood and third is the fast growing urbanisation process which has brought a further threat of land grabbing through the land brokers.

2. Uprooting a population forcibly from their land and livelihood and pushing them to totally temporary and uncertain avenues of livelihood under the name of development is a mockery to the humanity. Unfortunately, it is an ever-alarming situation that a democratic government body with its full administrative and political power acted against the interest of the common people.

3. The project has made an economically settled population into a socio-economic burden on the state.

4. A population, who used to supply food to the urban people now dependent on the urban society for their livelihood.

5. An active society who used to live on toil in land becomes jobless and inactive. This worklessness is a great problem for them as it brings many vices to the society. Syndicates are the best example.

6. Acquisition of a person's landed property does not restrict its impact on a single family but affect a number of families who were dependent on it over generations. Till 2011 a total of 2,421 hectares of land had been acquired for which 1.60 lakh of people were given compensation (Dey, 2011: 21) keeping apart the people who were deprived of compensations. Dey (*ibid*) observed that about 2.5 lakh of people will be deprived of their livelihood. In practice, at least five times greater number of people (if we consider the average family size is five in Indian context) would be the sufferers leaving apart even greater number of future populaton who are yet to born.

7. It is important to understand that small and marginal peasants cultivate their land not to produce surplus but to assure their consumption, i.e., the food security for the family. Therefore, in spite of earning cash money through other avenues they lost that sense of security. Won't they be called as 'economic refugee'? (We can recall here the statement by a land loser from Akanda Kesari village that 'our rice plate has been snatched away by the Left Front government').

8. A strong feeling of deprivation and exploitation is very prominent in their mental state that is hampering their normal way of life.

9. The harsh reality in Rajarhat is the ever worst example of the intentional exploitation of the voiceless marginal people by the then Left Front government, who violated the basic objective of the government of India to provide shelter to the poor and weaker section of the population as from this empirical study the fact came into surface speaks just an opposite picture. The multi-storied buildings brought up by the big real estate companies are priced for the rich and upper middle class affluent people from various corners of the city (Kolkata), from outside the city and even from abroad. Thus, the very basic intention of the then State government is under question.

10. There were protests from the part of the peasants under the banner Rajarhat Jami Banchao Committee (*Jami* = land; *Banchao* = save) against the ruthless decision of land acquisition by the then

government. It was a spontaneous movement where all the people of the affected villages irrespective of their caste, creed and political affiliation participated but unfortunately their voice was stopped rudely by the government functionaries with the help of the police force.

11. The observation of the Assistant Director of Fisheries, North 24 Parganas, Barasat through his letter (Memo No. 774, dated 26.08.99) addressed to the Deputy Director of Fisheries was totally ignored as it did not favour the project. The letter says 'The Rajarhat block is small in area but one of the potential block under North 24 Parganas in respect of water bodies, water resources, acquatic flora and fauna as well as aquaculture. The vast wet-lands surrounded with thousands of doba, Tank/pond, Nayanjali, jheel, beel, bilan, canal, Bypass canal dead river beds, swamp, low-lying area. In respect of water resources, there are saline, fresh and even waste water available in Rajarhat block. Apart from this, a vast low-lying thousands of hector areas from Dum-Dum Airport to Salt Lake area were recorded as Dhupir bil and locally known as Ghuni bil, Jatragachhi beel and in different names in diverse locations.' (Appendix-6).

12. This may be pointed out here that while government has made a planning for development of New Town out of acquiring vast area of land in this wet-land there was surprisingly no mention of the impact of destroying this vast eco-system and its long-run effect on the environment of not only Kolkata but also of the bio-diversity as a whole in any report submitted by different government and non-government bodies trusted upon for reviewing the situation. It is also not true that the Left Front government blindly depended upon those faulty reports as various departments of the government body submitted their reports stating the actual situation of the project area. Therefore, it can be inferred that being fully aware of the situation the government manipulated the data and passed the project.

13. It is unfortunate from the part of the democracy that the socially and economically marginal people were deprived of their basic rights and were pushed into wretched condition by a democratic government (Left Front government), who used these people earlier for assuring their vote bank.

14. In our country, while several welfare schemes are planned and implemented for the protection and uplift of these socially marginal backward people, the Left Front government on the contrary not only ousted them mercilessly from their livelihood but also ruthlessly deprived them from reasonable compensation, in many cases from compensation at all.

15. In the HIDCO report, it is observed that the New Town project was conceived and implemented in compliance with the Government of India's declaration of establishing hundred new towns of half million population by 2021. In this respect, it refers 'Lack of adequate shelter facilities, particularly of the economically weaker sections, has affected the quality of life, particularly of the children and women.

The shelterless people have been forced to squat on pavements and other places with an overall deterioration of health, hygiene and basic sanitation.' Thus, it welcomes the Government of India's declaration. In great contrast, we can refer FICCI report which speaks, '...an interesting phenomenon of the changing perception of New Town among prospective buyers from a predominantly MIG destination to a HIG destination. The number of applicants in the HIG segment is on the rise while those from the MIG segment have comparatively reduced' (c.f. Dey, 2011: 23). Is there any room for those shelterless people who have been forced to squat on pavements and other places with an overall deterioration of health, hygiene and basic sanitation as promised in the government report? Our data says 'no'.

16. There was no information with HIDCO about the actual number of affected people/families. A detailed survey was required.

17. Some points are coming up through analysis of the situation which has greater implication on the development aspect. The mega-city would accommodate huge urban population which would increase the congestion of CMA rather than decongest the city as claimed by the HIDCO backed reports.

The mega city requires huge water supply in contrast to earlier situation where per hectare population density was only seven while HIDCO proposes a population density of 244 per hectare of land initially, which will further increase through increased FAR (Floor Area Ratio) as declared by HIDCO Chairman in recent times (*Times of India Guide*, June, 2012). It is now an alarming situation in CMA in respect to high concentration of arsenic in water (*Times of India*, June, 28, and June 30, 2012) [Appendix-15].

18. Over-extraction of ground water is the cause of increase arsenic content in water. The areas affected under CMA are densely populated with high rise buildings. HIDCO estimated water requirement for the mega-city with residential as well as daily floating population (7.5 lakh) will be 100 million litres per day.

With the increasing population density in future years the requirement would be more. Can the future be imagined? In this context, we can mention of an article, Ganga Sindhu Narmada, by Jaya Mitra, that appeared in the editorial page of *Ananda Bazaar Patrika* on July 26, 2012; She expressed her concern for the destruction of the natural water drainage capacity of Kolkata in large scale filling up of its low lands, water bodies, ponds as well as natural slopes towards sea for the sake of high rises. She is afraid, whether we have to dig up the filled in lands again to restore the water bodies in future to save Kolkata.

There is a big gap in social, economic, educational, cultural and attitudinal levels between the two groups of population, one the old inhabitants, the villagers and the other middle and upper class urban groups of the cities and towns, living in very close physical proximity. The gap is very much visible and creates a sense of deprivation and a feeling of marginalisation among the villagers. It is also a great shock for their self-esteem. Such kind of social situations never lead a society towards a healthy state. Should we call it 'development'?

On the very thinking of development by the then Left Front government in respect of acquisition of lands for cities, mega-cities, malls, industries in imitation to the western model by applying the colonial Land Acquisition Act of 1894, we remember a part of the lecture delivered by Rabindranath Tagore during his tour to China in 1924, where he said 'we have for over a century been dragged by the prosperous West behind its chariot, choked by the dust, deafened by the noise, humbled by our helplessness, and overwhelmed by the speed. We agreed to acknowledge that this chariot drive was progress, and that progress was civilisation. If we ever ventured to ask, "progress towards what and progress for whom" it was considered to be peculiarly and ridiculously oriental to entertain such doubts about the absoluteness of progress. Of late, a voice has come to us bidding us to take count not only of the scientific perfection of the chariot but of the depth of the ditches lying across its path (c.f. Bagchi, 2007: 15).

10

Addendum

Introduction

From Rajarhat we winded up our field work for the desk work in early 2012. But we never withdrew ourselves from the people of the area, who trusted us and unfolded their saga to us. They knew that nothing miraculous would happen to rescue them from their struggle for a mere survival, to spare them from their daily hardship and toil for each and every requirement of daily life, to resuscitate their shattered dreams. They also knew that what they have lost is forever. Still they wanted to share their experiences, their saga with us. They wanted their saga to be noted down, recorded truly. There was never a gap at the level of interaction from their part. Those whom we could not meet during our field work for some reason or other came to us with the request to record their interview; sometimes people came to hand over their documents in support of their narrated stories, sometimes they came to meet us to share their recent struggle, sometimes they wanted us to visit some personalities whom they trust to be a speaker for their cause (in one such instance we met Nilotpal Dutta, who was in the leading role of the *Jami bachao andolan*, the movement against the land acquisition by the then State government). This continuous interaction helped us to understand the total scenario in a deeper way. But in the press, ready manuscript we could not do justice to all of them. Only two such interactions have been scripted under this section. One is our interaction with Nilotpal Dutta, and the other is that with Sukhen Mandol, a villager who is still struggling hard against the unethical acquisition of his *bil*-land.

Nilotpal Dutta recalled the early days of the movement against land acquisition (*Jami Andolan*) 'people from Aatghara, Kaikhali, Gopalpur, Sulanggari *moujas* were involved in the movement from the very beginning. They were mostly Muslims. The farmers of these *moujas* used to work as daily labourers also. The villagers of Laskarhat, Baliguri, and Patharghata joined in a later stage after being aware of the circumstances. Later this 'Andolan' came to a halt...

A total area of 3,075 hectare was acquisitioned in the name of development. But more than 2,085 hectare of water bodies including 'Dhupir bil' could not be acquitted for the developmental purposes without assessing its impact on the Environment according to 'Environment Impact Assessment Act'. Therefore, they did it with their own people and claimed that there was no water body. Then why they required such huge fund for filling up the land? ...

In 1993, an article by Sumit Kar published in *The Statesman,* which stated that foreign investments can be possible in two ways: 1) Building township, and 2) In Beverages. This is happening in our country. Just think, analyse and understand. But now in recent times, we find very few people are interested in buying flats. Hence, most of the flats in Rajarhat are lying vacant. Of course, flats coming up in Rajarhat are far more than the actual requirement. The importance of Rajarhat, its rivers, canals, khal, and water bodies is to be understood while talking of the massacre done by destroying its natural environment. Labanyaprabha River originated from the Ganges has its course as follows: flowing through Khardah to New Barrackpore to Jessore Road to the back of Rajarhat Police station to Beliaghata to Bidyadhari. Tantia Bil at Belgharia flows through B.T. Road, Teghoria, Raghunathpur, Jangra, and Mandalgathi to Bagjola (zero point). Total distance covered is 29 km. The point where Bidhyadhari meets Bagjola is known as Ekanno Gate. Earlier, in the Patharghata area the narrow water strips called *Khal* were directed straight. But later the course of these was changed. One such Krishnapur Bhangar *Khal* originates from Bagbazar, and flows through Ultadanga, Kestopur and flows to the channels of Bidhyadhari. There are three such *Khals* which surrounded Rajarhat. Four bypass canals originated from Dhupir Bil. The excess water of Dhupir Bil used to be channelised towards Bidhyadhari through the canals. Now water bodies have been filled up mostly. Roads have been constructed by filling up of the canals like that from VIP and like bypass-2. From these all one can foresee that Rajarhat shall no sooner be marked as an "Endangered City". For developing New Town there was uncontrolled felling of 15 lakh of trees in the initial days and it is (i.e., cutting of trees) still continuing. Many more trees are still being cut down to beautify the place artificially…

Rajarhat was once famous for its 'Himsaagar' variety of mango. But trees are being felled drastically and mango production is hampered largely. I can give you an impression of the situation; one Gopa Sen had a mango garden, she said that all 65 mango trees of her garden were cut down in the process of 'development'. This is only one case. There are many such people who had the same sad story. Khetawat Tower Pvt. Ltd had 86 mango trees in this locality, now you won't find them. In the year 2006, the Government took up a programme for plantation but only 575 trees were planted in lieu of 15 lakh of trees…These data clearly show that it's the unplanned growth of urbanisation and unwise application of technological advancement that bring forth pollution and environmental hazards. Where is the EIA report pertaining to all these acts? Who is responsible for this pollution? Losing a livelihood is much better than encountering pollution; pollution slow poisons a person and brings slow death…Dhupir Bil was extended from Chinar Park to Jatragachi, while Bagjola Basin was located on the left side of the road leading to Sector-V. All have gone in the name of development. An Arsenic plant has been constructed in Patharghata, due to the rapid decrease of groundwater level by 16 feet below the normal level…

On 2nd of June, 1995, '*Jami Bachao*' movement was initiated and a committee was also formed. But the movement could not sustain due to various reasons. No political party came forward to help....Rajarhat was very productive from agriculture as well as fisheries point of view apart from its environmental richness and bio-diversity. In Dhupir Bil and Ghunir Bil areas, cultivation was possible for three times annually. But unfortunately these lands were acquisitioned for township development. From the year 1998, land acquisition started.'

The '*Jami Bachao*' movement was led by Nilotpal Dutta as secretary of the committee. The president of the committee was

Topcher Miyan, from Raigachi. The farmers of Raigachi, Ghuni, Jatargachi, Pathorghata, Nababpur, Baliguri, and Laskarhati were associated with the movement. The committee comprised 11 members supported by 4,000 farmers and labourers. Dutta threw further light on the changed landscape of this wet land area, 'there were six panchayats in Rajarhat which indicate that human habitation exist in this locality. How the Government of West Bengal declared that there was no human habitation in Rajarhat? In 1962-63, the Congress Government proposed a satellite township in Dumdum area. For that purpose, the Government started acquiring lands. At that time, Rabin Mondal (a CPI-M leader) wrote a letter to the then Government of West Bengal and requested not to acquire these lands. He wrote that if the Government acquires the lands, many people will lose their age-old occupation of cultivation and they have to switch over from their traditional job. People may also become jobless. At that time, Government acquired some amount of land but the proposal for Satellite Township was not implemented. The land was acquired according to LA-3 (LA=Land Acquisition Act). The law under this section says if the proposed work can't be undertaken, the Government will be liable to return the lands to the owners. On 31st March, 1993, the Supreme Court rejected the law of LA-3 and introduced LA-4. Under this new law, the Government has to issue notice to the land owner informing that his/her land will be acquired by the Government. If the land owner has any objection he/she may submit it. Then another notice is to be issued to the land owner from the part of the Government stating that his/her land has been acquired and it should be followed by another notice requesting the land owner to collect the compensation cheque...

In case of Rajarhat, the Government sent the land acquisition notice under LA-4. In this notice, they stated that if any villagers have any objection, then he/she has to submit the objection within 42 days from the date of notification. But the notice was placed on the notice board at the Panchayat office, BDO office, etc., where the villagers seldom go and so they didn't know about the township, moreover, the notice was placed on the 40th day from the date of notification. So those poor people can't submit their objection to the respective office and Goutam Deb, the former Home Minister of West Bengal, declared that each and every one of this area is with us, no body has any objection. These are all known to the people.'

All these were not unknown to us because of our prolonged contact with the villagers during and after field investigation. Our query to him was 'why the *Jami Bachao Andolon* was not successful and came to a halt halfway?'

First, he analysed, in this movement, the share-cropper (*bhag chashi*) did not participate. Because they used to work hard in land but didn't get sufficient amount of crops or money or both. Only the land owners joined the movement. But the number of share-croppers was significant.

Secondly, Rajarhat was surrounded by the Salt Lake City on one hand and Dumdum on the other. So a large number of people from Tegharia, Ghuni, Sulanggari, Kadampukur, Jatragachi, Raghunathpur, Jangra Hatiara area used to work as labourer in the various industries/ factories of Dumdum and Salt Lake area. Thus, people had an alternative job option. They were also happy to get some amount of money in exchange of their land. Those people were also reluctant to participate in this movement. But now most of those factories are closed due to some or other problems and the workers are now jobless and facing severe hardship. But now it is of no use. Another point is that all the farmers who had other source of income did not join the movement and substitute jobs were available in the vicinity, hence it was easier for some people to find out alternative jobs.

But I feel that the major cause for the failure of this movement was lack of political support. Not a single party came to support this movement. The CPI-M and the TMC party made an agreement under the table. So, both of them were on the same side. The most unfortunate part was that all the political parties joined hands for their vested interest at the cost of these poor people. The TMC leader Tanmaoy Mondal said to the villagers that '*ei danobder sathe larai kore parbi na tar cheye jami ta die de*' (you cannot win over these demons, so it is better to give up your land). That means he also tried to convince people for giving their land. Would you believe that an opponent party leader convincing people in support of the ruling party without his own vested interest?

The Rajarhat New Town will be a dead city soon, because this city has no proper drainage system at all. The Left government filled up so many canals by dumping earth, like the Noapara canal. Besides, there are so many canals exist in this locality, but they need cleaning in every month which is not done in proper way. Gradually, those canals are getting blocked by the garbage and the drainage system is not functioning properly.'

Nilotpol Dutta and some people of the Rajarhat area along with the Howrah Ganotantric Nagoric Samiti filed a case at Kolkata High Court in 1998. In his own words, 'Justice P.K. Samanta was the judge and he said this case was not for the single bench, it must be put in the divisional bench. We again filed case for the second time in the year 2000 in the Green Bench of the Calcutta High Court. At that time, Justice A.K. Mathur was the Judge for this case and he said to these poor people, 'Environment ka kya thekadari liye hay?' ('Do you have taken contract over environment?'). In the year 2004, we filed case for the third time but again it was not succeeded. This time there were two judges handling this case, namely Justice Pinaki Chandra Ghosh and Justice Biswanath Sammadar.'

Dutta did not see any hope for the country where people, especially those who were at the whelm of affairs, did not give justice to the poor people rather exploited them for their vested interest. He felt sorry for the country.

The Experience of Sukhen Mondal

Sukhen Mondal's father bought a 13 bighas and eight cottah lands in Rajarhat area in the year 1956 from one Saikh Habibulla. It was a low-lying land and therefore was not much suitable for paddy cultivation, but still they cultivated some amount of paddy. The land was mainly used for coconut plantation. 'We had 160 coconut trees in that land,' Sukhen Mandal narrated his saga, 'in government records the land was identified as *bil*. In 1999 government, vested our land. During 2003-04 government acquired our land for New Town project. But we had RS record (according to 1962 records) and LR record (according to 1983 records). We submitted our land revenues regularly. Therefore, I found it irregular from the part of the government to declare their land as vested. My only query is that how my land could be declared as vested? A cheque of Rs. 24,41,949.00 was drawn in favour of the Collector against my land (as because the land was vested). Later in the year 2010 (18.03.2010), I received a letter from BLRO office, calling me to appear for hearing and correction of my land type. But till date it is not complete. During September-October, 2011 HIDCO started cutting down my coconut

trees in order to take up the project of Rabindra Tirtha. The site was marked for Rabindra Tirtha. I had a *kachcha* house in that land. On 22.10.2011, HIDCO destroyed that house, I tried my best to protect it but I could not succeed. They did it in the darkness of night. Rabindra Tirtha came up on my land and it was scheduled to be inaugurated on 07.08.2012 by the Chief Minister of West Bengal. On the previous day, i.e., on 6th August, 2012, I, along with my family started hunger strike in front of Ranbindra Tirtha. The TV channel '*Aj Tak*' started a live telecast. Police then came and asked me to vacate the place. I could understand why they came, because next day was the inauguration day. I told him that don't I have a right to sit at my own land? ('*amar jamite ki ami boseteo pari na*?'). Then the local leaders and the police men repeatedly asked me to withdraw the hunger strike but I could not agree on that with no bad intention, but I only wanted to get back my land which was occupied forcibly and I was not paid any compensation for my land. We are not rich people and we are claiming our own land; what is wrong in it? Still I am sticking to my one point agenda, 'give my land back'. I have filed a case also in this regard. At 10 O'clock in night, some local leaders came and threatened me, '*apni jodi amon kichu koren ja amader sarkar ke henostha kare tahole valo habe na*' ('if any of your doings hampers the image of our government we won't spare you'). Then the Minister In Charge, Urban Development and Town and country Planning and Municipal Affairs, local MLA and HIDCO Chairman came and assured me not to worry, they will solve the problem, '*katha dilam sob mitmata hay jabe*' (we give you the word that the matter would be solved). The Minister In Charge assured me that I can meet the Chief Minister the next day. I was very much hopeful for the meeting. He also invited me in dinner with them but I could not accept. I told him that, '*amar ato baro khati kore dilen apnara*'? (You have done such a great damage to me?). Next day, I did not go to that place and hoped that everything would be settled. But all in vain, I didn't receive any compensation till date. In the year 2011, I filed a case in the Kolkata High Court against the government in the division bench of Justice P.S. Banerjee and Justice C.R. Das. On August 8, 2012 the Minister, Firhad Hakim, called me in Writers Building and he told that they are feeling guilty because I did not get the compensation money. He assured that they will manage everything and suggested me to withdraw my case, '*akta din thik kore high court e gie sab mitmat kore nin*. Rabindra Tirtha *haye gache. Seta akta valo jinish. Apni ak koti taka nie chole jan'* (go to the Court one day and settle the case. Rabindra Tirtha has been built up. That is a good thing. You take rupees one crore and leave). But I cannot agree on this, I want justice only. For the sake of justice, I already spent 30 lakh rupees and I also gave my house on mortgage. I am now living like a refugee. How can I accept it?' Now, Sukhen Mandol is jobless, homeless, spending his days with the hope that one day he will get justice and will get back his land or at least will get proper compensation (Appendix 13).

Note: *Recently, it is informed that many of the land losers are now suffering from a severe economic and financial crisis as there is no alternative source of income from the part of the government and they are panting for a fresh breath. A person aged more than sixty years opted for a daily wage service of security guards to run his family and another nearing sixty is looking for daily wage labour. Both of them are educated and were affluent peasants and lost all their lands for the township.*

References

1. Ajzen, I., Fishbein, M., 1980. *Understanding Attitudes and Predicting Social Behaviour*, Prentice-Hall, New Jersey.
2. Bandyopadhyay, Debabrata, 2007: '*Paschimbange Unnayan Prakriyar Swarup*' in *Unnayan-Anunnayan*, (ed.) Sandip Das, Jayprakash Antyodaya Nidhi, Kolkata, pp. 33-41 (in Bengali).
3. Bagchi, Samar, 2007: '*Samayer Granthi Khule Gachhe*' in *Unnayan-Anunnayan*, (ed.) Sandip Das, Jayprakash Antyodaya Nidhi, Kolkata, pp. 14-23 (in Bengali).
4. Chattopadhyay, Kunal: 2001, *Environmental Conservation and Valuation of East Calcutta Wet-lands,* prepared for Environmental Economics Research Committee under The World Bank Aided 'India: Environmental Management Capicity Building Technical Assistance Project', Ministry of Environment and Forests, Indira Gandhi Institute of Developmental Research, Goregaon (East), Mumbai (India).
5. *Census of India* 2001: Data from the 2001 Census, including cities, village and towns (Provisional). Census Commission of India.

Archived from the original on 2004-06-16.http://www.censusindia.net. Retrieved 2008-11-01.

6. CMDA Report, May 1994, *Concept Plan,* New town at Rajarhat, prepared by Directorate of Planning and Development, CMDA. .
7. Datta, Dr R.N. and Prof Uttam Banerjeee, April 1996, *Physical Structure and Master Land-use Plan, New Town at Rajarhat,* Department of Architecture and Regional Planning, IIT, Kharagpur.
8. Dey, Pranab, 2011; *Rajarhat: Sarkar Jokhan Luthera*, Nagarika Mancha, Kolkata (in Bengali).
9. District Statistical Handbook, North 24 Parganas, Bureau of Applied Economics and Statistics, Government of West Bengal [cited from Pranab De, 2011: *Rajarhat: Sarkar Jokhan Luthera*, Nagarika Mancha, Kolkata, p. 23].
10. Dutta, Nilotpal (ed.), 2010: *Rajarhate Jami Dakatir Itihas*, Rajarhat Jami Bachao Committee, Kolkata (in Bengali).
11. Ghose Bose and Associates Pvt. Ltd., April, 2000, *New Town, Calcutta: Comprehensive Environmental Impact Assessment and Environmental Management Plan Report,* West Bengal Housing Infrastructure Development Corporation Limited (A Government of West Bengal Undertaking).
12. Government of West Bengal, September, 1995, New Town at Rajarhat, Project Report, Task Force, New Town Housing Department.
13. Government of West Bengal, 1995: New Town at Rajarhat Project Report, Task Force, New Town Housing Department.
14. Guha, Abhijit, 2007: *Land, Law and the Left: The saga of Disempowerment of the Peasantry in the era of Globalisation*, Concept Publishing Company, New Delhi.
15. HIDCO, May, 1999: New Town, Calcutta: *Project Report*, West Bengal Housing Infrastructure Development Corporation.
16. Joardar, Manas, 2007: '*Unnayan Silpayan Ebong Prajukti*' in *Unnayan-Anunnayan*, (ed.) Sandip Das, Jayprakash Antyodaya Nidhi, Kolkata, pp. 24-32 (in Bengali).
17. Rajarhat Gopalpur Municipality. Official website of the Department of Municipal Affairs, Government of West Bengal. http://wbdma.gov.in. Retrieved 2008-12-07.
18. Sangupta, Santanu, Sanhati, 2008: A history of the Brutal Rajarhat land acquisition, Bengal's new IT hub, Translated from *Rajarhat-Uponogorir Ontorale Arto Manuser Kanna* (Internet Source).
19. Yahoo maps location of Rajarhat Gopalpur. Yahoo maps. Retrieved 2008-12-07.

Appendices

Appendix – 1:

Appendix – 2: Tools of Anthropological Study
Anthropological Survey of India,
Eastern Regional Centre,
Kolkata.

Schedule - A: Socio-economy Survey of Household Census At the Level of Key Informants

Name of the Informant

Mother Tongue
Other language known
Migrated Religion
Community and Clan

House Type

Native place and if otherwise from
Agricultural implements and fishing net

S.N	Name of the family members	Relationship	Age	Sex	Marital Status	Age at Marriage	Education	Present Occupation		Past Occupation		Present Property Movable /Immoveable	Past Property movable /immovable	Remarks
								Prim	Sec	Prim	Sec			

Anthropological Survey of India
Eastern Regional Centre,
Kolkata

Land and Live-Stock

Schedule – B

Name of the Informant

S.N.	*Name of the head of the family*	*Present*		*Past*		*Present*		*Past*		*Remarks*
		Type of land	*Amt of land*	*Type of land*	*Amt of land in acres*	*Live stock*	*Nos.*	*Live stock*	*Nos.*	

Anthropological Survey of India
Eastern Regional Centre,
Kolkata

Information of Land and Perception

Schedule – C

Name of the Informant

Sl. No.	*Name of the head*	*Details of Sold out Land*							*Remarks*
		Type	*Area in acres*	*To whom*	*Sold out rate*	*Actual market price of that time*	*Present price of the land*	*Perception about urbanisation*	

Anthropological Survey of India
Eastern Regional Centre,
Kolkata

Information About New Habitants

Schedule – D

Community and Clan
Name of the Informant

Mother Tongue
Other language known
Religion

S.N	*Name of the head and members*	*Relationship*	*Age*	*Sex*	*Marital Status*	*Education*	*Occupation*		*Where from come*	*Type of residence*			*Cost*	*Remarks (mode of obtain) and perception*
							Pre	Past		Co-op	Indivi-H	Flat		

Anthropological Survey of India
Eastern Regional Centre
Kolkata

Schedule – E

Information at Official Level

1. Information about the area, history, background.
2. Total area acquired for the respective urban place like New Town, Gopalpur etc.
3. The names of the local community.
4. Distribution of area of land such as individuals, private companies, government offices and others.
5. Cost of the lands at respective levels individuals, private companies, others etc.
6. Initial price of land at the time of acquisition.
7. General land use figure. No. of *bheris*/ponds/water bodies and areas.
8. Future urban plans including type of urban land-use.

Psychological Tools

For the psychological study the subjects were selected purposively (the land losers were taken into consideration) and on availability. They were called individually and were made to reply the queries of the schedule. However, the queries were not merely confined to the schedule, rather, as a matter of fact prior to going through the schedule; a comprehensive interrogation was undertaken for thorough understanding of their family background and subsequently evaluating their eligibility to become an ideal subject. The subjects seemed to be very curious, encouraging and co-operative throughout the interaction.

For descriptive information about the socio-cultural background an interview was arranged, whereas questionnaire and schedule were used for quantitative measure of the attitude and mental state of affected people. The study variables included: (1) Demographic data/ Household Information, (2) Attitude and Mental State. The questions were designed to gather information about the attitude and mental state. The demographic questions included information on gender, educational qualification, age, caste, family structure etc. To assess the attitude and mental state relevant schedules were prepared.

(A) General Introductory Schedule: To get the respondent's personal bio-data like name, age, gender, education, marital status, religion, occupation, monthly income, type of family, number of family members, health related information etc., a general introductory schedule was prepared.

(B) Attitude and Mental State: The Attitude and Mental State mainly measured the attitude towards urbanisation and mental state of the affected people after land acquisition. The schedule included a total of 30 questions. Out of these 30 questions, some of the questions are open where the informant was allowed to answer in a descriptive manner.

Scoring

A short description of the psychological tests used in the present study for the collection of data and coding is presented below.

Description of Psychological Tools

Name of Tools Range of	*Variables*	*No. of Items*	*Scores*
(A) General Introductory Schedule	Name, Age, Gender, Education, Occupation, Monthly Income, Marital Status, Caste, Religion, Place of Origin, Birth Place, Mother Tongue, Type of Family, Total No. of Family Members, Address, Health related information etc.	16	
(B) Attitude and Mental State	A	07	7-14
	B	03	3-9
	C	10	10-30
	D	10	10-30
	Answer	**Score**	
	Often	1	
	Sometimes	2	
	Never	3	
	Yes	2	
	No	1	

* Some questions are descriptive in nature so that those of questions will be analysed in a different manner. Under section 'D', some statements are positive, so that the scoring would be done in vice-versa.

For most of the question Likert type of scoring was adopted to get proper response from the sample and in certain cases descriptive response was collected considering the nature of question. Maximum score was given for positive answer and minimum for negative answer in descending order.

Appendix – 3

Table 4.1: Land-use Break-up

	User Under	*Are in hectares*	*Percentage of Total Project Are*	*Percentage of Project Area Less Area under Item (vi) of Col. 1*
(i)	Residential including internal access roads, local open and community facilities	1555	50.5	70.2
(ii)	Industries	200	6.5	9.0
(iii)	New Business District and other commercial areas	140	4.6	6.3
(iv)	Regional, Cultural, Educational and Health facilities	20	0.7	0.9
(v)	Major Arterial road, Arterial road, Sub-Arterial road, LRT and Transport Terminals	300	9.7	13.6*
(vi)	Large Open spaces, Green areas, Water bodies, etc.	860	28.0	—

* Inclusive of internal and local roads, this figure will increase.

Appendix 4 (Genealogies)

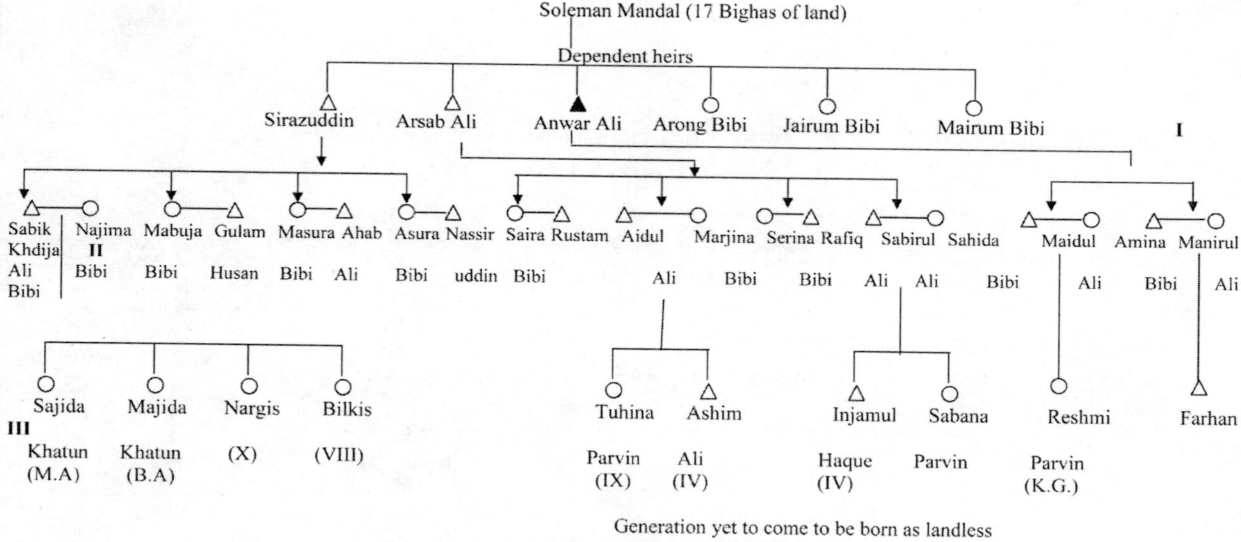

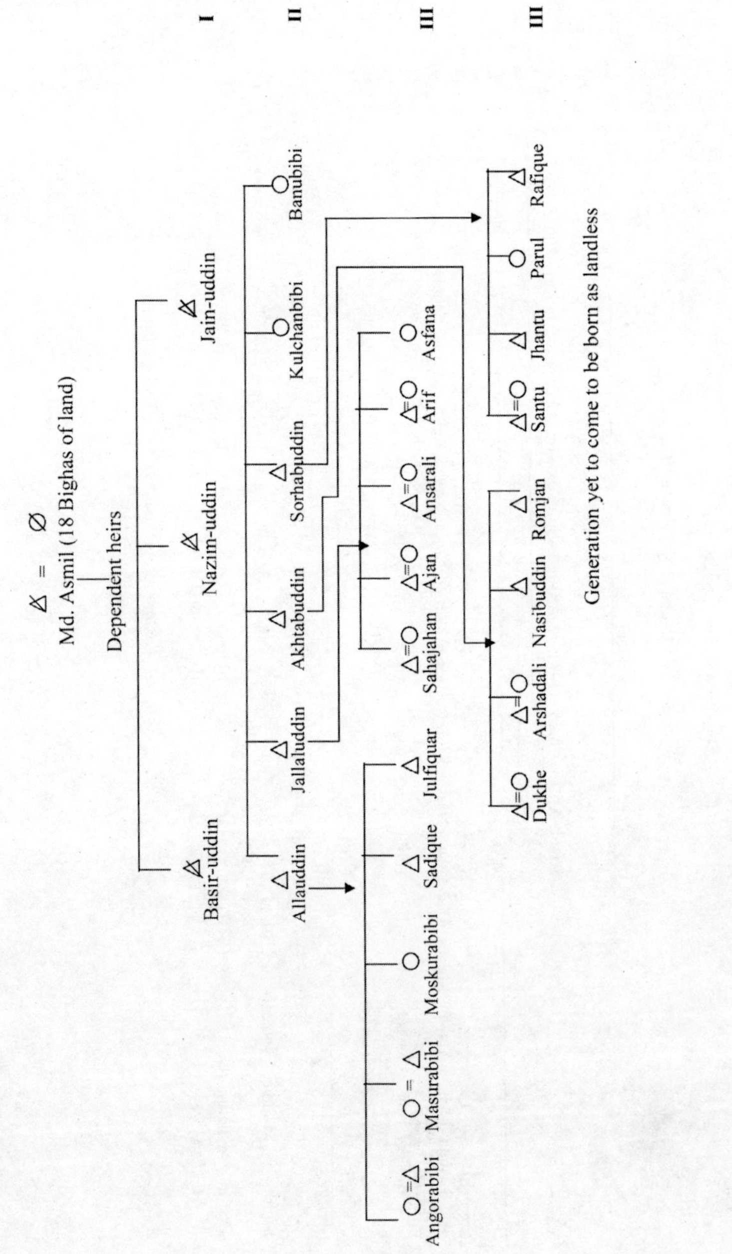
Md. Asmil (18 Bighas of land)
Dependent heirs
I
II
III
III
Basir-uddin
Nazim-uddin
Jain-uddin
Allauddin
Jallaluddin
Akhtabuddin
Sorhabuddin
Kulchanbibi
Banubibi
Angorabibi
Masurabibi
Moskurabibi
Sadique
Julfiquar
Sahajahan
Ajan
Ansarali
Arif
Asfana
Dukhe
Arshadali
Nasibuddin
Romjan
Santu
Jhantu
Parul
Rafique
Generation yet to come to be born as landless

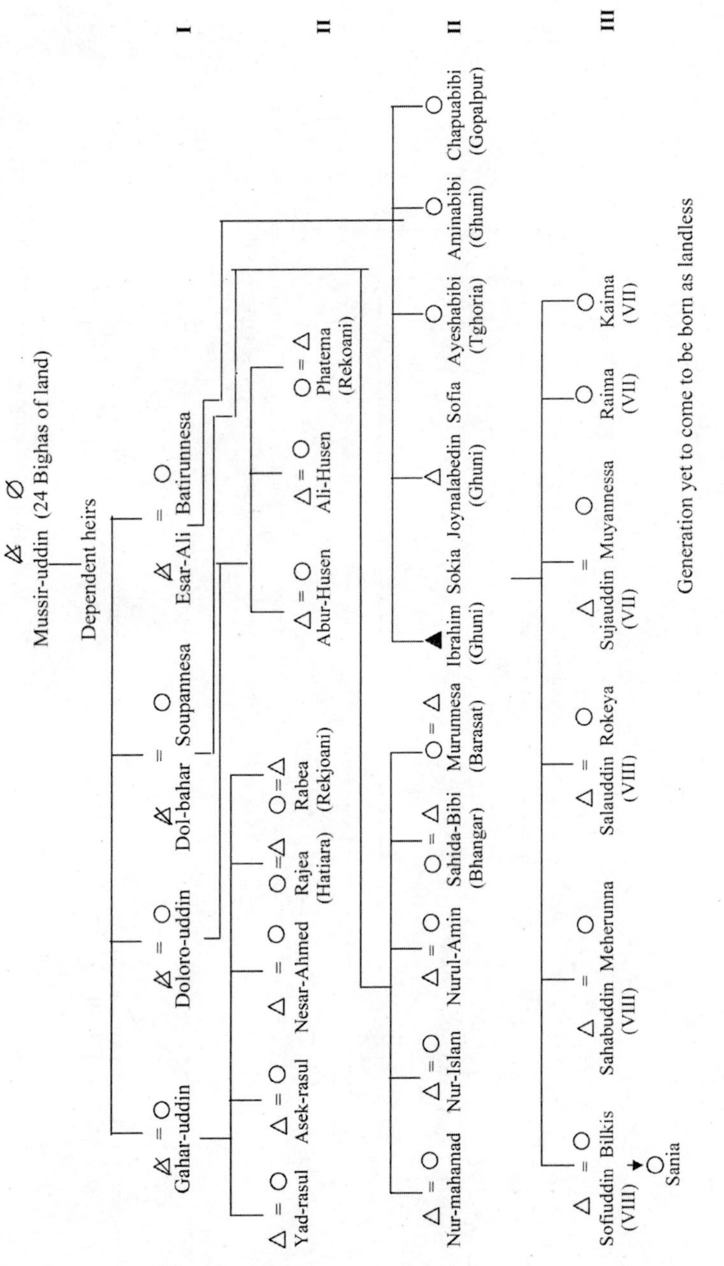
Mussir-uddin (24 Bighas of land)
Dependent heirs
I
Gahar-uddin
Doloro-uddin
Dol-bahar
Soupannesa
Esar-Ali
Batirunnesa
II
Yad-rasul
Asek-rasul
Nesar-Ahmed
Rajea (Hatiara)
Rabea (Rekjoani)
Abur-Husen
Ali-Husen
Phatema (Rekoani)
II
Nur-mahamad
Nur-Islam
Nurul-Amin
Sahida-Bibi (Bhangar)
Murunnesa (Barasat)
Ibrahim (Ghuni)
Sokia
Joynalabedin (Ghuni)
Sofia
Ayeshabibi (Tghoria)
Aminabibi (Ghuni)
Chapuabibi (Gopalpur)
III
Sofiuddin (VIII)
Bilkis
Sania
Sahabuddin (VIII)
Meherunna
Salauddin (VIII)
Rokeya
Sujauddin (VII)
Muyannessa
Raima (VII)
Kaima (VII)
Generation yet to come to be born as landless

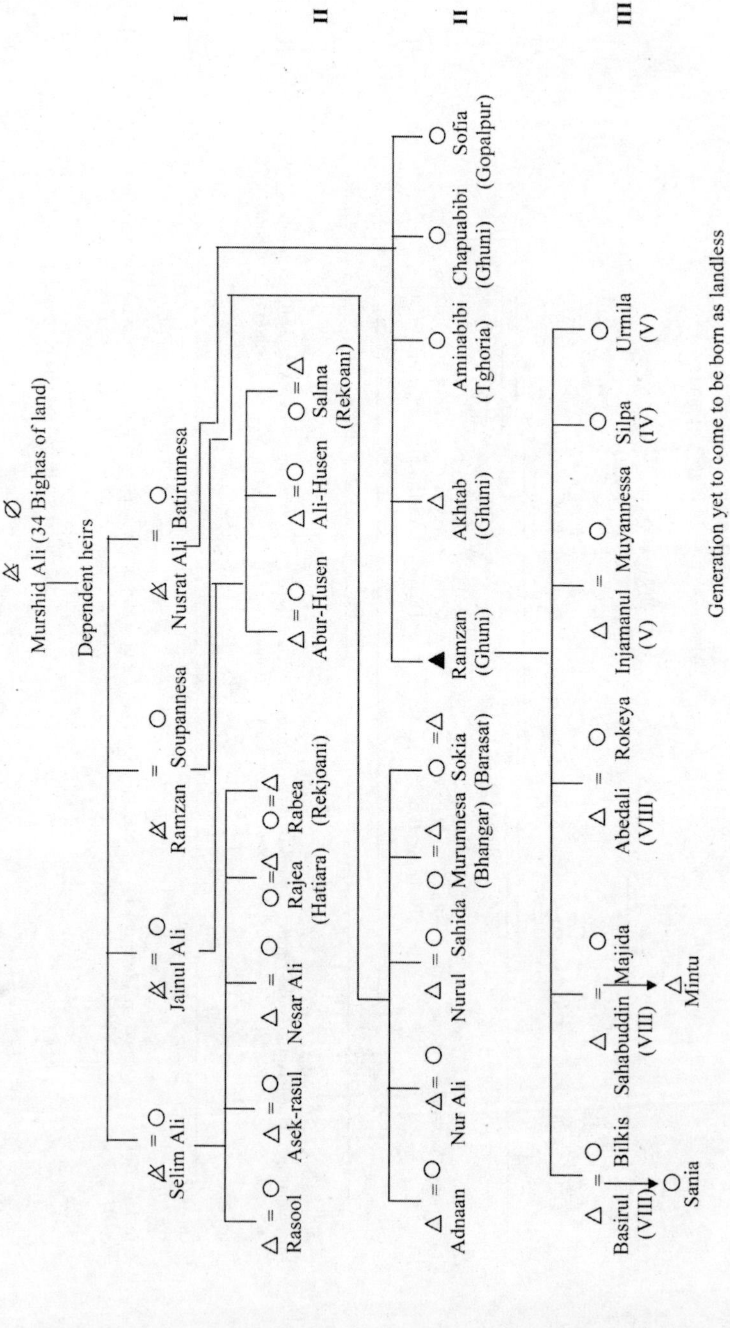
Murshid Ali (34 Bighas of land)
Dependent heirs
I
Selim Ali
Jainul Ali
Ramzan
Soupannesa
Nusrat Ali
Batirunnesa
II
Rasool
Asek-rasul
Nesar Ali
Rajea
(Hatiara)
Rabea
(Rekjoani)
Abur-Husen
Ali-Husen
Salma
(Rekoani)
II
Adnaan
Nur Ali
Nurul
Sahida
Murunnesa
(Bhangar)
Sokia
(Barasat)
Ramzan
(Ghuni)
Akhtab
(Ghuni)
Aminabibi
(Tghoria)
Chapuabibi
(Ghuni)
Sofia
(Gopalpur)
III
Basirul
(VIII)
Bilkis
Sahabuddin
(VIII)
Majida
Abedali
(VIII)
Rokeya
Injamanul
(V)
Muyannessa
Silpa
(IV)
Urmila
(V)
Sania
Mintu
Generation yet to come to be born as landless

Appendix – 5

IN THE ... CALCUTTA

CONSTITUTIONAL WRIT JURISDICTION
ORDINARY ORIGINAL CIVIL JURISDICTION
CIVIL APPELLATE JURISDICTION

c–1
Friday

ORIGINAL/ APPELLATE SIDE

Nilotpal Dutt & ors

VERSUS

The State of West Bengal

ON behalf of:

MR. Sakya Sen

Advocate/ Advocate

You with:
With you:
J. Kar,
Adv.

PURNA CH. PAUL CHOWDHURY
ADVOCATE
C/O. B.N. BASU & CO.
1, OLD POST OFFICE STREET (1st Floor)
CALCUTTA - 700001

Telephone: [illegible]

Contd…

STRICT : NORTH 24-PARGANAS

IN THE HIGH COURT AT CALCUTTA

CONSTITUTIONAL WRIT JURISDICTION

APPELLATE SIDE

Writ Petition No. 8159 (W) of 2004

IN THE MATTER OF :

An application Under Article 226

of the Constitution of India;

And

In the matter of :

A writ in the nature of Mandamus and/or

a Writ in the nature of Certiorari

and/or any other appropriate writ or

writs , order or orders, direction

or directions;

And

In the matter of :

Town & Country (Planning & Development)

Act 1979 and Rules framed thereunder.

And

In the matter of :

The New Township Project at Rajarhat,

District North 24-Parganas.

...2

And

In the matter of :
False declaration by the concerned authority about the nature & character of the land required for the project at Rajarhat area .

And

In the matter of :
Destruction of greeneries, wetlands of the Vast area required for the Rajarhat Township Project .

And

In the matter of :
Changing thecharacter of the land from agriculture and pisciculture to the Township without caring for maintaining ecological balance in the concerned areas .

And

In the matter of :
Spoiling and/or damaging the natural drainage and sewage system in the upper as well as in the lower Bagjola Basin .

...3

And

In the matter of :

Deliberate failure on the part of the concerned Respondents to evolve and/or plan an ecologically sustainable development of the area covered by the New Township Project, resulting in mass displacement of local populations without any rehabilitation scheme;

And

In the matter of :

1. NILOTPAL DUTTA
S/O Late Nirmal Krishna Dutta
of Debanjali Aptt. P.O Hatiyara
Ramkrishna Pally,
Kolkata- 700059. P.S. Rajarhat,
24-Parganas(N) .

2. MD. ABDULLAH GAZI
s/o Md. Alauddin Gazi
Vill- Baligori, P.O. Chakpachuria
Rajarhat 24-Parganas (N) .

3. PROSENJIT CHATTERJEE
S/O Pulak Chatterjee
Vill + P.O Patharghata, Rajarhat.
24-Parganas (North).

.... Petitioners

- Versus-

1. The State of West Bengal,
Notice through the Secretary,
Department of Housing,
Govt. of West Bengal,
Writers' Buildings, Kolkata-700001.

2. The Secretary,
Department of Housing & Development,
Government of West Bengal,
New Secretariat Building,
Calcutta.

3. The Secretary, Department of Town & Country Planning, Govt. of West Bengal'
xxxxxxxxx Writers' Building, Calcutta.

4. The Secretary,
Ministry, of Agriculture
Writers' Buildings, Kolkata-700001..

5. Secretary,
Ministry of Fishery Writers'
Buildings, Kolkata-

6. The Secretary, Ministry of
Irrigation, Writers' Buildings,
Kolkata- 700001.

7. The Collectorate, North 24-Parganas,
Barasat, 24-Parganas(North).

...5

8. Block Development Officer,
Rajarhat, 24-Parganas (North).

9. Agricultural Development Officer,
Rajarhat, 24-Parganas (North).

10. Deputy Director of Fisheries
Barasat, Meen Bhawan, Barasat,
24-Parganas.

11. West Bengal Housing Infrastructure
Development Corporation,
Salt Lake Stadium, Sector-III,
Bidhan Nagar, Kolkata- 91.

....Respondents.

To

The Hon'ble Mr. Ashok Kumar Mathur, Chief Justice And
His Companion Justices of the said Hon'ble Court.

The humble petition of the
petitioners abovenamed.

Most Respectfully Sheweth :

1. Your petitioners are the residents of the area which is covered under the New Town Project of the Government of West Bengal at Rajarhat.

....6

6.

2. That the Government of West Bengal has taken up a Scheme to set up a township called New Town - New Calcutta at Rajarhat. The foundation stone of the project was laid down by the Chief Minister, Govt. of West Bengal on 1st June, 1995. The photocopy of the brochure published on the occasion of foundation stone laying is enclosed and marked as Annexure 'P-1'.

3. It appears from the Brochure published by the Government of West Bengal in connection with the aforesaid project that initially a total of 2750 hectares comprising of 21 Mouzas was intended to be covered under the said Project. Subsequently from the application for obtaining consent from West Bengal Pollution Control Board filed by the Government authorities, four more mouzas were sought to be included covering an additional area of hectares aggregating to 3075 hectares.

4. Your petitioners states that the total area of 3750 hectares sought to be included in the said project comprises of high yield agricultural land and fisheries, on which a total number of 1,31,000 persons are dependent for their sustenance. According to a survey conducted by the Government, there are around 6179 marginal farmers 2105 small farmers 4605 landless labourers and more than 4000 people engaged in pisciculture.

..7

5. Your petitioners state that the annual yearly agricultural produce from the said land are as follows :-

	Items	Quantity
a)	Paddy	110000 mands
b)	Wheat	1000 "
c)	Oil Seeds	50000 "
d)	Vegetables	Huge quantity, cannot exactly be estimated
e)	Fruits	-do-
f)	Horticulture	-do-

6. Your petitioners state that in the past, the Government of West Bengal for facilitating agriculture in the said area had initiated and developed various types of irrigation facilities namely -

a) Minor Irrigations

I) Through deep tubewells installed by the Govt. of West Bengal.

II) Through shallow tubewells installed by Govt. of West Bengal.

III) Through huge number of shallow tubewells as well as shallow machines (203 nos) being run by Private individuals. A total of 868 bighas is tilled by shallow machine water.

....8

b) R.L.I(River Lifting Irrigation)

Through this process, water is lifted for irrigation from Kestopur Bhangar Kata Khal and from Bagjola Canal by the Govt. of West Bengal as well as by Private individuoals. There are about 58 nos. of RLI spout.

c) Irrigation by lifting water from innumerable water bodies, ponds, doba etc.

d) Irrigation through spout system at vast area. Details of Different modes applied for lifting water for irrigation purpose at Patharghata Mouza is shown in a schedule and marked as

P2 annexure 'P2'. The receipts granted by the office of B D O Rajarhat showing the purchase of water from the authority by different farmers are annexed hereto and marked with the letter

P3 'P3'. The said water is vastly issued for agriculture purpose.

7. Your petitioners state that the said area of the proposed township comprises of substantially agricultural land producing various crops of different types and providing sustenance to the population of about 1,50,000 approx residing in the said area. Your petitioners crave

..9

leave to refer to and rely upon some photographs showing cultivation in the said area at thetime of hearing, if necessary. Details of description of various modes of land in Patharghata Mouza and Baligori Mouza is shown in a schedule is annexed hereto and marked with theletter 'P-4'.

8. Your petitioners state that apart from large tracts ofagricultural land, there are large number of huge water bodies in the said area andmany of such water bodies are surrounded by coconut, betel nut and banana trees. Such water bodies are mostly fisheries. Your petitioners crave leave to refer to and rely upon some photographs of water bodies produced at the time of hearing, if necessary. In this connection a copy of a letter dt. 26.8.1999 addressed by Asstt. Director of Fisheries Barasat to Deputy Director of Fisheries, Microbiology & Parasitology, captain Bheri, Calcutta- 39 is annexed hereto and marked with the

P-4(i) letter P-4(i). From the said letter it transpires that the involved persons save their families from starvation by sailing commercial aquatic specius andby direct consumption from the beels. The said area is very rich for both fishery and agriculture.

9. The saidfact thatthe area proposed to be converted into a Township is a wet land and low land/area is also corroborated by draft project report published by the

...10

Government of West Bengal in September, 1995 wherein under Annexure 1 thereof, it has been stated under the caption " Land Filing " that 2095 HA out of 2750 HA of land need to be filledup at an average depth of 1.5 mt. and an amount of Rs. 241.4 crores has been earmarked as land filling cost for the project. Moreover, the said area which produces 1.1 million maunds of paddy in an approximate area of thirty thousand bighas is no doubt a huge wet land situated at the north-east verge of the city. There are also various large and deep water bodies in the said area.

10. ThePrimary source of sustainance of the population of the said area is the income earned from cultivation of the saidland. The saidlands in question are high yield commercial land producing 8.40 quintal of paddy on an approximate per bigha. Apart from paddy various forms of cultivation of other crops are carried on namely, sugar-cane, jute, wheat, oil , seeds, fruits and all kinds of vegetable. A schedule showing the details of agricultural yield from one particular mouza is annexedhereto and marked with theletter 'P-5'. P-5

11. That it is a matter of fact that Rajarhat area is not simply a low-laying area of wetland, vast area of this place, mainly Dhupir Bill and Ghuni-Jatragachi-Bagjola

...11

Basin act as a natural sewage for a large area which are heavily urbanized and densely populated namely localities like Dutta Bagan, Lake Town, Baguiati, Bangur Colooi, Baranagar, Panihati, Biruti, Kamarhati, North Dum Dum and South Dum Dum. In this connection a service map drawn by Calcutta Metropolitan, Water Sanitary Authority (CMWSA) is relevant, which shows the Dhupir Bill and Bagjola- Ghuni-Jatragachi Basin. A careful perusal of the said map will show that thexxxxxxxxx attitude of Dhupir Bill areas ranges from 2 feet to 6 feet from theses level. The names of the said area reveals that the same is an importent and large area of land, which acts as natural sewerage for the stom water and a part of the said bill remains under deep water even during theperiod of summer. The photocopy of the map printed by CMWSA is enclosed andmarked as

P-6 annexure 'P-6'.

12. Your petitioners have taken some photographs of the Dhupir-Bill area, which clearly indicate the exact characteristic of the rea . Some of the photographs are enclosed

P-7 and collectively marked as annexure 'P-7'.

13. As per the draft project report on New Town at Raharhat published by the Govt. of West Bengal in September 1995 Vide page 29, Paragraph 6.1.2 it has been admitted by the Govt. That " In recent years, the inhabited areas of Upper

..12

Bagjola Basin have experienced severe drainage congestion.. There have also been problems of drainage congestion in Lower Basin. There is a need to under-take major improvement measures for reducing the intensity of drainage congestion in these areas. * The problem will be further aggravated if the recent trend of unplanned growth in the present Project Area is allowed to continue, if even theplanned growth is allowed to continue. The programme for improving the drainage congestion in the Upper & Lower Basins of the Bagjola Canal required substantial investment, which may be difficult to provide through normal buggetary support of the State Govt. It may, however, be possible to make this investment as a part of the New Town Project. The cost of improvements necessary beyond the Project Area up to Kulti Gong may also be borne, at least partly, by the Project as & when such works are implemented *.

14. That thepresent position and function of Bagjola Basin, both upper and lower level, appear to be inadequate nd inapt to cater the large thickly populated urban area of the state . In the said draft project report vide page 59, Annexure '1' under the caption Major Infrastructure. II a, it has been stated that 40% of the total cost, amounting to Rs. 82.5 crores will be borne by the New Town Project. It is realy a matter of technical survey and review that by

...13

not having any Budgetary support and by spending a meager sum of Rs. 82,5 crores, whether the existing drainage congestion of upper and lower Bagjola Basin can at all be mitigated. On theother hand the question now arises that with the increasing load of sewage afor 5 lacks of permanent residents and 2.5 lakhs of floating people in the township, the entire drainage systems may collapse.

15. That if the Dhupir Bill and Bagjola-Ghuni-Jatragachi basin are allowed to face the natural death due to the construction of the township, there is a possibility that the storm-drain water from the airport of Kolkata, which stands at a distance of only 5 K.M may loose its naturel flow and thus may cause inundation of large new areas also.

16. Your petitioners were never aware of the said project initiated by the Government of West Bengal, Initially the respondents initiated irrigation measure for the development of agriculture in the said area for the benefit of the residents and farmers of the area. The respondents sought to sell the said project by luring the residents of the said Area to believe thatthe said area would be developed by introduction of electricity as well as by establishment of schools, college, factory, industries etc. But it was never disclosed to inhabitants of the area that actually and in fact by the said Project, the land belonging to the

..14

14.

agriculturalists of the area would be taken away for the ~~xxxxxxxx~~ profitable venture of Government of West Bengal in the garb of a ' Public interest '. Some of the ~~xxxxxxxx~~ cultivators being lured by the said offer of the Government surrendered their land for a paltry sum of Rs. 6,000/- per cottah. It now appears that those lands are being ~~gold~~ sold by the Government of West Bengal to private promoters for construction of housing project for promoting business thereon at an exorbitant amount of Rs. 1,61,000/- per cottah. In fact some of the cultivators have already surrendered the land belonging to them. The Government has taken substantial steps in and of their project and has earned huge profit in those areas and a huge Township is being constructed at present by private promoters namely — Sahara India, Srachi, Bengal Peerless Housing Development Co. Ltd, IFB etc.

17. Your petitioners state that so called project of the Government in the name of Public purpose if understood in its correct perspective would reveal that there is actually in fact no ' Public element ' involved in the project. The said project has actually and, in effect, purported to displace the cultivators from possession of their agricultural land resulting in deprivation of their only source of sustainence on the basis of an offer by the Government to purchase their land at Rs. 6,000/- per cottah

....15

The amount of Rs. 6,000/- per cottah was offered to tempt the poor mostly illiterate agriculturists to surrender their land, but the actual purpose of the Government is to deal with the said land and earn huge profit, income from the sale of the said land to private promoters and to portrary to the public that a new Township is being constructed for the benefit of public at large.

18. Your petitioners have approached this Hon'ble Court only for the purpose of determination whether the act of the Government in purporting to take away the agricultural land being the only source of sustenance of approximately 100 % of the population of the area for the purpose of construction of a new Township ultimately resulting in filling up the cofters of the State and enrichment of the Private promoters who have been allotted land in the said so called ' New Township' would actually fall within the ambit of ' Public Purpose ' under the garb of which such acquisition has been resorted to by the Government.

19. The right of the farmers to carry on agriculture in their own land is a part of the rights of life governed by Article 21 of the Constitution of India. The Public element allegedly involved in the measures initiated by the Government Authorities for development of the new Township on the agricultural land belonging to the inhabitants of the said area have to be prima-facie proved. The policy of the

....16

Government of West Bengal is in essence intended to mop-up substantial revenue for the Government of West Bengal by selling the said agricultural lands acquired from the cultivators to put promoters at exsorbitent prices for construction of multi-storied building and housing scheme which cannot by any stretch of imagination be deemed to be ' Public purpose'. Your petitioner states that in view of implementation of the so called ' Public project ', a large number of members of public are being sought to be not only disposed of their landed property but also are deprived of their right to earn their living which is dependent on cultivation of the said land. Hence the so called ' Public Project ' which is bound to result in substantial members of the public being deprived of the right to earn their living cannot be deemed to be a " Public purpose " in the eyes of law. In the instant case in order to determine whether the said project initiated by the Government of West Bengal is actually for ' Public Purpose ' one has to determine the ratio o f the public benefited against the ratio of the public to whom prejudice is likely to be caused. It is no doubt true that the said project is prejudicial to the interest of the majority of the public as the number of people who are likely to suffer on account of the said project far exceeds the number who may be benefited therefor.

20. Your petitioners are also aware that the said Township is not also intended for providing shelter or home to the homeless.

21. It appear from the project Report of Housing Infrastructure Development Corp (HIDCO) published on May,1999 that there are two paddy crops (Boro and Aman) are grown through double cropping practice in the said area. Such report is also silent about other crops (vegetables , & Oil seeds) grown on various seasons.

22. An earlier petition was moved before the Hon'ble Court when an order was passed on 16th February,2001 where the Division Bench was pleased to direct the Environment Department to apply their mind in respect of any further proposals if any mooted by the project authority not on the basis of permission granted in respect of 622 HA of land. A copy of the said order dated 16/2/2001 is annexed hereto and marked

P-8 with the letter 'P-8'. Government has not yet considered the same.

23. That being highly aggrieved thereby, the petitioner begs to move Your Lordships on the following amongst others:-

GROUNDS:

I. For that the purported project adopted by the concerned authorities without obtaining any opinion of experts on environmental and ecological aspects.

II. For that the proposed project of new township has been adopted in gross violation of the guidelines formulated by the Government of India under the name and style guidelines for the Environmental assessment of new township.

III. For that it is incumbent upon the concerned respondants to take recourse to the said guidelines before adopting the said project.

IV. For that in the connected brouchure published by the Government of West Bengal has shown the ~~guidelinesxbefore~~ proposed area of the project land as vacant land, deliberately and willfully suppressing the fact that the project area covers as may as forty villages having the total population to the extent of 1.50 lacs approximately.

V. For that a large portion of the land proposed for the construction of the new township being agricultural land yielding paddy, wheat and other agricultural products, it wouldbe total devastation of the agriculture in the event the project is being implemented.

VI. For that in as much as it is the adopted policy not to destroy or change the nature and character of the agricultural land, the autrorities concerne ought not to have taken the said project.

...19

19.

VII. For that the authorities concerned deliberately and wilfully made awrong declaration claiming non-existence of any fishery and permanent water body in the project area.

VIII. For that the Natural water Catchment area (the Dhupir Bill) and the natural drainage system in the area and also in the upper Bagjola Basins areas may get disturbed and or be destroyed if the project is allowed to take off without any technical review in the matter.

IX. For that the authorities concerned while choosing the proposed area for the said new township did not take into account the fate of around 6170 marginal farmers, 7105 small farmers, 4605 landless artisans, including the fate of more than x 400 people engaged in pisciculture.

X. For that in order to facilitate the people of a particular community and limited in number, a large section of the people is going to be uprooted.

XI) For that the respondents concerned did not take into account the foreseeable environment crisis bound to hover in the entire surround

20.

by virtue of the proposed project for new township effecting a large number of prople.

XII. For that so called project of the Government in the name of public purpose if understood in its correct perspective would reveal that there is actually in fact no ' Public element' involved in the project.

XIII. For that the said project has actually and, in effect, purported to displace the cultivators from possession of their agricultural and resulting in deprivation of their only source of sustainance on the basis of an offer by the Government to purchase their land at Rs. 6,000/- per cottah.

XIV. For that the act of the Government in purporting to take away the agricultural land being the only source of sustenance of approximately 100% of the population of the area for the purpose of construction of a new Township ultimately resulting in filling up the cofters of the State and enrichment of the private promoters who have been alloted land in the said so called " New Township" would actually fall within the ambit of ' Public purpose ' under the garb of which such acquisition has been resorted to by the Government.

...21

21.

XV. For that the said Township is not also intended for providing shelter or home to the homeless.

XVI. For that in view of the matter the so called project amounts to taking away and/or shortening life span of the people at large of the location and its surroundings due to the resultant enviornment and cological disorders.

XVII. For that the respondents concerned did not weigh the balance between the development and the destruction to adopt the so called project for construction of new township.

24. That the matter is extremely urgent and involves the fate and life of few lacs of people both with regard to their lives and livelihood and at any moment the said people would be thrown out from the respective place of residence and structural infrastructure would be set up.

25. That it appears that the foundation stone of the said project has already been laid and the respondent concerned did not even take any measure or scheme to rehabilitate such huge number of citizen at large having

..22

-6-

their home and hearth within the area proposed for new township which is nothing but a curse in disguise to them and under such circumstances no further demand of justice would yield result whatsoever.

26. Your petitioners further state that your petitioners are apprehending that the Government may take coersive forceable measure to recover the said land and therefore, it is necessary expedient and in the interest of justice the Hon'ble Court be pleased to intervene in the said matter to prevent the infructuous of the rights of the people of the area ~~petitioners~~ under Article 21 against forceable dispossession in the garb of so called public project initiated by the Government of West Bengal.

27. That there is no other speedy, efficacious, alternative legal remedy open to your petitioners and the relief as prayed if granted, would be complete.

28. That your petitioners are not persons from legal discipline and if there is an unintentional and procedural mistakes or wrong approaches in the petition, the same may kindly be overlooked and your petitioner may please be excused for the same.

29. That the relevant records are located outside the ~~xxxxxx~~ ordinary original civil jurisdiction of this Hon'ble Court.

50. That this application is made on good faith and to secure ends of justice.

In the circumstances it is prayed that Your Lordships may be graciously pleased to issue :-

a) A writ of and/or in the nature of Mandamus commanding the respondents, their agents, men, subordinates, superior, successor in office to forbear from giving any effect or further effect to the proposed scheme and/or project of setting up New Township-New Calcutta at Rajarhat in any manner whatsoever and to recall, rescind, withdraw and cancel the same.

b) A writ of and/or in the nature of Certiorari directing the respondant their agent, men, subordinate, superio successor in office to certify and transmit all the relevant records concerning the proposed scheme and/or project for setting up New Town-ship- New Calcutta at Rajarhat and doing conscionable justice by quashing the said project and/or scheme,

24

c) A writ of and in the nature of prohibitions forbidding the respondents, their agents, men, subordinates, superior successor in office from taking any step, actions measure towards implementations of the said scheme and/or project for setting up New Township-New Calcutta Rajarhat in any manner whatsoever.

d) A Rule Nisi in terms aforesaid and make the same absolute.

e) Any other or further, writ or writs, order or orders, direction or directions.

f) Cost and incidental thereto.

g) An interim order restraining the respondents their agents, men, subordinate, superior, successor in office from taking any step action, measure towards implementation of the scheme and/or project for setting up New Township-New Calcutta at Rajarhat in any manner whatsoever.

h) Such other order/orders as this Hon'ble Court may deem fit.

And your petitioners, as in duty bound shall ever pray.

Nilotpal Datta
Md. Abdullah Gazi
Prosenjit Chatterjee

Appendix – 6

Government of West Bengal
Office of the Assistant Director of Fisheries
North 24 Parganas
Meen Bhavan
Barasat

Memo No. 774 **Dated: 26-08-99**

To
The Deputy Director of Fisheries.
Microbiology & Parasitology.
Captain Bheri, Calcutta – 39

Sub:- Identification of endangered & rare species of aquatic lives and its areas of Rajarhat Block for publication of a block directory as a part of our on going project.

Ref:- Memo No 122/sch-3 dt 17th August'99 of the D D F (M&P)

Sir,

In reference to the above, a preliminary report are submitting on the basis of the first information.

The Rajarhat block is small in area but one of the potential block under North 24 Parganas in respect of water bodies, water resources, aquatic flora & fauna as well as aquaculture. The vast wetlands adon with thousands of Doba, Tank/Pond, Nayanjali, Jheel, Beel, Bilan, Canal, Bypass canal dead river beds, swamp, low lying area. In respect of water resources, there are saline, fresh and even wastewater available in Rajarhat block.

Apart from this, a vast low-lying thousands of hector areas from Dum-Dum Airport to Salt lake area were recorded as Dhupir beel and locality known as Ghuni Beel, Jatragachi beel and so on in different names in diverse locations.

This Dhupir beel were divided by Bagjola canal, which plays an important role in drainage system of the northern part of Calcutta Metropolitan areas carrying highly concentration wastewater. There are at least three nos of Bagjala bypass canal around Dhupir beel to let out the waters from this Dhupir beel in concept, for conversion of wetland to agricultural land. Throughout this process a part of Dhupir beel has been converted to agricultural land for double crops, some area has been converted as single crop and rest are still in natural condition.

Contd...

Most of the beel area has been distributed to the local farmers for agriculture and aquaculture purpose.

At present the average depth of water varies from two feet to six feet. The colour of the waters also varies from transparent, grayish, grayish-green, greenish in different zones. The beel water enrich in feeds and medicines of humankind and as well as of animal kingdoms. Simultaneously the beel is the dwelling of many aquatic flora & fauna in which many types of Phytoplanktons, Zooplanktons, Benthes, along with common endangered & rare species are available. Many types of aquatic vegetation including commercial & medicinal species were found as marginal, merged, sub merged, floating in nature. Various types of aquatic animals like snakes, frogs, creataseaus, fishes, etc. with a very long "feed chain" have also been found. A list of the same identified species are enclosed for ready reference.

Thousands of fisherman and fish farmers are praising aquaculture regularly, around and within the Dhapir beel following traditionally, extensively and improved extensive method. A few area of the beel is covered under FFDA and other departmental schemes. The involved persons save their families from starvation by soiling commercial aquatic species and by direct consumption from this beel. The wastewater fed aquaculture are also popular in Rajarhat Block.

The identification of resources in respect of areas and aquatic flora & fauna along with physico-chemical parameters are still going on.

Extensive work in this regard is needed with seasonal variations. The detail report of the Rajarhat Block will be submitted just after every phase of identification.

Yours faithfully,

26/8/99

Assistant Director of Fisheries,
North 24 Parganas,
Barasat

Appendix – 7

NEW TOWN PLANNING AREA

District North 24 Pargana

Notification No.	Sl. No.	Mouza	J.L. No.	Full/Part of The Mouza Included
1423/HG/NTP/ 1M-1/98 Dt. 27.08.99	1.	Raigachhi	12	Full
	2.	Recjuani	13	Full
	3.	Tarulia	21	Full
	4.	Sulangori	22	Full
	5.	Ghuni	23	Full
	6.	Jatragachhi	24	Full
	7.	Kadampukur	25	Full
	8.	Chakpachuria	33	Full
	9.	Baligori	34	Full
	10.	Chhapna	35	Full
	11.	Patharghata	36	Full
	12.	Akandakeshari	55	Full
737-HI/HG/NTP 1M-1/98 Dt. 26.07.01 in partial modification to Notification No. 1423/HG/NTP/ 1M-1/98 Dt. 27.08.99	13.	Mahisgot	20	Portion to the North of Krishnapur Khal
	14.	Thakdari	19	Portion to the North of Krishnapur Khal
	15.	Noapara	11	Plot Nos. 3,6-48,50,52-54,57-153, 270-277,281,320,321,327
	16.	Hatiara	14	Plot Nos. 379-398,402-405,437-440, 452-454,456-458,466-469,472-524,528,2001-3043,4556-4558
	17.	Chandiberia	15	Plot Nos. 263,384,407-417,435-443
737-HI/HG/NTP /1M-1/98 Dt. 26.07.01	18.	Mahisbathan	18	Portion to the North of Krishnapur Khal
	19.	Gopalpur	2	Portion to the South of Baguiati – Rajarhat Road
650-111/1M-1/98 Dt. 22.11.06.	20.	Jagadishpur	27	Full
	21.	Dharsa Moktarpur	26	Full
	22.	Mahammadpur	32	Full
	23.	Mandal Ganti	6	Full

NB. : Mouza - Jyangra, J.L.No. 16 in full was included in the NewTown Planning Area vide Notification No. 1423/HG/NTP/1M-1/98, Dt. 27.08.99 . But subsequently was excluded in full from the Planning Area vide Notification No. 737-H1/HG/NTP/1M-1/98, Dt. 26.07.01 .

Appendix – 8

প্রজ্ঞাপন

উত্তর ২৪ পরগণা নং ২৭৮৭ এল এ (২)/৪-এইচ-১১/৯৮ হাউজিং

তারিখ ২৮/৯/৯৮

যেহেতু রাজ্যপালের এরূপ প্রতীতি হইয়াছে যে নিম্নের তফসিলে বিবৃত রাজারহাট পুরসভার অন্তর্গত জমি জনস্বার্থে, যথা স্যাটেলাইট টাউনশিপ প্রকল্প নির্মাণের জন্য প্রয়োজন হইতে পারে।

এই প্রজ্ঞাপন সংশ্লিষ্ট সকলের প্রতি প্রদত্ত হইল যে, ১৮৯৪ এর ১ আইনের ৪ ধারার বিধান অনুযায়ী অর্পিত ক্ষমতা প্রয়োগক্রমে রাজ্যপাল উদ্যোগটিতে হাউসিং ডাইরেক্টরেট ও কালেক্টার উত্তর ২৪-পরগণার সকল আধিকারিকগণকে তাঁহাদের কর্মচারী ও শ্রমিকগণসহ জমিতে প্রবেশ, জরিপ এবং ঐ ধারায় অনুমত অন্য সকল কার্য করিতে প্রধিকৃত করিতেছেন। নিম্নবর্ণিত পথ নির্দেশিকা অনুযায়ী নিম্ন তফসিলভুক্ত মৌজাগুলিতে উক্ত প্রকল্পের জমি জরিপ সর্ব নিমিত্ত প্রবেশাধিকার থাকিবে।

সীমানা ও তাহার চৌহদ্দি

উত্তর প্রান্তভুক্ত মৌজাগুলি যথা, সালুয়া, গোপালপুর ও রায়গাছি হইতে দক্ষিণ পূর্ব প্রান্তভুক্ত মৌজা যথা বালিগড়ি পর্যন্ত এবং দক্ষিণ প্রান্তভুক্ত মৌজা যথা থাক্‌দাড়ি হইতে পশ্চিম প্রান্তভুক্ত মৌজাগুলি যথা, নওপাড়া, সুলানগুড়ি ও হাতিয়াড়া পর্যন্ত।

তফসিল

ক্রমিং নং	মৌজা	জে.এল.নং	থানা
১	তারুলিয়া	২১	রাজারহাট
২	গোপালপুর	২	,,
৩	সালুয়া	৩	,,
৪	চন্ডিবেড়িয়া	১৫	,,
৫	হাতিয়াড়া	১৪	,,
৬	আটঘরা	১০	,,
৭	কৈখালি	৫	,,
৮	তেঘরিয়া	৯	,,
৯	নপাড়া	১১	,,
১০	দশদ্রোন	৪	,,
১১	রাইগাছি	১২	,,
১২	মহিষগোট	২০	,,
১৩	সুলানগুড়ি	২২	,,

Contd…

১৪	মহিষ বাথান	১৮	,,
১৫	রেকজুয়ানী	১৩	,,
১৬	ঘুনী	২৩	,,
১৭	বালিগড়ী	৩৪	,,
১৮	থাকদাড়ী	১৯	,,
১৯	চক্ পাঁচুরিয়া	৩৩	,,
২০	যাত্রাগাছি	২৪	,,
২১	কদমপুকুরিয়া	২৫	,,
২২	পাথরঘাটা		,,
২৩	ছাপনা		,,
২৪	মহম্মদপুর		,,
২৫	জগদীশপুর		,,

রাজ্যপালের আদেশক্রমে
তপেন্দ্র নাথ খাঁ
উপ-সচিব, পশ্চিমবঙ্গ সরকার
আই সি এ ৩৪২৪(২)/৯৮

Notification

North 24 Parganas no. 2787 LA (2)/4-h-11/98 Housing
Date: 28/9/98

As the Governor has the impression that in the following Taphsil, the land under Rajarhat Municipality may be required for the public interest for the development of satellite Township.

This notice is published for all related people that, with the power vested under Section 4 of Law 1 under the Act of 1894, the Governor is allowing the officers along with their staff and labourers of Housing Directorate and Collector, North 24 Parganas to enter into the land and do the needful according the above law. According to the following directive, they will enjoy right to enter into land of the following Taphsil to measure the land for the said project.

Boundaries and Limit

From the *moujas* of northern limit like Salua, Gopalpur and Raigachhi to the *moujas* of south-eastern limit like Baliyari and the *moujas* on southern end like Thakdari to *moujas* on the western limit like Naopara, Sulanguri and Hatiyara.

Contd...

Taphsil

Sl.No.	*Mouja*	*J.L. No.*	*Thana Rajarhat*
1.	Tarulia	21	"
2.	Gopalpur	2	"
3.	Salua	3	"
4.	Chandiberia	15	"
5.	Hatiyara	14	"
6.	Atghara	10	"
7.	Kaikhali	5	"
8.	Tegharia	9	"
9.	Napara	11	"
10.	Dashadron	4	"
11.	Raigachhi	12	"
12.	Mahisgot	20	"
13.	Sulanguri	22	"
14.	Mahish bathan	18	"
15.	Rekjuyani	13	"
16.	Ghuni	23	"
17.	Baligaree	34	"
18.	Thakdaree	19	"
19.	Chak pachuria	33	"
20.	Jatragachhi	24	"
21.	Kadampukuria	25	"
22.	Patharghata		"
23.	Chhapna		"
24.	Mahammadpur		"
25.	Jagadishpur		"

As per order of The Governor
Tapendra Nath Khan
Dy. Secretary, West Bengal Government
I C A 3424(2)/98.

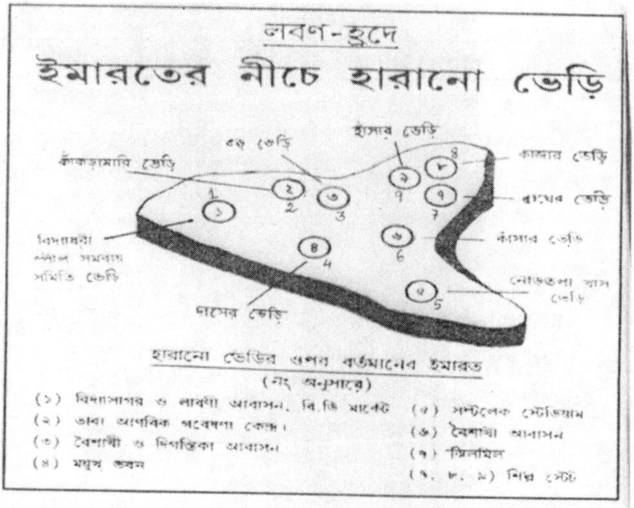

The *bheri* (fish embankments) lost forever under the Township of Salt Lake

1. Vidyasagar and Laboni Housing, B.D. Market (Bidyadhari Spill Samabay Samiti Bheri).
2. Bhaba Atomic Research Centre (Kankamari bheri).
3. Baisakhi and Digantika Housing (Bado bheri).
4. Mayukh Bhawan (Daser bheri).
5. Salt Lake Stadium (Nortala khas bheri).
6. Baisakhi Housing (Kansar bheri).
7. Jhil Mil [now Nicco Park] (Bagher bheri).
8. (Kajar Bheri)
9. (Hansar Bheri)

} Silpa state.

Appendix – 9

TABLE-5.5.2

Landholding Ownership Pattern

Name of Mouzas	Landowner engaged in Cultivation		Landowner not engaged in Cultivation		Total Number of Landowner	
	Upto 3 acre	Above 3 acre	Upto 3 acre	Above 3 acre	Upto 3 acre	Above 3 acre
Mahis Batan	-	-	2,000	-	2,000	-
Thakdari	700	-	-	-	700	-
Mahisgot	389	-	178	3	567	3
Tarulia	367	-	333	-	700	-
Raigachi	120	5	2,840	15	2,960	20
Chalkpachuria	562	8	6	4	568	12
Pathar̥ghata	793	-	7	-	800	-
Baligari	60	-	540	-	600	-
Sulangari	5	-	1,333	-	1,338	-
Kadampukur	465	6	25	4	490	10
Rekjuani	1,670	90	230	10	1,900	100
Naopara	11	1	238	-	249	1
Chandiberia	-	-	2,000	-	2,000	-
Jatragachi	196	8	1,369	-	1,565	8
Ghuni	1,110	8	1,110	18	2,220	26
Total	6,448	126	12,209	54	18,657	180

(c.f.: Ghosh Bose and Associates Pvt Ltd., 2000: Comprehensive Environmental Impact Assessment and Environmental Management Plan Report: 5.5-6).

The table is based on 1991 census data. Based on the said census report Ghosh *et al* observed that the two *maujas,* namely, Mahisbathan and Chandiberia cultivation is almost non-existent. Cultivation is found to be highly pronounced in Thakdari, Mohisgot, Tarulia, Raigachi, Chak Pachuria and Kadampukur *maujas*. It is submitted that small size land-ownership characterises the landholding pattern with barely one per cent of total land owners have more than three acres of land each. It further observed that around half of the land owners are not themselves engaged in cultivation. However, a greater proportion of big land-holders, the absolute number of whom is small, are engaged in cultivation.

What were overlooked by the firm were the engagement of share-croppers in cultivation and the nature of land. Empirical data shows Mahisbathan was under the water bodies including *bheris*, *gheris*, ponds and swamps. Besides cultivation on share-cropping was a regular practice in the pre-project scenario.

Appendix – 10

Persons who got plots at Rajarhat, New Town area through the Minister's Special Quota:

(Courtesy: www.thesundayindian.com/article_print.php?article_id=22076, Who will bell the cat? C.S. Bhattacharjee/New Delhi, September 18, 2011).

Sports Persons

1. Jyotirmoyee Sikdar,
2. Bhaskar Ganguly,
3. Sasthi Duley,
4. Dipankar Dey,
5. Saurav Ganguly.

IPS Officers

6. JC Mohanty (ADG, Administration),
7. MK Singh (IGP, Law and Order),
8. Gyan Dutt Gautam (Commandant 1st Battalion, State Armed Police),
9. Jawed Shamim (Joint Commissioner, HQ),
10. Raj Kanojia (ADG, State Crime Records Bureau),
11. AK Maliwal (ADG & IG, Provisioning),
12. Banibrata Basu (ADG, IB),
13. Siddhartha Gupta (Spl. IG and DIG, Presidency Range),
14. Somen Mitra (ACP II, KP), Kuldeep Singh, (ADG),
15. SK Purakayastha (ADG, Law and Order),
16. Praveen Kumar, Rahul Srivastava (IPS officers on Central Deputation, both),
17. Ajoy Ranade (IPS on compulsory waiting),
18. ZA Hasan (ADG, Western Range),
19. RK Mohanty apart from present Police Commissioner of Kolkata,
20. Ranjit Kumar Pachnanda. Pachnanda has been allotted plot number DF 61 in area AA-1, according to the document,
21. Harmanpreet Singh, the present IG (Headquarters),
22. Ashok Mohan and Gautam Mohan Chakrabarty – are in the list. Currently DG and IGP (Armed Police), Gautam Mohan Chakrabarty is the former police commissioner against whom the TMC had levelled allegations of being involved in the Rajarhat land scam in

December 2010. While Gautam was the police chief of Kolkata, his brother Ashok Mohan was the Chief Secretary of WB. And both of them grabbed two plots at AA-1 area of Rajarhat-New Town.

Bureaucrats

23. Basudeb Banerjee, former Chairman of Tea Board, who is now Secretary, Information Technology and present Deputy Chairperson of Tea Board,
24. Roshni Sen,
25. Anil Verma, who has been handling the administration of the defunct Darjeeling Gorkha Hill Council (DGHC),
26. Talleen Kumar, IAS on Central Deputation,
27. PS Kathiresan (Secretary, Food),
28. KS Rajendran (Secretary, Forest),
29. Alapan Bandopadhyay (Secretary, Municipal Affairs),
30. D Mukherjee (Secretary, Commerce and Industries),
31. Indevar Pandey (Secretary, Personnel and Administrative Reforms),
32. Gyan Dutt Gautam (Secretary, Home),
33. SK Das (Secretary, Public Health Engineering),
34. Dilip Rath (Secretary, Labour),
35. Subrata Gupta (Managing Director, Kolkata Metro Rail Corporation Limited),
36. Khalil Ahmed, (Director, MSSET),
37. Anup Chanda (Secretary, MSSET),
38. Anoop Kr. Agarwal (Secretary, ARD) ,
39. Atanu Purakayastha, Rajiv Sinha, Manoj Pant, Arun Kumar Bal and Arun Mishra, they are host of IAS officers on central deputation.

Politicians

40. Tarit Baran Topdar, former CPM MP,
41. Dines Dakua, ex-minister,
42. Forward Bloc MLAs Haripada Biswas,
43. Bithika Mondal,
44. Sardar Amjad Ali, a TMC candidate defeated in the last assembly election,
45. Manish Gupta, former Chief Secretary of West Bengal who served during Jyoti Basu and Buddhadeb Bhattacharya's reigns– and who defeated Bhattacharya in the last election and presently

holds charges of the Department of Power, Planning and Development,

46. The Animal Husbandry Minister of the present cabinet, Justice Nure Alam Chowdhury,
47. Wife of Manas Bhunia, Minister for Irrigation and Small Scale Industries,
48. Justice Pinaki Chandra Ghosh is still a sitting judge of Calcutta High Court and the said minister has favoured him with a 4.485 cottah plot in HIG category (plot no. AC-90 of AA-1 area) under the "chairman's quota",
49. Film Actor Deb has allotted plot no DE 43 of AA-1 area to one Karungulam Subramanian Ramasubban, who was secretary to Chief Vigilance Commissioner and presently a member of the Standing Conference of Public Enterprises (SCOPE).

Appendix – 11

The Times of India

Rajarhat New Town

RELATED KEYWORDS:

Popular Articles about Rajarhat New Town

KOLKATA

New Bypass to join Rajarhat and Kestopur

June 20, 2003 | TNN

KOLKATA: A new Salt Lake bypass would come up on the eastern fringe of the city, joining Nicco Park, Rajarhat New Town and Mahisbathan and meeting VIP road at Kestopur. A flyover to Baguihati Joramandir will be part of the project. West Bengal urban development minister Asok Bhattacharya said that the Rs. 100 crore project is likely to take off around the end of the year, after the funding patterns are finalised. Meanwhile, efforts are on to finish the construction of the flyovers at Lake Gardens and Bondel gate in the southern and eastern part of the city.

KOLKATA

Impressed Azad sees a New Town in all states

October 5, 2004 | Saugata Roy and Suman Chakraborti, TNN

KOLKATA: It's hot, it's happening, and it's here. That's Rajarhat New Town. Ask urban development minister Ghulam Nabi Azad. In Kolkata , the minister was so impressed by New Town that he wants to play up the satellite township as a model for other states to follow. "This could be really an eye-opener for the neighbouring states," Azad said in a meeting with state housing minister Gautam Deb at the Rajarhat site office. The minister asked state officials to send a representative to make a presentation on the New Town Project before the chief ministers of Delhi, Uttar Pradesh, Rajasthan and Punjab, who will meet in the Capital to attend a meeting on housing on October 28. "All these states now want to set up satellite townships, 20 years after Rajiv Gandhi mooted the idea.

KOLKATA

Civic status for New Town

September 5, 2005 | Suman Chakraborti, TNN

KOLKATA: The fast emerging New Town at Rajarhat, the state's showpiece township of the future will soon come under a new authority. The Rajarhat-Gopalpur Municipality that now looks after the backyard of New Town doesn't have the infrastructure to supervise the civic amenities of a township three times larger than Salt Lake. The government is likely to promulgate an ordinance in this regard, housing and public health engineering minister Gautam Deb told TOI. "An ordinance is in the pipeline.

KOLKATA

Get set for sports city in Rajarhat

June 3, 2007 | Swati Sengupta, TNN

KOLKATA: A sparkling new sports city is on the anvil at Rajarhat, which could give that much-needed boost to sports in a state that has a rich sporting legacy. Though the performance of the current crop of sportspersons is nothing to write home about, much of it could be attributed to the poor sports infrastructure in the state. All that is slated to change once the Buddhadeb Bhattacharjee government's plan to set up the sports complex materialises.

KOLKATA

Vedic shadow on New Town

September 3, 2009 | TNN

KOLKATA: Did the Vedic Village authorities encroach upon a part of the land purchased for the IT township project right next to the resort? The question has led Cabinet ministers and CPM veterans Abdur Rezzak Mollah and Gautam Deb? Who were initially at loggerheads ? To make peace for their own survival. The Vedic Village and IT township exposé is making things increasingly uncomfortable for the government. Three crucial CPM-controlled departments? Land and land reforms, IT and urban development?

KOLKATA

Report reveals anomalies in Rajarhat land deals

October 7, 2009 | TNN

KOLKATA: Land deeds were fudged and the character of land changed in many cases by none other than the officials of the land reforms department. The five-member committee probing the controversial land purchase process for the proposed IT hub between Vedic Village and Rajarhat New Town has pointed to such irregularities in its report to the land and land reforms department. Land and land reforms minister Abdur Rezzak Mollah conceded to such irregularities after going through the report.

KOLKATA

Jyoti Basu Nagar beckons Rajarhat New Town

August 26, 2010 | TNN

KOLKATA: Come October, Rajarhat New Town will be rechristened Jyoti Basu Nagar. The children's park here will also be named after the country's longest-serving chief minister. Housing Infrastructure Development Corporation (Hidco) plans to celebrate the naming ceremony of the township—close to Salt Lake aka Bidhannagar named after Basu's senior and former CM Bidhan Chandra Roy—with various cultural programmes through the month. "We will install a statue of Jyoti...

KOLKATA

Rajarhat: Deb to meet land-losers

December 5, 2010 | TNN

KOLKATA: State housing minister and Hidco chairman Gautam Deb will be meeting land losers in Rajarhat after persistent pressure from the Trinamool Congress, which has claimed that several landlosers have not received proper compensation. To counter the repeated Trinamool attack, Deb could also announce a new compensation package for the landlosers at the meeting. When contacted, Deb said that he would ask land-losers' co-opeartives if they have any complaints or grievances.

KOLKATA

Jobs and loans in new Rajarhat rehab plan

December 6, 2010 | TNN

KOLKATA: State housing minister Gautam Deb announced a new eight-point rehab package for the land-losers in Rajarhat New Town . The model township is the new land-acquisition battleground after Singur and Nandigram, with Trinamool Congress chief Mamata Banerjee and Deb locked in an increasingly aggressive war of words.

Trinamool plans to gherao the Hidco office on December 9. Deb is keen to beat her to the punch. On his platter is an array of sops?

KOLKATA

Progress at snail's pace puts IT plans on hold

December 23, 2010 | Suman Chakraborti , TNN

After Sector-V, Rajarhat New Town is now developing as the next IT destination in Bengal. Following the recent Wipro and Infosys deals, many IT companies are now making a beeline for New Town. The demand for land is such that Hidco has had to increase its reservation of land for the IT sector from 300 acres to 350 acres in Action Area-III. More than 50 IT companies have asked for 2-3-acre plots. As much as 288 acre of the original 300-acre IT land has already been given away.

Eco-tourism dreams for Rajarhat

July 20, 2011 | TNN

KOLKATA: The neglected water bodies at Rajarhat are all set to get a makeover. Chief minister Mamata Banerjee visited Rajarhat on her way to Writers' Buildings after landing in Kolkata from North Bengal and inspected the water bodies. The CM has instructed the Housing Infrastructure Development Corporation (Hidco) to engage reputed consulting firm Infrastructure Leasing and Financial Services Limited (ILFS) to make a study on how eco-tourism could be developed around the water bodies.

KOLKATA

New Town plot auction for health projects

September 27, 2011 | Suman Chakraborti, TNN

KOLKATA: The Housing Infrastructure and Development Corporation (Hidco) has decided to auction plots to set up specialised healthcare institutes. The Hidco authorities held a meeting in this regard. "It has been decided that two plots of two acres each will be sold in Action Area I near the new Hidco office building in Rajarhat New Town for setting up a geriatric health regeneration therapy centre and a trauma care centre. We are preparing the documents. The tender and auction will take place after the Pujas," said Hidco chairman-cum-managing director Debasis Sen. A tender notice will be put up soon.

KOLKATA

Land sought in New Town for airport modernisation

November 12, 2011 | Suman Chakraborti, TNN

KOLKATA: Union urban development department secretary Sudhir Krishna held talks with the Housing and Infrastructure Development Corporation (Hidco), and asked the state government to arrange for around five acres at New Town to assist in the airport modernisation project. Hidco chairman-cum-MD Debasis Sen said some extra land is required for the project. "About five acres will be required and discussions were held today on the possible location of the plot. More talks will follow," Sen said.

KOLKATA

Rajarhat to get eco park

November 23, 2011 | Suman Chakraborti, TNN

KOLKATA: The Infrastructure Leasing and Financial Services Limited (ILFS) made a detailed presentation at Writers' Buildings on its plans to develop a 480-acre water body in Rajarhat New Town into an eco-tourism park. Hidco chairman-cum-managing director Debasis Sen said meeting was aimed at coming up with a project plan. It was attended by senior officials of the urban development department and Hidco. "ILFS was engaged in preparing a plan and the survey has been...

KOLKATA

Rajarhat projects now in Hidco hands

December 6, 2011 | Suman Chakraborti, TNN

KOLKATA: The Housing and Infrastructure Development Corporation (Hidco) will henceforth plan and execute development projects in the entire 6,000-7,000 hectare area in Rajarhat, which was earlier under the now-dissolved Bhangor Rajarhat Area Development Authority (Brada). Hidco top brass is scheduled to hold a meeting on December 14 to take stock of the situation in the area and chart out plans needed to develop the area. Brada had jurisdiction over 24 *mouzas* - 15 in North and nine in South...

Rajarhat New Town Articles By Date

KOLKATA

Rajarhat 'irregularities': State issues notification for judicial inquiry

December 14, 2011 | TNN

KOLKATA: Left Front government's showpiece Rajarhat New Town is under scanner. Chief Minister Mamata Banerjee has ordered a judicial inquiry into the alleged irregularities in acquisition and distribution of New Town land under retired high court judge Ranajit Mitra. A notification has been issued in this regard. The termsof reference of the judicial inquiry is wide-ranging. The commission will examine the alleged forcible acquisition of land at Rajarhat New Town, the price offered to the landlosers and the rehabilitation, the alleged misuse of the chairman's quota while distributing plots - including the allotment of plots to politicians, bureaucrats, police officers and also those close to former Hidco chairman and housing minister Gautam Deb. The commission will also listen to complaints to ascertain whether the minister used muscle power to evict the rightful owner.

Hidco decides to sell more plots in Rajarhat

December 29, 2011 | Suman Chakraborti, TNN

KOLKATA: The Housing Infrastructure Development Corporation (Hidco) has decided to sell more plots at Rajarhat New Town for setting up hospitals, schools, colleges and other institutes. Hidco chairman-cum-managing director Debashis Sen said that the matter was discussed in the Hidco board meeting held . "It has been decided that 15 plots in Rajarhat New Town, in the range from a minimum of 20 cottahs to a maximum of two acres, will be sold through...

KOLKATA

Tourism hub at wetland

January 17, 2012 | Suman Chakraborti, TNN

KOLKATA: Chief Minister Mamata Banerjee recently re-visited the 480-acre Rajarhat water body where she wants to set up an eco-tourism park. The CM has asked the Housing Infrastructure Development Corporation (Hidco) to start work on the project. "We will now start work," said Hidco chairman-cum-managing director Debashis Sen. Earlier, ILFS was engaged to prepare a plan. After completing its survey, the firm has submitted an inception report to Hidco and also gave a detailed presentation on the proposed plan.

KOLKATA

Battery-run vehicles for Rajarhat roads

May 7, 2012 | Suman Chakraborti , TNN

KOLKATA: In keeping with the Trinamool-led government's green theme, the Housing Infrastructure Development Corporation (Hidco) wants pollution free, battery-operated three-wheelers to ply in Rajarhat New Town. The authorities have written to the power ministry seeking views on whether it's feasible to run such battery-powered vehicles. The concept is to have a personalised rapid transit system (PRTS) in place where vehicles will be battery-operated and will ply on short and dedicated routes.

KOLKATA

Rajarhat to get five-storey parking plaza

June 19, 2012 | Suman Chakraborti, TNN

KOLKATA: With the numbers of cars set to go up in the Rajarhat-New Town area, authorities have decided to set up a multi-storied community car parking plaza in the township. Rajarhat New Town is going to get its first multi-storied community car parking plaza, keeping in mind the future projection that thousands of cars will come at the area. The parking plaza, a first in the area, will be a five-storied building and will come up on a one-acre plot in Action Area-I. While 85 per cent of the built-up area will accommodate the car parking facilities, the remaining 15 per cent will be used for allied commercial activities like food stalls or a coffee shop.

KOLKATA

PWD submits report on potholed road repair

July 29, 2012 | Suman Chakraborti, TNN

KOLKATA: A few weeks after TOI reported on the precarious state of the PWD Road which links Rajarhat, New Town with Bantala, the state PWD sent a preliminary report to the Housing Infrastructure Development Corporation (Hidco) for repairing the important stretch. Hidco chairman-cum-managing director Debashis Sen discussed the project with PWD officials at Writers Buildings. "We discussed about the cost sharing for the project," Sen said. Earlier, Hidco had finished work for the east-west major arterial road that runs parallel to the site that has been earmarked for the Infosys and Wipro projects.

KOLKATA

Rajarhat land sold via e-auction

July 9, 2012 | Suman Chakraborti, TNN

KOLKATA: In a first in the state, a two-acre plot was sold off through e-auction. The West Bengal Housing Infrastructure Development Corporation (Hidco) conducted this e-auction, in which the two acres at Rajarhat, New Town was sold for Rs 10.10 crore for setting up a 10+2 high school. It plans to sell more such plots through e-auctioning. The auction was conducted by MSTC, a government of India public sector undertaking. "The process of on line e-auction is much more transparent than the conventional bidding and auctioning," a Hidco official said.

KOLKATA

Rajarhat hub gets one bid in four months

July 15, 2012 | TNN

KOLKATA: Chief Minister Mamata Banerjee had laid the foundation stone of the international financial hub at Rajarhat New Town in March amid huge publicity and expectations. Four months have passed since then, but the much-hyped hub has managed to attract only a single investment proposal all this while. Union minister of state for urban development Saugata Roy said he will call an investors' meet in Delhi to convince them to invest their money on the hub. Speaking at a seminar on 'Densification of Cities', organised by Hidco , Roy said, "The urban development ministry will hold a meeting in Delhi soon with big financial and banking institutes to discuss investment possibilities," Roy said.

KOLKATA

Urban planning team from Afghanistan meets West Bengal Housing Infrastructure and Development Corporation officials

August 7, 2012 | Suman Chakraborti, TNN

KOLKATA: A 10-member urban planning team from Afghanistan came at Rajarhat New Town recently and met officials of the West Bengal Housing Infrastructure and Development Corporation (Hidco) to discuss on urban planning. The team is designing a new city called Dehsabz city in the north of Kabul of Afghanistan. Officials came at Rajarhat to look into the way how Rajarhat New Town is coming up. "Dehsabz means Green Village", explained Ahmadi Mumtaz Ahmad, the team leader that met Hidco chairman cum managing director

Debashis Sen. The township will be designed for about three million people spreading over 700 sq km of area.

KOLKATA

New Town to get country's biggest convention centre

August 10, 2012 | Suman Chakraborti, TNN

KOLKATA: The city will soon get two Science City-like convention centres, one in Rajarhat New Town and the other in Alipore. The New Town centre will be one of the biggest in the country, Chief Minister Mamata Banerjee said at a programme in Rajarhat. The Housing Infrastructure Development Corporation (Hidco) has chalked out the artistic impression for the New Town project, which will have a seating capacity of about 6,000-odd people. The Centre will come up on a 10-acre plot in Rajarhat's Action Area II. According to plans, there will be a plenary hall and two other halls along with adjustable seating arrangements.

KOLKATA

New Town may get a civic body

August 13, 2012 | Suman Chakraborti, TNN

KOLKATA: Once a bill gets passed in the State Cabinet, the New Town Kolkata Development Authority (NKDA) may soon be entrusted to assess, levy and collect property tax from the residents of Rajarhat-New Town. The New Town Kolkata Development Authority may be soon entrusted to assess, levy and collect property tax from residents of Rajarhat New Town. The state urban development department had earlier mooted the proposal in the state cabinet for approval. The department was then asked to make some amendments in the New Town Kolkata Development Act so that the authority can be entrusted with the responsibility to act like a municipality or corporation and be able to collect tax. Sources said highly-placed government officials said that a proposal was presented, it has been mooted to the state cabinet to approve a bill to make certain amendments in the New Town Kolkata Development Act, 2007 to allow NKDA to collect tax. "The proposal has been placed before the state cabinet and the urban development department is working hard on it so that the proposal allowing NKDA to collect taxes gets passed in the cabinet," a highly-placed government official said.

KOLKATA

Record bid for Rajarhat plot

August 19, 2012 | Suman Chakraborti, TNN

KOLKATA: Rajarhat New Town seems to be on top of the list for investors. In the highest ever land auction in the area so far, a 2.5-acre plot for a retail-cum-office complex has fetched Rs. 51.13 crore for the Housing Infrastructure and Development Corporation (Hidco). The land, priced at more than Rs. 20 crore per acre or Rs. 34 lakh per cottah, has broken all land sale records in Rajarhat New Town. The 2.5-acre plot at Action Area-II of New Town is located beside the major arterial...

KOLKATA

CCTVs to watch over 'unsafe' New Town

August 21, 2012 | Suman Chakraborti, TNN

KOLKATA: In its spree to improve infrastructure in the township, the New Town Kolkata Development authority (NKDA) has decided to tighten security arrangements in Rajarhat. The administrative body has made amendments in the building rules, making installation of closed circuit televisions (CCTVs) and security alarms compulsory for all buildings constructed on plots having an area of one acre and above. The authorities are conducting a fresh review to take into count the number of high-rises that have CCTVs and security alarms installed.

KOLKATA

West Bengal government relaunches the international financial hub project at Rajarhat

August 24, 2012 | Suman Chakraborti, TNN

KOLKATA: The West Bengal government relaunched its much ambitious international financial hub project by holding a meeting recently at New Delhi's Vigyan Bhavan Hall-II. Union minister of state, urban development, Saugata Roy, West Bengal urban development minister Firhad Hakim, union urban development ministry, secretary Sudhir Krishna, West Bengal urban development secretary and Hidco chairman Debashis Sen and other senior central and Bengal urban...

Ferry project scrapped, launches rust in water

August 26, 2012 | Jayanta Gupta, TNN

KOLKATA: The previous government's ambitious ferry service project—and along with it several lakhs of public money—has met a watery grave. The Buddhadeb Bhattacharjee government had in 2006 announced the ferry service to connect Kolkata with Salt Lake and Rajarhat. Accordingly, two wooden launches were procured for several lakhs. Five years later, a few months after coming to power in 2011, Chief Minister Mamata Banerjee modified the plan and proposed a Singapore-like waterway along the network of canals connecting Kolkata to Rajarhat.

KOLKATA

'Magic' underpass to ease traffic rush

August 28, 2012 | Suman Chakraborti, TNN

KOLKATA: If the Housing Infrastructure Development Corporation (Hidco) has its way, Rajarhat New Town may soon boast of a magic box underpass—a concept widely used in Bangalore. Hidco, which plans to set up the underpass at the four-point crossing at Chinar Park, has engaged RITES to conduct a study on whether the project will prove feasible. The decision was taken to ease traffic congestion at the spot which is increasing each day with rise in vehicular traffic. "The crossing is already very congested.

KOLKATA

New Town Kolkata Development Authority starts anti-dengue drive in Rajarhat

September 7, 2012 | Suman Chakraborti, TNN

KOLKATA: The New Town Kolkata Development Authority (NKDA) has started an anti-dengue drive in Rajarhat New Town to prevent the disease from spreading into the township. Chief Minister Mamata Banerjee recently held a meeting on the issue as to how to combat the outbreak of dengue in the city, following which NKDA has started printing and distributing flexes and handouts for display. Officials said that two separate teams have started spraying mosquito killing oil and bleaching powder in the township.

KOLKATA

Street furniture to give Rajarhat a futuristic look

September 13, 2012 | Suman Chakraborti, TNN

KOLKATA: Taking a cue from the smart street furniture installed in New Delhi during the Commonwealth Games, the Housing Infrastructure Development Corporation (HIDCO) plans to give Rajarhat New Town a fresh and clean look. The Urban Mass Transit

Company (UMTC), which is working as a consultant for Hidco to develop the township's transport system, recently gave a presentation on street furniture as well. Officials said they are looking at smartly designed railings, bus-stops, public toilets, information boards, benches, traffic signal systems, variable message boards, garbage bins and food or magazine kiosks.

KOLKATA

Rajarhat New Town gets two new Childrens Parks

September 21, 2012 | Suman Chakraborti, TNN

KOLKATA: Rajarhat New Town recently got two new Childrens Parks. State urban development minister Firhad Hakim inaugurated the two parks, named as Rabindra Tirtha Sishu Udyan and Vivek Tirtha Sishu Udyan. The Housing Infrastructure Development Corporation has developed the parks. Authorities said that the parks have been named after Rabindranath Tagore and Swami Vivekananda so that the children who will come to the parks get to know about these two great luminaries. Not only for...

KOLKATA

Bengal to hardsell financial hub in Mumbai

September 22, 2012 | Suman Chakraborti, TNN

KOLKATA: In a desperate attempt to draw investors to the financial hub in Rajarhat New Town, state urban development minister Firhad Hakim along with his department and Hidco officials will be meeting bankers and investors in Mumbai. The financial hub which is being touted as the next in line to Mumbai's own Bandra Kurla has received only one application so far. Hard pressed over to attract investment in the much touted international financial hub in Rajarhat New Town that has only received one application from financial institutes so far, state urban development minister Firhad Hakim and other senior urban development and Hidco officials will be meeting bankers and investors and Mumbai on Saturday to attract investments for the financial hub which is being touted as the second such financial hub after Mumbai's own Bandra Kurla.

KOLKATA

West Bengal government organises roadshow to highlight the financial hub in Rajarhat

September 23, 2012 | Suman Chakraborti, TNN

KOLKATA: The Bengal government is trying hard to bring investments in the International financial hub in Rajarhat New Town. State urban development minister Firhad Hakim along with senior officials of the Housing Infrastructure Development Corporation organised a roadshow on the financial hub at Mumbai.. The meeting was organised at the Taj Lands End in Mumbai. Representatives of reputed institutions like Edelweiss Tokyo, IndusInd Bank, Yes Bank, Citibank, L and T Infra, DBS, IDBI Mutual, Dena Bank , SBI Capital, ICICI, Kotak Mahindra, Future Capital and others were present in the roadshow.

KOLKATA

Sculpture workshop ends at Rajarhat

September 28, 2012 | Suman Chakraborti, TNN

KOLKATA: The Housing Infrastructure Development Corporation is happy over the huge response and on the outcome of the sculpture workshop that was organised at Rajarhat New Town recently. The artists came up with beautiful statues in a very short time. The authorities are now working to install the statues in several places of the township. Not only with their works, the artists also recounted the old days. Renowned artist Bimal Kundu said how in the early days of the Salt Lake township that the then irrigation secretary had remarked that the government did not have any funds for coming up with statues but as a special favour he could only arrange a bit of raw material.

KOLKATA

State government trying hard to take forward financial hub project

October 5, 2012 | Suman Chakraborti, TNN

KOLKATA: With only another 25 days left for the state government to receive investment proposals for the much touted financial hub in Rajarhat New Town, the Housing Infrastructure Development Corporation (Hidco) is going all out to bring in investment proposals. Following the meeting with bankers at New Delhi and Mumbai, the authorities are further planning to hold more road shows. Hidco is trying hard to take forward the financial hub project and to attract investments, which has so far been proved to be a dampener.

KOLKATA

Firms keen to invest in financial hub

October 9, 2012 | TNN

KOLKATA: The government's ambitious financial hub project in Rajarhat New Town seems to be finally taking shape. State urban development minister Firhad Hakim said that five companies have given their offer letters to invest in the financial hub. "Out of the nine plots in the financial hub, offers have come for five plots. Besides, we are talking with several financial institutes like Dena Bank and Yes Bank," the minister said. The Hidco authorities are also making all efforts to highlight the hub when a 32-member delegation comes from the USA on a two-day visit to the city.

KOLKATA

World Bank team visits Rajarhat

October 12, 2012 | Suman Chakraborti, TNN

KOLKATA: A World Bank team visited the city a few days back to discuss on green city growth and on the National Ganga Mission. The team also visited Rajarhat New Town. The World Bank delegation comprising urban economist Zhiyu Jerry Chen, senior infrastructure specialist Raghu Kesavan and senior environment officer Tapas Paul met Hidco chairman and managing director Debashis Sen and discussed on the two issues. After visiting Rajarhat New Town, Chen and Kesavan later promised to come back for more discussions about formulating a technical assistance for capacity building in the township.

KOLKATA

US delegation visits Rajarhat

October 19, 2012 | Suman Chakraborti, TNN

KOLKATA: A 38- member US delegation recently visited Rajarhat New Town. The visit was facilitated by the US commercial service at the US Consulate in Kolkata. The delegation was from the American Institute of Architects and the US department of commerce. The members of the delegate held a meeting with Hidco officials at Rabindra Tirtha where a few investors were also invited. Hidco chairman and managing director Debashis Sen gave a presentation before the delegation on Rajarhat...

KOLKATA

Western model for Rajarhat addresses

November 11, 2012 | Suman Chakraborti, TNN

KOLKATA: If people complain that they have problems locating addresses in the city, they will certainly not grumble at Rajarhat New Town in near future. Soon houses there will have addresses with street numbers and plot numbers, having six-digit codes. The New Town Kolkata Development Authority (NKDA) has come up with this decision following the system in western countries. New Town will be the first township in the country to boast of this house-address system. ...

KOLKATA

Ring road to connect Sector V, Bantala

November 14, 2012 | Suman Chakraborti, TNN

KOLKATA: Here is good news for motorists and techies who have a harrowing time while on their way to work. The city's IT hub or Sector-V will soon be interlinked with Rajarhat, New Town and Bantala SEZ through new roads next year. The new road link will start with the Ring Road that is being set up at Sector-V and join the PWD road—that connects Rajarhat with Bantala on Basanti highway-at Bhojerhat. The Nabadiganta Industrial Township Authority (NDITA) is working to set up the 2.5 km long road that will form a ring surrounding Sector-V. This road connectivity will immensely benefit motorist and reduce the time taken to move through the three areas.

KOLKATA

State invites tenders for Rajarhat financial hub

November 19, 2012 | Suman Chakraborti, TNN

KOLKATA: The state government is all set to take the ambitious financial hub project in Rajarhat-New Town to the next stage. With applications from six financial and banking institutes, the authorities have now floated tenders to begin work on the second phase of the financial hub. After opening the bids that ended on October 31, Hidco received offers from United Bank of India (UBI), United Commercial Bank (UCO), National Insurance Company (NIC), West Bengal...

KOLKATA

HIDCO scanner on unutilised plots

November 27, 2012 | Suman Chakraborti, TNN

KOLKATA: The Housing Infrastructure Development Corporation (Hidco) has sent notices to forty companies asking them to furnish reasons as to why they are yet to start construction works on the plots allotted to them at Rajarhat New Town. Hidco chairman-cum-managing director Debashis Sen said they are keeping track of the matter and want full utilisation of the plots in Rajarhat. "We have already sent letters to forty such firms to give reasons for the delay to start work. We are planning to have a...

KOLKATA

Meet by infrastructure task force today

December 10, 2012 | Suman Chakraborti, TNN

KOLKATA: The task force on urban infrastructure that was set up by Chief Minister Mamata Banerjee recently to look into the problems of developers will hold its first meeting in the State assembly. The chief secretary and ministers and secretaries of the finance, industries and urban development departments are members of the task force and will report to the State cabinet committee on infrastructure. Representatives of the construction-builder community have also been...

KOLKATA

Government plans urban haat in Rajarhat

December 16, 2012 | Suman Chakraborti, TNN

KOLKATA: Small-time artisans from various districts of the state are all to get a major impetus with the government planning to set up an urban haat in Rajarhat New Town. The haat, to be christened as Banglar Haat, will have in display handicraft products from all districts. Visitors will also be able to buy the products. The project has been initiated by the Housing Infrastructure Development Corporation (Hidco). Tenders have already been floated to invite bids for...

KOLKATA

New Town bus stands to get digital time tables

January 10, 2013 | Suman Chakraborti, TNN

KOLKATA: Rajarhat New Town will soon get a passenger information system, which will help commuters know about the arrival time of buses by looking at a digital scroll board to be displayed at the bus stands there. Officials of the Housing and Infrastructure Development Corporation (Hidco) held a meeting with IT service providers, transport department officials and some bus operators to discuss the issue. "We had earlier operated the system on experimental basis. In the...

KOLKATA

Partha Chatterjee to follow up with IT giants

January 14, 2013 | Suman Chakraborti, TNN

KOLKATA: The State government is yet to receive any response from IT giants Infosys and Wipro over their proposed campuses in Rajarhat New Town. State IT and industries minister Partha Chatterjee has decided to discuss the matter with the firms soon. "I will again talk to them," Chatterjee said, adding that he will take up the matter after the Bengal Leads Summit. State IT and industries minister Partha Chatterjee will talk to IT giants Wipro and Infosys again...

KOLKATA

Appendix – 12

Papers related to the case of Nishikanta Mandal

নিরুদ্দেশ

উক্ত ছবির মানুষটি গত
২৭শে ফেব্রুয়ারী ২০০৭ তারিখে
সল্টলেক ময়ুখ ভবন থেকে
নিরুদ্দেশ হয়েছেন।

উক্ত ব্যক্তির নাম - শ্রী নিশিকান্ত মণ্ডল
বয়স - ৭২ বৎসর,
উচ্চতা - ৫ ফুট ৬ ইঞ্চি,
গায়ের রঙ - কালো,
পরনে ছিল ছাই রঙের খদ্দরের পাঞ্জাবী ও ধুতি,
মাথায় টাক আছে।
সঙ্গে লাউহাটী স্টেট ব্যাঙ্কের পাশ বই আছে।

**উক্ত ব্যক্তির সম্বন্ধে কোন রকম খোঁজখবর জানা থাকলে নিম্নের ঠিকানায় খবর দিন
সঠিক সংবাদদাতাকে ৫০০০ - (পাঁচহাজার) টাকা পুরস্কৃত করা হবে।**

যোগাযোগের ঠিকানা -

গোবিন্দ মণ্ডল
কলাবেড়িয়া, রাজারহাট-বিষ্ণুপুর, উত্তর ২৪ পরগনা, কোলকাতা - ১৩৫
ফোন - ৯৮৩৬০৪১৩৭৬ এবং ০৩২১৬ ২৭২৮২১ (বাড়ী)

এছাড়াও এখানে যোগাযোগ করতে পারেন -

গ্রাম ও পোঃ - আকন্দকেশরী, থানা - রাজারহাট, জেলা - উত্তর ২৪ পরগনা, কোলকাতা - ১৩৫
ফোন - ৯২৩৯০৬৫৭৯২ এবং ৯৮৩০১৮১১৩০

[This man is missing from Salt Lake, Mayuk Bhawan since 27th February, 2007.

Name	:	Nishikanta Mandal
Age	:	72 years
Height	:	5 feet 6 inches
Complexion	:	Dark

Wearing ash coloured Panjabi and Dhoti, bald headed.

He was carrying a passbook of State Bank of India of Lauhati branch.

For any information about this man please contact in the following address.

Prize money for correct information Rs. 5,000.

Contact address	:	Gobinda Mandal, Kalaberia, Rajarhat, Bishnupur, North 24 Parganas, Kolkata – 135.
Other contact address	:	Vill. and PO. Akandakeshri, P.S. Rajarhat, Dist. North 24 Parganas, Kolkata – 135.

DEPARTMENT OF HOUSING
N.T.P. BRANCH
NEW SECRETARIAT BUILDINGS., 1 ST FLOOR, BLOCK-'A',
1, K. S. ROY ROAD, KOLKATA – 700 001

NO. 1072/ SS/2005 **Dated. 04/10/2005**

Subject : Hearing of the Representation of Sri Nishi Kanta Mondal, S/o Late Nanilal Mondal of Vill & P.O. Akandakeshari P.S. Rajarhat Dist North 24-Parganas in pursuance of the order of the Hon'ble High Court. Calcutta in W.P. No 11256 (W) of 2005.

ORDER

04/10/2005

Today was fixed for passing a reasoned order in connection with the hearing of the petitioner, Sri Nishi Kanta Mondal in writ Petition No 11256 (W) of 2005 held on 30.09.2005 . The hearing was held in accordance with the order of the Hon'ble High Court, Calcutta dated 18.08.2005 in the said writ Petition directing me to pass a reasoned order after giving the petitioner an opportunity of hearing on his representation vide Annexure P8 of the writ Petition

The Petitioner was duly present on the date of hearing on 30.09.2005 with his Ld Lawyer . Additional L.A. Collector, North 24-Parganas as well as General Managers, W B H I D C O, Co-respondents in the writ Petition, were also present. Heard the Petitioner represented through his Ld Lawyer and the officials mentioned hereinabove .

The contention of the Petitioner as mentioned in details in Annexure P8 of the writ Petition was that he was the owner of a Brick Field built on his own plots of land as well as some lease hold plots namely 164/962, 363, 368, 372, 374, 362, 380, 381, 382, 383, 384, 385, 391& 392 in Mouza Akandakeshari , P.S Rajarhat, Dist North 24-Parganas . He started his Brick Field business a few years ago after taking loans worth several lakhs of Rupees from banks and other private agencies and had provided employment to some 200/250 Workers there . It was also the livelihood of his own and his two aged sons . He has been paying Royalty, Sales Tax , Income Tax etc due to the Government as well as local taxes to Gram Panchayat and Rajarhat Panchayat Samity .He, therefore, prayed for release of his land comprising the brick field from the Land acquisition Process particularly when many persons are being so exempted by the Government on humanitarian ground.The Petitioner also submitted some documents to substantiate his claim.

The submission of the Additional L.A Collector, North 24-Parganas, Co-respondent in the writ Petition was that the petitioner was actually the part owner of the three plots namely 363, 381 & 382 . He also stated that the so called lease of the petitioner in respect of other plots through unregistered deeds is illegal and Contravenes Section 7 of the W.B. Land Reforms Act

Further a portion of plots No 382 is actually a road belonging to Zilla Parished, North 24-Parganas. It was argued that the petitioner did not get any permit from B.L.L.R.O, Rajarhat for running brick field till date .An F.I.R. was lodged by the said official against the petitioner with Local Police Station on that ground for unauthorised extraction of earth from the land comprising the plots without any permission .He also stated that L A proceedings involving the land in question had been completed but the petitioner was not present to file his objection at the time of hearing . Award for compensation had already been declared and most of the awardees except the petitioner had already received their awards. Possession of the acquired land had been made over to R.B.

General Managers, W B H I D C O submitted that an area comprising about 20 acres of land including petitioner's land in New Town Project Area had been selected by a team of officials from HIDCO & WBSEB for installation of 220 KV Power Station for supply of electricity to the New Town . It was also stated that the plots of land falling within the New Town Project Area are not exempted and those falling outside the Project Area are being exempted from L.A Proceedings.

After hearing the Petitioner and the Officials present and on going through the documents submitted on their behalf it appears to me that the Government / WBHIDCO had no other alternative but to acquire the land comprising the brick field of the petitioner in Mouza Akandakeshari, P.S. Rajarhat Dist North 24-Parganas in the greater interest of the New Town Project particularly for installation of 220 KV Station for power supply to New Town .

It view of the above, I am of opinion that the representation of the Petitioner vide Annexure P8 of the writ Petition No 11256(W) of 2005 is not tenable since the land is acquired in the interest of New Town Project and as such the said representation is hereby rejected .

The Petitioner Sri Nishikanta Mondal to informed accordingly .

Dated , Kolkata the 4th October, 2005

Special Secretary
Housing Department
Government of West Bengal

NO. 1072/1(1)/ SS/2005 **Dated. 04/10/2005**

Copy forwarded for information to :-

1) Nishikanta Mondal
S/O Late Nanilal Mondal,
Vill. & P.O. Akandakeshari
P.S. Rajarhat
District - North 24-Parganas

IN THE HIGH COURT AT CALCUTTA

CONSTITUTIONAL WRIT JURISDICTION

(APPELLATE SIDE)

W.P. NO. [illegible] (W) OF 2005.

In the matter of :

An application under Article 226

of the Constitution of India;

And

In the matter of :

Nisikanta Mondal.

.... Petitioner

-Versus -

The State of West Bengal & Ors.

... .Respondents.

- P E T I T I O N -

BAPPADITYA [illegible]

ADVOCATE

HIGH COURT, CALCUTTA

BAR ASSOCIATION, ROOM NO.2.

মাননীয়

ইন্সপেক্টর ইন চার্জ

নিউটাউন থানা

রাজারহাট নিউটাউন, উত্তর ২৪ পরগণা, কোলকাতা - ৭০০১৩৫।

বিষয়ঃ আমার স্বামী নিশিকান্ত মণ্ডল একজন অবসরপ্রাপ্ত শিক্ষক বর্তমানে তিনি চক্রান্তের স্বীকার। শত্রুরা প্রায়ই তাকে ধমক দিত, প্রাণে মেরে ফেলার কথা বলত, গুম করে দেবার হুমকী দিত। তিনি গত ২৭/০২/২০০৭ তারিখ রহস্য জনক ভাবে সল্টলেক ময়ূখ ভবন থেকে নিখোজ হন। এই ঘটনার জন্য সল্টলেক উত্তর থানায় ও লোকান রাজারহাট থানায় ডায়েরি করি। হ্যাণ্ড বিল ছবি দিয়ে প্রচার ও পেপারে দিই এবং থানায় জানাই। কিন্তু অদ্যবধী খোঁজ পায়নি। তাই আমার স্বামীকে জীবিত বা মৃত খুঁজে বের করার জন্য আপনার নিকট আবেদন পত্র। অন্যথা আইনী ব্যবস্থা অর্থাৎ কোর্টে যেতে বাধ্য থাকিব।

রেফাঃ সল্টলেক উত্তর থানার ডায়েরী নং	3750, Date 28/02/2007
রাজারহাট থানার ডায়েরী নং	45, 01/03/2007
মিসিং স্কোয়ার্ডের ডায়েরী নং	MPB-F-No. 53/2007/A/M/22, Dated 02/03/2007
পেপার বর্তমান বিজ্ঞাপন	07-03-07 & 16-03-07
প্রতিদিন	16-03-2007

মহাশয়,

আমার বিনীত নিবেদন এই যে, আমার স্বামী একজন অবসরপ্রাপ্ত শিক্ষক, তিনি গত ইংরাজী তারিখ ২৭/০২/২০০৭ তারিখ সল্টলেক ময়ূখ ভবন থেকে রহস্যজনক ভাবে নিখোজ হন। ঘটনার দিন সকাল ৯ (নয়) টার সময় বাড়ী থেকে আমার মেজ পুত্রের সহিত মোটর সাইকেলে করে উকিল সাহেবের বাড়ীতে যান। সেখানে থেকে উকিলবাবুর সহিত উকিলবাবুর অন্য মক্কেলের গাড়ীতে করে আমার স্বামীকে ময়ূখ ভবেন ছেড়ে দেন এবং উকিলবাবু ঐ মক্কেলের সহিত চলে যান। তারপর আমার মেজপুত্র অশোক ওঁর বাবাকে নিয়ে ময়ূখ ভবন থেকে জমি সংক্রান্ত ব্যাপারে ট্রেজারির চেক তোলে। তারপর আমার পুত্র অশোক ওঁর বাবাকে ঐ অফিসেরই পাশে চায়ের দোকানে বসিয়ে রেখে পুনরায় উকিলবাবুর সহিত কথা বলেন এবং জমির ক্ষতিপূরণের টাকার ব্যাপারে হিডকো অফিসে উকিলবাবুকে নিয়ে যান (সল্টলেক স্টেডিয়ামে)। ঐখান থেকে ফিরে এসে ওঁর

বাবাকে আর দেখতে পায়নি, অনেক খোঁজ খবর করেও খোঁজ মেলেনি।

নিখোঁজ হবার সময় ওঁনার পরনে ছিল ধুতি ও ছাই রং এর খদ্দরের পাঞ্জাবী সঙ্গে ছিল লাউহাটি ব্যাঙ্কের একটি চেক বই এবং স্টেট ব্যাঙ্ক অফ্ ইণ্ডিয়া, লাউহাটি শাখার একিটি পাশ বই।

এই ঘটনা ঘটার পর সমস্ত আত্মীয় স্বজনের বাড়ি খোঁজ করি, না পেয়ে পরদিনই সল্টলেক উত্তর থানায় ডায়েরী করি যাহার নম্বর ৩৭৫০ ইংরাজী তারিখ ২৮/০২/২০০৭ এবং আমার লোকাল থানায় ডায়েরী করি যাহার নম্বর ৪৫ ইংরাজী তারিখ ০১/০৩/২০০৭ এবং বর্তমান পেপারে দুইদিন বিজ্ঞাপন দিই যথাক্রমে ইংরাজী তারিখ ০৭/০৩/২০০৭ ও ১৬/০৩/২০০৭, তাহা ছাড়া ভবানী ভবন মিসিং স্কোয়ার্ডে জানাই যাহার ফাইল নং ৫৩, নিশিকান্ত মন্ডল MPB F No. 53/2007/1A/M/(22), Date 02/03/2007 এবং হ্যাণ্ড বিলে ছবি ছাপিয়ে বিজ্ঞাপন দিই কিন্তু অদ্যবধী আমার স্বামীর কোন খোঁজ পাইনি। নিম্নের ঘটনাগুলি আমার স্বামীকে জীবিত বা মৃত খুঁজে বের করতে আপনাকে সাহায্য করবে মনে করে বর্ণনা করছি।

আমার কয়েকজনের উপর সন্দেহ হয় এবং আমার ধারনা আমার স্বামীকে কিডন্যাপ করে মের লাশ গায়েব করে দিয়েছে, (১) প্রভায মন্ডল, পিতা ঁহাবুল চন্দ্র মন্ডল, সাং ও পোঃ আকন্দকেশরী, থানা রাজারহাট, জেলা উত্তর ২৪ পরগণা, (২) বিনয় মন্ডল (প্রাক্তন এল. সি. এম), পিতা ঁসন্তোষ মন্ডল, সাং ও পোঃ আকন্দকেশরী, থানা রাজারহাট, জেলা উত্তর ২৪ পরগণা (৩) মাননীয় প্রাক্তন বিধায়ক রবীন মন্ডল, – এ বিষয়ে আমার কোন সন্দেহ নেই, এদের যদি ভালো করে প্রেসার দেওয়া হয় তাহা হলে আমার স্বামীর হদিস মিলবে।

আমার গ্রামের প্রান্তে ১১ বিঘা জমির উপর একটি ইটভাঁটা ছিল। ভূতপূর্বক রাজ্য সরকারের আবাসন মন্ত্রী গৌতম দেব, বিধায়ক রবীন মন্ডল, উত্তর ২৪ পরগণা জেলা সভাধিপতি আপর্ণা গুপ্তা ও HIDCO -র পদাধিকারীরা ক্যাডার, গুণ্ডা ও পুলিশ বাহিনীর যৌথ সাঁড়াশি আক্রমনে ২০০৬ সালের ৩রা জুন সকাল ৭টায় বুল ড্রোজার ও ডিনামাইট চার্জ করে উক্ত ইটভাঁটাটি ধূলিসাৎ করে দেয়। উক্ত বিষয়ে মহামান্য কোলকাতা হাইকোর্টে কেস করি যাহার নম্বর WP-11256(W) of 2005, মহামান্য কোলকাতা হাইকোর্টে কনসিডার করার জন্য হাউডিং ডেভেলপমেন্ট এর স্পেসাল সেক্রেটারী মিঃ পি. কে. নিয়োগী কে নির্দেশ দেন এবং সরকার পক্ষকে আমাদের ইঁটভাঁটার মামলা তিন সপ্তাহের মধ্যে মিমাংশা করে নিতে বলেন যাহার বিচারপতি ছিলেন মাননীয় শ্রী প্রনব কুমার চট্টোপাধ্যায়।

সে মোতাবেক আবাসন দপ্ত'র আমাদের নোটিশ দেন যাহার নম্বর 1072/SS ইংরাজী তারিখ ০৪/১০/২০০৫ এবং আবাসন দপ্তর আমাদের কোন কথা না শুনে জোর করে পাওয়ার হাউজের নাম করে জমি নেন অবশিষ্ট যাহা ছিল তাহা ভেঙ্গে দেন এবং এলাকার প্রভাবশালী লোকজন ক্ষমতাশীল পার্টির লোকের উসকানিতে যাতের এই প্রতিষ্ঠানে দাদন দেওয়া ও কয়লা সাপ্লাইয়ের টাকা বাকী ছিল তাদের লেলিয়ে দেন তাহা আমাদের বারধর করে টাকা এক্ষুনি দিতে হবে বলে শাসায় আমরা তাদের বলেছি আমরা ইঁটভাটার জমির টাকা পায়নি আমরা হাইকোর্টে কেস করেছি। কেস মিটলে টাকা দিয়ে দেব, কিন্তু তারা তাহা শোনেনি মদত দাতাদের কথামতো ইটভাঁটা থেকে ব্যাটস্ রাবিশ গাছপালা কেটে নেয় থানায় বারে বারে জানিয়েও কাজ হয়নি এবং তারাই বলত আমাদের টাকা দিতে হবে নইলে তোদের সবাইকে জানে মেরে ফেলব। আর সরকারকে এই জমি দিতেও হবে নইলে তোদের উপায় নেই হিডকোর একজন অফিসার বিকাশ ব্যানার্জী এলাকার লোকজনদের সহযোগীতা কিছু সাদা কাগজপত্রে বাড়ীতে এসে আমার স্বামীকে দিয়ে আমার ছেলেদের অবর্তমানে সই করে নিয়ে যান জোর পূর্ব্বক ফলে আমার স্বামী খুবই ভয় পান এবং ভেঙ্গে পড়েন। তার জন্য থানায় ডায়েরীও করি।

আবাসন দপ্তরে এই একতরফা সিদ্ধান্তের জন্য এবং খামখেয়ালি ও মহামান্য কোলকাতা হাইকোর্টের নির্দেশে অবমাননার জন্য আমরা আবারও কেস করি যাহার নম্বর 2899 (W) of 2005.

তাহা ছাড়া (S.B.I.) ব্যাঙ্কে বাগরী মার্কেট, UCO ব্যাঙ্ক দুটি শাখা থেকে লোন নিয়ে ছিলাম তারাও টাকা আদায় করার জন্য আমাদের বারবার চিঠি দেন।

এছাড়া যারা সবসময় আমাদের ক্ষতি করে, মারধোর করে কারনে অকারনে ভাঁটা থেকে মালপত্র সুঠ লুঠ করে সব সময় আমাদের ধ্বংস করতে চেষ্টা করে তাদের বিরুদ্ধে আমাদের ডায়েরীও করা আছে যথাক্রমে 536/06 Date 11-12-06 এবং 06 তাং 15-12-2006।

বিশেষভাবে উল্লেখ করা যেতে পারে যে, আমাদের যে সকল জমি হিডকো এ্যাক্যুইজিশান করেছে তার টাকা এবং ড্যামারেজ চার্জ অনেক, আমাদের গ্রামে আরো কয়েকজন নিশিকান্ত মন্ডল, পিতা ননীলাল মন্ডল আছে যে কোন মূহূর্তে তার একজনকে সাজিয়ে দালাল চক্র টাকা তুলতে পারে। অদ্যাবধী আমার স্বামীর কোন খোজ পাইনি। যদি আমার স্বামীকে জীবিত বা মৃত খুঁজে বের করার ব্যবস্থা না করলে আমি আইনী ব্যবস্থা অর্থাৎ কোর্টে যেতে বাধ্য থাকিব।

সে কারনে মহাশয়ের নিকট আমার আকুল প্রার্থণা যে কোন ভাবেই হোক আমার স্বামাকে জাবত বা মৃত খুঁজে বের করার জন্য আপনার যাবতীয় হস্তক্ষেপ গ্রহণ করিতে আজ্ঞা হয়। অন্যথা আইনী ব্যবস্থা গ্রহণ করা আমার একমাত্র অবলম্বন।

ইতি -

বিনীত নিবেদক

অমলা মণ্ডল

তাং ২২-০৮-২০১১

Mob No - 9836341578

শ্রীমতী অমলা মন্ডল

স্বামী- নিশিকান্ত মন্ডল

সাং ও পোঃ- আকন্দকেশরী

থানা- রাজারহাট-নিউটাউন

জেলা- উত্তর ২৪ পরগণা

কোলকাতা - ১৩৫

অত্র আবেদনপত্রের অনুলিপি প্রেরিত হইলঃ-

১। মাননীয়

হোম সেক্রেটারী, পশ্চিমবঙ্গ

রাইটার্স বিল্ডিং, কোলকাতা - ৭০০০০১

Received contents but not verified

Govt. of West Bengal

Writers' Buildings

২। মাননীয়

ডি. জি. পশ্চিমবঙ্গ

রাইটার্স বিল্ডিং, কোলকাতা - ৭০০০০১

RECEIVED

Contents not Verified

23/8/11

D.G. & I.G. of Police

West Bengal

৩। মাননীয়

ডি. আই জি, সি. আই ডি

ভবানী ভবন, আলপুর, কোলকাতা - ৭০০০২৭

CONTENT NOT VERIFIED

RECEIVED

C.I. D. West Bengal

23/VIII/X

৪। মাননীয়

ইন্সপেক্টর, মিসিং স্কোয়ার্ড

গোয়েন্দা বিভাগ

ভবানী ভবন, আলিপুর, কোলকাতা - ৭০০০২৭

[Respected,
Inspector-in-Charge
P.S. New Town
Rajarhat New Town, North 24 Parganas, Kolkata – 700 135.

Subject: My husband Nishikanta Mandal, a retired school teacher is a victim of deep-rooted conspiracy. Since 27/02/2007, he is surprisingly missing from Salt Lake, Mayukh Bhawan. He is not traced till date. So I appeal to you to find out my husband dead or alive, otherwise I will be compelled to go to the Court of Law.

Reference: Salt Lake North P.S. diary No. 3750, dated 28/02/2007
Rajarhat P.S. diary No. 45, dated 01/03/2007
Missing Squad diary No. MPB-F.No.53/2007/A/M/ 22, dated 02/03/2007,
Bartaman Newspaper, Advertisement 07/03/2007 and 16/03/2007,
Pratidin Newspaper 16/03/2007.

Sir,

My humble submission is that my husband is a retired teacher; he is surprisingly missing since 27/02/2007 from Mayukh Bhawan, Salt Lake. On the day of the incidence, he went to lawyer's residence along with my second son by motor bike. From there he had gone to Mayukh Bhawan. He received the treasury cheque from Mayukh Bhawan. After that my son went to meet the Lawyer, while my husband was waiting in a nearby tea-shop. My son also went to HIDCO office along with the lawyer. After returning from HIDCO office he could not trace his father. During the time of his disappearance, he was wearing a Dhoti and ash coloured Punjabi. He was carrying a cheque book and a pass book of SBI, Lauhati branch.

We made a thorough search for him and being unsuccessful to find him out we report the incidence to Salt Lake North Police Station vide diary No. 3750 dated 28/02/2007 and to local Police Station, vide diary No. 45 dated 01/03/2007 and publish advertisement in local daily '*Bartaman*' on 07/03/2007. Besides we reported to Bhabani Bhawan Missing Squad vide file No. 53 Nishikanta Mandal MPB F No. 53/2007/1A/M/ (22) dated 02/03/2007. We also distributed hand bill but till date there is no trace of my husband. The following incidences may help you to find out my husband either alive or dead.

I have doubt on the following people and I am afraid they might have killed him. (1) Prabhas Mandal, P.S. Akandakesari, (2) Binoy Mandal (Ex-LCM), Akandakesari, (3) Honourable Ex-MLA, Rabin

Mandal, I believe that if they are pressurised my husband can be traced out.

I have a brick kiln on 11 bighas land. The earlier State Governments' Housing Development Minister Gautam Deb, MLA Rabin Mandal, North 24 Pargana District, Sabhadhipati Aparna Gupta and HIDCO's officials in co-operation with cadres, goons and police force demolished the brick-kiln on 3rd June, 2006 at 7.00 am by charging dynamite and with bull dozer. On this issue, we filed a case to the High Court vide case No.WP-11256(W) of 2005. The High Court instructed. P.K. Niyogi, the special secretary of Housing Development to consider and settle the case within three weeks. The judge was Pranab Kumar Chattopadhyay. In spite of that the Housing Development Department forcibly acquired our land vide notice No. 1072/SS dated 04/10/2005 in the name of power house and destroyed the property. We were tortured physically on the provocation of the politically powerful people of the area. One of the HIDCO officials Bikash Banerjee forcibly got a signature on plain paper from my husband. We lodged a complaint to police station.

Again this one-sided game by the Housing Development Department and for contempt of High Court's instruction we file a case vide No. 2899 (W) of 2005.

Besides, we took loan from Banks for which they are also pressurising us for recovery of their loan.

Apart, we also lodged complain against the people, who looted our belongings from the brick kiln vide diary No. 536/06 dated 11-12-06 and 15-12-2006.

It may be noted that price of our land that has been acquisitioned by HIDCO and its demurrage charge is huge; we are afraid that the whole amount can be withdrawn by some conspirators unlawfully.

Therefore, I request you to find out my husband either alive or dead.

Yours sincerely

Sd/-

Date: 22.08. 2011 Amala Mandal

Copy to:

1. Home Secretary West Bengal, Kolkata
2. D.G., West Bengal, Kolkata
3. DIGCID, Bhabani Bhavan, Kolkata
4. Inspector, Missing Squared, Bhabani Bhavan, Kolkata.

বর্তমান
কলকাতা, রবিবার ১৩ সেপ্টেম্বর ২০০৯, ২৭ ভাদ্র ১৪১৬

জমি লুটের বিরোধিতা করায় নিশিকান্তবাবুকে খুন করে লাশ গায়েব, আশঙ্কা ছেলের

রাজারহাটে জমিহারা কৃষকদের কান্না • পাঁচ

BARTAMAN

KOLKATA, Sunday, 13 September, 2009

Headline: Nishikanta babu murdered and body concealed for resisting the land loot, apprehended by his son. The cry of Rajarhat land-looser—Part five.

Brief: Nishikanta Mandal of Akanda Kesari village is missing since last one and a half year. It is apprehended by his son that he is murdered and body has been concealed under the patronage of the government for raising voice against the land loot by the CPI-M.

The Mandal family had brick kiln on 13 bighas of land at Akanda Kesari. That has been brutally destroyed by the goons with the support of the CPI-M leaders. The labour quarters were pulled down with bulldozer and about 1,000 families became homeless and jobless.

Imdadul Dhali of Tegharia reported that he had 12 bighas of multi-crop cultivable land at Patharghata which was encroached brutally by the government with the help of RAF. They dumped soil also. It is observed by the villagers that the Engineer of HIDCO, who led the goons in the whole operation of land grabbing, is now becoming wealthy day by day. The question now arises among the land looser what is the secret of his sudden prosperity?

Abul Khayer Mandal of Tegharia reported that for Tata 26 acres of land has been acquired by HIDCO in the Patharghata and Chak Pachuria *mouja.* The peasants were paid Rs. 13 thousand per cottah of land while the government sold in Rs. 6 lakh per cottah. In the public meeting at Chhapna village Gautambabu announced that the land looser would get employment, training, business opportunity and alternative accommodation would be arranged for them. But everything proved false. Now, the peasants want to know why they will sacrifice for the profiteer of the housing department.

Now, it is a million dollar question that how far the demand of getting their land back by the peasants of Rajarhat is practicable at this stage. Still a large number of peasants from Rekjoani, Nababpur, Patharghata, Mahisbathan, Mahisgot, Ghuni, Jatragachhi, Baligari, Akanda Kesari etc., believe that a political turnover is expected and then they will get back their land.]

নিরুদ্দেশ

নিশিকান্ত মণ্ডল ২৭-২-০৭ সল্টলেক থেকে রহস্যজনকভাবে নিখোঁজ। 72/5'-6", কালো, পাতলা চেহারা, টাক, পরণে ছাই রঙের খদ্দরের পাঞ্জাবি, ধুতি। সঠিক সন্ধানদাতা পুরস্কার পাবে। ফোন : 9836041376/03216272821.

213/32

[*SANBAD PRATIDIN*

Wednesday, 21 March, 2007

MISSING

Nishikanta Mandal is missing mysteriously from Salt Lake since 27.2.07.

72 /5263, dark complexion, lean and thin, bald-headed, wearing ash coloured Khaddar Punjabi and Dhoti. Person providing correct information will be rewarded. Phone ….].

নিরুদ্দেশ

•শ্রী নিশিকান্ত মণ্ডল

উপরিউক্ত ছবিটি আমার স্বামী, বয়স 72/5'-6", রং কালো, পাতলা চেহারা, মাথায় টাক, ভাষা-বাংলা, অবসরপ্রাপ্ত শিক্ষক, পরনে ছাই রং-খদ্দরের পাঞ্জাবী ও ধুতি। গত 27-2-07 হইতে নিখোঁজ। সন্ধান জানাবার ঠিকানা-শ্রীমতি অমলা মণ্ডল, গ্রাম + পোঃ-

[*BARTAMAN*

KOLKATA, Wednesday, 7th March, 2007

MISSING

• Nishikanta Mandal

The above photograph is of my husband, aged 72 years/5263, complexion dark, lean and thin, bald-headed, mother tongue Bengali, retired teacher, wearing ash coloured Khaddar Punjabi and Dhoti. Missing since 27/02/2007. Contact address Amala Mandal, vill + P.O…]

ব্যক্তিগত

নিরুদ্দেশ

•শ্রী নিশিকান্ত মণ্ডল

নিশিকান্ত মণ্ডল সল্ট লেকের ময়ূখ ভবনের পাশের চায়ের দোকান থেকে 27.2.07 থেকে নিখোঁজ বয়স 72/5'6" রং কালো চেহারা পাতলা পরণে খদ্দরের পাঞ্জাবী ও ধুতি মাথায় টাক সাথে ব্যাঙ্কের বই আছে সঠিক সন্ধানদাতাকে সম্মানিত করা হবে। ঠিকানা: গ্রাম+পোঃ আকন্দকেশরী রাজারহাট নিউ টাউন কলিকাতা-135 ফোন: 9836041376/ 03216-272821.

08905/07(39)

[*BARTAMAN*

KOLKATA, Friday, 16th March, 2007

PERSONAL

MISSING

• Nishikanta Mandal

Nishikanta Mandal is missing from the tea-stall beside Mayukh Bhawan, Salt Lake since 27.2.07, aged 72 years/5263, complexion dark, lean and thin, wearing Khaddar Punjabi and Dhoti, bald-headed, carrying bank pass book. Person providing correct information will be duly rewarded. Address: Vill + P.O. Akanda Kesari, Rajarhat, New Town, Kolkata-135 ph…].

SAMAR BANERJEE
BCE., LLB,MIS,FIE,FIV
CHARTERED ENGINEER
VALUER & LOSS ASSESSOR & ADVOCATE
HIGH COURT, CITY CIVIL COURT,
ALIPORE COURT etc.

Presidency Small Cause Court
Bar Association, 4th Floor,
2 &3 K.S. Roy Road,
Kolkata – 700001
Phone 2248-2627,
2242-6190
Resi : 144/39, Dharmatala Road,
Salkia, Howrah 711106
Phone 2655-6325/9231638147/9830990983
Email : banerjee.samar@rediffmail.com

In the matter of :

Survey, assess and ascertainment of the extent and quantum of damage, suffered by the Nishikanta Mondal, Proprietor of Nishi Kanta Brick Field due to the malicious acquisition proceedings adopted on his brick field lying and situated at village & P.O. Akandakeshari comprising of Dag No. 363 (P), 381 (P) and 383 (P), J.L. No. 55, Khatian No. 253, Mouza – Akandakeshari, District – 24 Parganas (N) under the L.A. Act I of 1894 for the alleged installation of 220 KV Power station for supply of electricity to New Town for the development and ancillary to Rajarhat, New Town Project Area by the L.A. Collector, North 24 Parganas, Barasat at the instance of WBHIDCO, a Govt. of West Bengal undertaking.

REPORT

SAMAR BANERJEE VALUER

SAMAR BANERJEE
BCE., LLB,MIS,FIE,FIV
CHARTERED ENGINEER
VALUER & LOSS ASSESSOR & ADVOCATE
HIGH COURT, CITY CIVIL COURT,
ALIPORE COURT etc.

NISHIKANTA BRICK FIELD

Vill + P.O. – Akandakeshori, P.S.- New Town,
Dist.- North 24 Parganas, Kolkata – 700135

0.11.2. STRUCTURES VALUE OF NISHIKANTA BRICK FIELD

Sl. No.	Description	Qty	Unit	Rate	Amount (Rs.)
1.	Continuous working Hoffman's type Kiln made of 20" thick high quality fire bricks as well as burnt bricks, flue lines, guard wall 20" thick with 100 ft high Central Chimney made of bricks, and intermediate RCC Rims having 26 segments with fire controlling dampers etc. Area about- 22,243 sft- 303'-4" x 73'-4" x 14'-0" (Belowg G.L.) & 303'-4" x 73'-4" x 4'-6" (Above G.L.)	1 No.	L.S.	-	4217000/-
2.	Ranigunge Tile Shed Labour quarters made of 5" thick brick walls with 10" x 10" intermediate brick pillars, IPS floor, Cheap type wooden doors and windows, bamboo frame roof supporting structure etc. Av. Height- 10 ft; 14'-0" x 8'-6" x 130 Nos = 15,470 sft	15470	Sft	150/-	2320500/-
3.	1. Office Room: Specifications same as as in Sl. No 2 except Av. Height – 12 ft 15'-0" x 10'-0"x3 Nos = 450 sft	450	Sft	160/-	72000/-
4.	Toilet Block for labourers – specifications same as	480	Sft	140	67200/-

	Sl. No.2; Ht. – 10 ft.; 40'-0"x12'-0"= 480 sft.				
5.	-Do- for office 8'0"x6'-0" = 48 sft. (Superior construction)	48 sft.	Sft.	180/-	8,640/-
6.	5" thick masonry made boundary wall with intermediate 10"x10" brick pillars bonded with Cement and sand mortar. Height – 6 ft. Length – 1300 ft.	800 ft.	Rft.	220/-	1,76,000/-
				Price Cost	68,61,340/-
				Depreciation @ 30% (-)	20,58,402/-
				Therefore, depreciated value of structures	48,02,938/-

0.11.3 **TOOLS AND APPLIANCES :**

Sl. No.	Description	Qty.	Unit	Amount (Rs.)
1.	Pug Mill	4 Nos.	@ 6000/- each	24,000/-
2.	Hand Trolly	16 Nos.	@ 2000/- each	32,000/-
3.	Moulds	200 Nos.	@150/- each	30,000/-
4.	Wheel Barrow	20 Nos.	@ 1500/- each	30,000/-
5.	5 H. Power Diesel driven, Water pump set.	3 Nos.	@ 10000/- each	30,000/-
6.	Medium Dug 4" dia. Tube well	3 Nos.	@ 5000/- each	15,000/-
7.	M.S. Made Coal Drum	4 Nos.	@ 300/- each	1,200/-
8.	M.S. Bucket – medium sized	110 Nos.	@ 100/- each	11,000/-
9.	Spade	48 Nos.	@ 50/- each	2,400/-
10.	Shovel	25Nos.	@ 80/- each	2,000/-
11.	Axe	6 Nos.	@ 90/- each	540/-
12.	Basket cane woven	50 Nos.	@ 20/- each	1,000/-
13.	M.S. Poker, Damper extra, Hurricane etc.	-	L.S.	8,000/-
14.	**Office Furniture :**			

	i) Wooden Cot	3 Nos.	@ 800/- each	2400/-
	ii) Wooden Bench	3 Nos.	@ 300/- each	900/-
	iii) Wooden Chair	2 Nos.	@ 200/- each	400/-
	iv) Wooden Table	2 Nos.	@ 400/- each	800/-
			Total Rs.	191640/-

0.11.4 **TREES**

	i) Neem, Coconut, Mango, Jackfruit and Shiricer Trees etc.	80 Nos.	@ 600/- each	48000/-
	ii) Earthy tubs for plants	30 Nos.	@ 20/- each	600/-
			Total Rs.	48600/-

0.11.5 **RAW MATERIALS** : (As per Book)

i) Silver sand 100 lorry cft. @ Rs.1800/- per lorry Rs. 1,80,000/-
ii) Cut Soil 725 lorry @ Rs.800/- per lorry Rs. 5,80,000/-
iii) Mixed Soil (Dhuse) 100 lorry @ Rs.1000/- Rs. 1,00,0007/-
Rs. 8,60,0007/-

0.11.6 **SEMI-FINISHED BRICKS:** (As per Book)

2,30,000 Nos. @ Rs.1,500/-per thousand % Rs. 3,45,000/-

0.11.7 **FINISHED BRICKS:** (As per Bock)

8,00,000 Nos. @ Rs.2,500/- per thousand % Rs. 20,00,0007/-
Rs. 23,45,0007/-

Therefore, sum total depreciated value of structures, tool & appliances, office furniture, thus raw materials, etc.

Rs.(48.02,938/- + 1,91,6407/- + 48,6007/- + 8,60,000/- + 23,45,000/-) = Rs. 82,48,178/- (Rupees Eighty two lacs forty eight thousand one hundred seventy eight) only as on the year 2005.

0.12 **DAMAGE ASSESSMENT** :

This sudden, unexpected purported feat of acquisition as an inevitable result brought in its tally the following economic hazards and hardships,. viz.:-

i) Loss due to infructuous payment of ground rent @ Rs.10,000/- per Bigha per year from the period 03.09.05 to 03.06.06 i.e. for 9 months or 0.75 year in regard to leasehold land taken for this purpose in and around his own land. Dag Nos. of said leasehold lands are 364, 372, 373, 374 and 385 measuring more or less 7 (B) or 140 (K) which acted as incidental and supplemental to Brick manufacturing process.

Therefore, loss suffered on this count = Rs.10,000/- x7(B)x0.75 = Rs.52,500/- (Rupees fifty two thousand and five hundred) only as on the martial year 2005.

ii) Loan taken from the various Banks and private financiers & invested in improvement and in production growth as well as for the augmentation of business became dead/or close/ended due to this sudden, unforeseen, unpredicted, forceful, rule-less acquisition proceedings.

Loan taken from the banks (as reported)	Rs.30,00,000/-
Loan taken from private financiers	Rs.15,00,000/-
Total :	Rs.45,00,000/-

iii. Permanent loss of business as well as recurring monthly earning.

Taking modest earning @ Rs.5,000.00 P.M.

Therefore, yearly earning Rs.60,000/-

Therefore, capitalized value of the said earning taking @ 8% yield P.A. or 12.5 Y.P.

Therefore, Loss = Rs.60,000/- x 12.5 = Rs.7,50,000/-

iv) **Payment of labour compensation** :

Taking average payment of Rs.2,000/- for 6 months for 100 labourers.

= Rs.2,000/- x 6 x 100 = Rs.12,00,000/-

Therefore, loss/damage due to consequential severance of land = Rs.(52,500/- + 45,00,000/- + 7,50,000/- + 12,00,000/-) = Rs.65,02,500/- (Rupees sixty five lakhs two thousand and five hundred) only as on the material year 2005 – 2006.

The report is issued without prejudice.

SAMAR BANERJEE VALUER

26/12/06

SAMAR BANERJEE
BCE., LLB,MIS,FIE,FIV
CHARTERED ENGINEER
VALUER & LOSS ASSESSOR & ADVOCATE
HIGH COURT, CITY CIVIL COURT,
ALIPORE COURT etc.

NOTICE

LA Case : LA-4/159 of 04-05/NTP

In respect of acquisition of your land on the following Plot Nos. of mouza AKANDAKESARI J.L.No : 55 P.S.: RAJARHAT District :North 24 Parganas the verification of ownership is necessary.

You are requested to appear before the competent officer along with all relevant documents, regd. deeds, copy of records of right etc. on 19/07/2007 at 11.30A.M in office of the MAYUKH, GROUND FLOOR, SALT LAKE, KOLKATA - 700 091

LAND SCHEDULE

Mouza : AKANDAKESARI J.L.No(s) : 55
P.S. : RAJARHAT District : North 24 Parganas

Revisional settlement Plot Nos. in full :

383

Revisional settlement in part : NIL

Place :
Date :

Sd/-
Collector
Under Act-I of 1894

Copy forwarded for information and necessary action to :

NISHIKANTA MONDAL S/o NANI MONDAL
AKANDAKESARI

owner/occupier of the plot(s) mentioned above.

Place :
Date :

Collector
Under Act-I of 1894

NISHIKANTA BRICK FIELD

Vill + P.O. – Akandakeshori, P.S.- New Town,
Dist.- North 24 Parganas, Kolkata – 700135
PH-9836341598

Ref. No. ....

Date : 7-12-2011

To
The Addl General Manager (Admn)
West Bengal Housing Infrastructure Development Corporation Ltd.
HIDCO BHABAN
Kolkata – 700156

W.B. Housing Infrastructure Dev. Corpn. Ltd.
HIDCO BHABAN, 35-1111, M.A.R.
New Town, Kolkata-700 156
07 DEC 2011
RECEIVED
CONTENTS NOT VERIFIED

Kind Attention: **Mr. Krishnendu Basak** WBCS (EXE)

Sub: Total outstanding loan / or debt from private parties etc.

Sir,

Please note that total outstanding loan / or debt from standing now in our firms name is as under:-

1. **Private Loan of Nishikanta Brick Field (Due)**	**Rs.**	**16,16,000**
2. **Brick Loan of Nishikanta Brick Field (Due)**	**Rs.**	**10,78,270**
3. **Labour contractor payment due of Nishikanta Brick Field (Due)**	**Rs.**	**3,87,315**
4. **Fuel of Nishikanta Brick Field (Due)**	**Rs.**	**1,25,981**
5. **Manager / Munshi of Nishikanta Brick Field (Due)**	**Rs.**	**95,919**
6. **Tools & appliances of Nishikanta Brick Field (Due)**	**Rs.**	**95,919**
7. **Fireman of Nishikanta Brick Field (Due)**	**Rs.**	**1,02,570**
8. **Soil & sand of Nishikanta Brick Field (Due)**	**Rs.**	**22,400**
9. **Coal purchased by Nishikanta Brick Field (Due)**	**Rs.**	**1,21,100**
Total (Due)	**Rs.**	**8,63,000.00**
	Rs.	**44,12,555.00**

Rupees Forty four lacs twelve thousand five hundred fifty five only.

A comprehensive claim for the structural damages Rs. 8248178.00 and additional claim for damage assessment Rs. 6502500.00, Total: (Rs. 8248178.00 + Rs. 6502500.00) = **Rs. 1,47,50,678.00** (As per valuation Report)

Rupees **One crore forty seven lacs fifty thousand six hundred seventy eight** only.

In the above circumstances, I would humbly request to your honour to look into the matter radically and reasonably enough and the pass and order the "Award" along with all damages in connection with by said Brick Field in accordance with law.

Thanking you.

Yours faithfully,

Nandita Mondal

Enclosure: As above

To
The Panchayet Prodhan
Patharghata Gram Panchayet
Patharghata

তারিখ : ২৫-১১-২০১১

বিষয় :- ১) মৌজা ভগবানপুর, জে. এল. নং ১০, খতিয়ান নং ৯৬৮/১, দাগ নং ৮৬৫/১১১৪, জমির পরিমান ১ ১/২ কাঠা।
২) মৌজা আকন্দকেশরী, জে. এল. নং ৫৫, খতিয়ান নং ২৫৩, দাগ নং ৩৮১, জমির পরিমান, ৭ কাঠা, এবং দাগ নং ৩৬৩, জমির পরিমান ৩ কাঠা। মোট আনুমানিক ১১ ১/২ কাঠা জমি। উক্ত জমির উপর দিয়ে বিদ্যুৎ এর হাই পাওয়ারের পোষ্ট ও তারের লাইন যাওয়াতে জমির বর্তমান মুল্যে ক্ষতিপূরণের দাবী।

মহাশয়,

বিনীত নিবেদন আমাদের তিনটি জমির উপর দিয়ে হিডকো বিদ্যুতের হাই পাওয়ারের পোষ্ট ও তারের লাইন নিয়ে যাওয়াতে আনুমানিক ১১ ১/২ কাঠা জমি সম্পূর্ণ ক্ষতিগ্রস্থ হয়েছে। হিডকো-কে লিখিত ভাবে জানানো হয়েছে কিন্তু আজও কোন সমাধান হয়নি। হিডকো মৌখিক ভাবে প্রস্তাব দেন যে পঞ্চায়েতের মাধ্যমে জানালে আমরা ক্ষতিপূরণ দেব। অন্যান্য ব্যক্তিরা ক্ষতিপূরণ পেয়েছে, কিন্তু আমরা পায়নি।

অতএব মহাশয়ের নিকট বিনীত অনুরোধ, আপনি সরোজমিনে তদন্ত করিয়া পাওয়ার হাউসের তারের লাইন যাওয়াতে উক্ত জমি গুলির বর্তমান মূল্য বা ক্ষতি পূরণ ধার্য্য করিয়া হিডকো-কে জানিয়ে উক্ত ধার্য্যমূল্য যথা শীঘ্র পরিশোধের ব্যবস্থা করিলে বিশেষ ভাবে কৃতজ্ঞ থাকিব।

ইতি-

বিনীত -

১। শ্রীমতী অমলা মন্ডল, স্বামী নিশিকান্ত মন্ডল (নিরুদ্দেশ)
২। গোবিন্দ চন্দ্র মন্ডল, পিতা ঐ
৩। কৃষ্ণা মন্ডল, পিতা ঐ
৪। অশোক মন্ডল, পিতা ঐ
৫। অলোক মন্ডল, পিতা ঐ
৬। অসিত মন্ডল, পিতা ঐ

অনুলিপি :- মাননীয়া জাহানারা বিবি
সভাপতি, রাজারহাট পঞ্চায়েত সমিতি

Received
5/12/11
Prodhan
PATHARGHATA G.P.
North 24 Parganas

Received
05/12/11

[To
Panchayat Pradhan
….. Date: 25-11-2011

Subject: (1) *Mouja* Bhagabanpur, J.L. No. 10 Khatiyan No. 968/1, dag No. 865/1114, 1½ cottah land.

(2) *Mouja* Akanda Kesari, J.L. No 55, Khatiyan No. 253, dag No. 381, 7 cottah of land and dag No. 363,3 cottah of land. Total about 11½ cottah of land. Because of installing high tension Electricity wiring and post over the said land the claim of compensation for the damage at current rate of land.

Sir,

Humble submission is that because of installation of high tension electricity wiring and post about 11½ cottah of our land got damaged totally. The matter was informed to HIDCO in writing but in vain. It was communicated verbally from the part of HIDCO that if the claim is endorsed through Panchayat they would pay compensation. Other sufferers received their compensation but we did not. Therefore, our earnest request to you, Sir, after necessary inspection and fixing of compensation, please inform that to HIDCO and arrange us to get the compensation. We will be obliged to you.

Yours sincerely
Amala Mandal, w/o Nishikanta Mandal (Missing),
Gobinda Chandra Mandal, s/o Nishikanta Mandal,
Krishna Mandal, d/o Nishikanta Mandal,
Ashok Mandal, s/o Nishikanta Mandal,
Alok Mandal, s/o Nishikanta Mandal,
Asit Mandal, s/o Nishikanta Mandal].

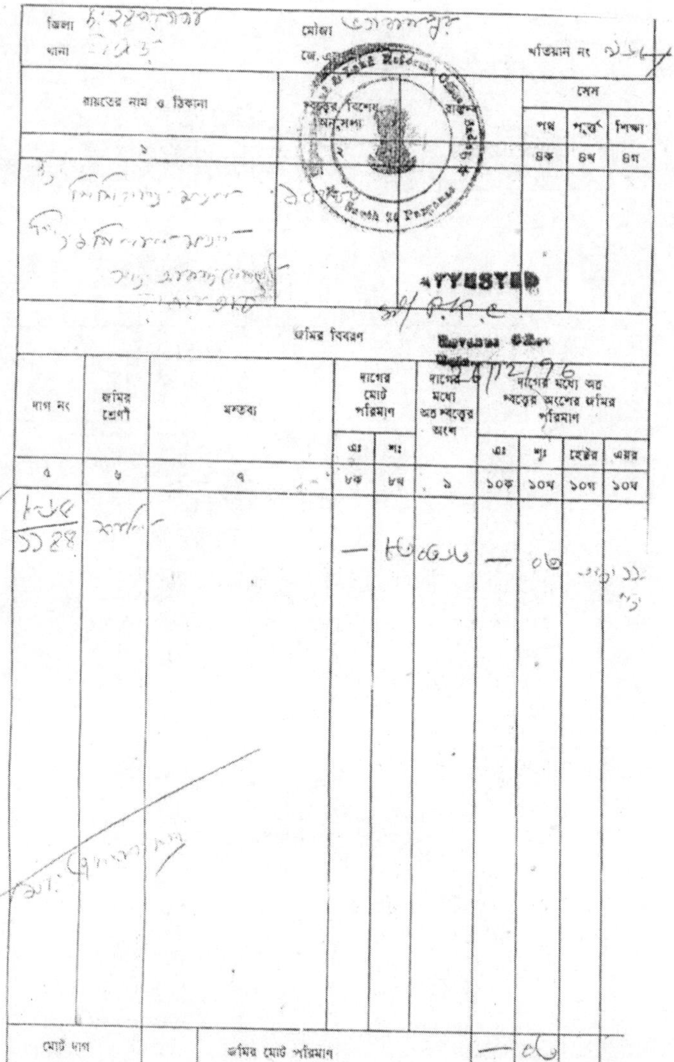

[Distt. South 24 Pargana, P.S. Bhangar *Mouja* Bhagabanpur, Khatiyan No. 968.

Name and Address of Rayat Nishikanta Mandal

Akanda Kesari

Dag no. 865/1144, Class of land: Sali].

উত্তর ২৪-পরগনা — খতিয়ান নং — ২৫২/২ — [১৫০৭০৫৫]

আকন্দ কেশরী — জে.এল.নং — ৫৫ — থানা — রাজারহাট

০.০০ টাকা

জমির মোট পরিমাণ — ৩.০২ একর (৩) মোট দাগের সংখ্যা — ৫৩

(৪) স্বত্বদের দখলকারের বিবরণ — (৫) স্বত্ব — (৬) মন্তব্য

নাম	নিশিকান্ত মণ্ডল	রায়ত	
পিতা/স্বামী	**** নন্দী মণ্ডল		
ঠিকানা	পশ্চিমপাড়া		

৭) অত্রস্বত্বে নিজ দখলীয় জমি ঃ

দাগ নম্বর	জমির শ্রেণী		দাগের মোট পরিমাণ	দাগের মধ্যে অত্র স্বত্বের	দাগের মধ্যে অত্র-স্বত্বের জমির অংশের পরিমাণ	
			একর	অংশ	একর	হেক্টর
২৫১	শালি			০.৩৯	০.০৬৮৭	০.০২
২৯২	বাস্তু			০.৫১	০.১১১১	০.০৬
২৯৭	শালি			০.৫২	০.১১১১	০.০৬
৩০১	শালি			০.১৮	০.২৫০০	০.০৪
৩৬৩	শালি			[illegible]	০.২০৭৩	০.১২
৩৮৩	ডাঙ্গা			২.৩০	০.০৬৮১	০.২১
৪২১	শালি			০.৬২	০.১১১১	০.০৭
৪৩০	শালি			০.৫২	০.০৯২৪	০.০৫
৪৩১	শালি			০.২৭	০.২৫০০	০.০৭
৪৩৫	শালি			০.০২	০.১১১১	০.০০
৪৩৬	শালি			০.০৪	০.২৫০০	০.০১
৪৪২	শালি			০.২২	০.১১১১	০.০২
৪৪৩	শালি			০.২২	০.০৫৫৬	০.০১
৪৫২	শালি			০.৬৮	০.০৭৮৬	০.০৬
৪৫৩	শালি			০.৩৫	০.১৬৬৭	০.০৬
৪৫৫	শালি			০.৪০	০.০১০৮	০.০১
৪৬০	শালি			০.৫৭	০.১৬৬৬	০.০৯

INDIA TEN RUPEES

দাগের মোট সংখ্যা — ৪(৪)ধারার বিরুদ্ধে নং

C.Copy-11240 — ২ / ৫ — 14/10/200

NAME:	NISHIKANTA MONDAL
S/o :	LATE NANI LAL MONDAL
VILL+PO:-	AKANDAKESHARI.
PS : -	RAJAR HAT NEWTOWN.
MOUZA:-	BHAGABANPUR.
JL NO.	10
KHATAN	968/1
DAG NO:	865/1188

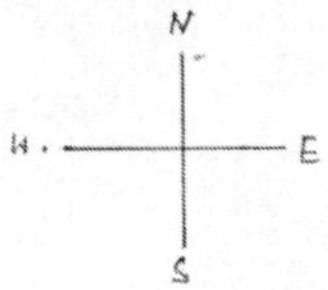

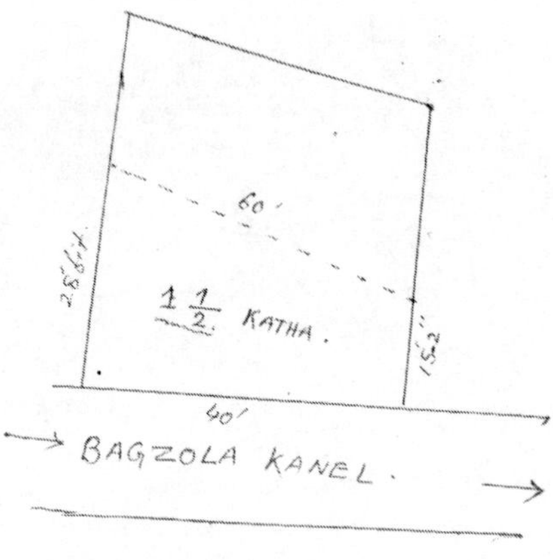

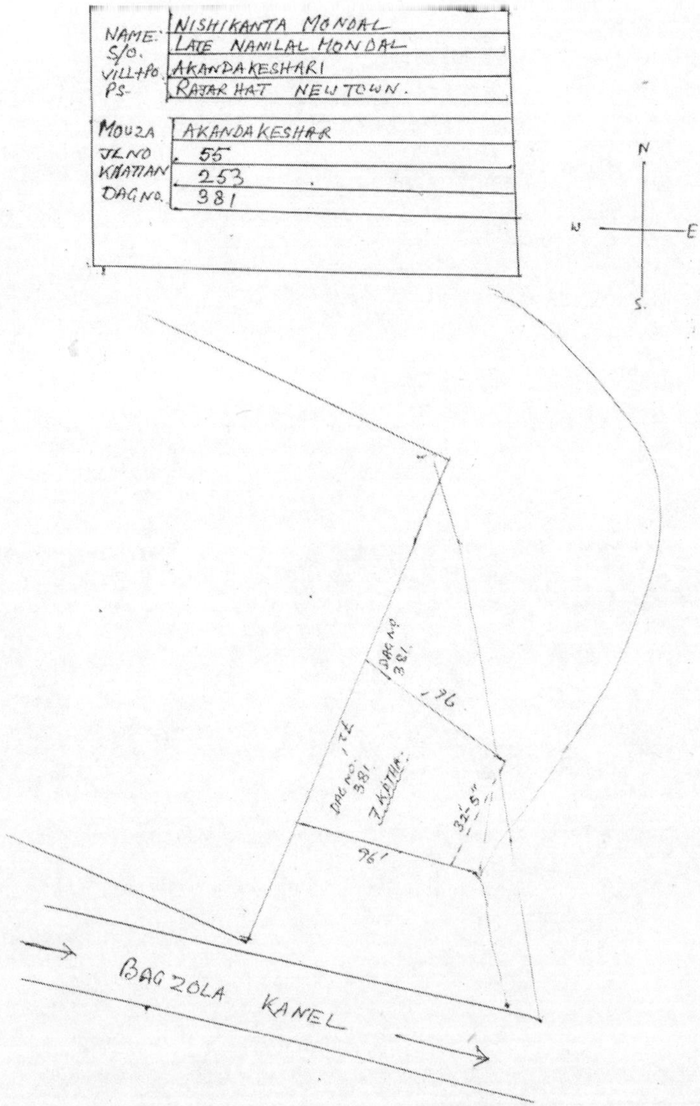
NAME: NISHIKANTA MONDAL
S/O. LATE NANILAL MONDAL
VILL+PO. AKANDAKESHARI
PS- RAJAR HAT NEWTOWN.
MOUZA AKANDAKESHAR
JL NO 55
KHATIAN 253
DAG NO. 381
N
W
E
S.
DAG NO. 381
96
DAG NO. 381
7 KATHA.
32'-5"
96'
BAGZOLA KANEL

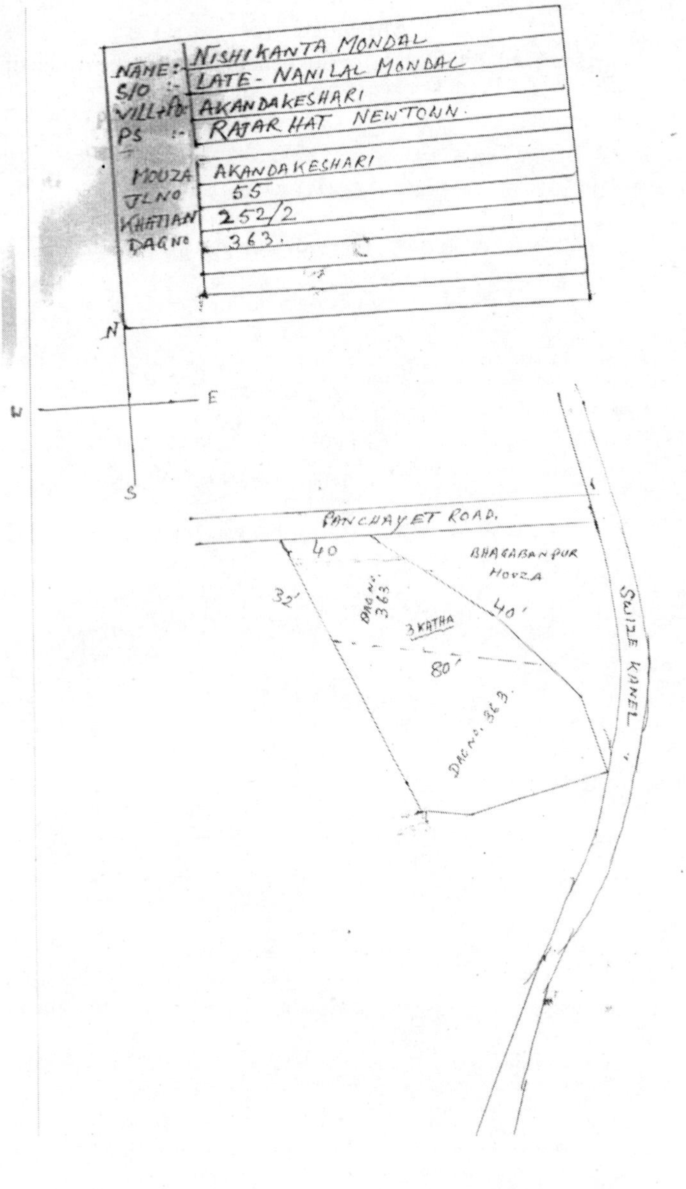
NAME: NISHIKANTA MONDAL
S/O :- LATE- NANILAL MONDAL
VILL+PO AKANDAKESHARI
PS :- RAJAR HAT NEWTOWN.
MOUZA AKANDAKESHARI
JLNO 55
KHATIAN 252/2
DAG NO 363.
N
W
E
S
PANCHAYET ROAD.
40
32'
DAG NO. 363
3 KATHA
40'
80'
BHAGABANPUR MOUZA
DAG NO. 363
SWIZE KANEL

Appendix – 13

Papers related to the case of i Sukhendu Mandal (see Addendum)

DISTRICT : NORTH 24 PARGANAS

IN THE HIGH COURT AT CALCUTTA

CONSTITUTIONAL WRIT JURISDICTION

APPELLATE SIDE

W.P No. 19676 (W) of 2011

AND

IN THE MATTER OF;

Jagannath Mondal & Anr.

.... Petitioners

-Versus-

The State of West Bengal & Ors.

.... Respondents

SUPPLEMENTARY AFFIDAVIT ON BEHALF OF THE PETITIONERS

I, Sukhendu Mondal, son of Sri Rakhal Mondal, aged about 39 years, by faith - Hindu, by occup[ation - Business, residing at - Canning, P.O. - Canning Town, P.S. - canning, District - South 24 Parganas do hereby solemnly affirmed and say as follows :-

2

1. That I am the son of petitioner No. 2 of the instant Writ Petition and have been duly authorized by petitioner No. 1 and petitioner No.2 to affirm this affidavit and as I am well acquainted with the facts and circumstances of the case and competent to affirm this affidavit.

2. That after due inspection and obtaining the photocopies of the original documents if is necessary to submit those documents before the Hon'ble Court thoroughly filling of supplementary affidavit before This Hon'ble Court for proper adjudication of the case.

3. That pursuant to the direction of this Hon'ble Court on 25.04.2013, The Ld. Advocate along with me had inspected the original records on 13.05.2013 at about 3.30 to 04.30 in the afternoon and having receipt the photocopies of those documents, the deponent has been advised to make this supplementary affidavit challenging the entries including the interpolated entries as follows. :-

i) At page No. 1 purported to be C.S. & R.S. Record of Right, Sk. Habibullah's name has been written subsequently although Government forgets to write his share because lands belonged to Laskar family. This is an interpolation. One Record of Right can not be C.S. & R.S. as there is a gap ranging from 1922 to 1956. Petitioner reserves their right to make suitable submission at the time of hearing.

ii) At page No. 2 purported to be C.S. & R.S. Record of Right by hand written interpolation recording of 'Beel' has been totally deleted and in its place 'Shali' has been written totally changing the nature and character of the property. Petitioner reserves their right to make suitable submission at the time of hearing.

iii) At page 3 depicted as L.R. Record of Right wherein name of Ranjit Roy depicting him as illegal occupier (Bina Anumati) putting the land in khatian No. 1, i.e. vested khatian. Petitioner reserves their right to make suitable submission at the time of hearing.

iv) It appears that in 5A proceedings 1st date 23.09.1968 and 2nd dated 05.05.1983 the land belonging to Habibullah was not mentioned whether retain or vested nor does it reflect name of petitioners then wherefrom the land is attributed to be vested. In the vesting schedule my plot namely C.S. Dag 1494 corresponding to R.S. Dag 1614 did not appear under the vesting schedule. Therefore the fact that the land is never vested squarely applies. Petitioner reserves their right to make suitable submission at the time of hearing.

The true copy of the documents collected from the Ld. Advocate for the State is annexed herewith and marked with the letter "X" collectively.

4. That your deponent submits unless His Lordship allow this supplementary affidavit is the part of the original

application Your petitioners will suffer irreparable loss and injuries for.

5. That the statements made in paragraphs 1 to 2 are true to my knowledge and belief and the rest is my respectful submission before this Hon'ble Court.

Prepared in my office DEPONENT

Advocate

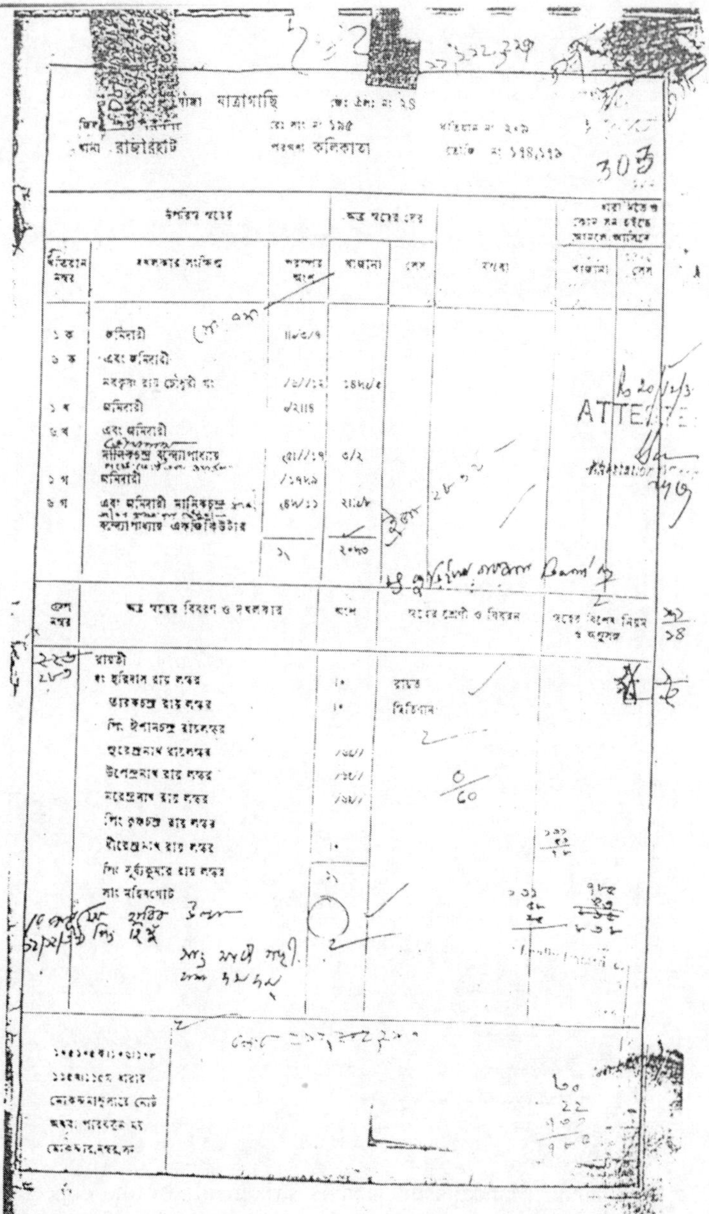
মৌজা দমদমগাছি
থানা রাজারহাট
পরগনা কলিকাতা

খতিয়ান নম্বর	দখলকার সংক্ষিপ্ত	অংশ	খাজানা	সেস
১ ক	জমিদারী			
১ ক	এবং জমিদারী			
			১৪৸৶৫	
১ খ	জমিদারী			
১ খ	এবং জমিদারী			
			৩/২	
১ গ	জমিদারী			
১ গ	এবং জমিদারী			
		১৲	২০৸৹	

স্বত্ব দখলের বিবরণ ও দখলকার

রায়তী
রায় লস্কর
রায় লস্কর
শিং ঈশানচন্দ্র রায়লস্কর
সুরেন্দ্রনাথ রায়লস্কর
উপেন্দ্রনাথ রায় লস্কর
নরেন্দ্রনাথ রায় লস্কর
শিং রায় লস্কর
রায় লস্কর
রায় লস্কর

ATTESTED

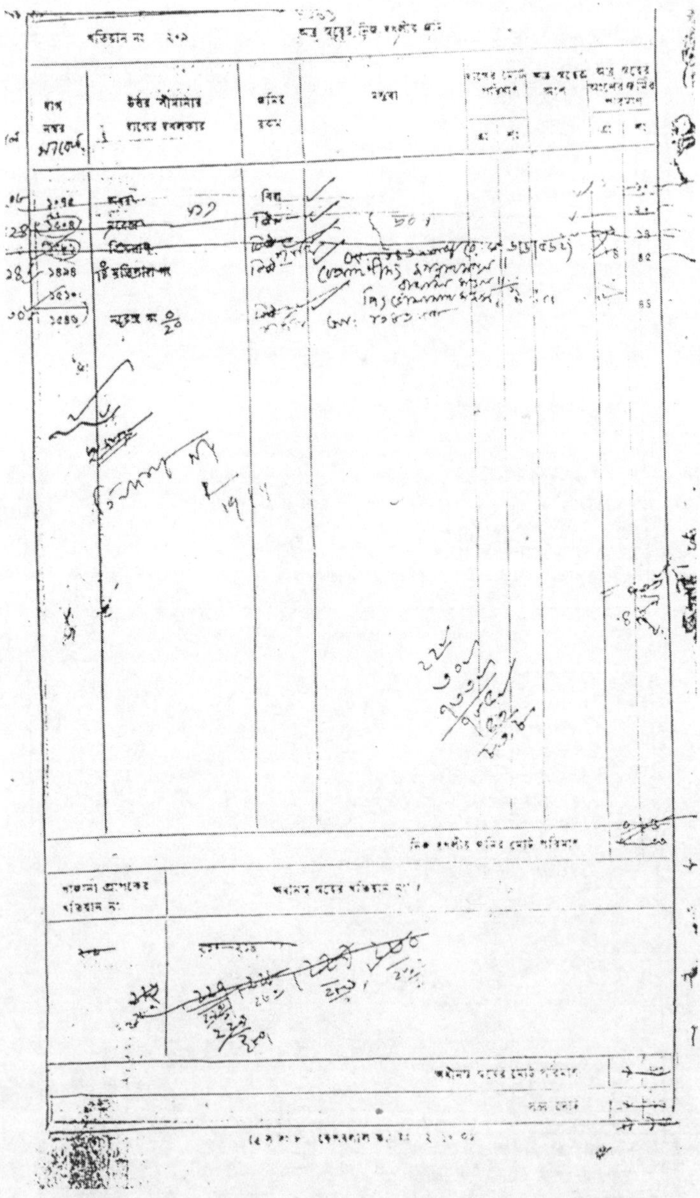

[Sukhendu Mandal's bil land is striken off by the concerned office without his knowledge (Row-3 from above)]

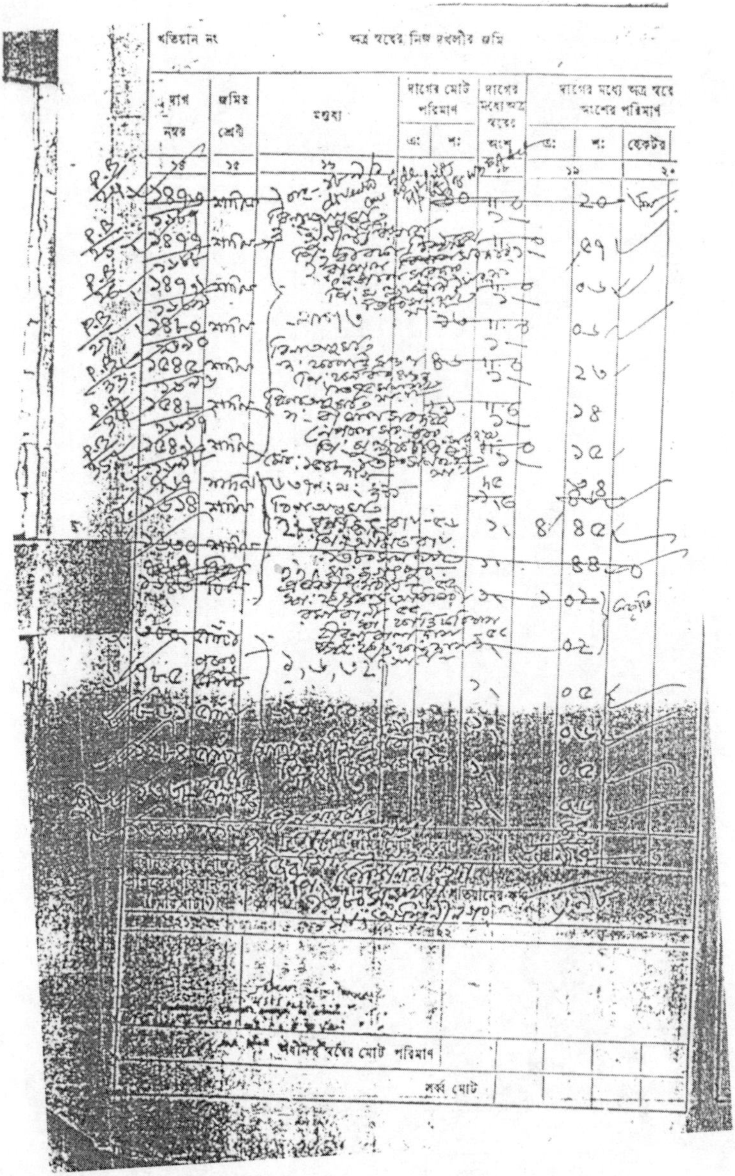

খতিয়ান নং

অন্য স্বত্বের নিজ দখলীয় জমি

দাগ নম্বর	জমির শ্রেণী	মন্তব্য	দাগের মোট পরিমাণ		দাগের মধ্যে অন্য স্বত্বের অংশ	দাগের মধ্যে অন্য স্বত্বের অংশের পরিমাণ		
			এ:	শ:	অংশ	এ:	শ:	হেক্টর

অধীনস্থ স্বত্বের মোট পরিমাণ

সর্ব্ব মোট

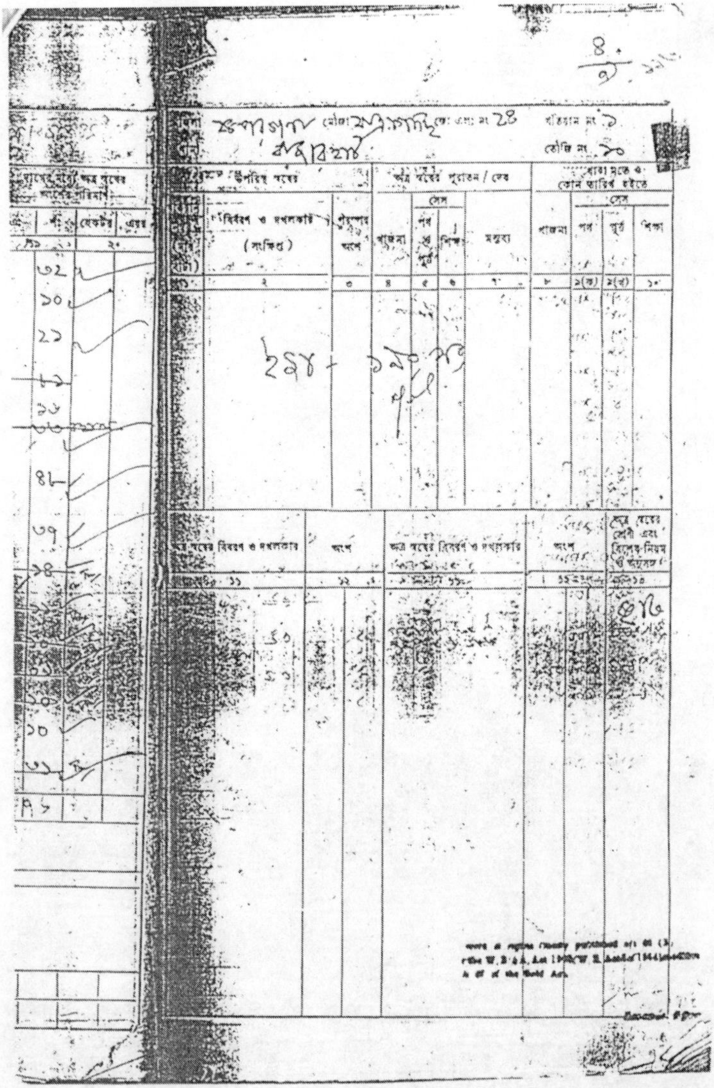

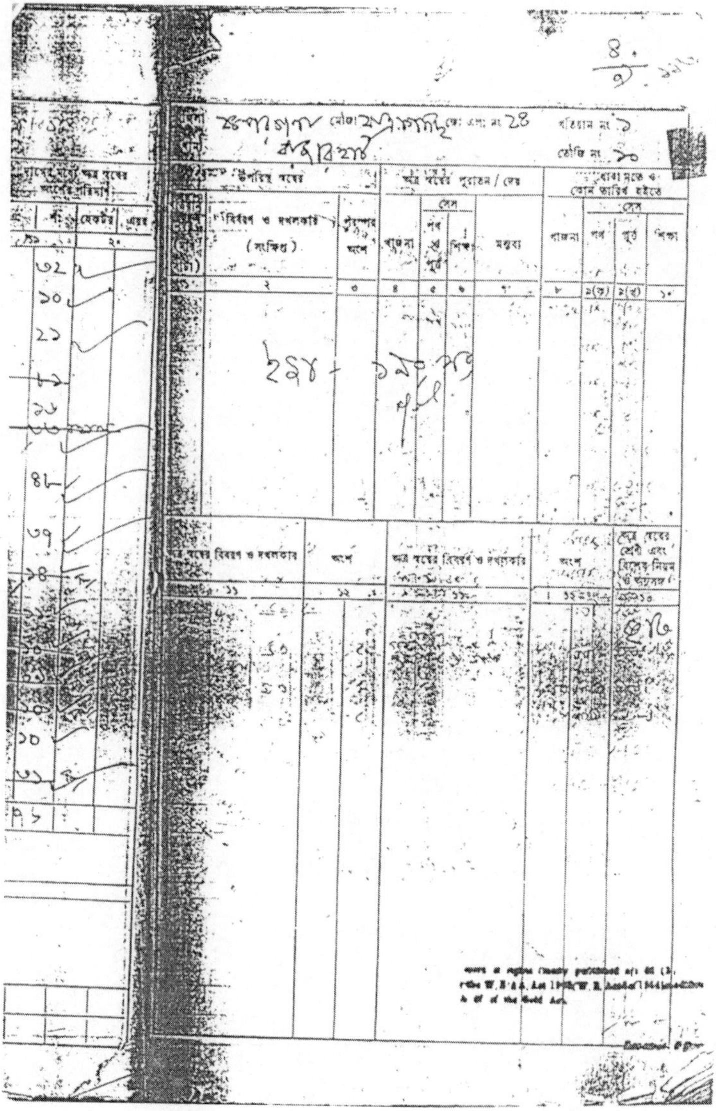

জে. এল. নং ২৪ খতিয়ান নং ৭

তৌজি নং ১০

বিবরণ ও দখলকার (সংক্ষিপ্ত)	অংশ	খাজনা	মন্তব্য	খাজনা
২	৩	৪	৭	৮

ORDER SHEET

(Rule-129 of the Records Manual, 191[illegible])

Order Sheet, dated from [illegible] to [illegible]

District 24-Parganas No. 8 of 1968

Nature of the case Proceedings u/s 6(5) read with [illegible] 47 of the [illegible] Act

Serial number and date of Order	Order and signature of Officer	Note of action taken on Order
1 / 15/5/68	Whereas it appears from the finally published record of rights that Shri S.K. [illegible] of [illegible] [illegible] [illegible] J.L. No. 23 etc. P.S. Rajarhat, Dist. 24-Parganas possessed khas lands above the prescribed ceiling u/s 6 of the West Bengal Estates Acquisition Act, 1953 (Act 1 of 1954) after 1st Baisakh, 1362 B.S. and, Whereas, it is necessary for me to [illegible] what lands Shri S.K. Habibullah [illegible] as admissible u/s 6(1) of the West Bengal Estates Acquisition Act, 1953. It is therefore ordered that [illegible] of the E.A. Act may be served on Shri S.K. Habibullah calling him to appear and to submit statement of lands he had in his khas possession [illegible] on the date of vesting. Sd/Illegible R.O.	
2 / 24.5.68	Notice duly served. Return filed with records. Sd/Illegible R.O.	
[illegible] / 30.5.68	Shri Fakiruddin appears and prays for 15 days time. Time allowed. He should [illegible] [illegible] 10. 6-68. Sd/Illegible R.O.	
6 / 10.6.68	Return is submitted [illegible] verify with R.O.R. & put up after complete [illegible] of S.A. [illegible]. Sd/Illegible R.O.	
5.9.68	Issue notice fixing date of hearing [illegible]. Sd/Illegible R.O.	
	Notice duly served and Return filed with records. Sd/Illegible	
12.9.68	[illegible] of S.A. Cases have not yet been completed. Shri Fakiruddin appears on behalf of his father. Date of hearing is fixed	

P.T.O.

... and date of Order	Order and signature of Officer	Note of action taken
	on 23/9/68. No further notice will be issued.	Sd/ Sk. [illegible]
23.9.68	Shri Fakiruddin appear on behalf of his father Shri Sk. Habibullah. It appears from the schedule of lands which is made part of the proceeding that Shri Sk Habibulla, is the possesses of 18.85 acres of agricultural and 6.32 acres of non agricultural land. All these lands have been recorded in his name in Mouza [illegible] (No. [illegible]) and [illegible] No 24. Apart from these land, he is in possession of 10.7[illegible] acres of non-agricultural land including home-stead land in mouza [illegible] No 20. P.S. [illegible] as it appears from the statement submitted by the C.O., Camp II, Barrackpore. This statement is also made part of the proceedings. But, Shri Sk. Habibulla has transferred 141.36 acres of agricultural and 4.81 acres of non-agricultural land between 5.5.53 and the date of vesting and these transfer were declared to be bonafide proceedings u/s 5A. This amount of lands transferred within the prohibited period requires to be taken into account in arriving the ceiling of land which he is entitled to retain u/s 6(1)(c) of E.A. Act. As he has already transferred 141.36 acres of land, so he is not entitled to retain any agricultural land. So, ordered that 18.85 acres of agricultural land which are recorded in khas possession of Shri Sk Habibullah be vested to the State but he is allowed to retain the non agricultural land. Sd/ Illegible. i) open Khanda [illegible] if necessary ii) Inform the C.O. Barrackpore Camp No.II for n/a	Certified to be true copy Sd/ [illegible] 25/7/85

Page No. 2

West Bengal Form No. 270.

Page - 2

ORDER SHEET

(Rule 129 of the Records Manual, 1917)

Order Sheet, dated from to

District 24-Parganas No. 8 of 1968

Nature of the case

Serial number and date of Order	Order and signature of Officer	Note of action taken on Order
iii)	Inform the Charge officer-I for favour circulation to all camps.	
iv)	Send a list of the vested land to the J.L.R.O. after complying the order.	
	sd/[illegible]	
[illegible]	On scrutiny of C.R.O. it transpires that a total [illegible] of agricultural land, as detailed below stands recorded in the name of Sri [illegible]	
	[illegible]	
	Total . 2.21 acres	
	As per order dated 13.7.68 of the instant proceeding the raiyat is not entitled to retain any agricultural land. Therefore, the above said lands are made vested to the State. Send the list of vested land to the J.L.R.O. concerned with the request to take over possession and arrange distribution. [illegible]	

Copied by [illegible] Certified [illegible]

PRESIDENT'S SECRETARIAT
(PUBLIC-II SECTION)
RASHTRAPATI BHAVAN
NEW DELHI - 110004

Sl.No.: P2/D/0712120160 **Date: 07 Dec 2012**

Enclosed please find for appropriate attention a petition addressed to the President of India, which is self explanatory.

Action taken on the petition may please be communicated to the petitioner directly under intimation to this Secretariat.

(Chirabrata Sarkar)
Under Secretary

To,
The Chief Secretary
Government of West Bengal
Kolkata

Copy to:

Shri SUKHENDU MONDAL
VILL. SANJOY PALLY
PO AND PS CANNING
DIST. 24 PARGANAS (S)
WEST BENGAL-743322

You are further requested to liaise with the aforementioned addressee directly for further information in the matter.

(Chirabrata Sarkar)
Under Secretary

BOOK POST

Serial Number :-
P2/D/0712120160

ON INDIA GOVERNMENT SERVICE
TO,
Shri SUKHENDU MONDAL
VILL. SANJOY PALLY
PO AND PS CANNING
DIST. 24 PARGANAS (S),WEST BENGAL-743322

FROM :
President's Secretariat
Rashtrapati Bhavan
New Delhi - 110004.

You may use website http://helpline.rb.nic.in for submitting your request/grievance online.

17/4/13

Section Officer
Public-II Section
President's Secretariat
Rashtrapati Bha...

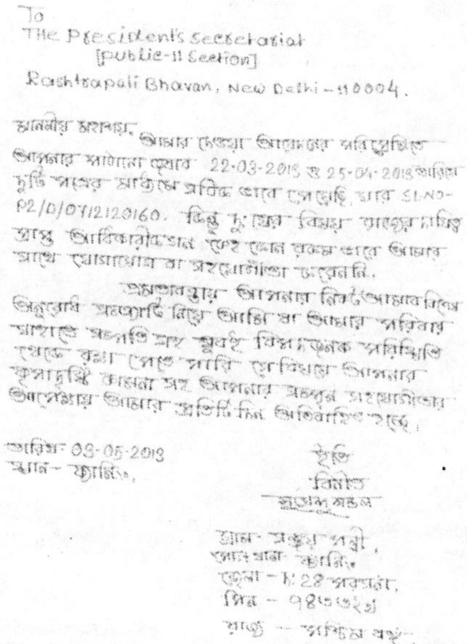
To
The President's Secretariat
[Public-II Section]
Rashtrapati Bhavan, New Delhi-110004.

[To,

The President's Secretariat
[Public-II Section]
Rashtrapati Bhawan, New Delhi-110004.

Respected Sir,

Your letter dated 22-03-2013 and 25-04-2013 with the SL. No. P2/D/0712120160 has been received by me. But unfortunately the concerned officers of the State Government did not co-operate with me.

Under such circumstances I appeal to you to relieve our family along with our property from this extremely distressful condition. We are spending each day looking for your mercy and co-operation.

Dated: 03-05-2013
Place- Canning

yours sincerely
sd/-
Sukhendu Mandal
Vill.- Sanjay Palli
P.O.+P.S. Canning
Dist. S.24 Parganas
PIN 743329
West Bengal]

GOVERNMENT OF WEST BENGAL
OFFICE OF THE ADDITIONAL DISTRICT MAGISTRATE &
DISTRICT LAND & LAND REFORMS OFFICER
NORTH 24 PARGANAS, BARASAT

No: L-15012(11)/14/2012-DL&LRO/39734 Dt: 26/11/2012

Notice U/S 19(1) of RTI Act, 2005 read with Rule 8 of WBRTI Rule 2006

Appeal Case No: 17 of 2012

APPELLANT	**RESPONDENT**
Sukhendu Mondal Vill-Sonjoy Pally, PO & PS: Canning Pin-743320	The Special L.A.O North 24 Parganas, Barasat

The above appellant and Respondent are hereby requested to attend the hearing at the chamber of the undersigned which has been fixed on .17.12.12 at.12 hr.with all relevant papers/documents.

Any default of appearing on the date fixed for hearing, decision will be taken as per provision of law.

Appellate Authority U/S 19(1), RTI Act 2005
Additional District Magistrate &
District Land & Land Reforms Officer
North 24 Parganas, Barasat

Sankar Prasad Dalapati
Advocate
High Court Calcutta
Bar Assaciation Room No.- 17

Residence : Gopalpur, P.O.- Hat-Gopalpur
P.S.- Patashpur, Midnapur (East)
Chamber : 12/2 Old post office street
(1st floor), Kolkata - 700 001
Mobile : 9836074135 / 9339001596

Date : 07/12/2012.

To

1) Mr. Shyamal Sanyal,
Advocate
High Court, Calcutta
Bar Association, Room No. 13.

2) Mr. Koushik Bhattacharjee
Advocate
8, Old Post Office Street
2nd Floor,
Kolkata – 700001.

Ref : W. P. No. 19676 (W) of 2011
Sri Jagannath Mondal & Another.
.... Petitioners.
– Versus –
The State of West Bengal
& Others.
... Respondents.

Dear Sir,

Please find enclosed herewith a copy of the Affidavit – In – Reply affirmed on 7th December, 2012 against the Affidavit – in – Opposition served by the respondent No. 5 and simultaneously I am withdrawing the copy of Reply served upon you earlier which is not at all filed before the Hon'ble Court.

Kindly acknowledge the receipt of the same and obliged.

Thanking you,

Yours faithfully,

Dalapati

Advocate.

To

The Addl. District Magistrate (L.R.)
North 24 Parganas,
Office at Barasat
P.O. & P.S. Barasat
Dist. North 24 Parganas.

Sub: An appeal under Right to Information Act.2005
An u/s (6) of Right to Information Act,
Ref: Application dated 10.05.2011 and your's
Memo No. 2745/LA(N)Bst/RTI/G-Misc.1077
dt. 09.08.2011.

Respected Sir,

With reference to above kindly supply the following records related with below schedule property, lying with your Office immediately to me as because the Owner of the property namely my Grand- father Late Bholanath Mondal and my father Rakhal Chandra Mondal.

1. C.S. Record of Right
2. R.S. Record of Right
3. L.R. Record of Right
4. Entire SA Proceeding including the vesting schedule.
5. Notice relating to the vesting of the land to the unlawful possessor.
6. Record of Right of the acquision of Land.

S C H E D U L E

District: North 24 Parganas, P.S. Rajarhat, under Mouza - Jatragachi, CS Kh. No-209 C.S. Dag No.1494 corresponding RS Dag No.1614, R.S. Khatian No. 283, J.L. No.24, measuring 4.45 acres of "BEEL" Land.

Please consider your goodself, so that I may get remedial measure and will remain ever greateful to you.

Thanking you,

Yours faithfully,

Sukhendu Mondal
(SUKENDU MONDAL)
Vill. Sonjoy Pally, P.O.& P.S. Canning Town, Dist. South 24 Pgs. Pin-743320.

Date: 19/10/2012

Contd....2/-

: 2 :

Copy to :

1. Block Land and Land Reforms Officer, Rajarhat, P.O. & P.S. Rajarhat, Dist. North 24 Parganas.

2. ~~Shri~~ Firhad Hakim, Urban Development Minister Govt. of West Bengal, Writers' Building, Kolkata - 700 001 - For information and taking necessary action please.

G.MISC-1077

RIGHT TO INFORMATION ACT. 2005

Dated 13-04-2011

To

The A.D.M (G) SPIO
North 24-Parganas.
Barasat,

Sub:- Prayer for R.S. C.S Information Realated to in Mouza - Ghuni J.L. No-23, Dag No-R.S- -3085, Khatian-1215, C.S. Dag 2508 According to R.T.I Act. 2005.

Respected Sir,

I beg to state That, I need ~~R.S.~~ + C.S. Dag-2508 Information of R.S. Dag, No,- 3085, R.S. Khatian No- 1215, Mouza- Ghuni, J.L. No-23, P.S- Rajarhat, Distt: North-24 Parganas.

There fore I am Praying to you to give me R.S. Information on said land, & obliged me,

Thank you

Sukhendu Mondal

From, Residential Address.

SUKHENDU MONDAL

Vill:- Sanjoypalli
P.O+P.S- Canning Town.
Dist- South 24 Parganas.
Pin- 743329.

RIGHT TO INFORMATION ACT, 2005,

G-MISC-1077

Dated 13-04-2011

Received
2042

To
The A.D.M. (G) SPIO
North 24-Parganas
Barasat,

Sub:- Prayer for L.R. (MATTH) K.B. Information Related to In. Mouza Ghuni, J.L. No-23 L.R.(K.B) Dag. 3085. R.S. Khatian, 1215 (K.B) Khatian '?' According to R.T.I Act. 2005.

Respect Sir,

I beg to state that I need L.R.(K.B) Information of Dag. No. 3085, Mouza-Ghuni, R.S. Khatian-1215, K.B '?' J.L. No, 23, P.S-Rajarhat, Dist- North-24-Parganas.

Therefore, I am praing to you to give me K.B. Information on said land and obliged me,

Thank you,
Sukhendu Mondal

From,
Residencial Address:-
S/O Rakhalchandra Mondal.
Vill. Sanjoypalli
P.O. + P.S - Canning Town
South 24 Parganas,
pin - 743329,

RIGHT TO INFORMATION ACT, 2005,

G. Misc - 1077
21-6-11

Dated. 13-04-2011

To
The A.D.M. (G) SPIO
North 24-Parganas
Barasat,

Sub:-
Prayer for L.R. (MATTH)
K.B. Information
Related to In. Mouza
Ghuni, J.L. No - 23
L.R. (K.B) Dag. 3085
R.S. Khatian, 1215 (K.B)
Khatian '?' According to
R.T.I Act. 2005.

Respect Sir,

I beg to state that I need L.R. (K.B) Information of Dag. No. 3085, Mouza-Ghuni, R.S. Khatian-1215, K.B-'?' J.L. No. 23. P.S-Rajarhat, Dist- North- 24-Parganas.

Therefore, I am praing to you to give me K.B. Information, on said land and obliged me,

Thank you.
Sukhendu Mondal

From,
Residencial Address:-
S/o Rakhalchandra Mondal.
Vill. Sanjoypalli
P.O. + P.S - Canning Town
South 24 Parganas,
pin - 743329,

Q. MISC-1076

20.5.11 U.C.D
8/06/11 From K.C.D

RIGHT TO INFORMATON ACT, 2005.

Dated-13-4-2011

To
The A.D.M.(G) SPIO
North 24-Parganas.
Barasat,

Sub:-
Prayer for L.R. Information Realated to in Mouza-Jat-ragachi, J.L. No-24 L.R. Dag No.-1614, According to R.T.I Act 2005.

Respected Sir,

I beg to state that I need L.R. Information of L.R. Dag No. 1614, Mouza-Jatragachi J.L. No-24, P.S-Rajarhat, Dist:- North 24-Parganas,

There fore, I am praying to you to give me L.R. Information on said land and obliged me,

Thank you,
Sukhendu Mondal

From,
Recident Address:-

S/o Rakhal Chandra Mondal.
Vill.-Sanjay palli,
P.O+P.S-Canning Town-
Dist-South 24 Parganas.
Pin-743329.

To
B.L.&.L.R.O
1043-14/06/11

-5 APR 2011
PARASAT, NORTH

B.L. & L.R.O. Barasat

Information

Sukhendu Mondal
8/04/11

[To,

B.L.& L.R.O
1043-14/06/11
Received by the office on 5 April 2011

The B.L & L.R.O, Barasat
24 Pargana (N).
Subject: Appeal for L.R. Information copy.

Applicant Rakhal Chandra Mandal s/o Bholanath Mandal, r/o. Gauranga Nagar (Ramkrishna Palli), P.S. New Town.

Sir,

My humble submission is that I require the LR list of RS 3085 under the address 23 No. Ghuni *Mouja.* I request you to kindly provide the same to me.

Yours sincerely
Rakhal Chandra Mandal
On his part sd/- Sukhendu Mandal 05/04/11]

To B.L. & L.R.O
918-9/06/11

To ... S.D.L.R.O. Barasat

[illegible]

-5 APR 2011
8

[illegible]

Sukhendu Mondal
5/04/11

5/04/11

[To,
B.L. & L.R.O
918-906/11 Received by the office 5 APR. 2011

The S.D.L.R.O. Barasat
Subject: Request for corrected LR Parcha.

Applicant: Rakhal Chandra Mandal s/o Bholanath Mandal, res. Gauranga Nagar (Ramkrishna Palli), P.S. New Town.

Sir,

My humble request is that the land having RS khatiyan No. 1215, Dag No. 3085, of 23 No. Ghuni *mouja* under P.S. Rajarhat was recorded in the math khata but I did not receive the LR Parcha. Therefore, I request you to kindly correct the LR record according to math khata.

Tapsil land
P.S. Rajarhat
Mouja: Ghuni No . 23
RS Khatiyan No 1215
RS Dag No. 3085
Amount of Land 35 satak.
Yours sincerely

Rakhal Chandra Mandal
On his part sd/-
Sukhendu Mandal 05/04/11]

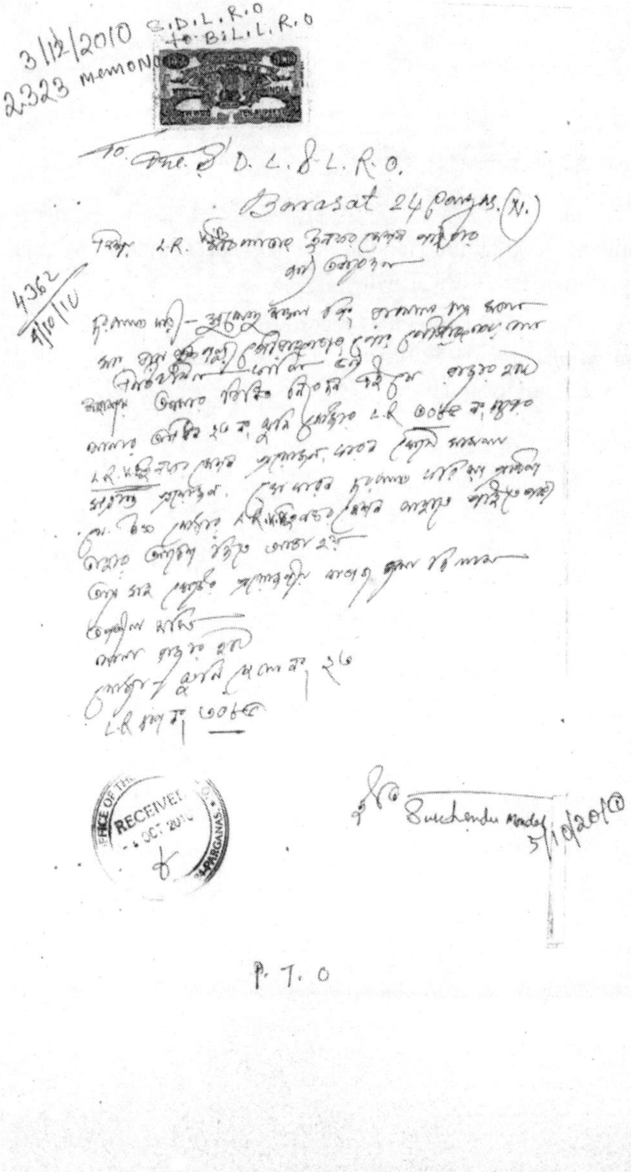
3/12/2010 S.D.L.L.R.O to B.L.L.R.O
2323 memo no

To
The S.D.L. & L.R.O.
Barasat 24 Pargs. (N.)

RECEIVED
OCT 2010

Suchendu Mondal
5/10/2010

P.T.O

[3/12/2010
S.D.L.R.O. To B.L.L.R.O
4362
4/10/10

To,
The S.D.L. & L.R.O.
Barasat 24 pargana (N)
Subject: Appeal for L.R.K.B. records

Applicant Sukhendu Mandal, s/o Rakhal Chandra Mandal, Gauranga Nagar, P.S. New Town.

Request for LRKB math khata record for LR Dag no. 3085, of 23 no. Ghuni *mouja* under P.S. Rajarhat for Court case.
SD/- Sukhendu Mandal
5/10/10].

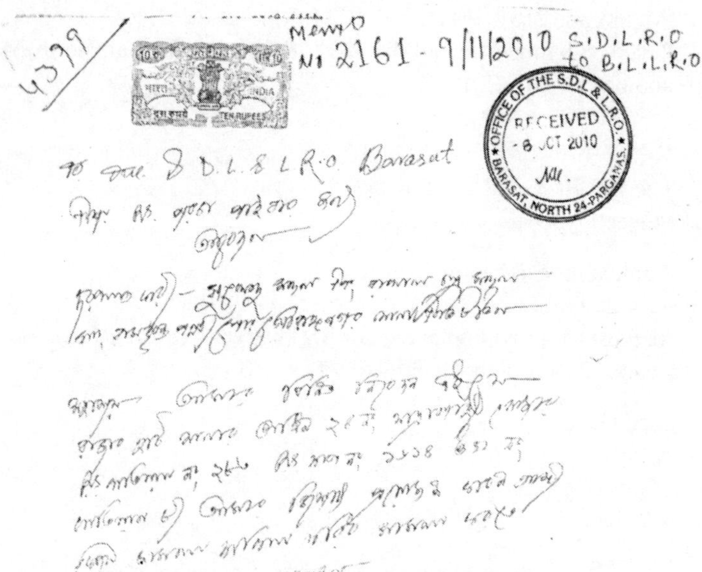
4399
Memo
No 2161 - 9/11/2010 S.D.L.R.O
to B.L.L.R.O
OFFICE OF THE S.D.L & L.R.O.
RECEIVED
- 8 OCT 2010
BARASAT, NORTH 24-PARGANAS.
INDIA
TEN RUPEES
S.D.L. & L.R.O. Barasat
Sukhendu Mondal
8/10/2010

[Memo no. 2161- 9/11/2010 S.D.L.R.O. to B.L.L.R.O

Received by the office of the S.D.L.& L.R.O., Barasat, North 24 Pargana on 8th Oct. 2010.

To,

The S.D.L. & L.R.O., Barasat

Subject: Appeal for Parcha

Applicant: Sukhendu Mandal s/o Rakhal Chandra Mandal, Ramkrishna Palli, Gauranga nagar, P.S. New Town.

Request for providing parcha of RS khatiyan no. 283 RS dag no. 1614 under 24 no. Jatragachhi *Mouja.*

Tapsil land

P.S. Rajarhat

Mouja Jatragachhi

RS khatiyan No. 283

RS Dag No. 1614

Sd/- Sukhendu Mandal, 8/10/2010.

N.B. the Xerox copy of the deed is attached herewith]

To
The S.D.L. & L.R.O
Barasat.

[illegible]

OFFICE OF THE S.D.L & L.R.O. BARASAT NORTH 24 PARGANAS
1 OCT 2010

4319
3/12/2010
2321 S.D.L.R.O
MEMO NO TO B.L.L.R.O

[illegible]

Sukhendu Mondal
1/10/2010

[To,

The S.D.L. & L.R.O., Barasat
Subject: Appeal for RS Parcha
Received by the office of the S.D.L. & L.R.O., Barasat, North 24 Pargana on 1st Oct. 2010.

Applicant: Sukhendu Mandal s/o Rakhal Chandra Mandal, Ramkrishna Palli, Gauranga Nagar, P.S. New Town.

Request for providing Parcha of RS dag no. 1614 under 24 no. Jatragachhi *Mouja.*

Tapsil land
P.S. Rajarhat
Mouja Jatragachhi-24
RS Dag No. 1614
Sd/- Sukhendu Mandal, 1/10/2010].

Dated : 13/12/2012

To
The Commissioner,
Presidency Division,
Kolkata – 700 001

Sub: Direction upon the Additional District Magistrate (L.R.) and/or to Block Land and Land Reforms Officer, Rajarhat to supply the documents upon the applicant.

Dear Sir,

That my father and my uncle purchased a piece and parcel of land measuring about 4.45 Acres of "BEEL" land under the Mouja – Jatragachi, C.S. Dag No.1494 corresponding to R.S. Dag No.1614, R.S. Khatian No.283, J.L. No.24, Police Station – Rajarhat, District – 24 Parganas (South) on 6th day of June, 1956.

Since Purchase they are in possession till 24th day of November, 2011, unfortunately on 25th day of November, 2011 the West Bengal Housing Infrastructure Development Corporation Ltd. with the help of the Police personnel disposes them and encroached the property for constructing the building over the said property.

On enquiry we came to know from the office of Housing Infrastructure Development Corporation Ltd. that the property had been acquisitioned by the State Government, on the other hand we came to another information from Block Land and Land Reforms Office, Rajarhat that the property has been vested upon the state in connection with a vesting proceeding under West Bengal Estate Acquisition Act, 1953.

We have take shelter before the court of law for adjudication and sought out the problem and in the mean time we have applied before the Block Land and Land Reforms Office, Rajarhat, the Chairman West Bengal Housing Infrastructure Development Corporation Ltd. and the Additional District Magistrate (L.R.), North 24 Parganas, office at Barasat asking the following documents for adjudication and settled the issue :-

1. C.S. Record of Right
2. R.S. Record of Right
3. L.R. Record of Right
4. Entire 5A Proceeding including the Vesting Schedule.
5. Notice Relating to the Vesting of the land to the unlawful possessor.
6. Record of Rights after acquisition of land.

RECEIVED

2

All the authorities neglected and denied to supply the above mentioned information purposefully, although all the documents are "Public Documents".

Therefore I humble prays before you kindly direct the Additional District Magistrate (L.R.) North -24 Parganas, Barasat and/or Block Land and Land Reforms Officer, Rajarhat to supply the copy within a stipulated period.

Thanking you,

Yours faithfully,

Enclo: Photocopy of all application Filed earlier.

Sukhendu Mondal
9874791258
9735563664

রাজারহাট কৃষি জমি, জীবন ও জীবিকা রক্ষা কমিটি

রাজারহাট, উত্তর ২৪ পরগণা, বেঙ্গল – ১৩৬

জমি হারা কৃষকের নাম	ঃ-
পিতার নাম	ঃ-
মোট জমির পরিমান	ঃ-
মৌজা	ঃ-
দাগ নং	ঃ-
খতিয়ান নং -	ঃ-

জমির অবস্থা ঃ-

L.A.4 হয়ে পড়ে আছে কি না ? ঃ-

Cheque নিতে বাধ্য হয়েছেন কি না ? ঃ-

Cheque আপত্তি সহকারে নিয়েছেন কি না ? ঃ-

কোন Referrance Case আছে কি না ? ঃ-

কোন আইনি পদক্ষেপ নেয়নি অথচ

মাটি ফেলে দখল করেছে কি না ? ঃ-

সঠিক দাম পেয়েছেন কি না ? ঃ-

বর্তমান দরে ঐ জমির দাম কত ? ঃ-

বাকী দাম পেতে চান কি না ? ঃ-

আন্দোলনের পথে এগোতে রাজি কি না ? ঃ- স্বাক্ষর

[RAJARHAT KRISHI JAMI, JIBAN O JIBIKA RAKSHA COMMITTEE
(Committee to save cultivable land, livelihood and occupation)

Name of the land-looser peasant and address:
Father's name:
Total amount of land:
Mouja:
Khatiyan no.:

Condition of land:
Whether the land is under LA-4:
Whether compelled to accept Cheque:
If there is any reference case:
Whether occupied forcibly by dumping earth without applying any legal procedure:
Whether received the fair price:
At current rate what is the price of that land:
Whether interested in getting the remaining price money:
Whether ready to join movement:
Signature:

(This form was circulated by the Rajarhat Krishi Jami, Jiban O Jibika Raksha Committee during the days of land acquisition by the then State Government)]

RIGHT TO INFORMATION ACT, 2005,

G. Misc - 1077
21-6-11

Dated. 13-04-2011

To
The A.D.M. (G) SPIO
North 24-Parganas
Barasat,

Sub:-
Prayer for L.R. (MATTH), K.B. Information Related to In. Mouza Ghuni, J.L. No - 23 L.R. (K.B) Dag. 3085 R.S. Khatian, 1215 (K.B) Khatian '?' According to R.T.I Act. 2005.

Respect Sir,

I. beg to state that I need L.R. (K.B) Information of Dag. No. 3085. Mouza - Ghuni, R.S. Khatian - 1215, K.B - '?' J.L. No, 23. P.S - Rajarhat. Dist - North - 24 Parganas.

Therefore, I am praing to you to give me K.B. Information on said Land and obliged me,

Thank you,
Sukhendu Mondal

From,
Residencial Address:-
S/O Rakhalchandra Mondal.
Vill. Sanjoypalli
P.O. + P.S - Canning Town
South 24 Parganas,
pin - 743329,

RIGHT TO INFORMATION ACT, 2005,

Dated 13-04-2011.

To
The A.D.M.(G) SPIO
North 24-Parganas.
Barasat,

Sub:- Prayer for K.B. Information Related to in Mouza Jatragachi J.L. No-24, Dag No-1614(R.S) Khatian No-283 According to R.T.I Act, 2005.

Respected Sir,

I beg to state that I need K.B. Information of K.B. Dag No,-1614, Khatian No-283, Mouza- Jatragachi, J.L. No-24 P.S.-Rajarhat, Dist.- North 24 Parganas.

There fore I am praying to you to give me K.B. Information on said land and obliged me,

Thank you,

Sukhendu Mondal

From-
Recidential Addreers:-

S/O Rakhal Chandra Mondal
Vill:- Sanjoy palli
P.O + P.S- Canning Town,
South 24 Parganas.
Pin - 743329.

(2) (4)

RIGHT TO INFORMATION, ACT, 2005,

Dated. 13-04-2011

To
~~The~~ A.D.M (G)/SPIO
North 24-Parganas,
Barasat,

Sub:- Prayer for R.S. Information Realated to in Mouza Jatragachi, J.L. No-24, R.S. Dag No-1614 R.S. Khatian No-283 According R.T.I Act-2005.

Respect Sir,

I beg to state that I need ~~to~~ R.S Information R.S. Dag No, 1614, R.S. Khatian -283, Mouza-Jatragachi, J.L. No-24, P.S.-Rajarhat, North 24 Parganas,

Therefore I am praying to you to give me R.S. Information on said land & obleged me.

Thank you

Sukhendu Mondal

From:-

S/o. Rakhal Chandra Mondal.
Vill.- Sanjay palli,
P.O. + P.S - Canning Town.
Pin-743329.

President's office intervenes in Rabindra Tirtha land row

statesman news service

KOLKATA, 9 APRIL: Following a complaint from a resident of Rajarhat that the state government had forcibly taken over 4.45 acres of land belonging to him without paying any compensation to set up Rabindra Tirtha, the President's office has instructed the chief secretary to take action and let it know the progress achieved.

The President's office has also asked the chief secretary to liaison with the complainant, Mr Sukhendu Mondol, directly for further information in the matter. The letter has been issued by Mr Chirabrata Sarkar, under-secretary in the President's secretariat.

The erstwhile Left Front government had acquired the land but did not formally take it over after it found the existence of a temple of the Matua community there. There is a water body and 160 coconut trees and because of this the area is called Narkelbagan.

After coming to power the Trinamul Congress government felled the coconut trees and began construction of Rabindra Tirtha, a centre for research on Tagore. Chief minister Miss Mamata Banerjee inaugurated the centre on 7 August 2012.

On 6 August, a day before the inauguration, Mr Mondol along with his spouse and children staged a fast in front of the centre. Police requested him to withdraw the fast and assured him that the state government would consider his appeal sympathetically. Senior police officers told him that the state urban development minister Mr Firhad Hakim would talk to him to resolve the issue.

CULTURE CLASH

Mr Mondol alleged that neither Mr Hakim nor the chairman of Housing and Infrastructure Development Corporation (Hidco) Mr Debashis Sen tried to address his problem. On one occasion Mr Sen left office without informing Mr Mondol who was waiting outside his chamber.

"It is most unfortunate that the state government did not do anything to resolve the impasse. Trinamul Congress government and the erstwhile Left Front government are two sides of the same coin," Mr Mondol maintained.

Finding no other option he approached the President, seeking his intervention.

Local Trinamul Congress leaders of Rajarhat said the matter was likely to affect the poll prospects of the party in the forthcoming panchayat election in the area.

Senior officials of Hidco said they would resolve the issue and a plan is being prepared.

No relief for Rabindra Tirtha plot owner

tarun goswami

KOLKATA, 30 AUG: Poor people are at the receiving end in Miss Mamata Banerjee's *maa mati manush* government.

Four weeks have passed the family members of Dhananjay Mondol, owner of the disputed plot where the chief minister's dream project Rabindra Tirtha *(in photo)*, has come up in Rajarhat, New Town are being lobbed like a shuttle cock between the offices of the chairman of Housing and Infrastructure Development Corporation (Hidco) and the state Urban development minister Mr Firhad Hakim at Writers' Buildings to know the status of the land or compensation.

"We have been treated like animals by some state government officials who are deliberately misguiding us. As the inaugural function is over the officials are not even recognising us," said Mr Sukhen Mondol, son of Dhananjay Mondol, owner of the disputed plot. "One year is a big time and we have realised that CPIM and Trinamul Congress are two sides of the same coin. This government is insensitive and it like its predecessor does not have any sympathy for the poor," said Mr Sukhen Mondol.

Sukhen and his family members including his wife and children stated a sit in demonstration at the site where the cultural complex has come up on 6 July. The police removed them from the spot and taken them to the New Town police station. The officers reportedly told them that if they continue to demonstrate they will be arrested and branded as "Maoists." The police officer at the thana provided them with a vehicle but dropped at their residence at Jatragachi. However, Sukhen on 7 July morning made another attempt to stage a sit in demonstration at the spot. He was stopped near the office of Techno India and said that Mr Hakim would meet him at Writers' Buildings on 8 July. Meanwhile, Miss Banerjee inaugurated Rabindra Tirtha on 7 July.

On 8 July Sukhen along with his lawyer met Mr Hakim at Writers' Buildings. He was told that within three weeks he would be told about the status of the plot and if the Mondol family is found to be the owner they would be given compensation.

Since then nothing has been done and Sukhen has been running from the pillar to post to know the result.

The erstwhile Left Front government had acquired 13 bigha and 8 cottah water body and 107 coconut tree describing it as vested. However, the state government could not show any document in favour of vesting of the water body. In 2010 the Mondol family went to court which directed the Block land and land reforms officer (BLLRO) to give a status of the water body. Till date no report has been filed by BLLRO.

Sensing some dispute the erstwhile Left Front government did not take possession of the water body.

After coming to power, Trinamul Congress led state government filled up the water body and fell 107 coconut trees to make room for Rabindra Tirtha. Because of the cluster of coconut trees the place is called Narkelbagan. "We want to know who is the real owner of the plot and the delay on the part of the state government shows that it is my fault," said Mr Sukhen Mondol.

Rabindra Tirtha: Land owners not compensated

statesman news service

deprived dejected

KOLKATA, 9 OCT: Two months have nearly passed but the state government is yet to give a single paisa as compensation to the owners of the land where the chief minister's dream project, Rabindra Tirtha, has come up in New Town, Rajarhat.

Miss Mamata Banerjee who was the then Railway minister had announced before the Assembly election in 2011 that the farmers from whom land was forcibly taken by the erstwhile Left Front government, would be given compensation.

On 6 August, descendants of Rakhal Chandra Mondol, Sukhendu, his wife and children staged a fast-unto-death at the site where Rabindra Tirtha has come up. Senior officials of North 24-Parganas district administration went to the spot and persuaded them to withdraw the fast and assured them that the Urban Development minister Mr Firhad Hakim would look into the matter sympathetically. On 7 August Miss Banerjee inaugurated Rabindra Tirtha, a centre to study the philosophy of Tagore.

Mr Sukhendu Mondol who had recently gone to Vellore Christian Medical College after he had a brain stroke said that "they have been forced to move like a shuttle-cock between the Housing and Infrastructure Development Corporation (Hidco) and the Urban Development department and no one is listening to them." He said that senior officials and Trinamul Congress leaders told them that it would not be possible for them to file a case against the state government and advised them to settle the matter amicably.

He added that some senior officials in private told them that the state government does not have a single document to prove its ownership over the land. The land measuring 4.45 acre is owned by Rakhal Chandra Mondol and Jagannath Mondol. The Left Front government forcibly took possession of the land in 2003-04 but did not do anything on it. There was a temple of Harichand Thakur, founder of the Matua cult and 150 coconut trees and that is why the area is called Narkelbagan.

Local people said: "The way Trinamul Congress leaders and workers in Rajarhat are oppressing poor farmers, chances of the party winning the gram panchayat and panchayat samitis in the forthcoming panchayat election are bleak."

Appendix – 14

Related documents (HIDCO Reports).

NEW TOWN PLANNING AREA

District North 24 Pargana

Notification No.	Sl. No.	Mouza	J.L. No.	Full/Part of The Mouza Included
1423/HG/NTP/ 1M-1/98 Dt. 27.08.99	1.	Raigachhi	12	Full
	2.	Reejuani	13	Full
	3.	Tarulia	21	Full
	4.	Sulangori	22	Full
	5.	Ghuni	23	Full
	6.	Jatragachhi	24	Full
	7.	Kadampukur	25	Full
	8.	Chakpachuria	33	Full
	9.	Baligori	34	Full
	10.	Chhapna	35	Full
	11.	Patharghata	36	Full
	12.	Akandakeshari	55	Full
737-HI/HG/NTP 1M-1/98 Dt. 26.07.01 in partial modification to Notification No. 1423/HG/NTP/ 1M-1/98 Dt. 27.08.99	13.	Mahisgot	20	Portion to the North of Krishnapur Khal
	14.	Thakdari	19	Portion to the North of Krishnapur Khal
	15.	Noapara	11	Plot Nos. 3,6-48,50,52-54,57-153, 270-277,281,320,321,327
	16.	Hatiara	14	Plot Nos. 379-398,402-405,437-440, 452-454,456-458,466-469,472-524,528,2001-3043,4556-4558
	17.	Chandiberia	15	Plot Nos. 263,384,407-417,435-443
737-HI/HG/NTP 1M-1/98 Dt. 26.07.01	18.	Mahisbathan	18	Portion to the North of Krishnapur Khal
	19.	Gopalpur	2	Portion to the South of Baguiati – Rajarhat Road
650-HI/1M-1/98 Dt. 22.11.06.	20.	Jagadishpur	27	Full
	21.	Dharsa Moktarpur	26	Full
	22.	Mahammadpur	32	Full
	23.	Mandal Ganti	6	Full

NB. : Mouza - Jyangra, J.L.No. 16 in full was included in the NewTown Planning Area vide Notification No. 1423/HG/NTP/1M-1/98, Dt. 27.08.99 . But subsequently was excluded in full from the Planning Area vide Notification No. 737-HI/HG/NTP/1M-1/98, Dt. 26.07.01 .

District South 24 Pargana

Notification No	Sl No.	Mouza	J.L. No.	Full/Part Of The Mouza Included
1423/HG/NTP/ 1M-1/ 98 Dt 27 08 99	1.	Kochpukur	2	Full
	2.	Jotbhim	3	Full
	3	Chandakanthalberia	8	Full
	4.	Hatisala	9	Full
650-HI/1M-1 98 Dt 22 11 2006	5.	Wari	26	Full
	6.	Paikan	28	Full
	7.	Sukpukuria	30	Full
	8.	Krolberia	31	Full
	9.	Chariswar	29	Full
	10.	Bhatipota	33	Full
	11.	Karaidanga	32	Full
	12.	Gangapur	35	Full
	13.	Ghunimeghi	44	Full
	14.	Jirangachhi	25	Full
	15.	Bamunia	45	Full
392-HI/HG/NTP 3C-2/2005 Dt 21.07.2008 in Supersession To Notification No 1418-HI/HG/ NTP/1M-1/98 Dt 26.08.1999	16.	Bhagabanpur	10	Plot Nos 865(P), 878(P), 879(P), 880(P), 881(P), 882, 883, 884(P), 885(P), 932(P), 933(P), 936, 942(P), 943(P), 944, 945(P), 947, 948(P), 949-961, 962(P), 963-967, 968(P), 971(P), 972(P), 973(P), 976(P), 978(P), 979, 980(P), 981(P), 989(P), 1049(P), 1050(P), 1110(P), 1124(P), 1125(P), 1126, 1127 & 1131

TABLE-1 AS ON 15.12.08

Action Area Break Up of New Town

Sl No.	Action Areas	Land Areas (Ha)
1.	Action Area - I	677.00
2.	Action Area - II	1310.00*
3.	Action Area - III	783.00
4.	Action Area - CBD	182.00
TOTAL		2952.00
5.	Water Treatment Plant	45.00
6.	Garbage Disposal Centre	90.00
GRAND TOTAL		3087.00

Action Area – IV .... 465.00 Ha

Total Area including Action Area – IV............ 3552.00 Ha.

*Including Added Area of 40 Ha.

E:\vamana 26 12.08\Action Area Break Up Of New Town table 1.doc

TABLE-2 AS ON 15.12.08

SUMMERY STATEMENT OF LAND USE BREAK UP – ACTION AREA- I, II, III & CBD

Land Use Zone including Local & Collector Streets, Local Open Spaces, Local Water Bodies, Local Utilities & Community Facilities	Total	
	Area (Ha)	**Percentage**
Residential zone	1292.45	43.78
Commercial zone	350.27	11.87
Information Technology zone	142.30	4.82
Social facilities (Health, Educational & Cultural) zone	251.05	8.50
Industrial zone	7.00	0.24
Major Roads, Large Open Spaces, Large Water Bodies & Peripheral Canals,	774.89	26.25
Town Level Utilities & Services	134.00	4.54
Sub total	**2952**	100
Garbage Disposal Area	90.00	--
Area of W.T.P.	45.00	--
Total Area	**3087.00**	--

* The area of AA-IV is 465 Ha. The total area after addition of area of AA-IV is 3552.00 Ha.

S. Bhattacharya

E:\sumana 26.12.08\tab 2 rev 26.12.2008.doc

TABLE – 4 AS ON 15.12.08

SALEABLE PLOTS & NON SALEABLE AREA – ACTION AREA- I, II, III & CBD

Use Categories of Saleable Plots	***Total Saleable Area (Ha)***
1. Residential Plots	879
2. Commercial Plots	280
3. Information Technology Plots	139
4. Plots for Social Facilities (Health, Educational & Cultural)	262
5. Industrial Plots	6
Sub Total of Saleable Plot Areas	**1566**

Use Categories of Non Saleable Areas	*Area (Ha.)*
1. Major Roads	362
2. Large Open Spaces, Large Water Bodies & Peripheral Canals	439
3. Town Level Utilities & Services	134
Local & Collector Streets, Local Open Spaces, Local Water Bodies & Local Utilities in :-	--
4. Residential Zones	361
5. Commercial Zones	33
6. IT Zones	7
7. Social Facilities Zones	49
8. Industrial Zones	1
Sub Total of Non Saleable Areas -	**1386**
Total	**2952**

E:\sumana 26.12.08\SALEABLE AREA table 4 dt 26.12.08 REV.doc

Sbhattacharya

TABLE-3 AS ON 15.12.08

Action Area and Design Population

Sl. No.	ACTION AREA	DESIGN POPULATION	
		RESIDENTIAL (Lacs)	FLOATING (Lacs)
1.	Action Area – I	2.42	0.70
2.	Action Area – II	3.02*	1.50*
3.	Action Area – III	2.81	0.70
4.	Action Area – CBD	0.53	2.00
SUB TOTAL		**8.78**	**4.90**
5.	Action Area – IV	1.20	0.60
TOTAL		**9.98**	**5.50**

I) Total Residential population : 9.98 lacs Say 10.00 lacs

II) Total Floating Population : 5.50 lacs

*Including added area population

TABLE – 5 AS ON 15.12.08

DETAILS OF SALEABLE AREA – ACTION AREA- I, II, III & CBD

Use Categories of Saleable Plots	Total Saleable Area (Ha.)	Already Sold (Ha.)	Remaining Saleable Area (Ha.)
Residential Plots	879	520	359
Commercial Plots	280	71	209
Information Technology Plots	139	76	63
Plots for Social Facilities (Health, Educational & Cultural)	262	98	164
Industrial Plots	6	-	6
Total	**1566**	**765**	**801**

Appendix – 15

TIMES CITY

THE TIMES OF INDIA, KOLKATA, JULY 3, 2012.

TIMES CITY

MADAN MITRA TRIES TO PLACATE CABBIES, BUT 72-HOUR TAXI STRIKE IMMINENT IN JULY | 3

STATE FORECAST WARNS OF RISE IN TEMPERATURE, MORE DISEASES IN FUTURE | 6

Arsenic Alarm Grips Kolkata

JU Study Reveals Signs Of Poisoning In Residents, Councillor Denies Threa

Prithvijit Mitra | TNN

Kolkata: If you live in or around Prince Anwar Shah Road, Ghulam Mohammed Shah Road, Golf Green, Jadavpur or Tollygunge and drink water drawn from tube-wells, better go for an arsenic poisoning test. Hundreds of Kolkatans have started showing the first signs of the illness, but are going unscreened and therefore, without treatment. Traces of arsenic have been found in the urine samples of scores of multi-storey residents of the areas mentioned. Scores of others have reported for treatment at Kolkata Municipal Corporation (KMC) clinics in recent weeks with arsenic-triggered lesions, but have been turned away, for the medics are not trained to identify arsenic poisoning.

A study carried out by Jadavpur University's School of Environmental Studies indicates that a fair number of residents on Prince Anwar Shah Road and Golf Green have been affected. Hair, nail and urine samples of several residents of two multi-storey apartments — Mecon Tower on Prince Anwar Shah Road and at Golf Tower in Golf Green — have been found to contain arsenic traces. While some residents have switched to bottled water, the rest are still drinking arsenic-contaminated water from the neighbourhood tube-wells and deep tube-wells.

B B Roy Sarkar, a resident of Mecon Tower, has arsenic traces in his urine. While Roy Sarkar and his family members have stopped consuming water from tube-wells and have switched to filter-cleaned KMC water, they haven't sought treatment or undergone further tests. "It was scary and we stay away from tube-well water now. Fortunately, we have no symptoms yet. Some of my neighbours have switched to bottled water, but some are still using water from the deep tube-well in the complex," said Roy Sarkar. He added that despite being warned about the contamination by the School of Environmental Studies, they have not approached the KMC. The latter is now installing tube-wells in the area despite the fact that it falls within the arsenic-affected zone.

"Water at most multi-storey apartments at Anwar Shah Road, Golf Green and Jadavpur are contaminated. We have repeatedly conducted tests, including one a few weeks back. The average arsenic count has been 190 microgram per litre which is way above the permissible limit of 10 mg/litre. The last test conducted at City High in Bikramgarh revealed an arsenic count of 60 mg, which is alarming," said Dipankar Chakraborti, director of the School of Environmental Studies who has been researching on arsenic contamination for the last three decades. He pointed out that a large number of victims were loathe to undergo tests or seek treatment even if they came from affluent, e[...] backgrounds.

Around 20 of the 80 residen[...] two apartments buildings who [...] arsenic test had traces of the p[...] chemical in their hair and urine[...] "We also tested the domestic h[...] watchmen who consume the [...] water. At least six of them had [...] traces. Only a handful have stopp[...] the contaminated local water, f[...] is no alternative. In time, they co[...] up lesions on their hands and fe[...] skin diseases, chronic diarrho[...] lung ailments and even canc[...] Chakraborti.

What makes the situation ev[...] is the civic authorities' failure [...] screen or treat patients. Hundre[...] tients from slums in the fringe o[...] davpur, Baishnabghata, Patuli, [...] ni and Garia are suspected to be [...] from arsenic poisoning. But the[...] diagnosed or treated due to the a[...] trained doctors at KMC clinics. [...] easy to identify arsenic-poisoni[...] doctors are trained adequately [...] skilled dermatologists for the [...] which we don't have. As a result [...] are being turned away with gene[...] cines. But doctors do suspect t[...] stantial percentage of those [...] could actually be victims of ar[...] soning," said a KMC health of[...] added that many of those who [...] clinics had lesions on their [...] were strikingly similar to those [...] by arsenic.

The civic authorities, howev[...] that the clinics lacked experts o[...] pected patients have been visit[...] "None of the KMC clinics in any [...] wards of Kolkata has received a[...] patient. If they do, the patient [...] ferred to a hospital. There's no q[...] not being able to identify an ar[...] tim, for there are none in the fri[...] city," claimed Atin Ghosh, MMI[...]

Chakraborti, on the other ha[...] ed out that he has repeatedly ap[...] the KMC with his findings an[...] them about the arsenic threat[...] written to them about the conta[...] at multi-storey buildings on An[...] Road and adjoining areas. But th[...] ready to accept that arsenic pois[...] ists in Kolkata. We are heading f[...] ter," said Chakraborti.

Many of the residents of Mecon Tower on Prince Anwar Shah Road have tested positive for aresenic poisoning. Also in the sample were residents of Golf Tower in Golf Green

Who did the study?

Jadavpur University's School of Environmental Studies

Sample

80 residents of two multi-storey apartments — Mecon Tower on Prince Anwar Shah Road and Golf Tower in Golf Green. Domestic helps and watchmen who consume the building water were also tested

Result

Around 20 of the 80 residents and six of the watchmen and domestic helps had traces of arsenic in their hair and urine samples

Only a handful have stopped using the contaminated local water, for there is no alternative. In time, they could develop lesions on their hands and feet, other skin diseases, chronic diarrhoea, liver, lung ailments and even cancer

Dipankar Chakraborti | DIRECTOR OF THE SCHOOL OF ENVIRONMENTAL STUDIES

No KMC clinic in any of the 141 wards of Kolkata has received an arsenic patient. If they do, the patient will be referred to a hospital. There's no question of not being able to identify an arsenic victim

Atin Ghosh | MMIC, HEALTH

TOI – JUNE 30, 2012 Saturday

KMC team to visit arsenic-prone areas

Saikat Ray | TNN

Kolkata: Following a TOI report that highlighted the threat of arsenic in some areas in Jadavpur, the Kolkata Municipal Corporation (KMC) has decided to send a team of officials to the affected areas next week. Though the team was supposed to visit these areas on Friday, the civic top brass asked officials to contact scientist Dipankar Chakraborty and ask him to lead them. The team will collect samples of water from tube wells in parts of Jadavpur from where arsenic-contaminated water was found by a study carried out by Dipankar Chakraborty, director (research) of Jadavpur University's School of Environmental Studies.

Tarak Singh, mayor-in-council member in charge of tube wells, held a meeting on Thursday with water supply department officials to chalk out measures to combat the arsenic threat. Singh had asked KMC health department officials to visit arsenic-prone areas on Friday and collect groundwater samples. "The samples will be sent to the laboratory at Palta waterworks for tests. If arsenic content is found, we will definitely take appropriate action," Singh said on Friday.

> It is quite unfortunate that lakhs of people in Garia and Jadavpur areas are forced to drink ground water that has arsenic content. There is no regular inspection by the KMC in these areas. We need to supply safe drinking water to these residents
>
> **Chayan Bhattacharya** | CPM COUNCILLOR

"We welcome any groundwater experts to assist us in our fight against arsenic," the MMiC said. Singh conceded that an arsenic threat exists in parts of the city. "It is not a new issue. We had found arsenic in large areas in Behala. After confirmation, we had to seal those tube wells," Singh added.

Sources in the KMC water supply department said that arsenic beyond permissible limits in ground water was found from areas such as Bairagi Para, P K Chandra Lane, P N Mitra Road, Chanditala Road and B L Saha Road in Behala. Singh did not dismiss chances of arsenic contamination in ground water in the southern fringes of the city. In fact, the KMC water supply and health department top brass are waiting for reports from experts of the State Water Investigation Department (SWID) on arsenic contamination in and around Kolkata.

After some KMC councillors pointed to an arsenic threat in the southern fringes, the civic authorities held a meeting with ground water experts from the Union government, SWID and West Bengal Pollution Control Board officials a month ago. However, the opposition Left Front councillors alleged that despite a serious arsenic threat in large parts of added areas such as Behala, Jadavpur and parts of Tollygunge, the Trinamool-run civic body was not taking any concrete steps to combat the menace. CPM councillor Chayan Bhattacharya, who represents residents in Garia and its adjacent areas, moved a resolution in the KMC monthly meeting a week ago alleging that residents in large areas of Garia and Jadavpur were being forced to drink water with arsenic content. "It is quite unfortunate that lakhs of people in Garia and Jadavpur areas are forced to drink ground water that has arsenic content. There is no regular inspection by the KMC in these areas. We need to supply safe drinking water to these residents," Bhattacharya said.

TIMES CITY

THE TIMES OF INDIA, KOLKATA, JULY 3, 2012

Over the last 15 years, I have sent around 100 letters and reports to the civic authorities. No one ever responded. While my findings have been published, they have never bothered to explain on what grounds they are rejecting them. I tested six tubewells in Jadavpur this year and all six showed very high levels of arsenic contamination

Dipankar Chakraborty | DIRECTOR, RESEARCH, JADAVPUR UNIVERSITY'S SCHOOL OF ENVIRONMENTAL STUDIES

STATE GOVT STUDY IN 2010

Arsenic in Ward No. 96 of Jadavpur which had recorded a count of 96 micrograms. Tests in multi-storey buildings in the Jadavpur area revealed an average arsenic count of 50-60 micrograms per litre. A multi-storey in Bikramgarh even recorded 199 micrograms. The maximum permissible limit is 10 micrograms per litre.
(Conducted by the state water investigation directorate)

City Suffers In Toxic Tussle

Political compulsion behind KMC stand on arsenic: Scientists

Subhro Niyogi | TNN

Kolkata: The city's scientific community is livid about the manner in which Kolkata Municipal Corporation (KMC) has brushed off warnings on arsenic poisoning of groundwater and continues to sink tubewells in the contaminated areas.

Despite warnings by Jadavpur University's School of Environmental Studies, the civic body has decided to install more tubewells in arsenic-affected Jadavpur because it cannot supply enough piped water to homes. KJ Nath, chairman of the state government's Arsenic Task Force, feels the controversy over the contrasting claims by JU's Dipankar Chakraborty and KMC could easily be resolved if the civic body conducted a blanket study of all tubewells in the conflict zone.

"The civic authority is responsible for providing safe drinking water to the citizens of Kolkata. Hence, the onus of examining all tubewells lies with KMC. What baffles me is why KMC refuses to test the tubewells checked by Chakraborty. There are plenty of laboratories in the city that can do the test for less than Rs 100. It is cheaper than a blood and urine test," he said, adding that each tubewell in use should be certified 'arsenic-free' by the civic body.

Though it is quite possible that the tubewells that KMC tested were free of arsenic while those tested by Chakraborty had high levels of contamination, Nath has no doubt that the belt has arsenic seepage in groundwater.

"When North and South 24-Parganas are among the arsenic-affected districts, Kolkata cannot escape since it is contiguous to these districts. The city does not figure on our list simply because the mandate of the task force was for rural areas serviced by the public health engineering department. We have always maintained that if KMC seeks our advice or help in testing the water, we are ready to help. But they have not done so. As chairman of the task force, I advice all house-owners, particularly the new ones being built along the southern fringes, to get the water tested," said Nath. The task force has tested 1.46 lakh public water sources in 79 blocks at 120 labs in rural Bengal.

Lashing out at KMC for ignoring years of scientific research that detected arsenic in tubewells in the Garia-Jadavpur-Lake Gardens belt, Society for Environment & Development director AK Ghosh said the move to install more tubewells in Jadavpur was a "deliberate act of negligence" that knowingly exposed citizens to arsenic poisoning.

"KMC is required to provide 'safe' drinking water. It can easily do so by getting the water treated. There are at least eight technologies available and some models are already in use in places like Chakdah, charging households Rs 1 for 100 litres," Ghosh said. Political compulsion, and not scientific truth, is leading the decision-making on the issue, Ghosh says. "Unless there is seriousness of purpose, recommendation will go one way and implementation the other," he said.

Geologist PK Sikdar, associate professor in environmental management at Indian Institute of Social Welfare & Business Management (IISWBM), rued the manner in which the decision-makers treated seminars and discussions on arsenic. "Politicians and bureaucrats inaugurate seminars and then leave as their schedules are busy. During the discussion, only those who know the subject are left to discuss it amongst themselves. After a while, scientists get frustrated, stop pursuing change and carry on with their own research," said Sikdar.

On whether installation of deep tubewells would ensure arsenic free water in Jadavpur locality, the scientists said it would not work as arsenic would seep through in a couple of years. Explaining the peculiar geomorphology of Adi Ganga channel along the southern fringe that contains fine sand and not clay till as low as 600 ft below the surface, he said sand allowed arsenic to easily seep down. Changes in the hydrological pressure has freed up the arsenite present in the natural rock stratum in the Indo-Gangetic plain. The arsenic then dripped into the lower aquifer level. With farmers in Bengal and Bangladesh practicing boro rice cultivation that uses irrigated water, a large number of tubewells were sunk, leading to the spread of arsenic into lower aquifers, he said.

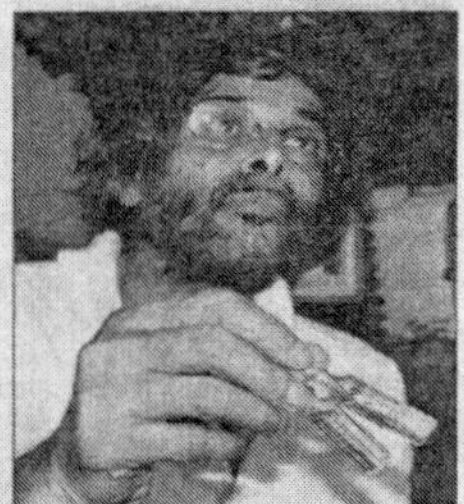

Dipankar Chakrabarti shows vials containing arsenic contaminated water

WAR OF WORDS

Chakrabarti has no authority to conduct the tests. He does not even have the SOES director's sanction to conduct them

Tarak Singh |

As research director of SOES, I don't need permission to conduct tests nor do I need a clearance from the director

Dipankar Chakraborty | SCIENTIST

Dipankar Chakraborty is very competent in the field of his research. There is no question of doubting his findings. He has a good laboratory, efficient technicians and arsenic detection is a routine scientific job that someone like him cannot goof-up

K J Nath | CHAIRMAN, ARSENIC TASK FORCE

DIPANKAR CHAKRABARTI TEST IN MAY 2012

Sample: Six tubewells in Jadavpur

Result: All six had an arsenic count far above the permissible limit. The lowest count detected was 30 micrograms and the highest was an alarming 190

I have interacted with Dipankar Chakrabarti on a couple of occasions. Kolkata Municipal Corporation does not take him seriously. Let him prove that the threat is as serious as he claims it to be

Sovan Chatterjee | MAYOR

KMC seals tubewells for arsenic threat, sets up new ones

Saikat Ray | TNN

Kolkata: Ringxing, a student from Sikkim, is scared of the water that comes out of the tap in his paying guest accommodation at Lake Gardens. He spends Rs 3,000 a month — almost as much as the rent and a meal-a-day — to buy filtered water. "I don't want to go deeper into the problem. But I'd be the last person to drink this unsafe water," the 23-year-old hotel management student told TOI.

Ringxing is not the only one paranoid about water in the Lake Gardens-Golf Green area. The Kolkata Municipal Corporation insists there is no arsenic contamination here but it is sealing off one tubewell after another because of the very threat. One such sealed tubewell stands in front of the Nava Nalanda School. It was sealed 15 days ago. Another, in front of the Lake Gardens post office, was sunk barely a month ago but has already been sealed.

> Students of the school drink water from this tubewell. If an arsenic alert is sounded, the civic authorities should cap this tubewell, too
>
> **Amit Deb** | RESIDENT OF LAKE GARDENS

Amit Deb, a resident of Lake Gardens who deals in electrical goods, is surprised that KMC has not sealed a tubewell opposite AK Ghosh Memorial School when two other hand pumps located in a 500-metre radius have been sealed. "Students of the school drink water from this tubewell. If an arsenic alert is sounded, the civic authorities should cap this tubewell, too," Deb said.

Lake Gardens residents have to depend on tubewells because the filtered water supply from Garden Reach is not enough. With the KMC sealing off many tubewells, several neighbourhoods are back in the grip of a severe water crisis.

Water being drawn from a tubewell in Golf Green right next to one that has been sealed due to presence of arsenic

> I pay someone to fetch drinking water. But I don't know if the bhari (water-carrier) gets it from a hand-pump or the filtered water taps
>
> **P R Narayanan** | LAKE GARDENS RESIDENT

P R Narayanan, a senior resident who runs a consultancy firm, concedes that the drinking water crisis is "above the arsenic threat" in Lake Gardens. "I pay someone to fetch drinking water. But I don't know if the bhari (water-carrier) gets it from a hand-pump or the filtered water taps," Narayanan said. The threat of arsenic contamination is indeed worrying, he says.

> The KMC sealed some hand-pumps in Narkelbagan, which is near our locality. But, they sunk a tubewell a fortnight ago in Golf Green because of the water crisis
>
> **Pampa Bardhan** | GOLF GREEN RESIDENT

Local councillor Mala Mahalanbis said the civic body had decided to seal some tubewells in Lake Gardens, as advised by experts, because of contamination of groundwater. Dipankar Chakraborty, an arsenic expert and director (research) of Jadavpur University's School of Environmental Studies, said that since a majority of the tubewells in Lake Gardens were sunk only 400 feet deep, the threat of arsenic was quite evident. "I had advised KMC to seal those tubewells long ago," he said.

Quite surprisingly, the KMC water supply department is still sinking hand-pumps afresh in Golf Green, where a number of tubewells have been sealed because of arsenic threat. "The KMC sealed some hand-pumps in Narkelbagan, which is near our locality. But, they sunk a tubewell a fortnight ago in Golf Green because of the water crisis this summer. I don't feel the KMC has done the studies necessary before deciding to set up new tubewells in the area," said Pampa Bardhan, a resident of Golf Green.

However, Tarak Singh, the mayor-in-council member overseeing groundwater, assured that an extensive survey would be carried out in all areas that are known to be arsenic-prone. "If we find traces of arsenic, we will take immediate action," Singh said.

Appendix – 16

From published news media sources

THE TIMES OF INDIA, KOLKATA
TUESDAY, NOVEMBER 13, 2012

Plot in Rajarhat fetches ₹6.85cr

Polyclinic Cum Day Care Centre To Be Set Up

Suman Chakraborti | TNN

Kolkata: The state government's plan to hardsell Rajarhat as a financial hub seems to be bearing fruit. A 22-cottah plot of land auctioned in Action Area I of Rajarhat has fetched Rs 6.85 crore, which is equal to Rs 18.45 crore per acre. The plot has been sold off to set up a polyclinic cum day care centre that can cater to the needs of local residents.

"We had put up a 22-cottah plot located in Action Area I for auction to set up a polyclinic cum day care centre. The last date of application was November 9. The plot has received a highest bid of Rs 6.85 crore, which is equivalent to Rs 18.45 crore per acre. We are working to complete the formalities quickly so that the process of setting up the day care centre can start at the earliest," said Hidco chairman cum managing director Debashis Sen.

So far, New Town lacks a hospital or polyclinic, said officials. Local residents hence depend on neighbouring areas of Salt Lake or VIP Road to attend to health issues. The number of people living in the township is estimated at 15,000. But with more highrises coming up in the area, the population is expected to shoot up further.

REALTY BOOM

- A 22-cottah plot in Action Area I of Rajarhat was sold at ₹6.85 cr
- Through e-auction, a 2-acre plot fetched ₹10.10 cr
- In August this year, a 2.5-acre plot in Rajarhat New Town had fetched ₹51.13 cr

Hidco planned to sell the land for a polyclinic keeping in mind the need of the residents. The news will come as a relief to them, felt officials.

In August this year, in the highest ever land auction for Rajarhat New Town, a 2.5-acre plot for a retail cum office complex fetched Rs 51.13 crore. The land, priced at more than Rs 20 crore per acre or Rs 34 lakh per cottah, broke all land selling records in Rajarhat New Town in terms of per acre price.

Though the authorities have been trying very hard to attract investments in the much touted financial hub, Hidco has been successfully selling small plots for commercial purposes.

The authorities had earlier put nine small plots in the area, ranging between 20 cottah and 2 acres, for sale through conventional bidding and auctioning. Out of the nine plots, seven of them were sold for a whopping Rs 58.5 crore.

Hidco authorities were also working on selling lands through e-auction. In the first such land sold through e-auction, a 2-acre plot for setting up a high school, fetched Rs 10.10 crore. More plots will be sold through this process, said Hidco officials.

TIMES OF INDIA
Nov. 19, Monday, 2012

State invites tenders for Rajarhat fin hub

Suman Chakraborti | TNN

Kolkata: The state government is all set to take the ambitious financial hub project in Rajarhat-New Town to the next stage.

With applications from six financial and banking institutes, the authorities have now floated tenders to begin work on the second phase of the financial hub. After opening the bids that ended on October 31, Hidco received offers from United Bank of India (UBI), United Commercial Bank (UCO), National Insurance Company (NIC), West Bengal Financial Corporation (WBFC), West Bengal Infrastructure Development and Financial Corporation (WBIDFC) and SREI. The authorities are working to scrutinize the bids.

Earlier, Allahabad Bank and SBI had already taken land near the hub. A few institutions like LIC Housing and Bank of India have requested for a little more time.

SECOND PHASE

In the second phase, the authorities want to hand over six vacant plots having an area of 12.5 acres on lease-hold basis for 99 years. The last date for submitting applications is January 31.

Hidco also plans to build an iconic building at a prime location of the central business district in New Town. The authorities have floated an expression of interest to invite best-in-class architect consultancy firm for this job.

Since chief minister Mamata Banerjee had launched the financial hub project earlier this year, the state government has been lobbying hard to attract investments. However, the initial response was very lukewarm. The authorities had only received one application after floating tenders and so they decided to extend the time for inviting applications.

Urban development minister Firhad Hakim, along with Hidco officials, went to Delhi and Mumbai to meet representatives of different financial institutions and convince them to invest. The authorities plan to hold more such meetings in Bangalore, Hyderabad and Singapore to highlight the hub.

TIMES CITY

SUNDAY TIMES OF INDIA, KOLKATA AUGUST 19, 2012

Record bid for Rajarhat plot

2.5-Acre Land At Action Area II Fetches Rs 51.13 Cr, Retail-Cum-Office Complex To Come Up

Suman Chakraborti

REALTY BOOM

IN DEMAND

> 2.5-acre plot for a retail-cum-office complex fetches ₹51.13 cr

> This is the highest bid ever in Rajarhat New Town so far

> Recently, seven small plots were sold for a total of ₹58.5 cr

OTHER LAND SALE RECORDS

SNAP-SHOTS

Sunday *Times of India,* Kolkata, August 19, 2012

Rajarhat plot sold for Rs. 20 cr/acre

Breaking all land auction records in Rajarhat-New Town, a 2.5-acre plot for a retal-cum-office complex in the township has fetched Rs. 51.13 crore. The rate works out to be more than Rs. 20 crore per acre or Rs. 34 lakh per cottah.

THE TIMES OF INDIA PRESENTS
times property guide
June, 2012 ISSUE IV ADVERTORIAL AND PROMOTIONAL FEATURE

THE FUTURE IS HERE

DEBASHIS SEN
CHAIRMAN, WEST BENGAL HOUSING INFRASTRUCTURE DEVELOPMENT CORPORATION LTD. (WBHIDCO) AND PRINCIPAL SECRETARY, URBAN DEVELOPMENT DEPARTMENT, GOVT OF WEST BENGAL

The slogan for New Town is — Be where it matters. New Town has emerged as a futuristic, smart, eco-friendly city. We are trying to develop it as an Eco 2 city; one that is both ecologically and economically advanced. We also want it to be a smart city, efficiently developed with energy saving devices, network, wireless and other technologies put together. Incidentally, the Government of India has already recognised New Town as a solar city. This was possible because we believe investments these days do not come only to places where land is cheap, especially high-class investments for eg as those in financial hubs. We think that the environment and surroundings really matter.

We recently had a one-on-one discussion with representatives of Yokohama, Japan. They had come to Kolkata to make a presentation. Yokohama has been recognised as an Eco2 city by the World Bank. They have shared with us some strategies regarding the Eco2 status, which will cost money now but will pay off in future.

As far as housing is concerned in New Town, there are different types of housing here, but now the strategy we are adopting is slightly different. In the last one year the strategy was to provide houses to the poor at affordable cost. But how do we provide affordable housing without getting any subsidy from the government? This is done by a system of cross subsidy wherein the profits made from the HIG sector is ploughed back in a no-profit-no-loss basis for the MIG sector and then leads to subsidised rates for the LIG sector. This has been the strategy so far.

For the Economically Weaker Section (EWS), the government has to directly step in. There is the need for great subsidy. But beyond that, there is a grey area. With a slight nudge, the private sector can come into play here.

This is the reason why the Government of India had formed a taskforce on affordable housing. I was part of this national level taskforce. With a little push those on the top of the poverty line can cross over. The private sector can also use this segment to make profits as well as provide housing for those who need it. However, normal market forces won't let it happen. It will need some kind of policy intervention, for eg faster plan passing period. One reason why the private sector is sceptical is that the plans take so much time to be sanctioned, and their capital remains blocked. In WBHIDCO the process of passing a plan is done online. You have to get a digital signature from a registered architect, submit your building plan parameters and you are given an online sanction. It is one of the few places in Bengal to have a thriving online process for passing building plans. Some kind of infrastructural support also needs to be given to private builders apart from faster sanction of plans. We think that the housing policy needs to concentrate upon the economically weaker section and the lower income group by making policy interventions and earmarking space for them.

This has already been done in New Town. Now

ALAKA PROJECT OF WBHIDCO IS A PERFECT EXAMPLE OF SUSTAINBLE DEVELOPMENT WHERE RESIDENTS CAN REST THEIR TIRED EYES WITH THE GREENERY ALL AROUND

what we are trying to move at is to support housing for people directly connected with the commercial sector. What does that mean in simple terms? Suppose we are trying to build a financial hub with a series of bankers, the question arises as to where are the executives going to stay? Where are the security personnel or cleaning staff going to stay? This is also another sector of society but since it is directly related to an economic activity that generates revenue, you should reserve land to cater to their accommodation needs.

Land is scarce, not much of WBHIDCO land is left. So it should be used up for those people who are involved in economy generating activities. Focus now is on generating the economy using housing as a tool to do so. WBHIDCO Ltd has taken the endeavour to open up discussion with national level financial institutions and banking units to offer ready plots for the expansion of their business in the eastern India.

As far as land allotment is concerned (for non-residential purposes), we are doing it strictly on an auction basis. The latest innovation that recently got approved during the board meeting held a few days ago is e-auction. It works very interestingly. The publicity and advertisement takes place on websites but it all happens in a particular span; say from 8am to 3pm on a particular day. But if there is a bid even 8 minutes before closing, the bidding is extended for another 10 minutes, so that people can compete more. E-auction is a very transparent process. We have talked with public sector organisations to set up such e-auctions on a national scale and we hope to set the ball rolling in June 2012 itself.

There is a lot of talk going on about rising price of property, but one must understand that the government needs money so as to engage in welfare activities for the poor. And if the market can afford it, I don't personally see why the government should be deprived of its revenue. There is a Chankaya saying I am fond of "A person who takes as government revenue less than what he is supposed to is cheating the government. But if he is taking more than double of what the revenue should be, he is killing the country." If I make my property prices too high, probably am not allowing development to set in. WBHIDCO has a very good pricing policy, absolutely scientific based on certain weightage factors.

We are holding a national seminar on July 14 on densification of cities. Since land is very scarce, we need to make full use of it as Singapore is doing, as downtown New York is doing, where the Floor Area Ratio (FAR) is around 11 or 14. Increased FAR means creation of more virtual land. What we are trying to say to builders is that we are encouraging compact, dense cities, which can enable maximum utilisation of existing land.

At a recent cabinet meeting, it was decided to form a committee to check the rampant mushrooming of high rises by private builders in New Town. An agency has been appointed to survey the area and chalk out land use maps. The committee would be headed by the chief secretary Samar Ghosh. It would comprise municipal affairs secretary Alapan Bandyopadhyay; Land Reforms Commissioner R D Meena and myself as the urban development secretary.

WBHIDCO land is running out. We would rather have vertical cities rather than urban sprawls. Of course that would require technology, but we would ask every builder to go tall as per the FAR permitted and leave green spaces in front. They should make use of rain harvesting, water harvesting to follow green building norms, use solar power wherever possible, efficient machines, airconditioners, so that our vision to make New Town an environment friendly green city is achieved soon. We appeal to all to make it aesthetically interesting as well.

New Town has a character of its own; it is not Kolkata, Kalyani or Salt Lake. It has a green character, an identity of its own. So that should definitely be kept in mind and the use of glass, steel, Teflon kept to a minimum. Builders should not stop at your property line, they should go beyond and make it a beautiful stretch.

I see Kolkata and especially New Town developing into a space where people are happy. We want to see an international community out here; we want to give people a sense of belonging. We envision healthy, happy families moving around shopping in malls and hardcore business taking place at the business centres, commercial hubs, IT and health hubs, in the IIT-KGP, Presidency University so as to meet the satisfaction levels of everybody residing here.

THE TIMES OF INDIA

For the poor?

Unused plots in Salt Lake under state scanner

Suman Chakraborti | TNN

Kolkata: The land issue has been gnawing at the Mamata Banerjee-led government ever since it has come into power. Soon after attaining office, the chief minister had therefore put a curb on land acquisition that was supposed to take place in Rajarhat. Currently, the state is determined to stall underutilization of land resources.

The urban development department is busy reviewing all unutilized plots that were handed over to private companies to implement projects through the public-private-partnership (PPP) model.

The private partners will be asked to give reasons for the delay in implementing projects. If the firms do not give any reply or fail to cite a satisfactory reason, the government will initiate steps to take back the plots and put them to proper use.

"A meeting was held on this issue last week. The status of all such plots is being looked into," said state urban development department secretary Debashis Sen.

Many plots were handed over to private companies during the Left regime for implementing projects through PPP, but the present urban development department has noticed that many of the plots are still lying unused. Most of these plots – located in Rajarhat, places off EM Bypass and other township areas – belong to the Housing Infrastructure Development Corporation (Hidco) and the Kolkata Metropolitan Development Authority (KMDA). The private partners had tied up with the two agencies to implement the projects through PPP. The urban development department is preparing a list of all such plots and the projects that were supposed to be implemented on them. A report will also be prepared on the present status of the plots and on the terms and conditions of financial agreement made with the private partners.

Plots were handed over to private companies during the Left rule for implementing projects through PPP model, but they are still lying vacant

For example, a water park cum entertainment centre was supposed to come up on a 33-acre area near Ruby hospital off EM Bypass for which a private company was also selected. The project was planned way back in 2005 but is yet to take shape.

Earlier, government agencies having land could make inter-department handover of the land and also could decide by themselves to sell or auction it. But now, The government land can be sold for any project only if the cabinet clears the proposal.

Apart from land for PPP projects that are lying unutilised, the urban development department is scrutising all land in Salt Lake area that are lying vacant for years. The authorities are sending notices to the leaseholders of these plots seeking reasons for not constructing houses yet.

TIMES OF INDIA, JULY 23, 2012

Times of India June 24, 2012

Don't use wetlands for even public projects, says panel

Suman Chakraborti | TNN

Kolkata: Filling up of wetlands and any construction on them should be banned across the state, says the committee tasked with preparing a draft policy on wetlands. The report has just landed on the environment minister's desk.

A major problem is that tracts of wetlands are declared as agricultural land and then converted to industrial or residential land, the report says, adding that this has to stop.

The report says that Bengal is blessed with a wide variety of wetlands, but the only Ramsar site is the 12,500-hectare East Kolkata Wetlands.

The draft policy advocates banning the use of any kind of wetland, irrespective of size, even for public interest projects. The government should reject all construction plans on wetlands or any other form of waterbodies like *jala, khal, bil, doba*, and even on paddy fields.

It calls for a 10-year awareness programme and restoration of all degraded and filled up wetlands and waterbodies. Apart from being vital to the ecological balance, wetlands are important for income generation, livelihood and well being of the communities, the report says. The draft policy speaks for a wetland inventory, and regular monitoring.

SAVE WETLANDS

The draft also points out that unregulated use of fertilizers and pesticides is having adverse effects on human health, food security and biodiversity stock. Also, since most of the larger wetlands lie outside any protected area under the Forest Act, the concept of catchment area is a necessity in conservation efforts.

সরকারি কোটায় জমি পেয়েছেন বিচারপতি ঘোষ: মন্ত্রী

নিজস্ব প্রতিনিধি, কলকাতা: বামফ্রন্টের আমলে সরকারি কোটায় জমি পেয়েছেন পিনাকীচন্দ্র ঘোষসহ মোট ১৭ জন বিচারপতি। শুক্রবার রাজ্য বিধানসভায় পুর ও নগরোন্নয়ন দপ্তরের বাজেট বিতর্ক চলাকালীন ‘পয়েন্ট অব অর্ডার’ এনে তৃণমূল কংগ্রেস বিধায়ক তাপস রায় পুরমন্ত্রী ফিরহাদ হাকিমের কাছ থেকে জানতে চান, বিগত সরকারের আমলে কতজন বিচারপতি সরকারি কোটায় জমি পেয়েছেন। সভায় তাঁদের নাম প্রকাশ করার জন্য পুরমন্ত্রীকে অনুরোধ করেন তাপসবাবু। তার জবাবে পুরমন্ত্রী জানান, প্রসেনজিৎ মণ্ডল, তপেন সেন, অসীম বন্দ্যোপাধ্যায় ও পিনাকীচন্দ্র ঘোষসহ মোট ১৭ জন বিচারপতি সরকারি কোটায় জমি পেয়েছেন। প্রসঙ্গত, হাইকোর্টের যে ডিভিশন বেঞ্চ সিঙ্গুর মামলার রায় দিয়েছে তার অন্যতম সদস্য হলেন পিনাকীচন্দ্র ঘোষ। বর্তমান ২৩ জুন ২০১২

[*Bartaman*, 23rd June, 2012 **Justice Ghosh Received Land in Government Quota: Minister**

During Left Front Regime 17 numbers of Justice including Pinaki Ranjan Ghosh received land in Government quota. In response to an enquiry by Tapas Roy, MLA, Trinamul Congress during a Budget session of the Ministry of Urban Development and Municipal Affairs in State Legislative Assembly, Firhad Hakim, the Minister in Charge of Municipal Affairs, said, altogether seventeen numbers of Judges including Prasenjit Mandal, Tapen Sen, Asim Bandopadhyay and Pinaki Chandra Ghosh received land on government quota during the regime of earlier government. Incidentally, Pinaki Chandra Ghosh is one of the members of the Division Bench, who delivered the verdict on Singurcase.]

Some news Head lines

আনন্দবাজার পত্রিকা বৃহস্পতিবার ১৩ জানুয়ারি ২০০০

পরিবেশের চূড়ান্ত ছাড়পত্র ছাড়াই জমি বিলি রাজারহাটে

(Anandabazar Patrika, Thursday 13, January, 2000, Headline: Distribution of land in Rajarhat without environmental clearance)

প্রতিদিন ৬ ফেব্রুয়ারি ২০০০

রাজারহাট উপনগরী : বিভ্রান্ত করছে আবাসন দপ্তর

(Pratidin 6th February, 2000, Headline: Rajarhat Township: Housing Department is misleading the people)

আনন্দবাজার পত্রিকা সোমবার ১৩ মার্চ ২০০০

লকলকে ধান উপড়ে ফেলে মাটি ভরাট

(Anandabazar Patrika, Monday, 13 March, 2000, Headline: Filling with earth on the riped crop)

বর্তমান ১ এপ্রিল ১৯৯৯

রাজারহাটে টাউনশিপ নিয়ে গ্রিন বেঞ্চে

নিজস্ব প্রতিনিধি, বারাসত: রাজারহাটে প্রস্তাবিত সাটেলাইট টাউনশিপের বিরুদ্ধে গ্রিন বেঞ্চে যাওয়ার সিদ্ধান্ত নিল রাজারহাট জমি বাঁচাও কমিটি।

(Bartaman 1st April, 1999, Headline: The Rajarhat Jamibachao Committee has decided to approach Green Bench against the proposed settelite Township at Rajarhat)

২৯ মার্চ ১৯৯৯ আজকাল

রাজারহাট

আন্দোলনে সমর্থন বুদ্ধিজীবীদের

আজকালের প্রতিবেদন: রাজারহাটে উচ্ছেদ বিরোধী আন্দোলনের পাশে দাঁড়ালেন বুদ্ধিজীবী ও সাংস্কৃতিক কর্মীরা।

(29th March, 1999, Ajkal Patrika, Headline: Rajarhat: Elites support movement; News: The elites and cultural Activists stand beside the movement against the land acquisition at Rajarhat)

The Times of India, Calcutta Saturday, January 8, 2000

Headline: File affidavit on Rajarhat HC tells Bengal Government.

MEENBARTA

A quarterly Organ of fisheries Department, West Bengal (Bilingual) February, 2009.

Global Warming and Endangered Wet-land

Kalyan Rudra

4) East Calcutta Wetland

The 12000 ha. wetland area has earned international recognition for its importance towards ecological balancing. of the city. It is necessary to have an idea about the Geomorphology of this wetland. This widespread 28 km. land between Hooghly river in the west and Kulti in the east, is slanting towards east. The east Calcutta wetland is situated between this two rivers. The drainage canal was dug in the British regime using the easterly slope. The waste water of Kolkata flows through this canal to the Kulti river. Waters of North 24 Parganas flows through Noai, Suti and Bidyadhari river. But during high tide in the Kulti river cause problem in the drainage system of Kolkata. To arrest the high tide of Kultialliock gates at Ghusighata are closed down. During this period east Calcutta wetland consumes all this waters. This is the natural reservoir of Kolkata during the period of high tide and rainy season.

286 Bheries of east Calcutta are being fed by this waste water for production of fish and vegetables. The sunlight and heat helps natural purification of this waste water. The waste water and the garbage meet 20% of the vegetables and 15% of the fish demand of the city. Calcutta is now spreading towards east, grabbing this wetland. 1500 ha. wetland has lost its character during the period from 1980 - 2000. The proposed township of Rajarhat will consume 2750 ha. agriculture and wetland. Though the Editorial of Meenbarta in the year 1988 commented -" the self interested people has caused degradation of biodiversity and environment. pollution on this wetland thereby disturbing the economic bouancy of the people of this area. The greed of such people has damped thousand of fisherman. The protest of the people living on this wetland for generation after generation has gone into the deaf ears. The survivility of the people of this area is struggling. This reminds the barbarism of the "Neelkuthi Saheb" of grabbing the agriculture land for the cultivation of Neel. The international traders were behind this conspiracy then. The multinational and transnational companies are now displacing the sun of the soil with the same motive" (Meenbarta, 9th June, 1998) The Metropolitan Development Plan, 1990 - 2015 of C.M.D.A. depicted "The agricultural lands as well as the wetland and large water bodies should be preserved as .such and no change in use such land should be permitted." This warning is corroborated in the reports submitted by G.SJ. which quoted - "urban expansion into low-lying interdistributory marshes should be avoided so as to conserve agricultural lands and to keep free sufficient area to accommodate spreading of flood spill." (G.S.I. Spl. Pub. No. 43 P. 121). The Rajarhat township is situated outside the protected area of K.M.D.A. So this warning does not apply to Rajarhat. But it is an offence in the eye of general rule to fill up the wetland. The enactment of 1994 to avoid the present act has quoted "Considering the locational advantages as well as the transport linkages of the eastern fringe of Calcutta, efforts shall be made to utilise some land for accommodating central functions of metropolitan level". (Landuse and development control plan, 1994). By this way Government has legalized this illegal filling of the wetland. This degradation was started since construction of Salt Lake City and Rajarhat New Township. The character of East Calcutta is rapidly changing since 80s. Anxiety always persists for the generation to come.

5) Benefits of Wetland

The importance of wetland is immensely felt in the social life. Some part of the vast water resources is preserved in this natural wetland. Therefore the wetlands help control of flood. 42% of the area of the State is flood prone and 2.51 % area is wetland. These wetlands are spread over in the flood prone areas. In the nine months period almost all wetlands, rivers, canals become dry and underground water goes down till the rains set in Rain water feds in all such water bodies and helps to raise underground water level.

High breed technology was introduced to meet growing demand of food during post independence five decades. Underground water was indiscriminately used for this. Now the underground water is contaminated with arsenic and people of nine districts of West Bengal are forced to drink such poisonous water. It is undisputed to meet the problem till restriction is imposed on lifting of ground water. Alternatively, the surface water could meet such demand and this is possible by conserving water in tanks, ponds, and wetlands. 50% annual demand of water in West Bengal is utilised in irrigation. The dams and reservoirs constructed 5 decades back have become silted. Construction of new reservoirs are not congenial in West Bengal. Thus the indigenous method of harvesting rain water is getting importance along with conserving water in wetlands. This is important in the light of scarcity of water.

The magnitude of wetland is multipurpose Restrains flood and helps deposition of underground water. Wetlands nourish 20% of world's biodiversity. Maintains balance of carbon di-oxideand Methen and effects rain by raising humidity in air during dry season. This imparallel natural resources is diminishing in the name of development. It's protection is indeed necessary for the sake of mankind. The verdict of Supreme Court is relevant here. "We are not obvious of the fact that natural resources have got to be tapped for the purposes of social development, but one cannot forget at the same time that tapping of resources have to be done with requisite attention and care so that ecology and environment may not be affected in any serious way, there may not be any depletion of water resources and long term planning must be undertaken to keep up the national wealth. It has always to be remembered that these are permanent assets of mankind and are not intended to be exhausted in one generation." (New Central Jute Mills Co. Ltd. V.U.P.E.B., Lucknow, AIR, SC-364) It is no longer a presumption but fact that climate on earth is warming. The report of Inter Governmental Panel of climate change (IPCC) has been published in the year 2007. It would be a matter of grave concern to all conscious citizens. The Expert Committee has said:

1. Out of hottest 12 years since 1850 last 11 years were significant.
2. Almost 7% of Glacier of North Pole has melted during twentieth century.
3. At the end of twenty first centre the world temperature will rise from 1.8°C to 4°C and sea water level will go up to 6.7 mtr. Causing inundation of wide coastal area.
4. Himalayan glacier will be vanished by 2035. Rivers originated from Himalaya may become in spate in few years, to come but ultimately will be dried.
5. The food production will reduce 4 - 10% in South East Asia.
6. The Ganges and Brahmaputra and their tributaries will go dry except in monsoon season.
7. The rainfall will be minimized between 10N - 30N i.e. all over India. Mentionably the deserted area has doubled during last 4 decades.

Consequently the wetland of India would gradually diminish. Soil humidity would be lost. Humidity of air would increase. And the ultimate result would be warming of climate affecting water cycle. Rainfall would be reduced since condensation of evaporation will be affected. All these would have a long term reaction. With the drying up of earth surface the trees and grass would not grow and the entire foodchain will be affected. Biodiversity loss will cause loss of lives on earth. Agriculture and drinking water will be hard hit due to insufficient underground water.

Finally the civilization will face monumental crisis.

THE TIMES OF INDIA, KOLKATA
TUESDAY, JUNE 12, 2012

State plans land use map for Rajarhat

TIMES NEWS NETWORK

Kolkata: Exactly a year after dissolving the Bhangar Rajarhat Area Development Authority (BRADA), the state government has taken it upon itself to create a land use map of the area around Bhangar and Rajarhat to control the mushrooming of highrises that are being constructed without taking into consideration the public infrastructure. This was decided at a cabinet meeting in the state secretariat on Monday.

"There is a lot of land around Rajarhat and Bhangar that has been allotted to private parties. We suspect that there will be rampant construction in the area. We have no problem with that, but unplanned construction cannot be allowed. We will prepare a detailed land use map that will earmark the roads, drainage and public utility. Based on this map, the allotees can go ahead with their construction," a Writers' Buildings source said.

The land use map will be prepared by a committee set up for this purpose. The committee will comprise urban development minister Firhad Hakim, urban development secretary Debashis Sen and municipal affairs secretary Alapan Bandyopadhyay. According to sources, there was unchecked distribution of land in the area after the dissolution of BRADA. It took some time for the government to realise that the situation has not shown any improvement even after BRADA was dissolved and promoters still call the shots. Sources believe that the cabinet decision may finally end up in the creation of a body like the BRADA. Only, this one will be controlled by the Trinamool Congress instead of the CPM.

The government took a decision to dissolve BRADA on May 31, 2011. It was then stated that the body was not functioning. It was then considered whether to hand over charge to Hidco. BRADA as it is had no control over the land and was primarily set up to formulate land usage. Unlike Hidco, BRADA had no control over land prices and a cottah of land that was barely worth Rs 20,000 till a few years ago changed hands recently for up to Rs 200,000.

Records show that nearly 2,000 acres were sold under BRADA. The area under consideration is over 6,000 to 7,000 hectares. It comprises 15 mouzas of North 24-Parganas and nine in the South. Among the prominent locations is the Vedic Village.

THE TIMES OF INDIA, KOLKATA
WEDNESDAY, JUNE 27, 2012

TIMES CITY

Ponds vanish in realty boom

Filling Up Of Waterbodies Continues As Land Sharks Bend Law To Encroach Upon Them

Subhro Niyogi & Saikat Ray | TNN

Four waterbodies along the EM Bypass are at various stages of being encroached by promoters and real estate developers

Kolkata: Chief minister Mamata Banerjee had asked the police top brass and Trinamool Congress councillors to ensure that waterbodies in their jurisdiction don't get encroached. But it seems the diktat has had little effect with police and party men turning a blind eye to indiscriminate filling up of ponds.

During a drive along EM Bypass on Tuesday, TOI encountered three waterbodies at various stage of encroachment and received complaints of another audacious attempt. While two ponds had been blatantly filled up with fly-ash in broad daylight, another had been filled up slyly at night.

After two-thirds of a pond was filled up in Anandapur, a local youth knocked on all doors, including that of the chief minister's office, and somehow managed to persuade the administration to stop the encroachment. He got in return threats and was finally beaten up by members of a local club that had allegedly been paid by a contractor to dump earth into the water body.

"I was on way home from work late one night when local youths thrashed me for raising a voice against the filling up of the pond adjoining my house. My family members were so terrorized that they shifted to a house in Dhakuria. I quit the job and stay at home now," said 25-year-old Surajit Bag of Anandapur.

Bag has lodged complaints with police and the Kolkata Municipal Corporation (KMC), but the encroachment did not stop. Local Trinamool Congress councillor Partha Roychowdhury conceded that there were attempts to encroach ponds in the locality but said he could do little unless police took more initiative.

A year ago, a member of NGO Public had been thrashed in Golf Garden for protesting against the filling up of a pond next to a burial ground. Though he had filed an FIR, he eventually withdrew it after both CPM and Trinamool Congress youths held separate rallies in the neighbourhood denouncing him.

Less than 1 km away from where Bag lives in perpetual fear is Collector bheri, a huge water body that was being blatantly encroached upon before a persistent TOI campaign finally led to concerted action by the East Kolkata Wetlands Management Authority, KMC and police. But after the walls that had been built around the pond overgrown with high weeds and grass. Now it appears to be a low-lying wasteland.

"That encroachment was stopped by decisive action is commendable. But the job is half-done unless it is filled up with water. Sadly that has not happened, leaving it vulnerable to encroachment at a later date," said green activist Bonani Kakkar.

With land price hitting the roof in recent times, land sharks are prying on water bodies to make a killing. In Purba Digantapur, opposite the locals. With the promoter hands-in-glove with local youths, no one dared to interfere.

"Over the past seven days, I have seen trucks enter the locality daily. It was only last evening that I discovered a pond that existed behind a four-storied building had disappeared," said local resident Suman Sinha.

Sandhita Mondal, mayor-in-council member overseeing the KMC environment department, promised action against the errant real estate

Further down the Bypass behind Apollo Gleneagles hospital, musclemen cordoned off a plot before filling up a pond. Scribes who went to probe were chased by hoodlums appointed by the realtor to guard the property. Though activist Subhas Datta filed a case and wrote to the CM, there has been no action yet.

In the evening, TOI received a call informing that a bheri in East Kolkata Wetlands was being filled up. Trucks of rubbish were being gradually

4 The Times of India, Kolkata June 23, 2012 TIMES CITY

Rajarhat plots fetch hefty prices

Hidco Receives ₹58.5 Cr Bid For Seven Plots

Suman Chakraborti | TNN

Kolkata: Just when the state is losing out on investment due to the government's hands-off acquisition policy and unavailability of land, Rajarhat New Town continues to be on top of the demand list with investors willing to pay as much as ₹21 crore for an acre of land.

Recently, the West Bengal Housing Infrastructure Development Corporation (Hidco) had put nine plots — ranging from 20 cottah to 2 acre — in Rajarhat New Town on the block for bidding and within days, the agency received highest bids for as many as seven plots. Deadline for receiving bid applications has been extended for the remaining two plots.

"It is very encouraging that investors have faith on Rajarhat and places surrounding the city," said Hidco chairman-cum-managing director Debashis Sen. The authorities have already given offer letters to the highest bidders. So far seven highest bids accumulate to ₹58.5 crore for about 3.6 acre and another three acre will be sold very soon.

Hidco had floated tenders for four institutional plots, one plot each for educational, mercantile retail, trauma care centre, geriatric centre and for setting up a restaurant, all within Action Area I and II. The agency received the highest bid of ₹34 crore for the four institutional plots on 2 acre of land. For the 20 cottah mercantile retail plot, Hidco received ₹7-crore bid. This amounts to ₹21 crore per acre.

For the 20-cottah restaurant project plot, a bid of ₹4.50 crore has been placed. For two health sector plots of 30 cottah each, the authorities have received bids of ₹7 crore and 6 crore respectively, which sum up to ₹14 crore and ₹12 crore per acre, respectively.

For two plots meant for the trauma care centre and a geriatric health care centre, Hidco has extended the time period to receive bid applications. The authorities have received only one bid for each of the two plots.

On an average, commercial plots in Rajarhat New Town now cost about ₹10 crore per acre. It was decided earlier that all plots in Rajarhat from now on will be sold through commercial bidding only. Earlier, the government had sold two 50-acre plots to Infosys and Wipro for ₹75 crore each, amounting to ₹1.5 crore per acre.

LAND PRICES BOOM

Price	Purpose	Price/acre
₹34 crore	4 institutional plots on 2 acre	₹17 crore
₹7 crore	20 cottah mercantile retail plot	₹21 crore
₹ 4.50 crore	20 cottah plot for restaurant	₹ 13.5 crore
₹7 crore	30 cottah healthcare facility	₹14 crore
₹6 crore	30 cottah healthcare facility	₹12 crore

TOI–JULY 9, 2012, MONDAY

Rajarhat land sold via e-auction

Suman Chakraborti | TNN

Kolkata: In a first in the state, a 2-acre plot was sold off through e-auction.

The West Bengal Housing Infrastructure Development Corporation (Hidco) conducted this e-auction, in which the 2 acres at Rajarhat New Town was sold for Rs 10.10 crore for setting up a school. It plans to sell more such plots through e-auctioning. The auction was conducted by MSTC, a public sector undertaking. "The process of on line e-auction is much more transparent than the conventional bidding and auctioning," a Hidco official said.

Officials said that the highest bid for the 2-acre plot was Rs 10.10 crore and was quite encouraging taking into the fact that the bid for the plot was made for setting up a school and not any commercial institution, like hotels or other profit making institutions. At present, commercial plots in Rajarhat New Town costs about Rs 10 crore per acre.

The entire process of e-auction is supervised by quality controllers, so that no malpractice can take place. The bidders are given passwords and asked to give digital signatures. The entire process takes place online.

> Hidco sells a 2-acre plot at Rajarhat for Rs 10.10 crore. It plans to sell more such plots through e-auctioning

Hidco has recently put nine plots, ranging from 20-cottah to 2 acres, in Rajarhat New Town on the block for conventional bidding and auctioning and till date seven plots have been sold for a total of Rs 58.5 crore. Two plots are yet to be sold off, for which the deadline for receiving bid applications have been extended. Officials said that it is encouraging that investors are keen on Rajarhat.

It has been decided earlier that all the plots in Rajarhat from now on will be sold through commercial bidding only and the process of e-auction, officials feel, will bring in more transparency.

Hidco authorities are framing a land use plan for the entire Rajarhat area, including the fringe areas that were earlier under the jurisdiction of Bhangor Rajarhat Area Development Authority (Brada). It was dissolved by the Mamata Banerjee government, so that the land could be put in good use.

বর্তমান

রাজারহাটে মমতার স্বপ্নপ্রকল্প রূপায়ণ করতে গিয়ে অশান্তি, শেষে পুলিশ প্রহরায় কাজ শুরু

জমিহারাদের হাতে হেনস্তা হিডকো প্রধানের

ইকো টুরিজম পার্ক

আয়তন ৪৮০ একর

[*Bartaman,* 12th May , 2012

ECO TOURISM PARK
Area 480 acre

- The Eco-Tourism Park will have 100 acres of water body
- Altogether four types of vegetation will be created
  1. Tropical Rain forest
  2. Harbs garden
  3. Bamboo forest
  4. Deciduous forest
- There will be restaurant in the water body
- Field for children
- Butterfly Park

In spite of objection from the land loser the work of Eco-Tourism Park started

The picture shows the northern part of the park

Head lines: Restlessness at Rajarhat on implementation of the dream project of Mamata Bandopadhyay, lastly the work started under Police protection.

Harassment of HIDCO Chief by Land-Loser

On 5th May the Chairman of HIDCO faced strong protest from the landloser of Jatragachhi *mouja* on the non-payment of compensation. The agitation was so strong that Police had to intervene... The agitation was for the non-payment of compensation to the land losers. HIDCO assured the land losers for discussion and it is assured that on submission of the related valid documents they will get compensation. But many do not have proper documents, informed by the local New Town Trinamool Congress leader].

Three kids enjoying at Eco-Park- Saubhik Dey.

(Some laugh many weep)

Anandabazar Patrika
A Land of Fairy Tales ...
Rajarhat Eco-park in the evening.

(At the cost of lakhs of people's livelihood ...).

The TOI, August 1, 2012

No takers for Rajarhat financial hub

Aparajita Gupta & Suman Chakraborti | TNN

Kolkata: It has been over four months since chief minister Mamata Banerjee flagged off the international financial hub project in Rajarhat. The government highlighted the potential of the hub in full swing, saying it will be only the second financial hub in the country after Mumbai's Bandra Kurla. However, quite unexpectedly, only one company has so far shown interest to invest in the financial hub.

Tuesday was the last day of application submission, but none turned up to show any interest in the last one month to set up shop in the much-touted financial hub of the city.

The project is implemented by the Housing Infrastructure Development Corporation Ltd (Hidco). A 25-acre plot has been identified for taking up the first phase of the financial hub, which could be extended up to 100 acres in the future in phases.

> This project needed a lot of promotions. That has not been done. We have to do aggressive marketing
>
> **Saugata Roy** | Union minister of state for urban development

Union minister of state for urban development Saugata Roy said poor marketing strategy by the department concerned is one of the root causes for this low turnout.

"This project needed a lot of space-selling promotions. That has not been done. We have to do aggressive marketing," he told TOI. He has convened a meeting with the financial institution heads of the country on August 23 at Vigyan Bhawan in Delhi to make them understand and convince about the facilities of this space so that more investment proposals come from the banking institutions.

Financial institutions include banks — both public and private — and insurance companies have been invited for the talks.

Hidco chairman-cum-managing director Debashis Sen said the authority will decide very soon as to whether a fresh expression of interest could be floated. "We will decide shortly whether we will float a new EOI with fresh terms and conditions. I will also be present at the meeting on August 23 where I will give a presentation on the financial hub," he said.

Earlier, April 24 was fixed as the last date of submitting applications. It was later extended till July 31 by Hidco, hoping that they will receive at least a few more applications. Only big financial houses and banking institutions, having an annual turnover of Rs 500 crore and above, could submit proposals for getting a space in the hub. The average market price of the land per acre is Rs 13 crore.

The TOI, May, 24, 2012

Land sharks gobble up 80-cottah pond

Rupali Shukla | TNN

Kolkata: Encroachment of waterbodies continues unabated. After a pond was filled up in Dum Dum and another in Nonadanga late last year, land sharks have struck yet again — this time in the city proper — filling up an 80-cottah waterbody to construct residential highrises. The encroached pond is at 51A Canal Circular Road behind Apollo Gleneagles Hospital in east Kolkata.

The controversial plot, that locals say rippled with water till three to four months ago, has now been filled up with earth. Though some claimed that the 80-cottah 'land' in question was a low-lying area where water accumulated during monsoon, giving the impression of a waterbody, others disputed it in hushed tones and informed that a pond had existed there for years. Sources said both muscle and money had played a part in suppressing voices in the neighbourhood.

The presence of shanties housing washermen is the only evidence of a 'waterbody'. In south Kolkata, too, washermen live in a cluster around a pond off Pramathesh Barua Sarani. "With the pond at Canal Circular Road now gone, the washermen have to make do with water from a well," said washerwoman Uma Razak.

It was a local resident who alerted environment activist Subhas Datta about the encroachment. The latter went on a recce on Wednesday afternoon, but was stopped by private security guards posted at the site. It was only after police arrived that the guards relented. What Datta saw left him in shock. "There is no sign of a pond now. It has been completely filled up," he said.

Aranya Roy Chowdhury

Environment activist Subhas Datta inspects the plot on Wednesday

Sources said the pond has been filled up over the past couple of months under blanket security. The entrance to the plot is shrouded with a black tarpaulin and entry strictly monitored. There is absolute secrecy over who the promoters are and what is to be constructed at the encroached site.

Some, however, brazenly claimed that the 'so-called pond' was a lowland. "It is good that it is being filled up," said Rajesh Sharma, who has been living here for 40 years. Activist Bonani Kakkar, who has fought many a legal battle for wetland conservation, clarified that any waterbody over 5 cottah comes under the purview of Inland Fisheries Act and any wetland, whatever be the condition, cannot be converted to dry land.

A 16-year-old spilled the beans. "The pond had a lot of water, but the people have been filling it gradually for years. The activity picked up steam over the past couple of months," he said.

An FIR has been lodged and Phool Bagan police have written to Kolkata Municipal Corporation for action. KMC has, in turn, asked police to maintain a 24×7 vigil and plans to inspect the site soon. "A joint inspection will be carried out with representatives of the pollution control board, inland fisheries department and KMC's project management unit," said KMC member, mayor-in-council (environment) Sanchita Mondol.

South Asian Forum for Environment chair Dipayan Dey isn't too enthused with the assurance of an inspection. "It is our collective responsibility to end the encroachment and filling of wetlands. But no one is doing anything about it. There are several cases like these, but they never come to our notice," he added.

THE TIMES OF INDIA, KOLKATA
THURSDAY, MAY 24, 2012

CITY MAIL BOX — SPEAK OUT

Land acquisition: Let the spirit of self reliance prevail

Though many of my compatriots may hold different views, I personally largely agree with the Parliamentary standing committee panel's proposed norms that land acquisitions by the government should be done mainly for infrastructure and social projects.

I feel any project in which private players are involved; the government should stay away from land acquisition. The fact of the matter is that few lakh private enterprises set up in India since Independence have, by and large, acquired land on their own for projects which they are successfully running. The private industrial sector in India has always fended for itself and has done a good job of setting up large enterprises and creating large scale employment without government support. Let this spirit of self reliance prevail.

Industry can acquire the land for itself and the land giver needs to be adequately compensated and resettled, if need be by re-training, etc. Government can of course intervene as a facilitator in such acquisition only when there is a need to resolve disputes and remove bottlenecks. It makes sense that the government should acquire land only for:

i) Rural or social sector development purposes like roads, schools, hospitals, sanitation, drinking water

ii) Projects of national interest and public service to create infrastructure like roads, power, irrigation

iii) For the purpose of creating land bank for supporting small /micro enterprises and land-linked employment generation activities

Private players — including realtors and SEZ developers — have often, through the government, received more land than they actually needed for their projects at a considered price which they later dispose off for profit. The standing committee's proposal would curb such profiteering, made at the cost of the farmers / land owners. Also, this would pave the way for optimal land usage in India and effectively address the issue of land shortage by indirectly making land available for industrial sector.

S K Birla

We want your views and comments.
Please write to us at Speakout (speakoutkolkata@timesgroup.com) with Times City, in the subject line

THE ECONOMICS TIMES

What To Do With New Fund Managers

PERSONAL FINANCE P4

'Architecture of Salt Lake is Commendable'

PRINCIPAL secretary of Urban Development of West Bengal, **Debashis Sen** *will be completing his one year as the chairman of West Bengal Housing Infrastructure Development Corporation Limited aka WBHIDCO this August. He strives to make "New Town the futuristic smart city boosting both economy and ecology." Leading WBHIDCO, which has been entrusted with the development of the second satellite city of Kolkata, it is Sen's open mindedness and willingness for change that has given New Town-Rajarhat a new meaning. In a conversation with* **Titash Roy Choudhury**, *he shares his views about the journey of New Town, since its inception to the hurdles he overcame and its bright future.*

Being a resident of Salt Lake, how do you perceive the growth of the first planned urban township of the city?

When we talk about expansion needs of a city like Kolkata, we cannot look at the western side of the city due to the presence of the Hooghly river. The only way Kolkata can grow is by expanding on the eastern fringes of the city taking into account that the wetlands are not affected. Salt Lake, when it was conceived 50 years ago, was a swampy area that was later filled up using various sophisticated technologies.

This was the first effort of planned urbanisation in the city and the project has fared well in my view. It is very exciting as an urban specialist to look back and see how planned towns grow in comparison unplanned towns. The way Salt Lake has been designed with its considerable wide roads, community centres, parks at that point of time, is commendable.

When the plan for Salt Lake was conceived it was planned as a housing township but with coming of several modern concepts that show how along with housing infrastructure, commercial viability of the place got enhanced and Sector V came into existence.

With its own governing body separate from Bidhannagar Municipal Corporation, Sector V has carved out a niche for itself by becoming the IT hub of the city.

What led the government to think of developing another township and how was the initial stage?

West Bengal has the second highest density of population in the country after the state of Bihar. Considering the growth Salt Lake has seen in the last few years, there was an acute shortage of land. As a result, rigourous unplanned urbanisation was taking place along the periphery of Salt Lake. To prevent this sprouting of disorganised settlements, the government decided to develop a green township in this area.

» Continued on Page 3

THE TIMES OF INDIA, KOLKATA
FRIDAY, JULY 27, 2012

A CONSUMER CONNECT INITIATIVE

Building Dreams

The essence of core sector development is the presence of proper infrastructure such as road-rail connectivity, water supply and other allied activities. In whatever little of HIDCO land is left, we are trying to build a financial hub too in New Town. What we are trying to move at is to support housing for people directly connected with the commercial sector. Many a time, people talk about the adverse effects of development activities, especially in relation to environment. However, the population is ever expanding. Majority of the people is gravitating towards the cities. The urban population contributes to 60 per cent of India's GDP. Hence for cities to function, one needs to set up core basic infrastructure.

***Debashis Sen**, principal secretary, urban development, govt of West Bengal and chairman, WBHIDCO*

SUNDAY TIMES OF INDIA, KOLKATA
JUNE 30, 2013

In another windfall for Hidco, Rajarhat plot fetches ₹57 cr

Suman Chakraborti | TNN

Kolkata: In the highest ever land selling bid in Rajarhat New Town so far, a 2.5-acre plot in the township has fetched the Housing Infrastructure Development Corporation (Hidco) a whopping Rs 57.33 crore. It amounts to Rs 23 crore per acre or Rs 38 lakh per cottah.

The previous highest bid for the same plot stood at Rs 51.13 crore. It was equivalent to more than Rs 20 crore per acre or Rs 34 lakh per cottah.

According to Hidco officials, the company that had placed the previous highest bid did not buy the plot — even after paying the earnest money — for reasons unknown to them. "Thus, the bidding was cancelled and the plot was put under the hammer for the second time," the official said. The bidding took place last week and this time, the highest bid surpassed the previous one.

The plot has fetched such a huge amount since it has a location advantage, a senior Hidco official said. the plot is off the Major Arterial Road that leads to the airport and is close to the second sharp bend near the sixth intersection.

Lately, Hidco has been reaping rich harvest by auctioning off plots in the township for commercial purposes. Only a few weeks ago, the authorities had fetched a total of Rs 10.81 crore by selling off two plots totaling 45.82 cottah.

Getting an encouraging feedback so far, Hidco authorities are now expecting to get similar response for two smaller plots that have been put up for sale.

IT'S RAINING MONEY

₹57.33cr: Latest bid for 2.5 acre
₹51.13cr: Previous highest bid

Why auctioned twice?

The previous bidder did not buy the plot even after paying the earnest money

Why's the land fetching astronomical amount?

Because of its location advantage

It is learnt that one of the plots — 1.13 acre — will be sold to an educational institution and the other — 1 acre — for an office complex. Officials said there were further plans to sell more such plots but "it has to checked whether it can be done after the panchayat election notifications are announced".

"Though the New Town Kolkata Development Authority (NKDA) area falls outside the panchayat jurisdiction, the pros and cons are being checked out," an official said.

Drinking water boost to Rajarhat

Suman Chakraborti | TNN

Kolkata: The state government will soon start work on the 11.5-kilometre water pipeline from Chitpore Lock gate to Rajarhat New Town, which will give a boost to the drinking water supply in several places on the northern fringes of the city surrounding the Rajarhat, Salt Lake and South Dum Dum municipality areas. The authorities held a review meeting on the project on Saturday.

Several government agencies like Housing Infrastructure Development Corporation (Hidco), Nabadiganta Industrial Township Authority (NDITA), municipal affairs department and state public health engineering (PHE) department are coordinating with each other to execute the project. Simplex Infrastructure Limited has been selected to build the intake jetty at Hooghly from where the water will be flowed in, and lay down the six feet diametre pipeline.

Survey work for the route alignment is over and soil testing work is almost complete. The survey drawings and other documents have been submitted to the irrigation department, railways and port authorities. Besu has been selected as the third party consultant for the work. The field work is likely to start from April-end and work will gain momentum after the pipe material are delivered next month. Hidco has already finished work on the raw water receiving reservoirs adjacent to the water treatment plant at Rajarhat.

The proposed intake point is at Rani Debendra Bala ghat. The pipeline, after moving along the Chitpore, RG Kar and Gajnabi bridges on BT Road, will cross Kolkata station and move towards Ultadanga crossing and Lalpole railway bridge near Bidhannagar rail station before entering Salt Lake's AA Block. It will then move parallel to Kestopur canal crossing the Lake Town footbridge, Baisakhi footbridge, 206 number footbridge and Nayapatti Bazar to enter Rajarhat New Town and move towards Kestopur Mission Bazar and Pass Khal.

It will end at the energy dissipation inlet at the 100 million gallon per day (MGD) treatment plant site.

RELIEF AT LAST

LENGTH OF PIPELINE: 11.5 kilometres

PROJECT COST: ₹435 crore

The capital cost is estimated to be around Rs 348 crore and the rest will be spent on operation and maintenance for five years

GOVERNMENT AGENCIES INVOLVED: Hidco, NDITA, municipal affairs, PHE

AREAS WHICH WILL GAIN: New Town, Salt Lake, Rajarhat-Haroa, Sector V, neighbouring areas of New Town and South Dum Dum

PIPELINE CONSTRUCTION AGENCY: Simplex Infrastructure Limited

The Times of India, Kolkata, April 8, 2013

THE TIMES OF INDIA

KOLKATA | FRIDAY, AUGUST 2, 2013

Development at the cost of thousands of hectares of wet-land and agricultural land…

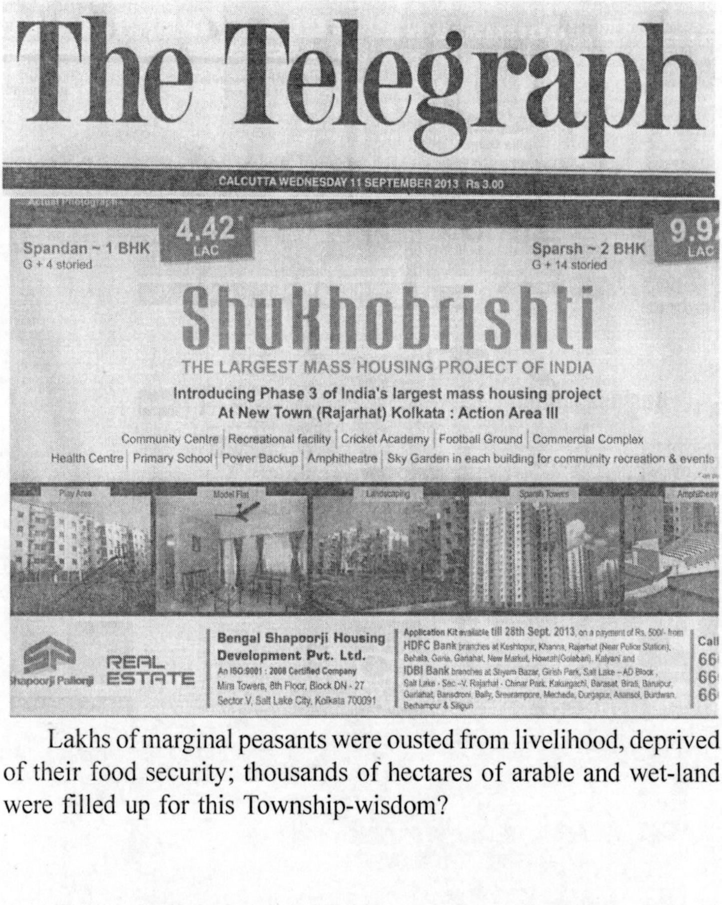
The Telegraph

CALCUTTA WEDNESDAY 11 SEPTEMBER 2013 Rs 3.00

Lakhs of marginal peasants were ousted from livelihood, deprived of their food security; thousands of hectares of arable and wet-land were filled up for this Township-wisdom?

More important than wet-land and food for the people?

Dream Town in place of Wet-Land and at the cost of livelihood of lakhs of marginal peasants.

TIMES CITY

THE TIMES OF INDIA, KOLKATA
WEDNESDAY, JANUARY 15, 2014

Rule to stop New Town vertical growth

Structures Higher Than 15 Metres To Require Stiff Compliances That May Put Off Realtors

Rohit Khanna & Suman Chakraborti | TNN

Kolkata: Have you been saving up to buy an apartment at a highrise on the north eastern fringes of the city at a lower price? Hold on. You might have to go slow on your plans. With new regulations from the Housing Infrastructure Development Corporation (Hidco) going to be in place very soon, the development of highrises in the fringe areas outside New Town jurisdiction in Rajarhat will come under a strong scanner, making it 'nearly impossible' for the realtors to comply with.

"Any developer planning to construct a building beyond a height of 15 metres will first have to get permission from New Town Kolkata Development Authority (NKDA)," said Hidco and NKDA chairman Debashis Sen. According to sources from the state secretariat, a notification is going to be issued shortly on the building rules.

While the new norms have not been notified by Hidco yet, sources close to the development said, "It will now be very difficult for realtors to construct any building beyond 15 metres in height. While Hidco may not impose a ban, the new set of regulations will require so many compliances, that most of the realtors will now stay back. Even if they comply with the new regulations, the project is unlikely to become viable at such huge costs."

There are rows of buildings on Rajarhat Main Road that have flouted norms

The narrow, bumpy road bifurcating at Derozio College near Rajarhat leads to Shashan on the right and Narayanpur on the left. The entire stretch is dotted with dozens of highrises. A minute's drive from Derozio College leads to Gopalpur Jagardanga where realtors have come up with large projects on both sides of the road. One of the hoardings, which reads "Tallest towers at lowest rates", was standing tall by an under-construction project.

"The big realtors have tried to comply with norms. But most of the smaller ones flouted norms while constructing highrises," said Prabir Kar, president of Rajarhat Panchayat Samiti. "You will find such highrises across Rajarhat Main Road from Narayanpur to Shashan," he said. "Many of these highrises are built on a stretch of road which barely allows you to drive a car," he said. The unplanned development without proper infrastructure has been posing a threat to the [illegible] lands at Sashan in North 24-Parganas.

According to locals, a lot of plans were sanctioned ignoring the flaws a few years back when Bhangar Rajarhat Area Development Authority (BRADA) was in place. BRADA had jurisdiction over 24 mouzas — 15 in North and nine in South 24-Parganas — covering 6,000 to 7,000 hectare where land prices were soaring. According to previous records, about 2,000 acres were sold by BRADA, while it had received applications for more than 1,500 acres. Land price shot up from around Rs 10,000 to Rs 20,000 a cottah to a range of Rs 5 lakh to Rs 10 lakh within 10 years. The Mamata Banerjee government had earlier dissolved BRADA after coming to the power.

According to Jitendra Khaitan, CMD of Pioneer Property Management Ltd, 15 metres will allow realtors to construct G+4 properties. "Land is limited now. So it is always better to go vertical. Highrises provide more floors on lesser land and makes way for more open space. In case of G+4 or G+5 units, construction costs are less but realization per unit is also less for realtors. Take-off of the properties become slow eventually," he said.

While both Sabyasachi Dutta, Trinamool MLA of New Town and Tapas Chatterjee, chairman of Rajarhat Gopalpur municipality, said they were unaware of any such regulation being planned, Prabir Kar said the district administration has already held a few meetings with local authorities.

Hidco identifies 16 unused plots

Suman Chakraborti | TNN

Kolkata: The Housing Infrastructure Development Corporation (Hidco) has identified 16 non-residential plot allottees in Rajarhat New Town who have yet to utilize their plots that were allotted in 2009 or earlier. The Mamata Banerjee government had earlier decided that no plot could be kept idle for more than six months after being allotted. Hidco authorities are now working out the process to impose a late fee of 10% of the total cost as penalty for each year of delay to these 16 identified plot allottees. This would be in addition to any other legal steps that the authorities may chalk out.

The Times Of India, Kolkata

TIMES CITY Thursday, August 23, 2012

With lone taker, govt hardsells fin hub

State To Promote Project At Bankers' Meet In Delhi

Suman Chakraborti | TNN

Kolkata: With only one investment proposal so far for the much-touted international financial hub at New Town, Rajarhat, the state urban development department plans to aggressively market the hub, the foundation stone for which was laid by chief minister Mamata Banerjee amid much fanfare in March. A foundation stone laying ceremony was earlier held during the Left regime.

The department has sought the Union urban development ministry's help to showcase the financial hub at a bankers' meet in New Delhi on Thursday, where state officials will interact with representatives of major banking and financial institutions and convince them to invest in the hub. The Housing Infrastructure Development Corporation (Hidco) authorities are also going to invite fresh applications after altering a few terms and conditions.

The state government wants large financial and banking institutions to come forward and invest in the financial hub in Rajarhat which has, so far, received lukewarm response from such institutions. Financial institutions include banks, both public and private, insurance companies and investment banks.

TOI

Mamata Banerjee had laid the foundation stone for the project in March

Union minister of state for urban development Saugata Ray, secretary in the ministry Sudhir Krishna, state urban development minister Firhad Hakim, his departmental secretary Debashis Sen and other senior urban development and Hidco officials will be present at Thursday's meeting to interact with the representatives of banks and financial institutions. "The financial hub will be showcased before them in the meeting. We want their investments," state urban development secretary and Hidco chairman Debashis Sen said.

The state has been highlighting the hub's potential, saying it will be only the second financial hub in the country after Mumbai's Bandra Kurla complex. However, quite unexpectedly, only one company has so far shown interest in investing in the financial hub. Hidco authorities informed Ray, who took up the matter with other central ministries and accordingly, the date of the bankers' meet was fixed.

In the fresh applications Hidco is inviting, officials said, the basic condition requiring a financial institution to have an annual turnover of Rs 500 crore will remain the same, but now one will be able to get a plot at a fixed price. Offers will be given to public sector institutions. Some of the plots will be auctioned, but one can also get a plot at a fixed price. This was discussed at the latest board meeting of Hidco. The deadline to submit applications will be October 31 this year.

After Banerjee had laid the foundation stone this year, April 24 was fixed the last date for submitting applications and Hidco authorities only received one application. Even after extending the deadline to July 31, no fresh application was received.

TSI on Mobile : http://m.thesundayindian.com

Enter search keyword here

THE SUNDAY INDIAN

Friday, June 8, 2012

Politics India Business Sports World Lifestyle & Entertainment Health Science Blogs Magazine Supplements Web Specials

ENGLISH | HINDI | URDU | BENGALI | TAMIL | KANNADA | BHOJPURI | TELUGU | MALAYALAM | GUJARATI | MARATHI | ASSAMESE | ORIYA | PUNJABI

Home Magazine Special Story

Article | Comments (0)

Who will bell the cat?

In a situation where everybody from politicians to bureaucrats to police and vigilance officers are among the beneficiaries of a no-holds-barred land dole out.

C S BHATTACHARJEE | Issue Dated: September 18, 2011, New Delhi

Seven years back, the Supreme Court had cancelled the allotment of a plot at Salt Lake to former Calcutta High Court judge Bhagawati Prasad Banerjee. The plot had been allotted by the then Chief Minister Jyoti Basu under Chief Minister's discretionary� "special quota". As directed by the Apex Court, the judge had to vacate the house for auction by the government � The SC observed, "He (Justice Banerjee) has misused his divine judicial duty...He has betrayed the trust reposed in him by the people. To say the least, this is bad."

Later, several other names were found to be involved in that scam including athlete-turned CPI(M) MP Jyotirmoyee Sikdar, sportspersons Bhaskar Ganguly, Sasthi Duley, Dipankar Dey and many others. A few months back, the same court had to order the cancellation of 'a plot given to cricketer Saurav Ganguly at a throwaway price. However, after the Justice Banerjee case, the state government did away with the CM's discretionary quota, but the quota system continued for the ministers.

��������������

A document recently made public by the West Bengal Housing Infrastructure Development Corporation (HIDCO) on July 1, 2011, contains details of more than 60 top officers of the Indian Administrative Service (IAS) and Indian Police Service (IPS) who got plots of prime land at Rajarhat-New Town area through the minister's "special quota" and discretionary quota.

And the minister in question, Gautam Deb – who has lost in the last assembly election – was the Housing Development Minister of West Bengal as well as chairman of HIDCO. Mamata Banerjee, Union Railway Minister at that time, had assured people of a thorough probe into the murky Rajarhat land deal if Trinamool Congress came to power.

The document bears names of a number of senior IPS officers including JC

Arindam Chaudhuri on Facebook

Like

1,240,892 people like Arindam Chaudhuri.

Facebook social plugin

CRICKET WIDGET

Issue Dated: Jun 17, 2012

SUBSCRIBE NOW

ARCHIVES

Mohanty (ADG, Administration), MK Singh (IGP, Law & Order), Gyan Dutt Gautam (Commandant 1st Battalion, State Armed Police), Jawed Shamim (Joint Commissioner, HQ), Raj Kanojia (ADG, State Crime Records Bureau), AK Maliwal (ADG & IG, Provisioning), Banibrata Basu (ADG, IB), Siddhartha Gupta (Spl. IG & DIG, Presidency Range), Somen Mitra (ACP II, KP), Kuldeep Singh, (ADG), SK Purakayastha (ADG, Law & Order), Rahul Srivastaua and Praveen Kumar, (IPS officers on Central Deputation, both), Ajoy Ranade (IPS on Compulsory Waiting), ZA Hasan (ADG, Western Range) and RK Mohanty apart from present Police Commissioner of Kolkata, Ranjit Kumar Pachnanda. Pachnanda has been allotted plot number DF 61 in area AA-1, according to the document.

The present IG (Headquarters), Harmanpreet Singh, is also one of those who got the favour from the minister. Interestingly, Mamata Banerjee fought a rigorous battle against the alleged misdeeds of Singh in Bhikhan Paswan case. And the names of two Chakrabarty brothers – Ashok Mohan and Gautam Mohan Chakrabarty – are in the list. Currently DG and IGP (Armed Police), Gautam Mohan Chakrabarty is the former police commissioner against whom the TMC had levelled allegations of being involved in the Rajarhat land scam in December 2010. While Gautam was the police chief of Kolkata, his brother Ashok Mohan was the Chief Secretary of WB. And both of them grabbed two plots at AA-1 area of Rajarhat-New Town.

The list of bureaucrats, too, is not shorter than the police officers in this regard. The names of former Chairman of Tea Board, Basudeb Banerjee, who is now Secretary, Information Technology and present Deputy Chairperson of Tea Board, Roshni Sen, also feature in the list. Anil Verma, who has been handling the administration of the defunct Darjeeling Gorkha Hill Council (DGHC), too, has a plot here like Talleen Kumar, IAS on Central Deputation.

The other powerful bureaucrats of West Bengal who feature in the list are PS Kathiresan (Secretary, Food), KS Rajendran (Secretary, Forest), Alapan Bandopadhyay (Secretary, Municipal Affairs), D Mukherjee (Secretary, Commerce & Industries), Indevar Pandey (Secretary, Personnel & Administrative Reforms), Gyan Dutt Gautam (Secretary, Home), SK Das (Secretary, Public Health Engineering), Dilip Rath (Secretary, Labour) Subrata Gupta (Managing Director, Kolkata Metro Rail Corporation Limited), Khalil Ahmed, (Director, MSSET), Anup Chanda (Secretary, MSSET), Anoop Kr. Agarwal (Secretary, ARD) and a host of IAS officers on central deputation like Atanu Purakayastha, Rajiv Sinha, Manoj Pant, Arun Kumar Bal and Arun Mishra.

And when bureaucrats and police officers abound in land grabbing, can politician be far behind? The list has the names of former CPM MP Tarit Baran Topdar, ex-minister Dines Dakua, Forward Bloc MLAs Haripada Biswas and Bithika Mondal among others. What's more interesting is that the list also features the name of Sardar Amjad Ali, a TMC candidate defeated in the last assembly election.

Manish Gupta, former Chief Secretary of West Bengal who served during Jyoti Basu and Buddhadeb Bhattacharya's reigns – and who defeated Bhattacharya in the last election and presently holds charges of the Department of Power, Planning and Development – has also received favours from Gautam Deb. The Animal Husbandry Minister of the present cabinet, Justice Nure Alam Chowdhury, is another recipient of a plot from Gautam Deb's "quota". Wife of Manas Bhuna, Minister for Irrigation and Small Scale Industries, is also another name in the present cabinet who has received favours from the "tainted" minister.

Though all those who have received a favour from the minister may not be involved in the scam, but the questions of morality and propriety remain intact. Is it proper to use your position to get a piece of land out of turn? The same yardstick can also be applied to the judges whose names figure in the list. Justice Pinaki Chandra Ghosh is still a sitting judge of Calcutta High Court and the said minister has favoured him with a 4.485 cottah plot in HIG category (plot no. AC-90 of AA-1 area) under the "chairman's quota".

If you think that's all, it's not. Deb has allotted plot no DE 43 of AA-1 area to one Karungulam Subramanian Ramasubban, who was secretary to Chief Vigilance Commissioner and presently a member of the Standing Conference of Public Enterprises (SCOPE). This brings us to the vital question: who will bell the cat?

With the change of guard in West Bengal, several things have changed, but as they say, the more they change, the more they remain the same. The orders for investigation into the scam is still awaited. Meanwhile, the State has told the High Court in a related case that "no irregularities [were] found" in land allotment at Rajarhat-New Town.

Amid all this mud-slinging, however, the "tainted" minister, Gautam Deb, deserves some accolades for he also allotted a piece of land to legendary singer Manna Dey, who had complained that he could not get a piece of residential land in and around Kolkata, despite several requests.

TIMES CITY

THE TIMES OF INDIA, KOLKATA | TUESDAY, JULY 17, 2012

Wetland being sold in pieces

Saikat Ray & Subhro Niyogi | TNN

Kolkata: A waterbody in the East Kolkata Wetlands — a Ramsar site that the state has committed to protect — has been filled up in broad daylight and demarcated into plots that are selling for Rs 3.25 lakh per cottah.

Located in Chowbagha, less than a kilometre from Collector bheri that TOI and environment activists had helped protect from land sharks in January, the 52-bigha waterbody was filled with sludge around the same time that concrete pillars and walls around Collector bheri were being torn down. In the ensuing summer, the water evaporated, leaving behind a stretch of fertile land where shrubs and bushes sprouted. There's no trace of the water. Instead, it looks like an island with water all around.

Workers build the boundary wall around what used to be a wetland at Pirtala; (right) construction material dumped on the encroached wetland

When TOI visited the encroached wetland at Pirtala in Kolkata Municipal Corporation area, a 5-minute drive from Collector bheri, located next to Heritage school and college, around a dozen masons and labourers were engaged in constructing a wall around the 1,040 cottah plot.

Overseeing the work, labour contractor Swapan Mondal surveyed the pristine area around and remarked how picturesque the location was. "The promoters want to sell off the land in 3 to 7 cottah plots. Those who build houses here will be in the lap of nature," he said.

But what was the surety that the adjoining bheris would also not be encroached upon and the wetlands replaced by a concrete jungle. "True, there is no guaranteeing that. Dozens of waterbodies have been encroached over the past few years and land sharks have become more active than ever. Anyway, it does not concern us so long as we get to earn," he said. In fact, large parts of the adjoining bheris are slated to be grabbed by the land shark once they build a 24-foot-wide road to woo investors to buy those plots.

Some locals, though, are distraught over the sweeping changes that have occurred in the neighbourhood and changed the very landscape. "A nexus of realtors, politicians and local toughs are wreaking havoc. They are grabbing land with impunity and no one dares resist. Tiljala police is aware of it but will not act because it too gets a share of the pie. While they monitor each truck entering and exiting major construction sites, they turn a blind eye to tankers dumping sludge into bheris and construction of walls around them," said a local.

Stone chips, bricks and sand were dumped on the adjoining kutcha road that meandered through bheris. "The road, built recently by dumping rubble, will be converted into a 25-foot-wide pucca road. Though around 5 feet of the adjoining waterbody needs to be reclaimed to construct the road, that will not be a problem. Book the plot within a month because the price will be revised upwards soon," said Sanjay, one of the middlemen engaged in selling the plots.

But is the land free of encumbrances? "There is a minor legal issue, but it will be sorted out within a couple of months. Apart from lawyers who are working on the case, there are arrangements in place to ensure that there is no trouble for buyers," said the agent who is available at Yuvak Brinda Club next to Ruby General Hospital.

East Kolkata Wetland Management Authority (EKWMA) chief technical officer Arijit Banerjee, who had initiated the drive to tear down the wall around Collector bheri, said he would take up the issue at the next meeting of EKWMA on July 19.

"This is shocking. There is a need for resistance from locals. Otherwise, the wetlands and the Ramsar tag will be lost. And that would be a shame for the city," he said. Though located in Ward 108, the KMC authorities are blissfully ignorant of the development. Sanchita Mondal, the member, mayor-in-council overseeing the KMC environment department, said she would definitely look into the matter. "I will send a team of civic officials to the spot to take stock of the situation," she said.

Kalyan Rudra, a member of the wetland conservation committee appointed by Calcutta high court, expressed dismay at the development. "Silt dredged from canals are being dumped into wetlands. We have already lost all waterbodies in Kolkata. Unless we protect the East Kolkata Wetlands, the very survival of the city will be at stake," Rudra said.

THE TIMES OF INDIA, KOLKATA
FRIDAY, MAY 17, 2013

6 TIMES

Win for wetland warriors

Court Says Character Of Dankuni Wetland Can't Be Changed

Subhro Niyogi | TNN

A file photo showing a man fishing on Mullarbaer that now lies covered with layers of fly ash

Kolkata: The Calcutta high court has ordered the state government to ensure that the character of Mullarbaer in Dankuni off Durgapur Expressway, is not changed, raising hope among locals as well as environment action groups that the sprawling wetland that was being filled up may yet be saved.

Responding to a public interest litigation filed by PUBLIC with the support of other NGOs, Chief Justice of Calcutta high court Arun Kumar Mishra and Justice Joymalyo Bagchi ruled on Wednesday that status quo be maintained and the nature and character of the land not be changed.

Pleading for the petitioners, Mr Sidhartha Mitra showed the court pictures of the destruction to get the order.

Since January this year, a group of NGOs — PUBLIC, WWF India, Disha and Forum for Human, Legal & Ecological Rights (LHLER) — have been fighting for the 500-hectare marshy land that is home to animals such as the jungle cat and the fishing cat as well as a migratory stop for birds whose breeding grounds stretch from Finland to eastern Siberia.

TOI, too, had visited the spot with the activists and reported on how hundreds of trucks were dumping fly ash on the marshy land.

"What galvanized the NGOs into action was the photograph of a yellow monitor lizard (protected under Schedule 1 of the Wildlife Protection Act, 1972 – the schedule that protects the tiger) crushed by the wheels of the trucks dumping fly ash into the wetlands," recounted Bonani Kakkar of PUBLIC.

Mullarbaer along with several other sites in the belt has been a favourite spot for birdwatchers. They discovered the destruction and alerted green activists. Moreover, activists added that the presence of at least one mammal, two birds and a reptile belonging to the Schedule 1 of IWPA, 1972, is bound to guarantee legal protection of the highest level. Also, the West Bengal Inland Fisheries (Amendment) Act, 1993, and National Environmental Policy, 2006 have enabling causes to protect wetlands.

"Despite repeated appeals to officials like the chief secretary to the environment secretary, the forest secretary and even to the district magistrate, the trucks — 100 to 150 a day — kept choking the area with fly ash," said Kunal Guha Roy of FHLER. Though delighted at the order, activists caution that this is only the first step. "So much damage has been done that restoration will be a real challenge," said Kakkar.

THE TIMES OF INDIA, KOLKATA
THURSDAY, JANUARY 9, 2014

TIMES

Now, buy a wetland plot and get freebies too

Firm Sells EKW Plots Openly, Offers Cars, Bikes And TV Free

Subhro Niyogi & Saikat Ray | TNN

Kolkata: In Kolkata, you can buy a plot at an internationally protected Ramsar site and develop it just the way you please. And, you can get freebies for doing that, too.

A private firm not only has chunks of land for sale at 300 sites in East Kolkata Wetlands (EKW), it is also offering cars, motorcycles and televisions free with the land parcels to entice buyers. The offer, advertised in posters strung up along Basanti highway, has led to a rush for plots at the firm's office in Anandapur, behind Ruby Hospital.

"If you want to buy land anywhere on a 5-km radius around our office or on either side of a 15-km stretch of Basanti highway, you have come to the right place. We have 300 sites spread across several hundred

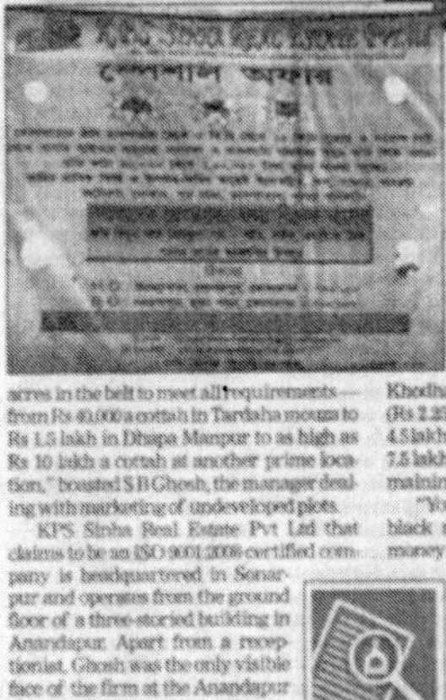

(Left) A poster offering plots in EKW (above) and (right) the office of KPS Sinha Real Estate Pvt Ltd in Anandapur

acres in the belt to meet all requirements — from Rs 40,000 a cottah in Tardaha mouza to Rs 1.5 lakh in Dhapa Manpur to as high as Rs 10 lakh a cottah at another prime location," boasted S B Ghosh, the manager dealing with marketing of undeveloped plots.

KPS Sinha Real Estate Pvt Ltd that claims to be an ISO 9001:2008 certified company is headquartered in Sonarpur and operates from the ground floor of a three-storied building in Anandapur. Apart from a receptionist, Ghosh was the only visible face of the firm at the Anandapur office. "Our directors are extremely powerful with links to politicians and police. Their names are confidential, but it suffices to say that they have enormous clout with the administration and have aggregated a huge quantity of land," said Ghosh.

TOI INVESTIGATION

The official also made it abundantly clear that buying land directly would be next to impossible due to obstacles from local youths, politicians, police and goons. "You won't face these problems when you buy it from us because our directors have a 'setting'. Once sale is done and land is registered, retaining possession is the buyer's responsibility. We advise you to wall the plot and develop a good rapport with boys from the local club to avoid trouble," he said.

Among the plots (and prices) that Ghosh mentioned to the TOI team were ones at Terdah Kapasati mouza (Rs 40,000 a cottah), Dhapa Manpur (Rs 1.5 lakh a cottah), Khodhati (Rs 2.25 lakh a cottah), Kheyada (Rs 2.25 a cottah), Bhagabanpur mouza (Rs 4.5 lakh a cottah) and Madurdaha mouza (Rs 7.5 lakh a cottah). Madurdaha apart, the remaining mouzas are all in EKW.

"You can buy the entire land with black money or a part of it. We accept money in both black and white," he said. In the plotted plans that Ghosh showed TOI, several were marked as registered while others were shown as booked.

"Check out the plots early because there is a huge rush on holidays and weekends. Decide on the budget and I will show you plots in multiple locations for a one-time registration fee of Rs 301. Once you have selected the plot, 30% of the money has to be paid in advance. The rest is to be paid after registration. Thereafter, I will put you in touch with people who will develop the low-lying land, get building plan sanctioned, do the mutation and undertake construction," Ghosh said.

But what about the ban on altering the land character in EKW, a Ramsar site? He brushes it off nonchalantly. "There is no

way anyone can stop development of a plot with a tenement or farmland. In fact, cabbage is cultivated in some of our plots in the area. And nearly all the prime plots are inundated and appear to be wetlands as it would otherwise be difficult to retain the plots," he explained.

Bonani Kakkar of environment action group Public, whose PIL had led to the protection of the wetlands, expressed dismay over the blatant manner in which land is being advertised and sold. "EKW land is being sold as though they were consumer goods. We have asked the chief technical officer (CTO) of East Kolkata Wetlands Management Authority to probe the matter as well the news report on wetland residents' eagerness to sell land," Kakkar said, referring to the TOI investigation that exposed the nexus between land owners, politicians, unemployed local youths and a section of land officials to sell land for Rs 1-1.4 lakh a cottah in Hatgachi mouza deep inside EKW. For every transaction of Rs 1.4 lakh, the seller made Rs 80,000 with the remaining Rs 60,000 being split between the local stakeholders.

THE TIMES OF INDIA, KOLKATA
FRIDAY, FEBRUARY 21, 2014

Pleas to stop wetland fill-up went in vain

Subhro Niyogi & Saikat Ray | TNN

Kolkata: Senior government officials living in cooperative societies in Patuli had approached various government agencies, including the chief minister's office (CMO) to prevent the construction of a building on a wetland and an extension of a sprawling 'jheel'.

Their pleas were, however, largely ignored resulting in the rapid construction of a five-storied building that appears to have forced the change in Metro Railways' Garia station-Airport route alignment.

Just over two years ago, retired bureaucrat Dipak Lal Ghosh, who resides in a cooperative society opposite the disputed building under construction, had written to the Kolkata Municipal Development Authority (KMDA), developer of the Baishnabghata-Patuli Township and Patuli police station, about the attempt to grab government land.

Debabrata Shome

The building (circled) being illegally constructed on Patuli wetland

The police initially refused to act. "The attitude of the police was disheartening. Having been in government service, it was my duty to alert authorities when government land is encroached. Since I was secretary of the cooperatives' association in Q block, the complaint was on everyone's behalf. But the police thought otherwise," Ghosh said.

The stretch between the township boundary and railway tracks for Sonarpur-Sealdah local trains should have belonged to either the Railways for future track expansion or the state government. In fact, Metro rail had even carried out soil tests for the Garia station-Airport link. But private parties then laid claim to it and constructed the building despite objections.

While the 6 cottah plot on which the building has been constructed is lost, a cat and mouse game is underway to grab the adjoining land and construct five-storied buildings that can fetch around Rs 6 crore (12 flats of Rs 50 lakh each).

Harjinder Singh, who served as district judge and chairman of West Bengal Cooperatives' Tribunal, has till date written at least half a dozen letters to various authorities to stop the construction. But with no decisive action, he is slowly losing the will to continue his fight.

"When I came here a few years ago, this was a low-lying land with grass and vegetation. Then, unscrupulous developers began dumping earth and rubbish in a clandestine manner. When I protested and wrote to several authorities, it stopped but by then some damage had been done," he pointed out. In February 2010, he alerted the CEO of KMDA. When a second attempt to grab land was made in August 2012, he alerted both Patuli police and KMDA. He wrote to both Patuli OC and KMDA CEO in February 2013 again. He even photographed the encroachment and emailed them to KMDA, railway officials and the CMO, but to no avail.

Kolkata Monday November 7, 2011
www.thebengalpost.com

Singur, Nandigram, Rajarhat to come under AnSI scanner

Mihir Bhonsale

Kolkata: Political flashpoints in the state have come under the scanner of the Anthropological Survey of India (AnSI) with the institution undertaking a study of Singur, Nandigram, Lalgarh and Rajarhat. The study would focus on economic and social deprivation inflicted on the people because of land acquisition for industrial and commercial purposes.

"A team has already left for Singur to collect data at the site. The project, which also includes Nandigram, Lalgarh and Rajarhat, is an initiative of the Eastern Regional Centre (ERC) of AnSI. Our goal is to study the social and economic deprivation of the people of these places," said a senior AnSI official. An AnSI team would also visit Lalgarh later this month to cooect data to understand the root of poverty in the area.

Over the past half a decade, Singur and Nandigram have witnessed strong local protests against the acquisition of land for industry while Rajarhat saw an industrial and commercial township growing over agricultural land.

The official said: "Some areas of Rajarhat were also part of the East Calcutta Wetlands,

Over the past half a decade, Singur and Nandigram have witnessed strong local protests against the acquisition of land for industry while Rajarhat saw an industrial and commercial township growing over agricultural land

which is a Ramsar site and protected under the Ramsar Convention. Increasing human activity for over a decade has brought about a rapid transformation of the marshy land into a township and is a matter of concern."

"A review of secondary data on Rajarhat has confirmed that vested interests had suppressed facts to develop residential and commercial townships and more facts would follow as we begin the fieldwork," said a principal investigator of the AnSI Rajarhat study.

The final reports are likely to be submitted by March next year.

Appendix – 17

Anandabazar Patrika, 11th February, 2012

সিন্ডিকেট নিয়ে সরব শোভনদেবও

নিজস্ব সংবাদদাতা: রাজারহাট, নিউটাউনে দলের 'সিন্ডিকেট' নিয়ে তৃণমূলের অভ্যন্তরে যে 'অস্বস্তি' রয়েছে, শুক্রবার ফের তা স্পষ্ট করে দিলেন রাজ্য বিধানসভার সরকার পক্ষের মুখ্য সচেতক শোভনদেব চট্টোপাধ্যায়। মুখ্যমন্ত্রী মমতা বন্দ্যোপাধ্যায় যখন উত্তরবঙ্গ সফরে, তখন মহাকরণের পোর্টিকোয় দাঁড়িয়ে শোভনদেববাবু বলেন, "দলকে কখনও আমার জন্য অস্বস্তিতে পড়তে হয়নি। আমাকে নিয়ে রাজনৈতিক বিতর্কের খবর বেরোতে পারে। কিন্তু কখনও সিমেন্ট, সিন্ডিকেট বা কোনও দুর্নীতির খবর বেরোয়নি। এটা আমার গর্ব। এখন কারও কারও নাম জড়িয়ে এ সব খবর বেরোচ্ছে এবং দল অস্বস্তিতে পড়ছে। তাঁদের নৈতিক দায়িত্ব, এ সব খবরের প্রতিবাদ করা।"

তৃণমূল নেতৃত্বের একাংশের ধারণা, নাম না করলেও শোভনদেববাবুর এই 'কটাক্ষে'র লক্ষ্য রাজ্যের শ্রমমন্ত্রী পূর্ণেন্দু বসু ও তাঁর অনুগামী, দলের শ্রমিক সংগঠনের (আইএনটিটিইউসি) নেতৃত্ব। পূর্ণেন্দুবাবু রাজারহাটের বিধায়ক। তিনি অবশ্য এই বিষয়ে কোনও মন্তব্য করেননি। কিন্তু তাঁর ঘনিষ্ঠ এক নেতার অভিযোগ, "মুখ্যমন্ত্রীর অনুপস্থিতিতে মহাকরণে দাঁড়িয়ে শোভনদেববাবু বিতর্কিত মন্তব্য না করলেই ভাল করতেন।"

আইএনটিটিইউসি-র সর্বভারতীয় সভাপতির পদ থেকে শোভনদেববাবুকে সরিয়ে সুব্রত মুখোপাধ্যায়কে দায়িত্ব দিয়েছেন মুখ্যমন্ত্রী। শোভনদেববাবুর অনুগামীদের অভিযোগ, তাঁকে 'অপসারণে'র মূলে রয়েছেন পূর্ণেন্দুবাবুরা। তারই প্রেক্ষিতে এ দিন নাম না করে পূর্ণেন্দুবাবুদের বিরুদ্ধে বর্ষীয়ান নেতা শোভনদেববাবু তোপ দেগেছেন বলে দলের একাংশের অভিমত।

মুখ্যমন্ত্রীর দফতরে কাজ ছিল বলে তিনি এ দিন মহাকরণে গিয়েছিলেন বলে শোভনদেববাবু জানিয়েছেন। তাঁর দাবি, যে সব কর্মী ইউনিয়নে তিনি নেতৃত্ব দেন, সেগুলি তেমনই চলবে বলে মুখ্যমন্ত্রী 'নির্দেশ' দিয়েছেন। বৃহস্পতিবারও মহাকরণে মুখ্যমন্ত্রীর সঙ্গে তাঁর বৈঠক হয়েছিল। তাঁর অনুগামীরা যাতে 'বিভ্রান্ত না হন' সেই কারণেই বৈঠকের কথা তিনি প্রকাশ্যে জানিয়েছেন। শোভনদেববাবুর কথায়, "মুখ্যমন্ত্রী আমাকে বলেছেন,'আপনি যে সব জায়গায় সভাপতি রয়েছেন, যেমন কাজ করছেন, তেমনই চালিয়ে যান।' ফলে কোনও সমস্যা নেই।" তারাতলায় তৃণমূলের শ্রমিক সংগঠনের গোষ্ঠী সংঘর্ষের ঘটনাকে 'দুর্ভাগ্যজনক' আখ্যা দিয়ে শোভনদেববাবু বলেন, "আশা করব, মুখ্যমন্ত্রী এর বিরুদ্ধে কড়া ব্যবস্থা নেবেন।"

[Headline: Shobhandeb is also Vocal about Syndicate
Shobhandeb Chattopadhyay made it clear that there is discomfort within the Trinamool Congress on the issue of syndicate at Rajarhat New Town. ...]

Anandabazar Patrika, 10 February, 2012

প্রশাসনের 'মাথাদের'ও রেয়াত করে না সিন্ডিকেট

দাম-মান-পরিমাণ, সবেতেই জবরদস্তির রফা

[Head line: Syndicate does not Care even for the Top Administrators

Each of them is a high ranking government official. But they are not exempted from the high handedness of the syndicates while constructing their co-operative building. These officials also dare not to raise their voice. Rather they were compelled to come to an understanding. A member of the local Contractor's Association informed that it is just impossible to go against the syndicates because they can do much harm. Their complaint is that the syndicates supply low quality of materials in high price; moreover in less quantity. The contractors wanted to come to an understanding with the syndicates in terms of quality of the supplied materials; they wanted to pay 20 per cent higher the market price against quality product and accurate quantity but in vain. From the part of the State government, it was said that strong action would be taken against syndicates. The Minister of Urban Development and Municipal Affairs, Firhad Hakim said that lawfully there is no existence of syndicates But if anyone lodge the complaint then action has to be taken by the Police irrespective of political affiliation. Rajiv Kumar, Police Commissioner of Bidhannagar Commissionerate says please avoid fearing them and inform and lodge complaint with Police against the high handedness of syndicates. Please give a chance to the Police and watch.]

Anandabazar Patrika, 8th February, 2012

সিন্ডিকেট-রাজ রুখতে হিডকো ‘নির্দেশিকা’ দিলেও মানছে কে

নিজস্ব সংবাদদাতা: নিউটাউনে সিন্ডিকেট-রাজ বন্ধ করতে রাজ্য সরকারের তরফে, নির্দেশিকা জারি করেছে হিডকো। তার চব্বিশ ঘণ্টাও কাটল না, নিউটাউনের এক নির্মাণসংস্থার মালিককে সিন্ডিকেটের কাছ থেকে লরিপিছু ছ'হাজার টাকা দরের বালি কিনতে হল ১১ হাজারে।

মঙ্গলবার দুপুরে নিউটাউনে নিজের অফিসে বসে টেলিফোনে সিন্ডিকেটের 'হুমকি' শুনছিলেন ওই ব্যবসায়ী। ফোনে তাঁকে পরিষ্কার জানিয়ে দেওয়া হয়েছে, সরকারি নির্দেশিকা যা-ই হোক না কেন, ইমারতির মাল সিন্ডিকেটের কাছ থেকে না-কিনলে 'বিপদ' বাড়বে।

গত বছরের ২৭ নভেম্বর কেষ্টপুরের তৃণমূল নেতা স্বপন মণ্ডল খুন হওয়ার পরে নিউটাউনে সিন্ডিকেটের 'জুলুমবাজি' ও তাকে ঘিরে রাজ্যের এক মন্ত্রীর নাম জড়িয়ে গোষ্ঠীদ্বন্দ্ব প্রকাশ্যে চলে আসে। তখনই মুখ্যমন্ত্রী মমতা বন্দ্যোপাধ্যায় ঘোষণা করেন, সিন্ডিকেট-রাজ বন্ধ করতে হবে। তার পরে আড়াই মাস কেটেছে। ইতিমধ্যে কিছু নির্মাণসংস্থার পক্ষ থেকে জুলুমের আরও কিছু অভিযোগ জমা পড়ে হিডকো-র কাছে। অবশেষে নিউটাউনে সিন্ডিকেট-রাজের অবসানের লক্ষ্যে হিডকো তৈরি করেছে নির্দেশিকা। যার মূল কথা: ইমারতি মালপত্র কেনা নিয়ে সিন্ডিকেটের জবরদস্তি কোনও মতেই বরদাস্ত করা হবে না। অভিযোগের যথাযথ তদন্ত চালিয়ে এবং অভিযুক্ত সিন্ডিকেটগুলোর সঙ্গে কথা বলেই নির্দেশিকাটি তৈরি হয়েছে বলে হিডকো-র দাবি।

সিন্ডিকেটের মাথারা কী বলছেন?

জুলুমের দাওয়াই

- নির্মাণসংস্থাগুলি যেখান থেকে খুশি মাল কিনতে পারবে।
- সিন্ডিকেট জোর-জুলুম করতে পারবে না।
- এ ব্যাপারে দায়িত্ব নিতে হবে সিন্ডিকেটের নেতাদের।
- সিন্ডিকেটকে বিক্রয়মূল্যের একটি তালিকা তৈরি করতে হবে।
- সামগ্রীর মান ও পরিমাণ যাচাই করার সুযোগ পাবেন ক্রেতা।

রাজারহাটের চিনারপার্কে ডায়মন্ড সিন্ডিকেটের সম্পাদক শাহনওয়াজ পুরকায়েত এ দিন বলেন, “হিডকো এমন কোনও নির্দেশিকা তৈরি করতেই পারে না।” তাঁর প্রশ্ন, “হাজার হাজার পরিবার সিন্ডিকেটের সঙ্গে যুক্ত। এ সব নির্দেশিকা মানবে কে?” হিডকো-এলাকার আটটি সমবায়-সিন্ডিকেটের সম্পাদক মোজাম্মেল তরফদারের বক্তব্য, “এখানে বড় বড় আবাসন, অফিস, শপিং মলে আমরাই মাল দিয়েছি। কোথাও কোনও অসুবিধা হয়নি।” এবং মোজাম্মেলের সাফ কথা, “হিডকো-র ওই নির্দেশিকার কথা আমরা জানি না। বৈঠকে আমাদের ডাকাও হয়নি। এ সব হতে পারে না।”

অধিকাংশ সিন্ডিকেট একই সুরে হিডকো-র নির্দেশিকাকে পত্রপাঠ 'খারিজ' করেছে। শুধু তারাই নয়, নির্দেশিকার বিরোধিতা করেছেন রাজারহাটের তৃণমূল বিধায়ক তথা হিডকো-সদস্য সব্যসাচী দত্তও। যাঁর প্রশ্ন, “সিন্ডিকেট নিয়ন্ত্রণ করার হিডকো কে?” বস্তুত ব্যাপারটা হিডকো'র মতো একটা সরকারি সংস্থার দেখার কথাও নয় বলে মনে করেন সব্যসাচীবাবু।

তা হলে কি সিন্ডিকেট-রাজ যেমন চলছে, তেমনই চলবে?

রাজ্যের নগরোন্নয়ন-সচিব তথা হিডকো'র চেয়ারম্যান দেবাশিস সেন এ দিন বলেন, “আমরা কঠোর হাতে সিন্ডিকেট-রাজ বন্ধ করার সিদ্ধান্ত নিয়েছি। এই পরিস্থিতি চলতে দেওয়া যায় না।” দেবাশিসবাবুর আশ্বাস, প্রশাসনিক স্তরে

এর পর সাতের পাতায়

[Headline: In spite of Enforcing Directives by HIDCO to End Atrocity of Syndicates, Nobody Cares.

Remedy for High handedness:

- Builders can buy construction materials on their own choice.
- Syndicate cannot force them.
- To implement these the responsibilities go to the syndicate leaders.

- Syndicate should prepare a selling price list.
- The buyers will get the opportunity to examine the quality and quantity of materials.

To bring an end to the atrocity of the syndicates HIDCO enforced a directive. But not even 24 hours passed a builder had to buy sand from the syndicate in Rs. 11,000.00 per truck while the actual price is rupees six thousand per truck. Syndicate warned the businessman that whatever is the directive of the government, if they don't buy the building materials from the syndicate they will be in trouble. On the issue of a murder case in Kestopur area last year the conflict between different syndicates in New Town came into surface. Then the Chief Minister announced that the atrocity of syndicate should come to an end. Even after that a few complaints have been received by HIDCO. As a result HIDCO enforced the directive. What the syndicate leaders say? Shahnawaj Purakayat of Diamond syndicate of Chinar Park, Rajarhat says HIDCO cannot enforce such directive. Thousands of families live on syndicate. Who will follow such directive? Mojammel Tarafdar, secretary of the eight co-operative syndicates in HIDCO area says in all big projects of housing, offices, shopping mall we only supplied building materials. There was absolutely no problem. His clear answer, we are not aware of such directive. Most of the syndicates dismissed the directive by HIDCO. The HIDCO Chairman, Debashis Sen says we have taken a strong decision against the atrocity of syndicates. Such situation cannot be allowed to continue.

The TOI, Kolkata, Feb 16, 2012

Syndicates bicker over supply of airport concrete

TIMES NEWS NETWORK

Kolkata: Discontentment brewing over controlling the supply of sand and stone chips to a concrete batching plant at the airport spilled out in the open on Wednesday morning, leading to a faceoff between syndicate operators owing allegiance to leaders of Congress and Trinamool Congress.

The clash partially affected supply of ready-mix concrete to the airport modernization project. Already delayed by several months, any further disruption in supply could deal a crippling blow to the project. Everyone breathed a sigh of relief when the imbroglio was resolved with syndicates agreeing to split the supply.

According to sources, Trinamool supporters from the neighbourhood have been eyeing the lucrative supply contract to the ACC plant. Since 2006, four syndicates — Ma Manasa, Jonaki Enterprise, P&F Enterprise and Dey Enterprise — controlled by Congress and CPM and allegedly backed by Bablu Ghosh of Congress controlled all the supplies to the plant. Following Trinamool's resounding victory in the assembly elections last year and Congress joining hand to form the government, the CPM backed suppliers switched to Congress.

Left in the cold, Trinamool supporters began to pressure local party councillors Barun Natya and Jawhar Upadhyay. Matters apparently came to a head on Tuesday evening when Natya and Upadhyay met the ACC management and asked them to take supplies from locals. When the company told them that they could not take on more syndicates, the men allegedly threatened to stop supply of stone chips and sand. The plant purchases stone chips and sand worth nearly Rs 40 lakh a month.

Sources said the Trinamool leaders demanded that their men be given 70% share of the spoils. On Wednesday morning, its supporters gathered in large numbers at the plant site to force the issue.

The ACC plant at the airport

By 8 am, hundreds of Congress supporters had also gathered to retain their turf.

Fearing a fight would break out any moment, police kept a vigil at the spot. "The situation was very tense. Had someone provoked a clash, the situation could have spiralled out of control in seconds. Thankfully, the leaders intervened and worked out an amicable solution," said a police officer.

According to sources, both parties have decided to split the supply. While Congress supporters involved in the syndicates will supply 50% of the material, those belonging to Trinamool will supply the rest. Natya clarified that he had gone to negotiate on behalf of the locals and had nothing to do with the party.

Appendix – 18

THE HISTORIC ORDER OF THE HON'BLE SUPREME COURT BY WHICH THE FIRST GREEN BENCH OF THE COUNTRY HAS BEEN CONSTITUTED AT THE HIGH COURT OF CALCUTTA

IN THE SUPREME COURT OF INDIA
CIVIL ORIGINAL JURISDICTION
WRIT PETITION (C) NO. 380/95

Howrah Ganatantrik Nagarik Samity & Ors. Petitioners.

–Vs –

State of West Bengal & Ors. Respondents

ORDER

This public interest petition under Article 32 of the Constitution of India has been filed by Mr. Subhas Datta. General Secretary, Ganatantrik Nagarik Samity, Howrah. The petition relates to the city of Howrah. It is stated that Howrah is one of the most polluted cities in the country and no attention is being given to the environment protection and pollution control by the Howrah Municipal Corporation and other authorities responsible for the said work. Various issues have been raised in the Writ Petition. We may mention some of the issues :-

1. Garbage and Solid Waste Removal & Disposal
2. Garbage from Fish & Betel Markets
3. Drainage & Sewage-system
4. Supply of clean water
5. Afforestation
6. Destruction of greenery for commercial exploitation
7. Centenary Park at Howrah Maidan
8. Afforestation in particular regarding Centenery Park at Howrah Maidan, Dalmia Park & Belilious Park.

Affidavits have been filed before us by the Howrah Municipal Corporation and various other authorities. The Commissioner, Howrah Municipal Corporation has placed before this court various suggestions which the Corporation intends to implement regarding cleaning and improving the sanitation in the city of Howrah. We are of the view that the environment preservation and pollution control are to be given utmost priority by the courts in the country. Despite various enactments by the Parliament and the State Legislatures regarding pollution control and environment protection, nothing much is being done in this respect. It is common knowledge that all the big cities including Howrah are littered with garbage, household waste etc. and there are no satisfactory arrangements for collecting and disposing of the same. Even the sewage treatment plants have not been constructed. Needless to say that much attention is required to be given in this field of law. This court meets more than once in a week to attend to the environment problems in the country.

We are of the view that it would be appropriate to transfer this petition to the Calcutta High Court for consideration and necessary action. Because of the distance and various other problems it would be better that the matter is dealt with at the High Court level. We request Mr. Justice V.N. Khare, Chief Justice of the Calcutta High Court to designate an appropriate Bench to consider and deal with environmental and pollution control matters including the present petition. The Bench can consider and monitor various issues involved in this Writ Petition and other petitions as and when they are filed before the High Court. We give liberty to the petitioner to approach this court as and when it becomes necessary for him to do so.

We transfer this petition to the Calcutta High Court. This petition shall be treated to be a petition under Article 226 of the Constitution of India and shall be dealt with in accordance with law. The parties to appear before Registrar of the Calcutta High Court on 3rd June, 1996. The registry to send the records along with this order to the Registrar of the High Court within one week from today. The Registrar of the Calcutta High Court shall place the matter before the Chief Justice of Calcutta High Court within one week thereafter. The Writ Petition stands disposed of.

Sd/-

(Kuldip Singh)

Sd/-

(S. Saghir Ahmed)

New Delhi,
Dated: 16th April, 1996.

Ref.: SOUVENIR on the 4th Anniversary of the Constitution of the First Green Bench of the Country at the High Court at Calcutta, 17th June, 2000, Ganatantrik Nagarik Samity, Howrah.

The Historic order of the Green Bench of the High Court at Calcutta in the matter of Construction of Buildings at parks and green verges of the SALT LAKE CITY, CALCUTTA

IN THE HIGH COURT AT CALCUTTA
Appellate/Revisional Civil Jurisdiction

Present :
The Hon'ble Mr. Justice S.B. Sinha, J.
and
The Hon'ble Mr. Justice R.K. Mitra, J.

W.P. No. 15871(w) of 1997 — Howrah Ganatantrik Nagarik Samity & Ors. Vs. The Chief Secretary & Ors.
with
(Original Side Matter)

G.A. No. 3300 of 1999
W.P. No. 1823 of 1994 — Sri Parimal Kumar De Vs. Chief Secretary, Govt. of West Bengal & Ors.

For Appellant/Petitioner — Mr. Subhas Datta. (W.P. 15871 W/97)
Mr. Ranajit Chatterjee (W.P. 1823/94 & Ors.)

For State Respondent/Opposite Party — Mr. S.C. Ukil, Ld. Govt. Pleader
Ms. Chhabi Roy (Das)

For Bidhannagore Municipality :- Mr. M.C. Das
Mr. Goutam Mukherjee

For Respondent No. 7 in W.P. 1823/94 – Ms. Chaya Das

Heard on : 17.9.99

Judgement on : 16.12.1999
S.B. Sinha, J.:-

The questions which arise for consideration in these two applications are as to whether any construction can be allowed in a Public Park.

Contd...

The Salt Lake City which consisted of water bodies having a large area. Keeping in view the growing population it was considered necessary to turn into a Model Town. Subsequently named as 'Bidhannagar', the town stands at the extreme eastern end of Town of Calcutta having a total area of around 15 square K.M. The layout plan of Bidhannagar City indicates that 35.10% of the total land would be open space, out of which 23% had been earmarked for roads and the rest 12.10% for exclusive greenery, parks etc. The present estimated population is about 5 lakhs.

There are about parks in the said area and some green verges which act as lungs of the residence of the area. A piece of land had been leased out to the applicants for 999 years it is accepted that persons those who wanted allotments facing open spaces park were required to pay a premium and those who wanted land near green verges were required to pay a premium of 3% of the used charges. The Policy of the State, thus, there can not be any doubt, was to maintain the greenery. It, however, appears that in the name of Community Centre or Ward Office of the Bidhannagar Municipality, constructions were allowed on portions of the Parks as a result whereof hardly any area is left aside as open-space for the neighbouring building owners. One of such buildings had been constructed in BH Block.

Various photographs have been annexed with the writ application to show that vats have been placed in the green verges, as a result whereof a vicious atmosphere had been created.

It is, thus, not denied that 30 numbers of parks exist in the Salt Lake City. It is further not denied that in some of the parks including B.H. Block which is the subject matter of Writ Petition No. 1823/94 a Community Hall had come up resulting in frustrating the purpose for which the petitioner had paid the extra premium. Photographs placed before us clearly depict that construction had been raised even without leaving the required space between two buildings.

How the State Government had allotted a portion of the park in deviation of its policy decision in the name of building of Community Hall is a matter of great surprise that there are several statutes governing the field is not in dispute. A layout plan has to be made under the provision of the West Bengal Town and Country (Planning and Development) Act, 1979. The Calcutta Metropolitan Development Authority has issued a hand-book laying down the procedure and guidelines for environmental clearance. Although the same is meant for certain purposes, viz, industrial projects, the same is a pointer to show that the state had been also eager to maintain the greenery and the ecological balance. Therefore, we fail to understand as to how the state could allot the lands in question within a park which is contrary to the representation made by it to the residents particularly in view of the fact that any excess premiums had been charged for those who had opted for settlement of land near the park or green verges.

It is also surprising as to how the Bidhan Nagar Municipality also sanctioned the building plan within a park. The said action, in our opinion was not commensurate with the professed policy decision of the State and the Municipality. This aspect of the matter has recently been considered in M.I. Builders Pvt. Ltd. -vs- Radhey Shyam Sahu & Ors. reported in Judgement Today 1999(5) SC 42 wherein it has been held that the Municipality is a Public Trustee in respect of Parks.

Contd...

Clauses (a) and (1) of Sub-section (3) of Section 63 of the West Bengal Municipal Act, 1993 read thus:-

"(3)(a) - devising town planning within the limits of the municipal area in accordance with the laws relating to town planning for the time being in force:

(1) - measures for beautification of the township by setting up fountains and statutes, providing recreational area, improving river ranks, landscaping and the like."

Clauses (k) and (1) of sub-section (4) of Section 63 read thus :-

"(4)(k) - protecting public properties in general and civic properties in particular;

(1) - abatement of pollutions of all kinds."

The obligatory functions leave no manner of doubt that park being a property having vested in the Municipality, it has the duty to maintain and develop the same. It, of course, has a discretionary duty, interalia, to construct and maintain a Community Hall but the same can not be done at the cost of ecology and greenery. The State, as noticed hereinbefore, has a duty to look after the environment, safety and improvement. Such functions can only be transferred in terms of Section 65 of the Act but the same has not been done. It was in this situation the Municipality could not have sanction any building plan inside the Park. The respondents have constructed their building at their own risk during pendency of the Writ Petition. They, therefore, can not take any benefit thereof and, thus, there is no difficulty in directing demolition of those buildings and a further direction that the Parks should be restored to their original position. It is directed accordingly.

These writ applications are disposed of with the aforementioned directions but without any order as to costs.

(S.B. Sinha, J.)

(R.K. Mitra, J.)
I agree

Appendix – 19

Minbarta, No. 78-P/C M, 9th June, 1998

The Chief Minister, West Bengal

I am happy that the forth coming issue of Minbarta is enriched with the important discussion on wet-land. It is urgent need to develop mass awareness regarding the conservation of wet-land. *Wet-land cannot be sacrificed for the cause of urbanisation/ development of cities.* Protection of ecology and development activities should go together. Conflict between the two is not desirable. Through conservation and proper utilisation of wet-land we can resolve many problems and can promote development in a better way. Keeping in view the present situation and future all concerned parties are to work together. I wish all the success of this special issue of Minbarta.

s/d

Jyoti Basu

Appendix – 20

No Hidco /Planning – 13/97 Calcutta, the 13.11.97

To,

The Secy. to the Govt. of West Bengal.

Fisheries Department.

Writers Building, Cal- 700001

Sir,

Re : Permission for relaxation of the provisions of Inland fisheries Act 1984 & West Bengal Inland Fisheries (Amendment) Act 1993 for filling up of Water areas for implementation of New Town. Calcutta Project by HIDCO.

I have to inform you that Govt. of W.B. has decided to set up a "New Town" covering about 3075 ha. in the Rajarhat and Bhangar P.S. Comprising 25 Mouzas. Tentative location of the Township is shown in the enclosed plan Out of the total area immediate Action Area- I (AA-1) has been earmarked as 640 ha. between Bagjola &. Krishnapur Canal and the same has been shown by red border in the plan.

The said Action Area-I includes some water areas/depressed land holdings as shown in the annexed list which requires filling for the purpose of implementation of development scheme as stated above for puting the area for use other than fishery.

Application for necessary permission for filling up of the water areas/depressed land holdings is being made as per provisions of chapter III A, Sec. 17A (9) (b) of W.B. Inland Fisheries (Amendment) Act 1993 (W.B. Act XIX of 1993).

You are therefore requested to kindly accord approval of filling of water areas/depressed land holdings for the purpose of development of the Township Project, in relaxation of the provisions under chapter IIIA, Sec. 17A(9) (b) of the West Bengal Inland Fisheries (Amendment) Act 1993.

It may kindly be noted that an area of about 70 ha (more or less) has been kept reserved for new water bodies within AA-I which is much more than the area of water areas/depressed land that would require filling.

Yours faithfully,

Managing Director.

19.11.99

Enclo : As stated.

West Bengal Housing Infrastructure Development Corporation LTD.
(A Govt. of West Bengal Undertaking)
Regd. Office: Salt Lake Stadium Complex, Gate No. 3, Sector III,
Salt Lake, Calcutta 700 091
Telephone : 337 7146, 337 7227, Fax : 337 6677

Appendix – 21

Extract from:. Land Conversion Act

Sec.4c. Permission for change of area, character use of land

1. A raiyat holding any land may apply to the Collector for change of area or character of such land or for conversion of the same for any purpose for which it was settled or was being previously used or for alteration in the mode of use of such land.
2. On receipt of such application the Collector may, after making such enquiry as may be prescribed and after giving the applicant or the persons interest in such land or affected in any way an opportunity of being heard, by order in writing either reject the application or direct such change, conversion or alteration, as the case may be, on such terms and conditions as may be prescribed.

R. 5A. Inquiry to be made and terms and conditions to be imposed, under subsection (2) of section 4C.

1. An inquiry shall be held under sub-section (2) of section 4C in ascertain any or all of the following:
   (i) If the change of area, if any, prima facie attracts the provision of section 14U;
   (ii) If the proposed change of character or conversion of a land conforms to the general pattern of use of land in the locality;
   (iii) If the change or conversion is likely to cause inconvenience to the residence of the locality where the land is situated;
   (iv) If the application is for conversion of any agricultural land for any purpose other than agriculture and if such conversion will interfere with the normal agricultural activities in the surrounding area;
   (v) If the object of change or conversion is to use the land for a purpose for which permission of license from and appropriate authority is necessary and if the same has been obtained necessary.
   (vi) That the permission is without prejudice to any of the provisions of Chapter IIB of the Act.
   (vii) That where the land situated within any urban agglomeration within the meaning or the Urban Land (Ceiling and Regulation) Act. 1976 (33 of 1976), the permission is without prejudice to any of the said Act, and
   (viii) That where the land is situated within the jurisdiction of a

Development Authority constituted under the West Bengal Town and Country (Planning and Development) Act, 1979 (West Beng. Act XIII of 1979), the permission is without prejudice, to the Provisions of the said Act.

Appendix – 22

Some news headlines

The Statesman, 30 November, 1997

'Megacity plan will drain state'

Statesman News Service,

Calcutta, Nov.29- The Rs.1,600-crore megacity project would empty West Bengal's coffers, Ms Medha Patkar said here today. "All funds will now go towards the project," the environmentalist said at a press conference."Around 7,000 acres are being taken away from farmers for industry. It is horrifying to see what is happening to the state's land and water resources."

The leader of the Narmada Bachao Andolan and convenor of the National Alliance of People's Movement criticized the state government also over its Rajarhat township project. Farmers were being forced to sell off their lands at throwaway prices for the township, she said. Condemning the 'conversion of agricultural land for constructing residential and commercial complexes at Rajarhat', she asserted: 'this is an unplanned urbanization. These projects are unjust, unequal and non-sustainable.' ...

The Statesman, 17 December, 1997

Rajarhat construction ban

Tarun Goswami, Statesman News Service,

Calcutta, Dec.16- The state government has banned the construction of buildings in areas located close to the proposed new Calcutta Township at Rajarhat in North 24-Parganas. A senior official of the state housing department said that the ban was imposed so that the state government could acquire land without any difficulty for the proposed township.

A notification (memo No.1538 (6)/(M)ZP/T&C/115) was given on 6 December by the North 24 Parganas zilla parishad...The notification has asked them not to sanction any building plan in these areas. When any plan for proposed building is submitted to the gram panchayat or municipality it should be sent to the zilla parishad within 15 days from submission of the building plan.

The zilla parishad in turn will send it to the state housing department for necessary action. The notification further states that the gram panchayats are not allowed sanctioning building plans for areas which do not come under the jurisdiction of the Calcutta Metropolitan area.

Another reason for the ban is to save the state government from having to pay more money as compensation if structures come up on land to be acquired. In many cases the owners of structures move the court and get a favourable order against the proposal to acquire the plot…

The state finance department had issued a notification (No.3044-FT) on 6 December last year banning purchase, sale and subsequent registration of land in 21 moujas. The proposed township is likely to come up in these areas covered by the moujas. …

The Statesman, 21 November, 1997

Ponds filled for garment complex

Statesman News Service,

Calcutta, Nov. 20 – Builders are filling water bodies at Mahishbathan in Salt Lake to make room for a proposed garment complex. The Chief Minister, Mr Jyoti Basu, will lay the foundation stone of the complex on 29 November. Builders constructing the complex are learnt to be close to some CPI-M leaders. Local people have lodged complaints with the Bidhannagar Municipality and the state fisheries department seeking their intervention. Hectic filling of water bodies is on round the clock. Heavy duty pumps are being used to drain out the water. Embankments separating water bodies have been severed. Lorries offload rubbish daily to expedite the filling operation. It was learnt that builders the water bodies, had been marked as 'land' in the Record of Right (ROR)…A senior district administration official said that the work, which started last year, was suspended after the state fisheries department intervened. The work resumed again on 7 November.

Mrs. Chameli Naskar, councilor of Ward 14 where the complex is coming up, said that the drainage system in the area would collapse if the water bodies were filled. She said that despite repeated complaints lodged with the fisheries and urban development departments, nothing has been done. She demanded stern action against officials of the Block Land and Land Reforms Office. The latter had issued conversion certificates without visiting the spot.

Mr. Dilip Gupta, Chairman of Bidhannagar Municipality, said that the municipality could not do anything because the plot owners had obtained conversion certificates from the district administration. A senior official said that the municipality was totally in the dark on the setting up of the garment complex. He said that the builders had not submitted any plan for the proposed complex as yet....Fisheries department officials said they had received complaints that the water bodies were being filled and were looking into the matter. They expressed their inability to take action against the builders as the state government had cleared the project and also because of their political clout.

The Statesman, October 1, 1998

Supervisory body for Rajarhat Township

Statesman News Service,

Calcutta. Sept.30- The state government has set up a Housing Infrastructural Development Corporation to look after the allotment of land and infrastructural development of the proposed New Calcutta Township at Rajarhat. The proposed township will come up on 7,000 acres of land in North 24 Parganas. The three directors of the corporation are the State Housing Department Secretary, Mr. Amal Ghosh, the Commissioner of state Housing Department, Mr. Chinmoy Mazumder, and the Joint Secretary, State Housing Department, Mr. Tapan Mazumder. The numbers of directors in the Corporation will be increased to 11 later....

The state government has already allowed three private firms to procure land in the proposed township. Gujrat Ambuja, Peerless and Srachi will buy 100 acres each in Mahisbathan, Mahisgoat and Thakurdari Moujas.

The state government has now stopped purchase and sale of land in these three moujas along with 18 others to set up the township....

The Hindustan Times, November 22, 1998

Peasants up against 'second Calcutta'

HT Correspondent

Threatened with eviction by the West Bengal Government's plan to set up a second Calcutta at Rajarhat near the Calcutta airport, local peasantry locking horns with the State Government on the issue have sought the help of Ms Medha Patkar of Narmada Bachao fame. Ms Patkar had already expressed solidarity to their cause and assured them of her full support to the protest movement, said members of the Rajarhat Jami Bachao Committee, comprising local farmers, students and youth groups coming out in support of the farmers cause.

And as the West Bengal Government draws up ambitious plans of setting up a second Calcutta and a grand prix circuit at Rajarhat, local peasantry have come out on the streets to fight what they claim is a blatant attempt at "land grab" by evicting the poor farmers.

The projected township is proposed to be built on 2750 hectares of land, mostly agricultural, with water bodies covering 653 hectares. Threatened with risk of eviction are 6170 marginal farmers, over 2000 small farmers, 4600 landless labourers and 4000 others, working in local bherries (fisheries), according to Rajarhat Jami Bachao Committee (save the land of Rajarhat Committee). The area is also primarily a Scheduled Caste and Tribe area, the population of backwards here being around 44,000 against the total population of 1,31,000. They have already lodged sharp protests against the government move, but it has not yielded tangible benefits so far mainly because of the lack of any patronage from political parties.

The job has been made further difficult for them by the fact that the CPI(M) enjoys commendable clout in the envisaged township project area. For the farmers the attitude of CPI (M) has come as an 'abject betrayal' to their cause as the left party has consistently worked on the slogan 'land to the tillers' to gather wholesome support from the poor farmers and marginal labour....

Mr. Nilotpal Datta, secretary of the committee points out that apart from dispossessing the farmers, the new township will lead to a big ecological problem as well. There are four big canals, which serve the irrigation needs of local farmers and equally importantly serve the sewerage purpose of the city. The township projects providing shelter to 5,00,000 people, but the committee points out that the State Government only plans to give away the job of building residential complexes to joint sector housing companies, public sector corporations, housing board and allied bodies, for which it would be more a project to serve the affluent sections of people. The protesting peasants allege that while they were being given a more Rs.6000/- as compensations per cottah of land, the State Government sold the same land to the Coal India at a whopping price of Rs.95,000/- per cottah.

The Statesman 1st January, 1999

A Township for the New Millenium

We at West Bengal Housing Board know your dream – a Home of your own ! And so our new Township project around Rajarhat is fast nearing completion – it is close to Calcutta and closer to Dum Dum International Airport and Bidhan Nagar.

Convenience within your reach:

All daily necessities will be there for your-markets, shape schools, hospitals, playgrounds, lakes-you name it, we have it. All really, as we would really love to give you a comfortable living in great style.

Within your budget:

The flats that are being constructed here come in different sizes and are priced accordingly. To suit the needs of all income groups – lower, middle and upper.

Green and peaceful:

No noise pollution! No smoke no grime – No. only fresh air amidst sprawling greenery. Health for you, after all, is prime on our mind.

Car parking facility:

Some car parking facilities will be available on the ground floor for HIG flats. There is provision of car parking space for 60% of successful candidates in HIG category selected through separate lottery. An amount of Rs.50,000/- will be charged extra for parking space. So, Own your Own Home and relax! would feel happy to see you, bask in the glory of fulfilling your dream. Application forms and brochure can be obtained on payment of Rs.50/- for LIG / MIG category and Rs.100/- for HIG category from the following banks during banking hours.

Category	Area	Type	Number	Price Rs.	Income Group	Application Money (Rs.)
HIG 'A' 82	Sq.M	G+4 with lift and above	32	10,15,000/-	Rs.10,001	50,000/-
HIG 'B' 72	Sq.M	G+$ with lift	64	9,20,000/- p.m. and above	Rs.10,001	50,000/-
MIG 'C' 49.8	Sq.M	4-storied walk up to 10,000 bldg. p.m.	64	4,50,000/-	Rs.4,501	25,000/-
LIG 'D' 34.7 Sq.M		4-storied walk up bldg. p.m.	64	1,50,000/-	Rs.4,501 to Rs.10,000	8,000/-

West Bengal Housing Board

105, S.N. Banerjee Road, Calcutta-14

Contact No. P.RO. (Phone): 2441965, 24411967

The Statesman February 15, 1999

Rajarhat pond filled up despite stop-work notice

CALCUTTA: Feb 14: A real estate agent along with some local youths filled up a 13 cottah water body at East Narayanpur, Rajarhat, floating, provisions of the West Bengal Inland Fisheries Acquisition and Requisition Act. The Act bans filling up water bodies above five cottah and any one erring can be imprisoned for three years and fixed up to Rs.50,000/-. The Rajarhat Gopalpur Municipality had issued a stop work notice on the real estate agent last year.

A visit to the area revealed that that over 11 cottahs have been filled up. Local youths are guarding the reclaimed land as the agent is trying to divide the land into smaller plots and sell them. A senior official of the municipality said after complaints from the local residents, the municipality had issued the stop work notice. But the agent flouted the order and filled up the water body.

Index